Strategic Information Technology:

Opportunities for Competitive Advantage

Raymond Papp
Quinnipiac University, USA

IDEA GROUP PUBLISHING
Hershey • London • Melbourne • Singapore

Acquisition Editor:	Mehdi Khosrowpour
Managing Editor:	Jan Travers
Development Editor:	Michele Rossi
Copy Editor:	Maria Boyer
Typesetter:	Tamara Gillis
Cover Design:	Deb Andre
Printed at:	Sheridan Books

Published in the United States of America by
      Idea Group Publishing
      1331 E. Chocolate Avenue
      Hershey PA 17033-1117
      Tel: 717-533-8845
      Fax: 717-533-8661
      E-mail: cust@idea-group.com
      Web site: http://www.idea-group.com

and in the United Kingdom by
      Idea Group Publishing
      3 Henrietta Street
      Covent Garden
      London WC2E 8LU
      Tel: 44 20 7240 0856
      Fax: 44 20 7379 3313
      Web site: http://www.eurospan.co.uk

Library of Congress Cataloging-in-Publication Data

Strategic information technology : opportunities for competitive advantage / [edited by] Raymond Papp.
    p. cm.
   Includes bibliographical references and index.
   ISBN 1-878289-87-X (paper)
    1. Information technology--Management. 2. Strategic planning. 3. Competition. I. Papp, Raymond, 1966-

 HD30.2 .S7883 2000
 658.4'012--dc21   00-050553

British Cataloguing in Publication Data
A Cataloguing in Publication record for this book is available from the British Library.

Strategic Information Technology: Opportunities for Competitive Advantage

Table of Contents

Chapter I
Introduction to Strategic Alignment 1
    Raymond Papp, Quinnipiac University, USA

Chapter II
Sustainable Competitive Advantage from Information Technology:
Limitations of the Value Chain 25
    David L. Bahn, Metropolitan State University, USA

Chapter III
Alignment Through Cross-Functional Integration 40
    Mark R. Nelson, Rensselaer Polytechnic Institute, USA

Chapter IV
Information Systems Strategy, Structure and Alignment 56
    Yolande E. Chan, Queen's University, Canada

Chapter V
Communicating Strategic IT Vision to Organization Members:
A Conceptual Framework 82
    Mary Elizabeth Brabston, University of Manitoba, Canada
    Robert W. Zmud, University of Oklahoma, USA
    John R. Carlson, Baylor University, USA

Chapter VI
Assessing Business-IT Alignment Maturity 105
    Jerry N. Luftman, Stevens Institute of Technology, USA

Chapter VII
Outsourcing Decisions: Using Porter's Model 135
    Anne L. Powell, Southern Illinois University-Edwardsville, USA

Chapter VIII
The Changing Roles of IT Leaders 150
        Petter Gottschalk, Norwegian School of Management

Chapter IX
Strategic Information Systems for Competitive Advantage: Planning,
Sustainability and Implementation 169
        Gareth Griffiths, Manchester Metropolitan University, UK
        Ray Hackney, Manchester Metropolitan University, UK

Chapter X
Aligning IT Resources for E-Commerce 185
        Makoto Nakayama, DePaul University, USA

Chapter XI
Competitive Force/Marketing Mix (CF/MM) Framework 200
        Brian J. Reithel, University of Mississippi, USA
        Chi Hwang, California State Polytechnic University-Pomona, USA
        Katherine Boswell, University of Mississippi, USA

Chapter XII
The Importance of the IT-End User Relationship Paradigm in Obtaining
Alignment Between IT and the Business 218
        A.C. Leonard, University of Pretoria, South Africa

Chapter XIII
Strategic Human Resource Forecasting for an Internal Labor Market 237
        Wilfred S.J. Geerlings, Delft University of Technology, The Netherlands
        Alexander Verbraeck, Delft University of Technology, The Netherlands
        Pieter J. Toussaint, Delft University of Technology, The Netherlands
        Ron P.T. de Groot, Royal Netherlands Navy, The Netherlands

Chapter XIV
Strategic Alignment for Electronic Commerce 258
        Christian Bauer, Electronic Commerce Network, Western Australia

Chapter XV
Strategic Significance of Information Technology to Developing Countries 273
        Muhammadou Kah, Rutgers University-Camden, USA

About the Authors 292

Index   298

Preface

In the area of strategic information technology, strategic alignment is an often discussed but frequently misunderstood term. Alignment has been defined in many ways in recent years in the popular press, yet in the information technology realm, it is most commonly defined as the implementation of information technology (IT) in the integration and development of business strategies and corporate goals. Its importance has been well known and documented since the late 1980s and it remains one of the primary areas in which businesses are focusing their attention. In fact, it has become an area of prime interest to managers, eclipsing even such topics as e-commerce and the Internet.

Traditional methods of developing business strategies have failed to take full advantage of IT. In the past, technology was typically treated as a "cost center" or viewed as an "expense" rather than an enabler of business value. Strategic alignment sheds new light on IT and its role in the development of business strategies. It is no longer economically feasible to treat IT as a lower level support tool; failure to leverage IT may seriously hamper the firm's performance and viability in today's global, information-intensive world. Alignment of business strategies with IT goals and objectives to evaluate and assess the level of integration of business and IT strategy within firms is paramount. By concentrating on the alignment of strategy and infrastructure, firms may not only achieve synergy and facilitate the development of business plans, but also increase the profitability and efficiency of their firm within its industry. These tangible benefits allow management to focus on the application of IT as a means to leverage their core competencies, skills, and technology scope, resulting in improved efficiency.

In the quest for alignment, some key questions executives must begin to ask themselves include "Are our business strategies and plans leveraging information technology (IT)?", "Are our company's business and IT organizations aligned?" and "What are the implications of a misalignment between business and IT?" to determine appropriate strategies which take advantage of IT capabilities. Alignment enables a firm to maximize its IT investments and achieve harmony with its business strategies and plans, leading to greater profitability and effectiveness. Alignment is important to firms for many reasons. The major reason is to ease the development and implementation of cohesive organization and IT strategies that enable firms to focus on the application of IT to improve the business. By understanding and leveraging the business/IT partnership, organizations can concentrate on the application of IT to enable the business strategy. This harmony can be extended and applied throughout the organization as new opportunities are identified.

The primary objective of this book is to explore the myriad of issues regarding the application of business strategy and IT strategy, specifically focusing on ways to achieve, implement, and measure strategic alignment and what can be done to facilitate its use in the firm. The chapters presented herein address strategic use of IT and what can be done to facilitate its implementation in the firm. They are based on research from both academia and industry to provide managers and students alike with an understanding of and appreciation for the development of business and information technology strategies.

Use of this book by practicing managers and academics

Managers and consultants may find this book an invaluable "field guide" to the alignment process. Although it is authored by both academics and practitioners, it incorporates many real-world examples and focuses heavily on how executives can implement strategic alignment to achieve competitive advantage within their organization and industry. Consultants and executives will also find this a good resource for understanding alignment and keeping current on an important topic in the information systems field.

This book could also be used as a college text for a senior level undergraduate or graduate-level course in information systems and is particularly well suited for a course on strategic information systems and its implementation. Additionally, this book would be suitable for use by non-IS majors to study the development of business and technology strategy within a business framework.

Format and contents

This book begins with an overview of the strategic alignment process and focuses on how alignment is used to assess the degree and extent of business/information technology synergy within a company. The remainder of the book focuses on the application and/or implementation of strategic information systems using various constructs and includes implications and suggestions for managers to implement strategic alignment.

The objective throughout the book is to present the reader with a comprehensive look at strategic information technology and how it can be applied by focusing on real-world scenarios. The papers presented in this book represent leading research in the area of strategic information technology by an international cadre of academics and practitioners. Their expertise and knowledge are combined in one text whose premise is that a successful firm must utilize information technology effectively, efficiently, and appropriately if it is to remain competitive in a changing world.

Acknowledgments

This book comprises a compilation of chapters from leading practitioners, teachers, consultants and researchers from around the globe. Each of the authors shares his/her findings regarding the implementation and/or application of strategic information systems for competitive advantage. Bios of each of the authors follow. I wish to thank all the authors whose contributions appear in this book. Much of the work presented here represents cutting-edge research on strategic information technology that cannot be found elsewhere.

I also wish to acknowledge Idea Group Publishing, specifically Medhi Khosrowpour for his assistance with my original proposal, and Jan Travers and Michele Rossi for their help in assembling this book.

Thanks are also due to Tom Brier and IBM for their assistance with the collection of the raw data from which much of the theoretical research on alignment has been based and to the many companies who have assisted in the empirical validation and application of the strategic alignment model.

Finally, I wish to thank the many students I've had who have suggested that I assemble a contemporary textbook on strategic information systems. It is because of them that this book is a reality.

This book is dedicated to the families of all the contributors. I especially want to dedicate it to my family, whose support and indulgence have made this possible.

Raymond Papp
January 2001

Chapter I

Introduction to Strategic Alignment

Raymond Papp
Quinnipiac University, USA

The concept of strategic alignment is more than two decades old (McLean and Soden, 1977; IBM, 1981; Earl, 1983; Mills, 1986; Brancheau and Wetherbe, 1987; Parker and Benson, 1988; Henderson and Venkatraman, 1990; Dixon and John, 1991; Niederman, et. al., 1991; Watson and Brancheau, 1991; Liebs, 1992; Luftman, Lewis and Oldach, 1993; Goff, 1993), however it has never been more timely than in today's fast-paced, dynamic business environment (Papp, 1998; Rogers, 1997). The original alignment model was a largely theoretical construct that studied only a single industry (Henderson & Venkatraman, 1990; Henderson & Thomas, 1992) but has since been adapted for use by virtually any industry looking to integrate their business strategies with their information technology strategies (Papp, 1995; Luftman, Papp, & Brier, 1995).

THE STRATEGIC ALIGNMENT MODEL

The Strategic Alignment Model is composed of four domains or quadrants. Each of the four quadrants is composed of three components, forming a triad, which can be used to operationally define the quadrants as shown in Figure 1. It is these 12 components, working in harmony, which can be used to determine the extent and type of alignment within a corporation.

Business Strategy

The upper left-hand quadrant is the traditional business strategy domain. It consists of three components: business scope, distinctive competencies, and business governance. Business scope, also known as market scope, focuses on the type of business the organization is engaged in, the products and/or services it offers, market segmentation (geography, diversification, customers), competition, and the values and mission of the organization. Distinctive competencies include the areas in which the company excels—its distinguishing strengths. These competencies determine the extent to which the firm will be able to compete with the rest of the market, the decision of customers to buy from that firm, and the ability to differentiate its products and/or services from its competition. Also included are the critical success factors necessary to achieve these competencies. Examples would include a customer satisfaction strategy, service, pricing or quality focus, or the creation of a first-rate marketing channel. The third component, business governance, focuses on ownership. It specifically looks at the establishment of business alliances and partnerships with other firms, government regulations and their effect, as well as outsourcing strategies.

Organization Infrastructure

The lower left-hand quadrant is the organizational infrastructure domain. The components in this quadrant are administrative structure, processes, and skills. Administrative structure consists of the authority structure, responsibilities, and roles within the organization. It specifically addresses the number of levels of management (i.e. the organizational structure), the extent to which decision-making is centralized or decentralized, and the geographical orientation of the firm. Business processes are those activities that drive the business. They determine the extent to which work flows can be integrated with respect to information technology. Improvements to business processes can be the result of information technology, or new processes may be designed to incorporate emerging information technology. Business skills, the third component, focus on the human resources of the firm. Specifically, it concentrates on the training and experience of employees, the creation of a corporate culture, opportunities for outsourcing,

Figure 1: Strategic Alignment Model

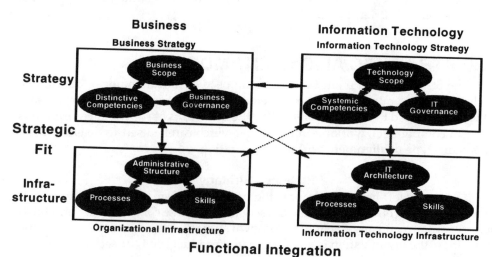

definition of competencies, norms and values, salaries and rewards, and the assessment of human resources for the achievement of the business goals.

Information Technology Strategy

The upper right-hand quadrant, information technology strategy, is the information technology counterpart to business strategy. It consists of technology scope, systemic competencies, and information technology governance. Technology scope, like business scope, focuses on the key technologies and applications the business should and/or must employ. It looks at what specific information technology is needed to achieve the critical success factors as well as what the competition uses. Systemic competencies include information about the company's customers and clients (i.e., customer/product databases), accessibility, reliability, and other vital characteristics and strengths of information technology. The third component, information technology governance, addresses many of the same issues as business governance. Specifically, it focuses on the decision to make-or-buy, the prioritization of applications, and the possibility of technological alliances and partnerships (including outsourcing).

Information Technology Infrastructure

The fourth and final domain is the information technology infrastructure quadrant. The components include information technology architecture, processes, and skills. Information technology architecture includes the hardware, software, data, applications, and communication platforms that the organization uses to achieve its information technology and business strategies. The processes focus on the development of specific information technology practices and how they can be improved. They include application development, systems management, and maintenance functions. The final component, information technology skills, addresses the experience, competence, and values of technology employees. It includes the information technology culture and its associated norms, employee salaries, and hiring and training practices.

LINKAGES

The interrelationships between the domains of the strategic alignment model reflect the linkages between the four domains. While each of the four domains is important in its own context, they only gain value when employed as a cohesive whole. To achieve this goal, various linkages are used as illustrated in Figure1. The first such linkage is a vertical one, that of strategic fit. It concentrates on the need to make business decisions that determine the position of the firm in the marketplace as well as the infrastructure, processes and skills that determine the internal focus necessary to achieve the desired market position. The use of strategy to determine infrastructure typically yields these vertical linkages.

The second major linkage is the corresponding horizontal one that is referred to as functional integration (Henderson & Venkatraman, 1990). This extends the principle of strategic fit to the functional domains of business and information technology. The information technology strategies must change as business strategies change and correspondingly, infrastructure and processes must keep pace as either business or information technology undergoes change. The ability to successfully position the firm in the technology marketplace is vital in the leveraging of information technology; functional integration yields competitive advantage (Reich & Benbasat, 1993; Thomas & DeWitt, 1993) and maximizes the value of information technology (Barua et al., 1995; Goren et al, 1994; LaPlante, 1994a; LaPlante & Alter, 1994).

STRATEGIC ALIGNMENT PERSPECTIVES

Given the importance of strategic fit and functional integration, the use of cross-domain alignment (focusing on three of the four quadrants at a given time) permits both strategic fit and functional integration to be addressed simultaneously (Papp, 1995; Luftman, Papp, & Brier, 1995). When this is done, eight

Table 1: Alignment Perspectives

	Strategy Execution	Technology Potential	Competitive Potential	Service Level
Anchor	Business Strategy	Business Strategy	IT Strategy	IT Strategy
Pivot	Business Infrastructure	IT Strategy	Business Strategy	IT Infrastructure
Impact	IT Infrastructure	IT Infrastructure	Business Infrastructure	Business Infrastructure
	Organization IT Infrastructure	**IT Infrastructure Strategy**	**IT Organization Infrastructure**	**Organization IT Infrastructure**
Anchor	Business Infrastructure	IT Infrastructure	IT Infrastructure	Business Infrastructure
Pivot	IT Infrastructure	IT Strategy	Business Infrastructure	Business Strategy
Impact	IT Strategy	Business Strategy	Business Strategy	IT Strategy
	Organization Strategy Fusion	**Organization Infrastructure Fusion**	**IT Strategy Fusion**	**IT Infrastructure Fusion**
Anchor	IT Infrastructure	IT Strategy	Business Infrastructure	Business Strategy
Pivots	IT Strategy & Business Infrastructure	Business Strategy & IT Infrastructure	Business Strategy & IT Infrastructure	IT Strategy & Business Infrastructure
Impact	Business Strategy	Business Infrastructure	IT Strategy	IT Infrastructure

perspectives result as the domains are combined in various ways using a triangle construct to encompass three quadrants and address both strategic fit and functional integration at the same time.

There are three components of a strategic perspective: the anchor, pivot, and impacted domains. The anchor domain is the area of greatest strength among the four domains. This is the area that drives the changes that will be applied to the pivot domain; it is the catalyst of the perspective. The pivot domain, or weak quadrant, is the area that will receive focus and where changes will be addressed by the anchor quadrant. The impacted domain will be directly affected by the change to the pivot domain (Henderson & Venkatraman, 1993; Luftman, Lewis, & Oldach, 1993).

Thus, there are a total of eight possible perspectives resulting from the use of cross-domain alignment as well as four fusion perspectives that combine two of the individual ones (Papp, 1995).

Strategy Execution Perspective

The perspective that receives the most focus is the strategy execution perspective. Business strategy is the anchor domain and the company traditionally has a strong and well-established strategy. The weak domain is the business infrastructure, often the business processes and employee skills. The information technology infrastructure is the impacted domain and usually results in major changes to the information technology architecture as a result of changes in the business processes. Top management is frequently the leader in this perspective and information technology management is more of a functional subordinate. The organization's mission-critical areas and critical success factors must be defined and communicated to everyone. The information technology manager implements and supports the business priorities, hence information technology's role is largely reactive or responsive; the goal is to meet the demands of the business strategy. Performance measurement is typically of a financial nature (Venkatraman, 1989a). The perspective focuses on information technology planning or business transformation. There is frequently a tight linkage to information technology planning methods, and prototyping is often deployed in the operational environment (Fitzgerald, 1993). The goals are usually along the lines of reducing delays and errors, enhancement of services, and time savings (e.g., routing of paperwork, redefinition of tasks, etc.). Companies that have successfully employed a strategy execution perspective include IBM Credit Corporation (who reduced the time required to process orders from six days to less than two hours), Mutual Benefit Life (who reduced costs by 40% through the use of reengineering), and McGraw-Hill (who redesigned its textbook work-flows through its revolutionary PRIMIS database), among others (Luftman, 1995, Venkatraman, 1993a, 1993c).

Technology Potential Perspective

The Technology potential perspective is driven by business strategy, much like strategy execution; however, the pivot is information technology strategy, resulting in a clockwise direction with information technology infrastructure as the impacted domain. Top management's role is that of a technology visionary who

Figure 2: Original Alignment Perspectives

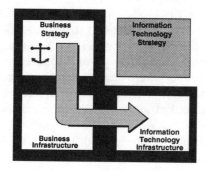

Strategy Execution Perspective
- Business Strategy - The domain anchor
- Organization Infrastructure - The pivot domain
- IT Infrastructure - The impact domain

Technology Potential Perspective
- Business Strategy - The domain anchor
- IT Strategy - The pivot domain
- IT Infrastructure - The impact domain

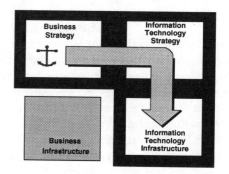

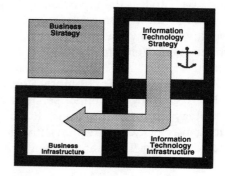

Competitive Potential Perspective
- IT Strategy - The domain anchor
- Business Strategy - The pivot domain
- Organization Infrastructure - The impact domain

Service Level Perspective
- IT Strategy - The domain anchor
- IT Infrastructure - The pivot domain
- Org. Infrastructure - The impact domain

identifies how the firm can apply technology, what the strengths and weaknesses are of the information technology infrastructure, and how to manage the risks of new information technology. The information technology manager's role is one of a technology architect whose job is to design and manage the technologies defined by top management, apply information technology so as to add value to the business, and address how information technology can be used to enable the business strategy (Luftman, 1995; LaPlante & Alter, 1994). The value of information technology is its contribution to the final product or service. The relationship between the customer and the firm are important, and information technology strategy drives the planning perspective. Some examples of technology potential include USAA, which has attempted to build a paperless office using imaging technology (Elam & Morrison, 1989); Rosenbluth travel, which combined several reservation databases together to create a customized, highly functional reservation system (IBM, 1991); as well as Frito-Lay, Otis Elevator, and Levi Strauss (Otisline Case Studies A & B, 1990; Frito-Lay, Inc., Case Studies A-D, 1991; Halper, 1994).

Competitive Potential Perspective

The competitive potential perspective focuses on how emerging information technologies can influence and enable new business strategies. From these new business strategies come competitive advantage. Information technology strategy is the anchor domain in this perspective, business strategy is the pivot domain, and organizational infrastructure is impacted. The role of top management is that of a business visionary whereby the potential of emerging information technology is realized and its strategic importance is assessed relative to the business. Top management must also be cognizant of how to leverage information technology to transform the business to achieve their vision. The role of the information technology manager is that of a business architect whose function is to ensure awareness of information technology and how it can be applied. The information technology manager is an integral part of the management team, and an ability to communicate the value of information technology is paramount, along with sound business knowledge (Luftman, 1995). The information technology focus is to provide "value-add" to the business strategy and enable new opportunities for the business (Barua et al., 1995; Katz, 1993; LaPlante, 1994a). The application of information technology to influence business strategy and create competitive advantage is vital. Information technology performance is assessed with respect to how the application of information technology influences clients and customers. The strategic planning method is business strategy based on information technology whereby technology scans are used to identify information technology that could be applied to the business. Some examples of firms that have utilized this perspective are American Airlines, which through its SABRE reservation system manages more than 50 million fares, 2,000 messages/second, and 500,000 passengers/day using high-speed networks and EDI (Hopper, 1990; Adcock, Helms, & Wen-Jang 1993); Baxter Healthcare, which integrated American Hospital Supply's ASAP system to create a network of hospitals linked to its order entry and tracking system (Konsynski & Vitale, 1991); and McGraw-Hill, which reengineered the textbook creation process by using the PRIMIS database to quickly produce customized textbooks (Venkatraman, 1993b, 1993c).

Service Level Perspective

The Service level perspective, with information technology strategy as the anchor, information technology infrastructure as the pivot, and organizational infrastructure as the impacted domain, focuses on how information technology can improve the delivery of products and services to processes. It also assesses how information technology can improve its own business processes. The role of top management is to define priorities for information technology projects. The role of information technology and its executives is to support key areas of the business and balance short-term objectives with long-term investment in information technology. Steering committees frequently identify and set priorities for information technology projects and, in effect, function as a "business within the business." The information technology manager's major role is to act as a service manager and satisfy the users of information technology. Performance is usually measured by the degree of end-user satisfaction. Prolonging this perspective may lead to the outsourcing of information technology (Luftman, 1995).

Organization Information Technology Infrastructure

The organization information technology infrastructure perspective results in process improvements from information technology and the application of value to business processes. The organization infrastructure provides the direction for IT, serving as the anchor. IT infrastructure is the pivot or weak area and changes made here impact IT strategy. The strategic planning method used is business process reengineering (BPR). For example, the role of top management is that of a leader or sponsor and information technology management's role is that of business process architect to enable BPR. Less than 10% of the companies studied over the past seven years fall into this perspective.

Information Technology Infrastructure Strategy

The information technology infrastructure strategy perspective focuses on the improvement of information technology strategy based on the implementation of emerging and existing information technology infrastructures. The anchor is IT infrastructure, which enables IT strategy. Object-oriented systems or e-commerce applications, for example, are tools frequently used to enable changes in the delivery of applications in the firm. In McGraw-Hill's PRIMIS application, information technology management serves as the project manager while business management's role was that of a sponsor and visionary. Thus, information technology provides customer satisfaction through system support. While less than 5% of companies studied followed this perspective, the influx of e-commerce applications will probably result in an increase in the use of an information technology infrastructure strategy perspective.

Information Technology Organization Infrastructure

In the information technology organization infrastructure perspective, top management takes on a leadership role similar to that followed by the strategy

Figure 3: Additional Alignment Perspectives

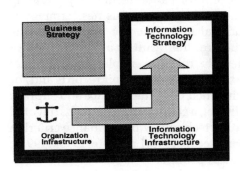

Organization IT Infrastructure
- Organization Infrastructure - The domain anchor
- IT Infrastructure - The pivot domain
- IT Strategy - The impact domain

IT Infrastructure Strategy
- IT Infrastructure - The domain anchor
- IT Strategy - The domain pivot
- Business Strategy - The impact domain

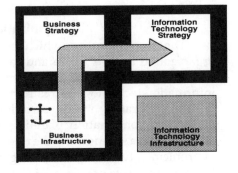

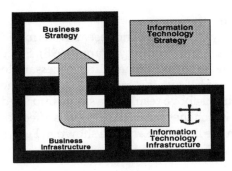

IT Organization Infrastructure
- IT Infrastructure - The anchor domain
- Organization Infrastructure - The pivot domain
- Business Strategy - The impact domain

Organization Infrastructure Strategy
- Organization Infrastructure - The anchor domain
- Business Strategy - The pivot domain
- IT Strategy - The impact domain

execution perspective; however, IT becomes the architect by which the visions and processes are carried out. For example, BPR or information technology planning methods are used to enhance organizational infrastructure. Business strategy is impacted, this time through the organizational infrastructure pivot. Since the anchor is information technology infrastructure, the result is a combination of service level and strategy execution leadership roles to enable organizational capability. Numerous companies that have begun to digitize their records and/or make them Internet-accessible have found that their customer service and support processes needed to be changed as a result. In fact, a chapter in this book is devoted to the strategic use of e-commerce. Information technology performance criterion focuses on information technology value (Barua et al., 1995; LaPlante, 1994a, 1994b; Katz, 1993) of IT to enable value to the business process.

Organization Infrastructure Strategy

Organization infrastructure strategy exploits the capabilities to enhance new products and services, influence strategy, and develop new relationships; it enables enhancements to business strategy, hence business strategy is the pivot domain, impacting information technology strategy. This perspective combines the leadership roles of strategy execution and competitive potential. Information technology management functions as a project manager and business management is a sponsor. The role of information technology is to deploy value to business processes using the value of information technology to the product or service. Currently, many companies are using the Internet to provide customer access and/or implementing e-commerce solutions that are developed and supported by IT.

Fusion

Fusion occurs when there are two equally weak areas, and research has found that more than 35% of firms studied exhibited this tendency (Papp, 1995). Since there are two "paths" from the anchor to the impacted domain, it is necessary to identify the weaker of the two pivots and carry out this perspective first. The combination of two of the perspectives outlined above results in a single impacted domain; there are two possible routes with which the impacted domain is affected. Four types of fusion have been identified in the literature and are shown in Figure 1-4 (Papp, 1998).

Organization Strategy Fusion

The two perspectives which impact business strategy, information technology organization infrastructure and information technology infrastructure strategy, are combined to produce a perspective that fuses toward business strategy from an information technology infrastructure anchor. The two weak points, information technology strategy and organization infrastructure, are the areas that will receive focus. This combination planning approach is technology driven. Information technology is a solution and the role of information technology management is that of problem-solver. Business management must be receptive to changes and accept the dominant role of information technology.

Figure 4: Fusion Perspectives

Organization Strategy Fusion

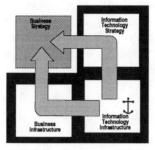

Combination of:
- IT Infrastructure Strategy Perspective
- IT Organizational Infrastructure Perspective

IT Strategy Fusion

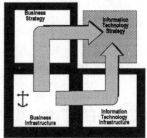

Combination of:
- Organizational Infrastructure Strategy Perspective
- Organizational IT Infrastructure Perspective

Organization Infrastructure Fusion

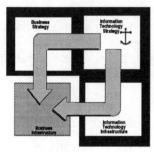

Combination of:
- Competitive Potential Perspective
- Service Level Perspective

IT Infrastructure Fusion

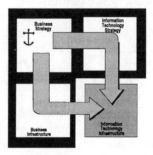

Combination of:
- Strategy Execution Perspective
- Technology Potential Perspective

Organization Infrastructure Fusion

The combination of competitive potential and service level perspectives results in a combined planning approach where organization infrastructure is impacted from an information technology strategy anchor. The two pivot points, information technology infrastructure and business strategy, result in the use of information technology as a competitive weapon. The business management's role is responsive and information technology's role is general. The performance criterion of information technology is the determination of information technology's value in the organization.

Information Technology Strategy Fusion

Two perspectives impact information technology strategy. They are organizational information technology infrastructure and organizational infrastructure strategy. The combination of these two perspectives toward information technology strategy from an organization infrastructure anchor yields the pivots business strategy and information technology infrastructure. Business management's role is to develop information technology for the purpose of strategic change. Information technology management's role is to accept such changes and focus on a cost/ benefit performance criterion.

Information Technology Infrastructure Fusion

The final fusion perspective combines strategy execution and technology potential. The anchor is business strategy and the pivots are organization infrastructure and information technology strategy, which directly impact information technology infrastructure. In this combination approach, information technology management's role is that of a technology manager with a focus on a new and emerging information technology architecture. Business management is focused on the future and information technology is seen as the cost of success.

MANAGEMENT IMPLICATIONS

These 12 alignment perspectives defined above can be used to assess the level and type of strategic alignment within an organization. They underscore the need to carefully examine both the business and information technology strategies and infrastructures to determine whether they are working in harmony or whether they are working in opposition.

Inappropriate alignment can cause problems not only with the development and integration of business and information technology strategies, but actually prevent technology from being leveraged to its maximum potential in the firm. Since information technology plays an increasingly vital role in corporate decision-making, its correct application will facilitate both a more competitive and profitable organization. The next section will focus on how companies can implement the model to determine which perspective they fall into and how they can use this information to maximize their information technology investment and develop their business and technology strategies.

ASSESSING ALIGNMENT

A company interested in assessing the level and extent of its strategic alignment first needs to determine where it is headed with respect to business and information technology strategy. The two best people to determine those strategies are the CEO (or highest ranking business executive) and the CIO (or highest ranking technology executive), respectively. These two individuals, along with other top executives, sit down and assess where the company is headed with respect to business and technology (see Table 2). Although several approaches exist to determine the level of integration of strategies within a company, the strategic alignment model can be used to successfully determine, by individual analysis of the company's top executives, the direction the company is headed and the areas that need attention.

A tool to determine the company's alignment perspective has been developed in conjunction with IBM (Luftman, Papp, & Brier, 1995). The first step is to answer a series of questions that address each of the components of the alignment model. The resulting alignment perspective is based on a mathematical weighted average calculation of the individual's objective assessment of each of the components. The questions used to assess alignment are found in Appendix 1 and have been adapted for multi-industry use (Luftman, Papp, & Brier, 1995; Papp & Luftman, 1995) from

Table 2: Components of the Strategic Alignment Model

I. BUSINESS STRATEGY

1. **Business Scope** – Includes the markets, products, services, groups of customers/clients, and   locations where an enterprise competes as well as the buyers, competitors, suppliers and potential competitors that affect the competitive business environment.
2. **Distinctive Competencies** – The critical success factors and core competencies that provide a firm with a potential competitive edge. This includes brand, research, manufacturing and product development, cost and pricing structure, and sales and distribution channels.
3. **Business Governance** – How companies set the relationship between management stockholders and the board of directors. Also included are how the company is affected by government regulations, and how the firm manages their relationships and alliances with strategic partners.

II. ORGANIZATION INFRASTRUCTURE & PROCESSES

4. **Administrative Structure** – The way the firm organizes its businesses. Examples include central, decentral, matrix, horizontal, vertical, geographic, and functional.
5. **Processes** - How the firm's business activities (the work performed by employees) operate or flow. Major issues include value-added activities and process improvement.
6. **Skills** – H/R considerations such as how to hire/fire, motivate, train/educate, and culture.

III. IT STRATEGY

7. **Technology Scope** - The important information applications and technologies.
8. **Systemic Competencies** - Those capabilities (e.g., access to information that is important to the creation/achievement of a company's strategies) that distinguishes the IT services.
9. **IT Governance** - How the authority for resources, risk, and responsibility for IT is shared between business partners, IT management and service providers. Project selection and prioritization issues are included here.

IV. IT INFRASTRUCTURE AND PROCESSES

10. **Architecture** -The technology priorities, policies, and choices that allow applications, software, networks, hardware, and data management to be integrated into a cohesive platform.
11. **Processes** - Those practices and activities carried out to develop and maintain applications and manage IT infrastructure.
12. **Skills** - IT human resource considerations such as how to hire/fire, motivate, train/educate, and culture.

original work done on a study of hospitals in the early 1990s (Henderson & Thomas, 1992).

As a service to executives, an abridged version of the assessment tool is available online at *http://strategic-alignment.com* and any results and suggestions should first be verified with the developers before undertaking any corporate strategy modifications. Please visit the Web site for complete information.

CYCLICAL ANALYSIS

Once the company's alignment perspective has been identified, it is important to determine where future iterations will lead to facilitate long-range planning and strategy formulation. For example, if an organization follows a *Strategy Execution* perspective (counter-clockwise direction), it is quite likely that the next perspective will be *Organization Information Technology Infrastructure*, maintaining the counter-clockwise "flow". By adhering to the same direction or flow, the four domains will be kept in balance. When the equilibrium is upset, the domains will not operate optimally until each has the ability to support the change. The cycle will typically continue, with the pivot becoming the new anchor, the impacted domain the new pivot, and the quadrant previously not addressed will become the next impacted domain. While this cycling through the model usually continues in the same direction, it is suggested that the firm continuously reassess the domains for the direction of change. The cycle is a continuous process of transformation, and not simply a single event. The ability to reassess the values, area of focus, and roles of the executives and employees involved is vital. Strategic alignment is achieved by continual reassessment and adjustments with respect to the perspectives (Papp, 1995; Henderson & Venkatraman, 1990 and 1996).

Once the firm has assessed its alignment, it needs to identify which area(s) deserve immediate focus based on the recommendations of the tool. Firms that are identified as following a fusion perspective, which is the combination of two individual perspectives as previously outlined, face a more difficult decision as they will need to determine which one of at least two courses of action to follow. The model is just the first stage in the alignment determination. Executives must also focus on identifying those factors that aid and hinder the achievement of alignment as well as focus on the activities that firms should undertake to either reach alignment or keep themselves aligned (Luftman, Papp,& Brier, 1999).

Alignment is a dynamic, complex process that takes time to develop and even more effort to maintain. Companies that have achieved alignment can facilitate building a strategic competitive advantage that will provide them with increased visibility, efficiency, and profitability to compete in today's changing markets. The importance of cooperation between business and IT to maximize investment in technology remains clear. The careful assessment of a firm's alignment is important to ensure IT is being used to appropriately enable or drive the business strategy. The strategic alignment model is a dynamic construct and cannot be explained with an isolated look at firms' perspectives. The model is designed to encourage and facilitate response to changing business conditions; a firm may be comfortable in one perspective at the current time, but may desire (or be forced) to change its

Figure 5: Cycling Through the Alignment Perspectives

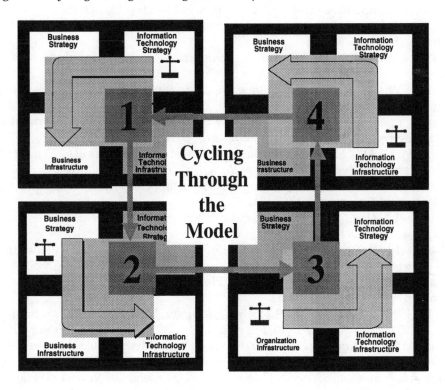

perspective in the future depending on its environment and competitors. Subsequent chapters will focus on the application of various components of strategic alignment and provide illustrative examples of how organizations can work toward the achievement of synergy between business and information technology.

REFERENCES

Adcock, K., Helms, M., & Wen-Jang, K. (1993). "Information Technology: Can it provide a sustainable competitive advantage?" *Information Strategy: The Executive's Journal*, (Spring), 10-15.

Alter A. (1995). "The Profit Center Paradox," *Computerworld*, (April 24), 101-105.

Baets, W. (1996). "Some Empirical Evidence on IS Strategy Alignment in Banking," *Information & Management*, 30, 155-77.

Boynton, A., Victor, B., & Pine II, B. (1996). "Aligning IT With New Competitive Strategies", *Competing in the Information Age*, Luftman, New York, Oxford University Press.

Brancheau, J., & Wetherbe, J. (1987). "Issues In Information Systems Management," *MIS Quarterly*, 11(1), 23-45.

Broadbent, M., and Weill, P. (1993). "Developing Business and Information Strategy Alignment: A Study in the Banking Industry," *IBM Systems Journal*, 32 (1).

Cardinali, R. (1992). "Information Systems—A Key Ingredient To Achieving Organizational Competitive Strategy," *Computers in Industry*, 18, 241-45.

Chan, Y., & Huff, S. (1993). "Strategic Information Systems Alignment," *Business Quarterly*, 58(1), 51-56.

Cook, T., & Campbell, D. (1979). *Quasi-Experimentation*, Boston: Houghton-Mifflin Co.

Creswell, J. W. (1994). *Research Design: Qualitative and Quantitative Approaches*, Thousand Oaks, CA: Sage Publications.

Davenport, T., & Short, J. (1990). "The New Industrial Engineering: Information Technology and Business Process Redesign," *Sloan Management Review*, 11-27.

Davidson, W. (1993). "Managing the Business Transformation Process," *Competing in the Information Age*, Luftman, New York, Oxford University Press.

Dixon, P., & John, D. (1989). "Technology Issues Facing Corporate Management in the 1990s," *MIS Quarterly*, 13(3), 247-55.

Earl, Michael J. (1983). *Corporate Information Systems Management*, Homewood, Illinois, Richard D. Irwin, Inc.

Earl, Michael J (1993). "Experience in Strategic Information Systems Planning," *MIS Quarterly*, 17(1), 1-24.

Faltermayer, E. (1994). "Competitiveness: How US Companies Stack Up Now," *Fortune*, 129(8), (April 18), 52-64.

Foster, R. (1986). *Innovation: The Attacker's Advantage*, New York: Summit Books.

Goff, L. (1993). "You Say Tomayto, I Say Tomahto," *Computerworld*, (Nov. 1), 129.

Hammer, M., & Champy, J. (1993). *Reengineering the Corporation: A Manifesto For Business Revolution*, New York: Harper Business.

Hammer, M., & Stanton, S. (1995). *The Reengineering Revolution*, New York: Harper Business.

Henderson, J. & Thomas, J. (1992). "Aligning Business and Information Technology Domains: Strategic Planning In Hospitals," *Hospital and Health Services Administrative*, 37, (1), 71-87.

Henderson, J., Thomas, J., & Venkatraman, N. (1992). "Making Sense Of IT: Strategic Alignment and Organizational Context," Working Paper 3475-92 BPS, Sloan School of Management, Massachusetts Institute of Technology.

Henderson, J., & Venkatraman, N. (1990). "Strategic Alignment: A model For Organizational Transformation Via Information Technology," Working Paper 3223-90, Sloan School of Management, Massachusetts Institute of Technology.

Henderson, J., & Venkatraman, N. (1996). "Aligning Business and IT Strategies," *Competing in the Information Age*, Luftman, New York, Oxford University Press.

IBM (1981). *Business Systems Planning, Planning Guide*, GE20-0527, IBM Corporation, 1133 Westchester Ave, White Plains, New York.

Ives, B., Jarvenpaa, S., & Mason, R. (1993). "Global Business Drivers: Aligning Information Technology To Global Business Strategy," *IBM Systems Journal*, 32(1), 143-161.

Jick, T. (1979), "Mixing Qualitative and Quantitative Methods: Triangulation in Action", *Administrative Science Quarterly*, 24, December, pp. 602-611.

Kador, J. (1996). "CEO's Take the Wheel," *Beyond Computing*, January/February, 50-53.

Keen, P. (1996). "Do You Need An IT Strategy?" *Competing in the Information Age*, Luftman, New York, Oxford University Press.

Keen, P. (1991). *Shaping the Future*, Boston, MA: Harvard Business School Press.

King, J. (1995) "Re-engineering Focus Slips," *Computerworld*, (March 13), 6.

Liebs, S. (1992). "We're All In This Together," *Information Week*, (October 26), 8.

Luftman, J. (1997). "Align in the Sand," *Computerworld Leadership Series*, (February 17), 1-11.

Luftman, J. (1996). *Competing in the Information Age: Practical Applications of the Strategic Alignment Model*, New York: Oxford University Press.

Luftman, J., Lewis, P., & Oldach, S. (1993). "Transforming the Enterprise: The Alignment of Business and Information Technology Strategies," *IBM Systems Journal*, 32(1), 198-221.

Luftman, J., Papp, R., & Brier. T. (1995). "The Strategic Alignment Model: Assessment and Validation," In *Proceedings of the Information Technology Management Group of the Association of Management (AoM) 13th Annual International Conference*, Vancouver, British Columbia, Canada, August 2-5, 1995, 57-66.

Luftman, J., Papp, R., & Brier, T. (1999). "Enablers and Inhibitors of Business–IT Alignment," *Communications of the AIS*, I (11), March 1999.

McLean, E., & Soden, J., (1977). *Strategic Planning for MIS*, New York, John Wiley & Sons,

Mills, P., (1986), *Managing Service Industries*, New York Ballinger.

Niederman, F., Brancheau, J., & Wetherbe, J. (1991). "Information Systems Management Issues For the 1990s," *MIS Quarterly*, 15(4), 475-95.

Papp, R. (1998). "Alignment of Business and Information Technology Strategy: How and Why", *Information Management*, 11, #3/4.

Papp, R. (1995). *Determinants of Strategically Aligned Organizations: A Multi-industry, Multi-perspective Analysis*, (Dissertation), Hoboken, NJ: Stevens Institute of Technology.

Papp, R., & Luftman, J. (1995). "Business and IT Strategic Alignment: New Perspectives and Assessments," In *Proceedings of the Association for Information Systems, Inaugural Americas Conference on Information Systems*, Pittsburgh, PA.

Parker, M., & Benson, R., (1988). *Information Economics*, Englewood Cliffs, New Jersey, Prentice-Hall.

Pyburn, P. (1991). "Redefining the Role of Information Technology," *Business Quarterly*, (Winter), 89-94.

Robson, W. (1994). *Strategic Management and Information Systems: An Integrated Approach*, London: Pitman Publishing.

Rogers, L. (1997). "Alignment Revisited." *CIO Magazine*, May 15.

Rockart, J., Earl, M., and Ross, J. (1996). "Eight Imperatives for the New IT Organization." *Sloan Management Review*, Fall 1996, 43-55.

Rockart, J., & Short, J. (1989). "IT in the 1990's: Managing Organizational Interdependence," *Sloan Management Review*, 30(2), 7-17.

Wang, C. (1997). *Techno Vision II*, New York, McGraw-Hill.

Watson, R., & Brancheau, J. (1991). "Key Issues In Information Systems Management: An International Perspective," *Information & Management*, 20, 213-23.

Yin, R. K. (1984), *Case Study Research: Design and Methods*, Newbury Park, CA: Sage Publications.

Yourdon, E. (1997). *Death March: The Complete Software Developers Guide to Surviving Mission Impossible Projects*, New Jersey: Prentice Hall.

FURTHER READING

Earl, Michael J. (1983). *Corporate Information Systems Management*, Homewood, Illinois, Richard D. Irwin, Inc.

Luftman, J. (1996). *Competing in the Information Age: Practical Applications of the Strategic Alignment Model*, New York: Oxford University Press.

Papp, R., "Business - IT Alignment: Productivity Paradox Payoff?", *Industrial Management & Data Systems*, 99(8).

Papp, R.(1988)."Achieving Business and IT Alignment", *Effective Utilization and Management of Emerging Information Technologies*, Hershey, PA: Idea Group Publishing.

Luftman, J., Papp, R., & Brier, T., "Enablers and Inhibitors of Business-IT Alignment", *Communications of the AIS*, Volume 1, Article 11, March, 1999.

Robson, W. (1994). *Strategic Management and Information Systems: An Integrated Approach*, London, Pitman Publishing.

APPENDIX 1:
STRATEGIC ALIGNMENT MODEL
ASSESSMENT QUESTIONS

Using the Strategic Alignment model previously described, you can better understand your organization and your planning perspective. This assessment tool consists of 36 questions about your organization. Each question asks you to rank how the issues, opportunities, and risks associated with the choices and decisions of strategic alignment are made regarding your enterprise on a scale from 1 to 7 (see below). Based on your responses, we will determine your current planning perspective.

Poor	Inadequate		Sufficient	Strong		Extraordinary
1	2	3	4	5	6	7

Your planning perspective is determined by first identifying the quadrant (or box) that your responses suggest has the largest opportunity (lowest ranking) for enhancing the enterprise. This quadrant will be used as the pivot domain. That quadrant that your responses suggest has the highest ranking will be used as the anchor domain. Given the selection of your anchor and pivot, the flow/direction of your perspective and impacted domain can be identified.

There are cases where the determination of your perspective does not fit the process described. This perspective is called "fusion" and should be discussed with an instructor.

The questions are divided into two parts. The twelve questions in Part 1 address the four quadrants of the Strategic Alignment Model. There are three questions (one page) for each quadrant of the model.

Part 1

To what extent do you believe the following components are defined, communicated, effective, efficient, valuable:

__(1 of 12)__ the SCOPE of your business, encompassing the products, services and geography your organization serves and the services you provide.

__(2 of 12)__ the DISTINCTIVE COMPETENCIES or unique characteristics of your products or services, such as pricing, distribution channels and quality of service.

__(3 of 12)__ how you carry out the GOVERNANCE of your BUSINESS, the manner in which you choose to operate and compete, either as a single entity or by forming alliances with customers, suppliers, and other providers.

To what extent do you believe the following components are defined, communicated, effective, efficient, valuable:

__(4 of 12)__ your ADMINISTRATIVE STRUCTURE, which defines organization arrangement and responsibilities, including centralized, decentralized, and networked structures.

__(5 of 12)__ the design of your essential PROCESSES, such as standard operating procedures, cross-functional processes, and associated information flows.

__(6 of 12)__ the acquisition of new SKILLS, the modification of the existing skills, and other human resource considerations of those who will carry out your strategy.

To what extent do you believe the following components are defined, communicated, effective, efficient, valuable:

__(7 of 12)__ your I/T SCOPE, the determination of the range and type of information technologies critical to your organization, such as image processing, expert systems, and local area networks.

__(8 of 12)__ the SYSTEMIC COMPETENCIES or important characteristics of your information technology infrastructure, including access to information, reliability, speed, and connectivity.

__(9 of 12)__ your GOVERNANCE of I/T, including steering committees, contracting for I/T services, and establishing partnerships with other organizations to obtain needed services.

To what extent do you believe the following components are defined, communicated, effective, efficient, valuable:

(10 of 12) your I/T ARCHITECTURE, which defines the choices and policies that enable the systems, applications, data, software, and hardware in a cohesive platform.

(11 of 12) your I/T work PROCESSES associated with the development, delivery, and use of information systems, including application development, standard security procedures, and other system management controls.

(12 of 12) the acquisition or modification of SKILLS and experience related to the development, operation, and use of information systems in your organization to match I/T skills to your business needs.

The 24 questions (8 pages) in Part 2 address the relationships among the four quadrants of the Strategic Alignment Model. The vertical relationships are called "strategic fit". The horizontal relationships are called "functional integration". These relationships are illustrated in the figure below. The relationships are two-way between adjacent quadrants of the model. There are three questions for each relationship. The next 12 questions pertain to "strategic fit". The last 12 questions relate to "functional integration".

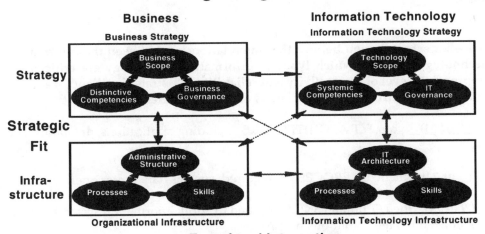

The Strategic Alignment Model

Part 2

To what extent do you believe that the relationship between the business strategy (entering new markets, changing services) and the following organizational infrastructure decisions are defined, effective, efficient:

  (1 of 24) your ADMINISTRATIVE STRUCTURE, including reporting relationships and roles.

  (2 of 24) the design of your critical work PROCESSES, such as work flows and standard operating procedures.

  (3 of 24) the SKILLS needed for human resources for line or functional areas to carry out the strategy.

To what extent do you believe that the relationship between the organizational structure and processes (authority structure, business processes and skills) and the following business strategy decisions are defined, effective, efficient:

  (4 of 24) the SCOPE of your business, including clients and services.

  (5 of 24) the DISTINCTIVE COMPETENCIES of your products and services, such as quality of service.

  (6 of 24) the GOVERNANCE of your BUSINESS, or the way in which you operate.

To what extent do you believe that the relationship between the information technology strategy (which types of information technology are critical, the appropriate level of connectivity and reliability, I/T strategic alliances) and the following I/T infrastructure decisions are defined, effective, efficient:

  (7 of 24) your I/T ARCHITECTURE, including applications, databases, and hardware.

  (8 of 24) the work PROCESSES required, such as data center operations.

  (9 of 24) the I/T human SKILLS needed to apply information systems in your organization to meet your business needs.

To what extent do you believe that the relationship between the information technology infrastructure (specific hardware, databases, and development processes) and the following I/T strategy decisions are defined, effective, efficient:

__(10 of 24)__ I/T SCOPE, such as networks, image processing, and knowledge-based systems.

__(11 of 24)__ the SYSTEMIC COMPETENCIES of your I/T infrastructure, such as reliability and connectivity.

__(12 of 24)__ the GOVERNANCE of I/T, whether you build your own systems or establish partnerships to obtain needed services.

To what extent do you believe that the relationship between the business strategy (entering new markets, changing services) and the following I/T strategy decisions are defined, effective, efficient:

__(13 of 24)__ I/T SCOPE, such as image processing and networks.

__(14 of 24)__ the SYSTEMIC COMPETENCIES, such as reliability, connectivity, and speed.

__(15 of 24)__ your I/T GOVERNANCE, such as application ownership or alliances to develop software or other products.

To what extent do you believe that the relationship between the I/T strategy (which types of I/T are critical, the appropriate level of connectivity) and the following business strategy decisions are defined, effective, efficient:

__(16 of 24)__ your BUSINESS SCOPE, the essential products and services you provide.

__(17 of 24)__ the DISTINCTIVE COMPETENCIES of your products and services, such as quality, and service level.

__(18 of 24)__ the GOVERNANCE of your BUSINESS, operating as a single entity or in partnership.

To what extent do you believe that the relationship between the organizational infrastructure (administrative structure, work processes, and human skills required to carry out your business strategy) and the following I/T infrastructure decisions are defined, effective, efficient:

__(19 of 24)__ your I/T ARCHITECTURE, including critical applications, databases, or hardware.

__(20 of 24)__ your I/T PROCESSES and operations, such as systems development, application development, and data center operations.

__(21 of 24)__ the I/T human resources and SKILLS you need to meet business requirements.

To what extent do you believe that the relationship between the information technology architecture (I/T architecture and processes such as specific hardware and development processes) and the following organizational infrastructure decisions are defined, effective, efficient:

__(22 of 24)__ your ADMINISTRATIVE STRUCTURE, including authority levels, roles, and responsibilities.

__(23 of 24)__ the PROCESSES of your business, such as standard operating procedures and cross-functional processes.

__(24 of 24)__ the SKILLS required of your people to carry out your business strategy.

Chapter II

Sustainable Competitive Advantage from Information Technology: Limitations of the Value Chain

David L. Bahn
Metropolitan State University, USA

The strategic benefit of IT (information technology) in supporting business functions is often seen as the basis for competitive advantage that is sustainable. The value chain concept has been a handy tool widely utilized in business strategy analysis to match firm competency in performing business activities with the achievement of sustainable marketplace advantage. When it comes to the assessment of the competitive value of information technology, the value chain concept seems to either categorize IT as a support activity or to overly narrow the scope of IT's role in achieving sustainable competitive advantage.

This chapter reviews the concepts of the value chain and sustainable competitive advantage. Short case studies from a number of industries are presented in order to illustrate the limitations of using the value chain to describe information technology's role in achieving sustainable competitive advantage. These examples demonstrate the subtle and often complex relationship between information technology and competitive advantage.

Information technology and systems are often cited as having a strategic role in achieving competitive advantage. Beyond the achievement of simple competitive advantage, the strategic benefit of deploying information technology to support business functions is often seen as the basis for competitive advantage that is *sustainable*. While there have recently been questions about the reality of sustainable competitive advantage (Oliver, 1999), this concept nevertheless often underlies characterizations of information technology's value to the firm.

The value chain concept has been a handy tool widely utilized in business strategy analysis to match firm competency in the performance of business activities with the achievement of sustainable marketplace advantage. This concept works rather well for assessing firm activities such as sales, manufacturing, retailing, and purchasing. Nevertheless, when it comes to the assessment of information technology competency, the value chain concept seems to imply either categorizing this competency as a support activity or overly narrowing the scope of IT's role in achieving sustainable competitive advantage.

This chapter will review the concepts of the value chain and sustainable competitive advantage. It will then present case examples that illustrate the limitations of using the value chain to describe information technology's role in achieving sustainable competitive advantage. These case examples will also be used to demonstrate the subtle and often complex relationship between information technology and competitive advantage.

THE VALUE CHAIN CONCEPT

The value chain concept is one particular paradigm that has often been utilized for describing the achievement of sustainable competitive advantage. The value chain concept, as introduced by Porter (1985), states that a firm's activities can be viewed as part of an array of sequential processes that transform unfinished inputs into finished outputs suitable for customer use. The sequential string of activities was referred to as the value chain because each activity is considered to add perceived or real value for the customer or end-user of the product. Porter regarded five primary business activities as being constituent of a generic value chain. Figure 1A illustrates these five generic activities.

The manifestation of value chains differs from firm to firm. Value chains also significantly differ according to the product or service being produced. Moreover, even as each component activity of a value chain presumably adds some value to the finished output delivered to the customer, each activity also incurs some cost. Figure 1B illustrates a typical value chain for a producer of butter.

One of the most powerful insights of the value chain concept is that some of the significant activities in the value chain for a firm's products could lie outside the boundaries of the firm's own activities. For example in the value chain for butter production presented in Figure 1B, the actual sale of butter to the consumer is accomplished by retailers and the marketing of butter to the consumer may also be handled largely by intermediaries rather than by the producer.

A related strength of the value chain concept is that it can be applied at the level of an industry rather than being pertinent only at the level of the firm. The *value*

Figure 1A: A Generic Firm Value Chain

Figure 1B: A Value Chain for a Firm Producing Butter

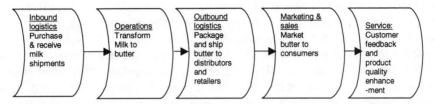

system for a given product describes the vertically linked and sequential activities of several firms within an industry involved in the transformation of raw materials into a completely finished product that is available and suitable for consumption (Porter, 1985; Armistead & Clark 1993). Figure 2 expands the butter producer's value chain described above into a value system for butter manufacture and distribution. Essentially, the linked value chains of several firms comprise the value system for producing butter and delivering it to the consumer.

This depiction of the value system for butter also demonstrates how the value chain activities that a firm is involved in can leapfrog the linked activities performed by another firm. In this example the butter manufacturer not only performs production and packaging activities prior to marketing and sales by the retailer, it also performs service-related activities that succeed the sales activity. This too illustrates the strength of the value chain concept (as it has been extended into the value system) for demonstrating that firms must develop competitive strength not

Figure 2: A Value System for Producing and Delivering Butter

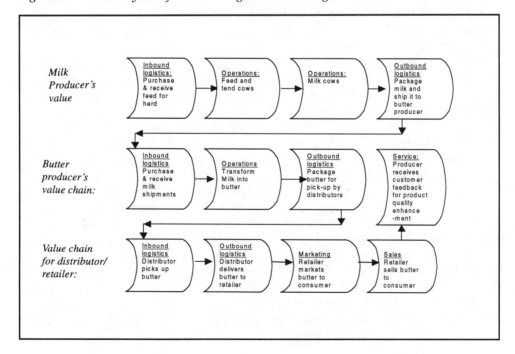

just by enhancing their own business activities, but by creating effective linkages with the value chains of suppliers, distributors and retailers (Morrow & Ashcroft, 1994). Depending on the level of analysis and the degree of atomization in description, the value chain concept can flexibly serve as a window onto one firm's own activities with its products or into the activities of an entire vertical industry with respect to the same products. This windowing capability makes the concept rather helpful as a tool for assessing firm strategy in the context of an industry.

A further useful aspect of the value chain concept is the idea of activity-based costing. In breaking down the entire of range of production activity into precisely delineated component activities, a firm can measure the costs and benefits of each of these activities. This data can be significant in a firm's determination of which activities need improvement or even outsourcing. An allied benefit of this activity-based costing of activities is the potential for benchmarking a firm's performance of value chain activities against the performance of comparably defined activities of competitors (Thompson & Strickland, 1999; Morrow & Ashcroft, 1994).

All told, the value chain is a highly useful strategy concept with utility for simplifying the view of two complex relationships: the interaction between a firm and its upstream/downstream industry, and the comparison of a firm's activities with those of its competitors. Not surprisingly, the value chain concept has taken a strong place in business jargon.

THE VALUE CHAIN AND SUSTAINABLE COMPETITIVE ADVANTAGE

In a sense, the notion of achieving sustainable competitive advantage has been the 'holy grail' of much of what has been written in the business strategy literature for the past 20 years. The efforts in this body of literature to descriptively define sustainable competitive advantage have been inextricably bound up in prescriptive research on how it can be achieved.

One recent analysis (Duncan et al., 1998) defined sustainable competitive advantage as the outcome of "an enduring value differential between the products or services of one organization and those of its competitors in the minds of customers". Sustainable competitive advantage has been described as being manifest in three distinct forms (Ghemawat, 1986): benefits from the size of a firm's volume or market share in the potential market, superior access by a firm to resources or customers, and restrictions on competitors' options. If a firm has significant size in production volume it can: (a) achieve economies of scale in mass production, (b) benefit from longer term experience in production activity in order to reduce costs and improve quality of outputs, and (c) achieve economies of scope that enable it to differentiate more of its products without increasing costs. A firm's superior access to raw materials or to production technology could enable it to achieve significant cost advantages over its competition. Similarly, superior access to customers or markets can place prohibitive costs upon competitors seeking the same customers. Sponsorship of government regulation that delimits business activity within an industry, or being a first mover in respect to a new product or industry, can both potentially create competitive advantage by restricting competitors' options in the same industry.

There have been two primary schools of thought in the strategic management literature on how competitive advantage is achieved (Dyer & Singh, 1998). One school of thought sees the characteristics of a firm's membership within a particular industry as the primary determinant of sustainable competitive advantage. In this view, competitive advantage can result if the characteristics of an industry allow a firm to establish barriers to entry that prevent other firms from initiating competition. A firm could also use its size or resources to gain a stronger measure of bargaining power in respect to the suppliers or buyers in its industry. Another school of thought regards a firm's resources and capabilities as being the source of competitive advantage. According to this perspective, the extent to which such capabilities and resources cannot be matched or imitated ('trumped') by other firms determines the degree of sustainability for the competitive advantage.

Particularly according to this resource-based view of the firm, a breakdown of organizational activities using the value chain is often the basis for assessing competitive advantage and its degree of sustainability. In the context of an internal assessment of an organization's potential for achieving competitive advantage, firm resources or capabilities are evaluated to see if they contribute to the superior and distinctive performance of value chain activities (Duncan et. al., 1998). If this match of a resource/capability to the superior performance of a value chain activity is also not subject to being imitated by competitors, then the competitive advantage is characterized as being sustainable (Collis & Montgomery, 1995). For example, the match of Wal-Mart's cross-docking capability to the enhancement of its value chain activity of distribution has been characterized as not being replicable by competitors and hence serves as a basis for sustainable competitive advantage over its competitors in the retail industry (Dess & Picken, 1999).

THE VALUE CHAIN CONCEPT AND INFORMATION TECHNOLOGY

The value chain concept is often used implicitly or explicitly as the basis for evaluating information technology's role in strengthening firm operations to achieve competitive advantage. For example, a recent study of information technology's use in international business operations utilized the configuration and coordination of value chain activities as two primary measures of how an appropriate information technology platform could benefit planning and coordination of business activities (see King & Sethi, 1999). The competitive value of electronic commerce is routinely described in terms of efficiency improvements to value chain activities of supply, manufacturing, operations, sales and distribution. Another recent and common metaphor is the idea of information technology's application to tightly integrate separate value chain activities and so gain competitive advantage from efficiency (Cahn, 1999; Morash & Clinton, 1997) or effectiveness (Steidtmann, 1999; Radcliff, 1999).

Nevertheless, the value chain concept also possesses significant limitations that can often contribute to obscuring the full nature of information technology's role in achieving competitive advantage. In Porter's (1985) original conception of the value chain, the information technology function was categorized as belonging to administrative support activity (a net cost) rather than as belonging to primary revenue-enhancing activity directly on the firm's value chain. To the extent that information technology is perceived as adding value, it is only in the context of adding value directly to a firm activity that is a primary component of the value chain. Generally this value-added benefit is assessed with respect to a single primary value chain activity in isolation from others. Even to the extent that information technology is perceived as beneficial to multiple value chain activities, it is typically defined in terms of efficiency benefits resulting from the integration or consolidation of primary value chain activities, a phenomena usually described as "supply chain management" (Fein & Jap, 1999). Competitive advantage yielded from a systematic impact on firm activities that results from an information technology capability (or, for that matter, from any organizational capability) is not easily depicted in value chain terms (Porter, 1996).

Notwithstanding these limitations of the value chain concept, it has become so semantically and metaphorically significant in assessing information technology's contribution to competitive advantage that a new version of the concept has been adopted: the virtual value chain. This refers to the sequential execution of value-adding activities that transform "raw information into new marketspace services and products that are unique to the information world" (Rayport & Sviokla, 1995, p. 77). Five information-processing task activities are seen as constituent of a virtual value chain activity: gathering, organizing, selecting, synthesizing, or distributing information. The virtual value chain concept does categorize information technology activity as a primary value-adding activity rather than as a support activity. However, this manifestation of the value chain concept still parses the competitive value of information technology into the discrete enhancement of sequential organizational activities, albeit that these are information-processing activities. Thus the modified concept of a virtual value chain also seems incapable of readily describing the systemic impacts of information technology upon a firm's business activities.

In as much as the value chain concept offers a handy means of comparing a firm's activities and costs to those of its competitors, it is not surprising that it is used for characterizing any particular basis for competitive advantage, including information technology. Nevertheless, as the ensuing examples will illustrate, the actual impacts of information technology on a firm's activities are both obvious and yet also more subtle and complex than what is projected by the value chain concept.

HARLEY DAVIDSON: COORDINATING MANY IT INITIATIVES IN PARALLEL

Harley-Davidson, a prominent American manufacturer of motorcycles, has seen its share of ups and downs during the course of its 96 year history. Recently, Harley-Davidson has accomplished a remarkable turnaround strategy to regain leadership in its industry. The firm has sought to retain and strengthen its dominant competitive position through the use of advanced information technology in a broad spectrum of business activities.

In the area of design engineering, Harley-Davidson utilizes information technology to transform product development into a coordinated cross-functional activity. While a design plan for a new model of motorcycle is initially under development by the design engineers, the plan can be reviewed and critiqued for feasibility by both purchasing and manufacturing staff (Minihan, 1998). Drastic reductions in cycle time for new product development have been achieved with even greater reductions anticipated. In its manufacturing operations Harley-Davidson has utilized information technology to boost production while concurrently cutting operating costs (Caldwell, 1998). In the activities of supply and inbound logistics, Harley-Davidson has made use of its parts database to track and streamline the number of its suppliers. Even the firm's marketing and sales activities have utilized both customer relationship management software to nurture relationships with purchasers of its motorcycles and a business-to-consumer Web site to provide pre-sales product information to prospective customers.

These information technology applications can be considered individually in light of the value chain activities that they support. With respect to the sustainability of the competitive advantage that each application yields, there is nothing that inherently renders the firm immune to imitation by industry rivals. Yet the very breadth of Harley-Davidson's information technology activities gives us pause in asserting that the competitive advantage is not sustainable. Harley-Davidson's competitive advantage from information technology does not reside in any one of these value chain activities individually but in its organizational capacity to successfully and continually engage in multiple information technology development efforts simultaneously. Given the complexity of information technology development projects (as well as the ever-present risk of failure), this is not a capability that can be readily duplicated by other firms. Furthermore, it represents a managerial competency that is systemic in nature and that ranges across several distinct value chain activities.

RAINFOREST CAFÉ: MINIMIZING IT TO ENHANCE COMPETITIVE ADVANTAGE

As a mature industry, the restaurant business has been undergoing much fragmentation and segmentation in the past few years. One of the most exciting new wrinkles in this sector is the advent of theme restaurants such as Planet Hollywood, the Hard Rock Café, and Rainforest Café. These recent entrants to the industry are characterized by significant investment in the physical and operational infrastructure of food service in order to create a distinct atmosphere and unique theme-based experience for their customers. The Rainforest Café provides a total atmosphere involving the experience of being in a tropical rain forest, including mechanically induced sound effects of waterfalls, lightning, and wildlife as well as live tropical birds. In adjoining storefronts, each Rainforest Café restaurant sells retail merchandise related to the rain forest theme. The particular theme is intended to foster in adult and child customers a sense of excitement about nature, concern for the survival of the tropical forest ecosystems and a strong loyalty to the firm's food service and retail products.

One of the distinguishing facets of Rainforest's operations is its rapid turnover of table space in its restaurants. This results in a capacity utilization of retail space that has been significantly higher than most of its competitors. Moreover, the firm's sales per table, along with its ability to generate repeat customer visits, have been quite high for its industry. While Rainforest Café does utilize information technology to support its food service operations, its use of information technology is remarkably simple and direct. The point-of-sale system it utilizes enables its retail managers to easily track revenue generation and table productivity accomplished by the restaurant service staff. The point of sale system is also remarkably user-friendly and requires very little training on the part of the servers in order for them to enter and update transaction data effectively. To coordinate rapid server and table assignment for customers, the restaurant utilizes a particularly inexpensive form of information technology: two–way radio (e.g. 'walkie-talkies'). To coordinate the effective delivery of meal orders to its customers, the restaurant bypasses the pager technology favored by many of its competitors for server notification and instead employs independent staff called runners to deliver the food to the tables. This maximizes order-taking opportunities by enabling the servers to remain in constant physical proximity to the customers. Rainforest Café also utilizes customer relationship management software to track customer purchasing behavior and to offer promotions that stimulate more customer visits during periods of diminished capacity utilization. Although the financial performance of theme restaurant chains has recently faltered, Rainforest Café's performance seems to have suffered less than several other competitors.

In assessing the role of information technology in Rainforest Café's success, it is useful to consider the place of information technology investment in the restaurant industry. Restaurant chains typically view information technology as a burdensome expense that negatively impacts on the profit and loss statement for each restaurant location. Restaurant chains also usually employ staff who either are not well suited to use sophisticated information technology or whose terms of employment are often too brief (due to a high industry-wide labor turnover rate) to achieve a level of skill necessary to effectively exploit the capabilities of advanced information technology.

From a competitive standpoint, what makes Rainforest Café's utilization of information processing technology noteworthy is that it is expertly minimal. The simplicity of its point of sale systems enables the firm to almost completely bypass the costs of technology training for its service staff. The organization of its table assignment and order delivery operations allows Rainforest Café to greatly minimize equipment costs while maximizing revenues. Although utilized to organize efficient table assignment and order delivery operations, the information technology also has a minimal and discrete physical presence in the restaurant that does not overshadow the rain forest atmosphere that is the basis of the retail experience provided to customers. To the extent that the Rainforest Café has a competitive advantage from its revenue-enhancing food service operations, the role of information technology in supporting this competency is sophisticated in concept, simple in execution and inexpensive to boot. These are all process attributes that have a rather good fit with the operational requirements of the restaurant industry. With respect to information technology, it could be asserted that the firm has a managerial competency of knowing how to effectively invest in and to deploy information technology without incurring excess resource costs or a loss of customer focus in store operations.

We could employ the value chain concept in describing the role of information technology to support the food service activity on the Rainforest Café's value chain. This description might even depict a beneficial enhancement for the firms of some key performance indicators in comparison with other restaurants (e.g., customer turnover and revenue per table). However, this description would not necessarily capture either the unique fit of the information technology application to the operational characteristics of the theme segment of the restaurant industry or the nature of the managerial competency that is the basis for this enhancement of the firm's competitive performance.

CHRYSLER'S EDI IMPLEMENTATION: USING IT TO DOMINATE SUPPLIERS

Chrysler, along with General Motors and Ford, has long utilized information technology in many of its business areas: inventory management, design engineering, manufacturing, sales, marketing, and even in service/warranty operations. One of the more recent information technology applications has been in the widespread implementation of electronic data interchange (EDI) for inbound logistics. EDI is used by Chrysler and by the other large auto firms to integrate information on parts supply and ordering with the information systems of their suppliers. This enables Chrysler, like many other manufacturers, to order parts inventory on a just-in-time basis. By transmitting parts orders immediately and only when inventory is required, EDI implementation has reduced inventory costs by almost eliminating the need for Chrysler's manufacturing plants to maintain stocks of unused parts inventory (Mukhopadhyay et al., 1995). This shorter lead-time and more direct process for inventory resupply has also resulted in reducing the costs of parts inventory that become obsolete when new models of automobiles are introduced. EDI implementation has also cut shipping costs by reducing the number of situations where parts have to be ordered and shipped from suppliers on an emergency basis. In a sense, Chrysler's implementation of EDI is a textbook case of using information technology to integrate the respective value chain activities of outbound logistics for suppliers with inbound logistics for customers.

Although this description of EDI implementation is straightforward, it overly simplifies the impact of EDI for Chrysler. First of all EDI implementation is, in a sense, unremarkable in that many manufacturers and large buyers of manufactured parts and products have adopted it in order to yield reduction of inventory-related expenses. Thus, the competitive advantage within any given industry that results from the cost savings EDI yields would seem ephemeral.

In fact, the strategic benefit of EDI is more complex. Within many manufacturing industries, EDI implementation has been hastened by the championing of its adoption by the industry's major manufacturers. Typically, this advocacy manifests itself as a requirement imposed upon industry suppliers to adopt EDI or risk losing the manufacturer's business. Within the auto industry EDI implementation has been dictated to parts suppliers as a precondition to doing business with the major automakers. Within any given industry, the benefits of EDI implementation tend to accrue more for the buyers than the suppliers (Riggins & Mukhopadhyay, 1994). However, this is particularly true for the auto industry where the buyers are few and large and the suppliers are many and not of such large size. The buyers (or manufacturers) can better absorb the costs of EDI and can use EDI to minimize inventory cost across a very large number of purchasing transactions. In contrast, for the auto parts suppliers, EDI can be an expensive cost of doing business that is harder to absorb because of a small transaction volume (relative to the buyers). Chrysler's implementation of EDI could almost be characterized as a means of passing off costs to its suppliers, thus gaining a competitive advantage more with respect to parts suppliers than to competing automakers.

Augmenting this competitive advantage is that EDI implementation in the auto industry has been manifest through proprietary data standards such as EDIFACT and with proprietary telecommunication networks for transmitting transactions. The implementation of ANX, the industry's proprietary EDI network, has effectively required suppliers to pay for duplicate TCP/IP connections: one for regular Internet connectivity and one for ANX (Borchers and Demski, 1999). Essentially, suppliers have incurred additional costs for an information technology application that primarily benefits Chrysler and the other large buyers in the industry.

The vertical nature of the competitive advantage gained by Chrysler is hardly abnormal in the context of the auto industry. In general, strong competitive pressures are routinely exerted upon parts suppliers in order that the automakers can report better profit margins. Indeed what is remarkable is how well matched Chrysler's implementation of EDI is to the competitive dynamics of the industry, which typically pit manufacturers against suppliers almost more than against each other. Once again we see that the value chain concept yields a description of the competitive advantage afforded by information technology that is not quite sufficient. The value chain concept does not depict just how nicely the information technology application of EDI both matches the strategic characteristics of competition in the auto industry and augments existing competitive advantage in respect to parts suppliers.

YOU NAME IT, WE'LL GET IT: USING IT TO REINVENT THE OFFICE SUPPLY BUSINESS

The retail office supply industry in the U.S. is fairly large, with annual sales of about $200 billion (Zitner & Reidy, 1997). Although increasingly consolidating with the advent of office supply superstores, it still contains a wide variety of merchandisers. Retailers, who sell to consumers and businesses, range in size from small to large and range from local to national in scope. Office supply dealers, who sell primarily to businesses (often through catalogs), maintain modest warehouses in order to ensure an adequate stock of commonly sold items. Wholesalers, who maintain comprehensive inventories in very large warehouses, are both regional and national in scope. Wholesalers sell primarily to retailers and dealers but also sell directly to large customers in some instances.

You Name It, We'll Get It, Inc. ™ (YNIWGI) is a local office supply dealer in the twin cities of Minneapolis and St. Paul, Minnesota. YNIWGI and several other office supply dealers primarily sell to large corporate customers in this metropolitan area. What distinguishes YNIWGI from its competition is that it has no warehouse and no supply trucks. It also maintains no inventory on hand. Essentially, YNIWGI sells over the phone and more recently through the Internet. It also pledges to obtain any office supply item requested by its clients within several days time. All of this is accomplished by maintaining agreements with several wholesalers to deliver customer orders directly from their own warehouses with either their own trucks or though drop shipping (Federal Express, etc.). YNIWGI's clientele place orders for office supplies using a web based order system that is customized to each client's purchasing preferences, corporate mandates and unit budgets. YNIWGI's information system then transmits the order electronically to the wholesalers. To top it all off, YNIWGI also completely guarantees satisfaction on each order with a 30-day return policy. Within a two-year period the firm has increased its client roster twenty-five fold (Ojeda-Zapata, 1999) and has become the fastest growing and sixth largest office supply dealer in the Minneapolis-St. Paul area (Hahn, 1998).

From the standpoint of the value chain for the office supply industry, YNIWGI's seems to have a profound competitive advantage over other dealers. Without incurring inventory expenses such as operating a warehouse or a fleet of delivery trucks, it utilizes electronic commerce to service its customers and link to its supply chain of wholesalers. This would appear to be a competitive advantage that is based on reorganizing and consolidating the value chain for selling and delivering office supplies. Furthermore there is an apparent benefit of yielding cost savings to customers by disintermediating costly inventory-related business activities routinely performed by most local office supply dealers.

However, this apparent scenario of competitive advantage is not the reality. In fact, YNIWGI charges its customers as much as (or even more than) other dealers for its office supply products. Its 30-day, no-questions-asked returns policy also increases its expenses. Moreover, the large office supply superstore chains have also made significant continuous efforts to consolidate their supply chain and to disintermediate wholesalers in order to establish their own direct-to-manufacturer purchasing and logistics.

Instead, the basis of YNIWGI's competitive advantage lies in the capabilities of the web-based order entry system that is customized for the preferences, mandates and budgets of each client's organization. This IT application provides some unique benefits for YNIWGI's customers. YNIWGI's system provides constant up-to-date management reports that can detail and summarize all expenditures for office supply products. The client organizations themselves are thus freed of much of the onerous and often confusing tasks of trying to exercise centralized fiscal control over office supply purchases. At the same time, each individual business unit or employee can directly order supplies from a range of approved products within a designated budget, thus optimizing their own effectiveness. If certain purchases require approval of senior managers, the order entry system can place an order on hold until such approval is electronically submitted. This removes often cumbersome and costly layers of bureaucracy that can plague what should be essentially routine transactions. Each YNIWGI client gets a unique interface to the order entry system that is completely customized in fine detail to the particular requirements of the customer's purchasing processes. YNIWGI's information technology concurrently maximizes both: (a) the freedom and ease with which the individual business units of client organizations can purchase office supplies, and (b) the capacity of the senior financial managers of each client to monitor and control both the aggregate expenditure and ultimate selection of office supplies that are purchased.

Effectively YNIWGI's clients have outsourced to it a significant portion of the inbound logistics activity of their value chain (at least with respect to office supplies). However, this is not an example of a Kamban system where physical delivery and stocking are the primary activities outsourced. The primary and most valuable outsourced functions fulfilled by YNIWGI are the information management and control activities associated with enabling the clients to obtain best value for their office supply budget. Of course, any competitor could replicate what is essentially an information management function. However, since YNIWGI keeps busy customizing its information technology for each new client, it is highly unlikely that the competition will easily catch up with either YNIWGI's capability to rapidly deploy effective information technology in this domain or with YNIWGI's expertise in comprehending the evolving business requirements of its customers for executing fiscal control over office supply expenditure. Furthermore, the detailed knowledge of customer purchasing preferences that is provided by the strong degree of customization expertise also yields YNIWGI an enhanced capability to bargain and link with suppliers. Therefore, the sustainability of the firm's competitive advantage seems assured, at least in the short or medium term.

Once again we have an example of the limitations of the value chain concept in describing information technology's role for achieving sustainable competitive advantage. In strict value chain terms, YNIWGI's information technology provides little to no direct economic benefits resulting from efficiency or consolidation of business activities. Instead, the information technology plays a role in enhancing the customer's own value chain activity of inbound logistics. Indeed the essential benefit of the information technology is most pronounced in a management and control function associated with the customer's inbound logistics, rather than in the direct execution of those logistics activities themselves.

CONCLUSIONS

The value chain concept has gained wide usage because it is applicable to describing and comparing business activities at the levels of both a firm and an industry, thus providing a way for business people to summarize the complexity of the internal and external environments of real-life organizations. The cognitive value of this summarization should not be underestimated in as much as managerial decision-making is routinely characterized by the necessity of coping with a very complex, unstructured and often quite disordered reality.

At the same time though, the simplicity of the value chain is also the source of its limitations. In as much as the value chain concept presents a sequential view of business activities, it is well suited for describing business activities that center on machine-oriented and sequentially performed manufacturing processes. It is not well suited to describing the creation of value that is derived from services or experiences bundled with products, or the creation of value derived from information content that is appended to physical products or processes (Cartwright & Oliver, 2000). The value chain thus inadequately portrays YNIWGI's competitive advantage from customizing information technology to manage the inbound logistics and purchasing on behalf of its clients. Moreover, since the value chain is a snapshot of a sequence of business activities, it does not easily depict the fit of specific information technology to the requirements for success over time within a particular industry. This longer-term fit is exemplified by the Rainforest Café's expertly minimal use of information technology to minimize cost and maximize operational efficiency and the customer experience. It is also exemplified by the synergy of Chrysler's EDI implementation alongside the automaker's generally competitive approach towards suppliers.

The purpose of this chapter has been to illustrate some of the limitations of utilizing the value chain, a key concept from the strategy literature, in describing the role of information technology in achieving sustainable competitive advantage. In each of the brief case studies that were presented, the value chain concept fell short of a comprehensive description of the role and purpose of business information technology. However, this does not mean that the value chain concept provides no advantage whatsoever in comprehending the benefits of information technology, only that the concept has particular limitations with respect to describing how information technology can support or yield sustainable competitive advantage. Concepts such as the value chain that summarize a complex reality do provide a common lexicon for communicating about business strategy and for comprehending the messy organizational and industry context in which business strategy is formulated. Nevertheless, such summarizing concepts also create cognitive traps for those employing them. The role of academics should not only be to originate such concepts, but also to utilize them to parse out the real-life context of business practice through the thorough demarcation of their limitations.

Many organizations in the developed world are approaching a point where information technology capability becomes synonymous with elementary organizational continuity and function. As information technology becomes more ubiquitous in both life and business activities, it becomes increasingly difficult to separate out the role of information technology in business activities from a description of the business activities themselves. For example, in the context of extranets, the quality of the information technology becomes largely equivalent with the quality perception of the organization by its customers and stakeholders (Prahalad, 1999). The information technology of an organization is evolving into becoming a ubiquitous element in the transactional interface between an organization and all of its external constituencies. Accordingly, the chances that we will find one single concept that can adequately describe the role of information technology in achieving sustainable competitive advantage seem quite dim. A more promising approach could be to develop a range of alternative strategy concepts, each of which has distinct strengths and limitations when utilized to describe information technology's role in competitive advantage. Furthermore, the illustrative value of these concepts should stem as much from their comparative limitations as from their strengths.

REFERENCES

Armistead, C. & Clark. G. (1993). "Resource activity mapping: The value chain in service operations strategy." *The Service Industries Journal*. Vol. 13, Oct., 221-239.

Borchers, A. & Demski, M. (1999). "ANX®: An EDI standard in search of a business model." *Proceedings of the 1999 Americas Conference on Information Systems*, 429-430.

Cahn, D. (1999). "Achieving cyber efficiency."Manufacturing Systems, April 1999, 132.

Caldwell, B. (1998). "Harley shifts into higher gear." *Information Week*, November 30, 55-60.

Cartwright, R. and Oliver, R. (2000). "Untangling the value Web." Journal of Business Strategy, January/February, 22-27.

Collis, D. & Montgomery, C. (1995). "Competing on resources: Strategy in the 1990s." *Harvard Business Review*; Boston, July, 118-128.

Dess, G. & Picken, J. (1999). "Creating competitive (dis)advantage: Learning from Food Lion's freefall." *The Academy of Management Executive*, August , 97-111.

Duncan, W., Ginter, P. & Swayne, L. (1998). "Competitive advantage and internal organizational assessment." *The Academy of Management Executive*, August, 6-16.

Dyer, J. & Singh, H. (1998). "The relational view; Cooperative strategy and sources of interorganizational competitive advantage." *The Academy of Management Review*, October , 660-679.

Fein, A. & Jap, S. (1999). "Manage consolidation in the distribution channel." *Sloan Management Review*; Fall, 61-72.

Ghemawat, P. (1986). "Sustainable Advantage." *Harvard Business Review*, 65(5), Sept/Oct ., 53-58.

Hahn, S. (1998). "Top 25 List: Office Supply Companies." *City Business: Minneapolis/ St. Paul*, November 13th, 20.

King, W. & Sethi, V. (1999). "An empirical assessment of the organization of transnational information systems." *Journal of Management Information Systems*, Armonk; Spring, 7-28.

Minihan, T. (1998). "Harley-Davidson revs up development process." *Purchasing*, May 7.

Morash, E. & Clinton, S (1997). "The role of transportation capabilities in international supply chain management." *Transportation Journal*, Spring , 5-17.

Morrow, M. & Ashworth G. (1994). "An evolving framework for activity-based approaches." *Management Accounting*, February, 32-36.

Mukhopadhyay, T., Kekre, S. & Kalathur, S. (1995). "Business value of Information technology: A study of Electronic Data Interchange." *MIS Quarterly*, June, 137-156.

Ojeta-Zapata, J. (1999). "Raising the Net case study: E-strategies that paid off." *St. Paul Pioneer Press*, January 29th, 1E.

Oliver, R. (1999). "The Red Queen rules." *Journal of Business Strategy*, May/June, 8-10.

Porter, M. (1985). *Competitive Strategy*. New York: Free Press.

Porter, M. (1996). "What is strategy." *Harvard Business Review*, November/December, 61-76.

Prahalad, C. & Krishnan, M. (1999). "The new meaning of quality in the information age." *Harvard Business Review*, Sept/Oct., 109-118.

Radcliff, D. (1999). "Power struggle." Computerworld, Oct 25, 46-50.

Rayport, J. & Sviokla, J. (1995). "Exploiting the virtual value chain." *Harvard Business Review*, November/December, 75-81.

Riggins, F. & Mukhopadhyay, T. (1994). "Interdependent benefits from interorganizational systems: Opportunities for business partner reengineering." *Journal of MIS*, Fall , 37-57.

Steidtmann, C. (1999). "The new retail technology." *Discount Merchandiser*, November, 23.

Thompson, A. & Strickland, A. (1999). *Strategic Management*. New York: Irwin/McGraw-Hill.

Zitner, A. & Reidy, C. (1997). "Staples' $4 billion merger rejected." *The Boston Globe*, April 5, .A1.

ACKNOWLEDGEMENTS

The encouragement and critique of Karen Schnatterly and Alfred Marcus is humbly and gratefully noted.

Chapter III

Alignment Through Cross-Functional Integration

Mark R. Nelson
Rensselaer Polytechnic Institute, USA

ABSTRACT

The strategic alignment model presented in the first chapter of this book clearly identifies cross-functional integration as a critical dimension of IT alignment. This chapter focuses on the assessment and improvement of functional integration and presents a model for understanding how cross-functional integration between IT and other functional areas leads to more effective IT alignment at the functional level. By moving to higher levels in this "integration hierarchy" model, organizations can expect to achieve a higher degree of IT alignment. To provide context, the chapter presents the integration hierarchy model by focusing on the marketing and IT units. This cross-functional interface is a particularly important area for IT alignment given the environmental demand for effective e-commerce and data warehousing solutions. However, as later sections of this chapter will discuss, there are implications for the model for both practitioners and researchers beyond the marketing and IT interface.

Insights into why some organizations are better than others at making effective use of information technology (IT) to support business units will help us better understand the processes for achieving IT alignment. A key factor that affects the alignment of IT resources to an organization's business needs is the integration of the IT unit with the rest of the organization. Integration is "the quality of the state of collaboration that exists among departments that are required to achieve unity of effort by the demands of the environment" (Lawrence & Lorsch 1967:11). Also termed "cross-functional integration," how to successfully manage the interface between IT and business units is not particularly well understood. Therefore, new insights and models that help managers and researchers better understand this interface will improve the firm's ability to achieve more effective IT alignment.

For years, many firms have maintained functional boundaries (e.g., marketing, finance, operations, etc.). However, there is substantial evidence that cross-functional integration improves goal achievement (Sashittal and Wilemon 1994), innovation success (Sashittal and Wilemon, 1994; Hitt, Hoskisson, and Nixon, 1993; Rothwell and Whiston, 1990; Gupta, Raj and Wilemon, 1986), information system success (Sabherwal, 1999), and organizational performance (Slater and Narver, 1994; Rockart and Short, 1989). More importantly, it can also improve the speed of response to environmental change (Rockart and Short, 1989), a critical issue for today's organizations. This chapter provides a hierarchical framework for understanding and assessing the state of cross-functional integration between IT and other units in an organization. By moving to higher levels in this "integration hierarchy" model, organizations can expect to achieve a higher degree of IT alignment.

Henderson and Venkatraman's (1990) strategic alignment model clearly identifies functional integration between business and IT as a critical linkage for IT alignment. This chapter focuses on functional integration and provides a model for assessing and eventually improving the state of integration between IT and other business units. To provide context, the model focuses on the integration of marketing and IT as two units where improved IT alignment will benefit the firm. Effective alignment between marketing and IT is particularly important at this time as the success of e-commerce, data warehousing, and other emerging applications require both marketing and IT to work more closely together to define and execute both business strategy and IT infrastructure. However, as later sections of this chapter will discuss, there are implications for the model for both practitioners and researchers beyond the marketing and IT interface.

THE LINK BETWEEN INTEGRATION AND IT ALIGNMENT

Woolfe (1993) identified four stages in the alignment process where IT can provide value to the business. These stages are: 1) functional automation, 2) *cross-functional integration*, 3) process automation, and 4) process transformation. He argues that strategic IT alignment really occurs only after the fourth stage. The first two stages focus primarily on improving efficiency, while the latter two concentrate on changing the way work is done. Woolfe (1993: 21) summarizes the role of cross-functional integration in the alignment process as follows:

Integration involves coordinating the development of creative business uses for IT to support business processes that transcend the boundaries of business units. Information services integration can save money by encouraging a common approach, but more important, it contributes to corporate added value by exploiting synergies that exists between business units.

Woolfe (1993) details the difficulties of aligning the information services function with the business at each stage, in particular, that cross-functional integration, the second stage, is complex and not easily accomplished. Reasons cited for the difficulty include a lack of communication and complications in managing interdependence between information services and other business functions. Along similar lines, Miller (1993) found that information services performance ratings were higher when the information services function aligned itself closely to important business objectives. The key to alignment was agreement between the information services staff and the non-information services staff as to what business objectives are important.

Other studies also confirm the importance of cross-functional integration in the IT alignment process. Chan and Huff (1993) identify three stages for achieving IT alignment: awareness, integration and alignment. The integration stage is characterized by acceptance of the need for information services to mesh its plans with those of the organization. They suggest that, for information-intensive industries, integration occurs best when the business plans and IT plans are developed *simultaneously*. This finding is in line with other studies (e.g., Goldsmith 1991; King 1978; King and Teo, 1997) that emphasize the importance of integrating business planning with information systems planning activities. Lederer and Mendelow (1989) point out multiple reasons why the integration of information systems and business planning is important. These reasons include assuring development of the most critical applications for the organization, and completing projects that are related to overall business objectives and are of value to the organization. Furthermore, a recent study by Sabherwal (1999) indicates that these information systems projects will be more successful when cross-functional integration is higher.

Boar (1994) pulls together the work of several people, including Henderson and Venkatraman (1990, 1993), and points out that alignment must occur along two dimensions: functional and process. Functional alignment deals with cooperation and collaboration among functional areas, i.e., cross-functional integration. Process alignment involves the creation and redesign of processes so that they are synchronized with business strategy. In both cases the alignment should extend beyond the firm boundaries to include customers and suppliers. In the process of achieving IT alignment within a firm, Boar notes that cross-functional integration plays an early and crucial role.

Finally, the work on IT alignment by Henderson, Venkatraman and Oldach (1996) points out that functional integration of IT with business strategies can enhance IT alignment in two ways. First, by creating opportunities for information services to contribute to both shaping and supporting the strategic initiatives and plans of other functional units. Second, functional integration between information services and other units improves the link between the organizational infrastructure and processes, and the information services infrastructure and processes. Thus, models and methods for improving cross-functional integration should contribute to improved IT alignment.

Table 1. Sample Organizational Profiles

	Integration Status	Interface Topics	Characteristic Statements
Org Alpha	Well integrated	Most energy spent on making the most effective use of data, very strong communication and participation patterns, systems are sophisticated, useful and used	"The relationship with marketing has never been as good or as close or as productive as it is now." And, "Communication? We don't really think about that. It works so well, we just take it as a given."
Org Beta	Moderately integrated	Concerned with data quality issues and what data is in the systems, and improving the effectiveness of participation and other decision-making activities	"I think that we [marketing] should play a bigger role in the decision making. … We aren't getting involved until they're [IT] already at the 'we've decided to do this' stage."
Org Gamma	Marginally integrated	Concerned with communication quality and participation problems, areas have a weak understanding or appreciation of each other, systems rarely meet needs well	"I know if the reports aren't there they [marketing] get really cranky. So they must use them. … I'm not really sure what they do with them. I'm sure they do something."
Org Delta	Poorly integrated	Concerned with basic communication and participation issues, problems with trust and understanding are prevalent, systems often limited to simple reporting or used rarely	"There is a clear need for improved communication." And, "The problem is that decisions are made without our input and without providing rationale."

AN EMERGING HIERARCHY

The concepts reported in this chapter stem from data collected through a number of sources. The primary study began with interviews of marketing executives at several organizations who were asked to identify key information technology issues facing their organizations. An extensive review of industry and academic journals and the business press supported development of a holistic model of marketing and IT integration.

Figure 1: Integration Hierarchy

STRONG		
	Effective Partnerships	Effective cross-functional integration, seamless interaction, sophisticated systems, effective use of information technology to achieve goals of another area, strong and transparent communication structures
	Data and Needs Resolution	Developing more proactive participation and collaboration mechanisms, efforts focused on developing a shared understanding of data and support needs, access to data, and resolving data quality issues
	Communication Development	Working towards better inter-department understanding and developing quality communication, begin getting more inter-department input in planning and decision-making processes, basic participation and collaboration occur
	Basic Understanding	Trust, basic understanding and appreciation are all issues to be resolved, interaction begins to focus on communication of basic information such as priorities and rationales for decision making, the medium and frequency of communication is very important
	"Dis - Integration"	Integration does not exist, open hostility or complete lack of understanding or trust might be present, there is little to no effective interaction related to the work relationship
NONE		

Degree of Cross-Functional Integration

Refinement of the model involved surveys and in-depth interviews with both marketing and IT professionals in four large organizations. Each organization was selected based on the degree of integration present between the two functional areas. Table 1 presents brief profiles of the four organizations, each with a different degree of cross-functional integration between the IT and marketing units. The profiles also identify typical issues found at the interface between the two units.

Some interesting patterns emerged upon examination of the data from the selected organizations and those patterns led to the creation of the model presented in Figure 1. The model explains how integration takes place within a hierarchy and that needs at one level must be fulfilled before an organization can move to a higher level of integration. The lower levels of the integration hierarchy address basic needs for an effective working relationship, such as communication, trust, appreciation, and understanding. The higher levels focus on the work-related dimensions of integration unique to the collaboration of the two functional areas, in this case, marketing and IT. Thus, without basic understanding, communication, and trust between IT and marketing, an organization will not be able to make effective use of technology to support marketing in its goal achievement. An expert panel of CIOs, heads of marketing, and marketing information systems consultants reviewed the model and suggested both refinements and directions for future research and application.

THE LEVELS OF THE HIERARCHY

At the lowest level of the integration hierarchy is what might be best termed "dis-integration" or the complete absence of an effective working relationship between IT and another functional area. This may happen because the two functional areas never had a reason or incentive to interact previously, or it could be rooted in deeper problems related to internal politics or battles. At this level there is usually little understanding regarding how each department operates, makes its decisions, sets its priorities, or even the work it performs. This lack of understanding and communication may lead to mistrust and other anti-productive conditions.

At the second level of the integration hierarchy, issues of trust and appreciation are most prevalent. Individuals in the units typically focus interface time on communicating basic information between units. Organization Delta (see Table 1) is an example of an organization typical of this level – where integration is poor to nonexistent, but the organization has begun to address the problem. Organizations at the lower levels of the integration hierarchy are likely to have very unsophisticated systems, and perhaps little more than standardized "green bar" reports whose format and data are mostly predetermined, inflexible, and are produced on a regular schedule, and quite possibly only on paper.

At the third level in the integration hierarchy, the quality of communication becomes a greater concern. Organization Gamma is more characteristic of an organization at this level. The emphasis here is on communicating effectively. At this level, developing quality communication with IT is more important to help marketing achieve its goals than the data infrastructure or system sophistication. Cross-functional work groups are more likely to act and perform like committees than teams as participation and collaboration mechanisms are initiated and residual lower-level issues are further addressed. Some lower level organizations, such as Organization Gamma may have a sophisticated marketing information system, such as a decision support system of some type, but marketing users report that the system does not meet their needs and therefore is not used.

At the fourth level, the two departments focus on resolving data issues and building a shared understanding of data and support needs. Organization Beta is characteristic of this level of integration. Data problems are an important issue, as are further improving joint participation in decision making and system development. Unlike the lower levels where communication was a significant problem or focus, at this level there is more a sense that "we do a pretty good job of communicating." Cross-functional work groups begin to function more like teams than committees. Similarly, individuals in the one business unit appear to have a better understanding and respect for the work of individuals in the other functional area. Integrated data sets, data warehousing, and initial data mining tools emerge that are driven by marketing's needs for information. These refinements in the systems and data infrastructure will lead to marketing information systems that are often more sophisticated and more effective.

Finally, at the top level of the integration hierarchy, the focus is clearly on making effective use of available data. Organization Alpha is representative of this level, where the marketing information systems are used more often and are more sophisticated than at lower levels. The marketing information systems are likely based on a data warehousing infrastructure with advanced decision support tools and flexible, real-time inquiry and reporting capability. System changes and enhancements required to meet changing business needs often occur very quickly and marketing users report a high degree of satisfaction with the systems and data. While individuals in organizations at other levels might be quick to point out problems in their interaction between departments, at this level the interface is more seamless. Less energy is spent on managing the interface and is spent instead on cooperation for effective achievement of goals.

Table 2: Sample Assessment Measures

	Sample Assessment Measures
Outcome	- % of joint goals achieved - % of joint projects completed successfully - perceived integration - perceived effectiveness of the cross-functional relationship
System Variables	- sophistication of marketing information systems - perceived effectiveness of marketing information systems - frequency that marketing information systems are used - purposes or activities that marketing information systems are used for
Technical Resource Allocation	- % of total IT budget invested in marketing - % of IT budget invested in marketing compared to other functional areas - amount of marketing-specified data stored on computer - amount of marketing-specified data accessible to marketers
Participation	- role each department plays in decisions of other department - role each department plays in cross-functional decision making - role each department plays in developing new information systems - perceived effectiveness of integrative mechanisms (participatory roles)
Communication	- frequency of communication between the two departments - methods of communication between the two departments - perceived effectiveness of the communication between the departments - % of communication time spent in conflict
Cross-functional Understanding	- % of employees participating in cross-functional training - % of employees with work experience in other functional area - % of employees with exposure or other experience in other functional area - % of employees who can identify the goals or priorities of the other functional area

ASSESSMENT MEASURES

A formal assessment instrument based on the integration hierarchy has yet to be developed and validated. As an initial step in that direction, Table 2 provides a short list of measures useful for establishing where an organization falls within the integration hierarchy. The outcome variables (Lawrence and Lorsch, 1969; Ruekert and Walker, 1987) evaluate the most visible outcomes of cross-functional integration between two areas, such as the percentage of joint projects achieved and the perceived effectiveness of the relationship. The system variables (Li 1995; Stone and Clarkson, 1989; Talvinen and Saarinen, 1995) measure the effectiveness of the marketing information systems in place within the organization in terms of sophistication and usage patterns. The technical resource allocation variables (Li, 1995; Talvinen and Saarinen, 1995) concentrate on evaluating the direction and focus of the IT functional area and its priorities as reflected by both financial allocations and the data infrastructure. The participation and communication variables (Hutt and Speh, 1984; Li 1995; Lim and Reid, 1992; Miller and Friesen, 1982; Ruekert and Walker, 1987; Sabherwal, 1999; Williams, Guinipero, and Henthorne, 1994) are the more traditional measures of cross-functional integration. They cover communication patterns, joint decision making and other "integrative mechanisms" such as joint committees and participatory roles. Finally, the cross-functional understanding variables (Whiston, 1991; Williams et al., 1994) evaluate "domain similarity" or the degree to which employees in one functional area can understand or relate to the goals, priorities, or activities of the other. While Table 2 provides an initial set of metrics for managers to assess their own departments' integration with IT, additional work in this area by academics and practitioners should lead to both a general integration hierarchy assessment tool and a more specialized set of instruments that each evaluates a particular cross-functional interface (e.g., IT and marketing, IT and HR, marketing and manufacturing, etc.).

Placement in the integration hierarchy can be determined through several mechanisms. Members of the expert panel who helped refine the model suggested that many of them could identify where their organizations fell within the integration hierarchy. This suggests that managers could use the model and their own observational experiences to identify position within the integration hierarchy. In doing so, managers in one functional area (e.g., marketing) should compare their evaluation to those of managers in the other functional area (e.g., IT) and engage in discussion around the points where conclusions differ. Managers might also consider gaining a wider range of input to the evaluation, including a sample of staff at different reporting levels from both departments. This could be done through a short survey instrument or perhaps as part of a short staff meeting.

In order to evaluate observational experiences or other data collected in the assessment process, managers should look for patterns that are similar to those described earlier in this chapter. For example, a set of poorly integrated functional areas should find that sophisticated marketing information systems (if any) are rarely used and/or do not meet marketing's needs. Integrative mechanisms, such as group participation patterns and quality of communication, are likely to be weak, and employees will place a high importance on the frequency and method of communication employed. There will likely be a higher degree of conflict or perception of a low degree of communication effectiveness between the functional areas.

In contrast, a well-integrated set of functional areas would place less importance on the communication and integrative mechanisms based on the assumption that they are working well. Marketing information systems are likely to be more sophisticated and have stronger usage patterns. Higher importance will be placed on data infrastructure issues and wait time. There will likely be a lower degree of conflict and a much higher degree of perceived communication effectiveness. Joint participation in decision making is also likely to be perceived as having higher degree of importance and probably occurs more frequently across a range of decisions. Domain similarity values, such as the degree of cross-functional understanding and cross-functional training or experience, will likely be higher; however, the perceived importance of these variables is likely to be lower as a common understanding is more assumed or taken for granted.

MOVING UP THE INTEGRATION HIERARCHY

Given a sense of where an organization "fits" in the integration hierarchy, the next step is to develop an action plan to move up the hierarchy and to monitor improvement. This could be done using a modified balanced scorecard approach[1]. The balanced scorecard is a framework for translating strategy into concrete objectives that drive both performance and behavior. It accomplishes this by viewing all the activities of an organization from four key perspectives: financial (or outcomes), customer, internal, and learning and growth. Linked to one another in a hierarchical fashion, these perspectives define the strategy of an organization, such as improving cross-functional integration or IT alignment, in terms of actionable objectives, measures, and initiatives.

As a management system, the balanced scorecard requires that information about the four perspectives be communicated to *all* employees because each individual needs to understand how their actions can impact, positively or negatively, the overall organizational strategy. The balanced scorecard provides the tools to bridge this gap. It is called a *balanced scorecard* because it includes measures that are both quantitative and qualitative, that include historical, present and future-oriented data, and measures that are both leading and lagging indicators of performance. It also facilitates the process of organizational change by shifting internal focus from the question, "How well did we do?" to asking, "What can we do to improve our performance or create new value?" The mix of measures that the perspectives encompass provides a broader, or more comprehensive, view of organizational strategy and performance that is easy to communicate and monitor.

Developing and monitoring strategies to improve cross-functional integration, and subsequently IT alignment, is an ideal application of the balanced scorecard model. The variables related to the integration hierarchy include both quantitative and qualitative measures, and leading and lagging indicators. The lagging indicators are those variables that represent or indicate where an organization is within the hierarchy at a given point in time. These lagging indicators or "status" variables include those that appeared in Table 2. The leading indicators

Table 3: Sample Balanced Scorecard Measures

	Sample Lagging Indicators	Sample Leading Indicators
Financial or Outcomes Perspective	- perceived integration - perceived quality of decisions made - perceived MKIS effectiveness - frequency of system use - purpose of system use - MKIS sophistication	- # of unresolved data issues - # of unresolved functionality problems - % of joint projects completed successfully - % of joint goals achieved
Customer Perspective	- perceived priority among departments - perceived effectiveness of working relationship - perceived relevance of available data - perceived usefulness of system - degree of access to available data	- degree of top management support - % change in amount of conflict - % of communication that is conflict - perceived sense of crisis
Internal Process Perspective	- amount of communication - frequency of communication - participation patterns - perceived quality of communication - perceived effectiveness of communication processes - amount of joint development of systems (esp. at early stages) - amount of joint system selection - amount of participation in decision processes	- amount of IT dollars or re-sources invested in marketing - % of IT dollars or resources invested in marketing compared to other functional areas - amount of wait time (turn-around time) on requests - communication mediums used
Learning and Growth Perspective	- language commonality - degree of appreciation/respect of other area - understanding of what each area contributes - perceived sensitivity of other area - degree of trust - degree of understanding	- %/amount of employees with cross-functional training - %/amount of employees with cross-functional experience - %/amount of employees who understand decision rationale, goals or activities of other area - co-location of functional areas

measure variables that influence, positively or negatively, an organization's ability to move up the integration hierarchy. These variables can be used within the balanced scorecard framework to monitor current levels of integration and drive the cross-functional integration process.

Table 3 illustrates a range of sample variables that might be included within an integration-oriented balanced scorecard. An actual scorecard will most likely have a smaller selection of variables that are selected based on where an organization currently resides in the integration hierarchy. In addition, it is easy to argue that some of the variables listed could be interpreted as both leading and lagging indicators depending on a particular organization's place in the integration hierarchy, its particular strategy for moving up the hierarchy, and specific variables the organization selects.

MANAGEMENT IMPLICATIONS

For organizations pursuing IT alignment, the integration hierarchy provides an additional tool for improving internal strategy and infrastructure relationships. Luftman (1996) identified a number of inhibitors to strategic IT alignment, and he notes that, "The primary problem [is] one of affiliation. Business and IT are going in different directions with poor communication and interaction between them" (1996:46). Luftman further refines this description through a listing of specific inhibitors to alignment, which include: no close relationship between IT and other business units, IT does not understand other business units, no communication, plans not linked, as well as several others. As the material in this chapter shows, however, these inhibitors are *characteristic qualities* of a poorly integrated unit. Thus, as the alignment model in the first chapter of this book suggests, identifying and improving functional integration between IT and other business units is a critical component for IT alignment. The integration hierarchy provides an easy-to-communicate framework for accomplishing this task.

This chapter focused primarily on the marketing and IT interface; however, it is also possible to generalize the framework to the integration of IT and non-marketing functional areas such as Human Resources, logistics or manufacturing. Indeed, improving the integration of IT with other functional units is critical to the successful implementation of new strategic initiatives, such as e-commerce applications, ERP systems, and modern supply chain management (Kalakota and Robinson, 1999). These strategic initiatives require application, data and end-to-end process integration, which implies that integration must occur between multiple business units and possibly even between multiple organizations. The integration hierarchy does not address the technical aspects of integration as much as the organizational dimensions, and for that reason the framework can be adjusted to evaluate the relationship between any two functional areas, any two organizations, or even an organization and its customers. Thinking more broadly about business strategy and infrastructure relationships will lead to a broader array of useful applications for the integration hierarchy model within an organization.

There are also key lessons for leadership that emerged from the research to develop the integration hierarchy. For one, top management in both departments must support better integration between the two units and is a key enabler of movement up the hierarchy. Conflict among executives in different functional areas is likely to be a greater barrier to improved integration than conflict at lower managerial levels. If two departments are at a low position in the integration hierarchy relative to each other, leadership should focus first on building cross-functional understanding and communication. Decision processes and rationale should be laid open and explained. As trust and communication quality improve, more focus on participatory decision making and planning should take place.

Provided these basic integrative mechanisms are in place, the next focus should be on improving the data infrastructure and end-to-end processes through joint effort. This path to improving integration will yield integrated data, application and process infrastructures that are more effective and useful in achieving the business objectives at the departmental level.

Finally, it is possible for organizations to address multiple levels of the integration hierarchy at once. For example, two departments can work on improving data quality while developing better communication and participatory mechanisms. However, this approach requires leaders to monitor and place their emphasis on developing the basic integrative mechanisms first and then gradually shift their attention to higher-level issues. In other words, until the basic integrative mechanisms are in place, the goal of effectively aligning strategy and infrastructure relationships cannot be achieved. Improving those mechanisms is a top responsibility of the executive leadership.

RESEARCH IMPLICATIONS

The integration hierarchy presents several interesting avenues for further research. One is further refinement of the model among functional areas beyond marketing or information services. However, research should also determine if the model presents explanatory power for relationship effectiveness or alignment between an individual functional area and an organization as a whole, or between one organization and the external entities with which it associates. More basic research on the model itself is also required to further validate and refine the model and its component variables.

The first avenue for additional research is further explication of the integration hierarchy for different relationships in an organization. At one level, examining the interaction of information services or marketing with other areas of an organization is an obvious place to start. In the case of IT and marketing in the organizations examined in this study, the IT functional area contributed more to meeting marketing's goals than the contrary condition, thus the relationship was somewhat unidirectional. What would the upper levels of the hierarchy look like for two departments that *both* rely on each other to achieve their individual functional goals, such as the interaction of sales and marketing, or human resources and IT?

Expanding on this theme, if the integration hierarchy were altered somewhat, it might also be used to illustrate integration of a functional area, such as IT, with the overall organization. In this scenario, the integration hierarchy becomes a tool for assessing and improving functional alignment to corporate goals and objectives. Assuming that further research proved this hypothesis correct, the resulting implication is that a tool could be developed to help organizations determine how well the IT function is aligned with the goals of the organization. Based on the results of that assessment, top management could then quickly identify an action plan for improving the integration of the IT function with the rest of the organization. Further exploration of using the balanced scorecard model to achieve this objective might be an effective direction for future work.

Lawrence and Lorsch (1967) observed that different industries require different balances of integration and functional specialization. It would be interesting to compare the data from organizations in multiple industries that are perceived to be better or worse at using information technology to support the needs of marketing. By applying the model to different industries, one could further explore antecedents to effective marketing and information services integration, and IT alignment at the functional level. These antecedents might include the role of culture, regulation, or historical events within a particular industry as well as several other variables. Industries that might be particularly interesting to look at and compare are the consumer packaged goods industry, heavy industrial (business-to-business) organizations, and financial services organizations.

A fourth direction for research is application of the integration hierarchy to cross-industry or cross-organizational integration. With the number of strategic partnerships and mergers or acquisitions among companies in similar or different industries, it would be interesting to see if a similar integration hierarchy exists between organizations. This line of research could also examine whether the integration hierarchy exists between an organization and its suppliers, or an organization and its customers. Where information systems span these relationships, identifying and using the integration hierarchy could improve the effectiveness of the resulting IT solutions.

Finally, out of necessity, a number of variables were not included within this research. Future research should include additional variables and clarify which variables are "critical" to becoming better integrated, and which are "nice to have." For example, the support of top management appears to be critical to improving integration, along with some degree of domain similarity. Other factors, such as co-location, while helpful, do not appear to be critical to achieving integration between two areas. In addition, a more rigorous quantitative study would help further validate and refine the existing model.

CONCLUSIONS

By improving the interface between IT and other business units, organizations will be better at aligning their technology resources to their strategic goals and objectives, and ultimately at adapting to rapid environmental change. The key implication of the integration hierarchy for management is that it provides the groundwork for assessing and improving cross-functional integration in an organization. Using the integration hierarchy, organizations can identify their degree of integration as it relates to developing effective information systems. Given that information, a plan to improve the integration of the information technology area with other functional areas becomes a more manageable objective.

The integration hierarchy that emerged from this study can serve as a theoretical model or hypothesis to explain how the information technology function contributes to goal achievement at the functional, if not the individual and organizational, level of the firm. The model's focus on creating information systems that effectively meet the needs of another functional area directly addresses how to use cross-functional integration to improve IT alignment. However, it is also clear that additional research is needed to both refine the existing model and develop validated measurement tools and practices for managers.

ENDNOTES

1 For more detailed information on the balanced scorecard approach, see Kaplan and Norton (1992, 1993, 1996a, 1996b), and Olve, Roy and Wetter (1999).

REFERENCES

Boar, B.H.(1994). *Practical Steps for Aligning Information Technology with Business Strategies: How to Achieve a Competitive Advantage,* John Wiley and Sons, Inc., New York , NY.

Chan, Y.E., and Huff, S.L.(1993). "Strategic Information Systems Alignment," *Business Quarterly,* Autumn, 51-55.

Goldsmith, N.(1991). "Linking IT planning to business strategy," *Long Range Planning* (24:6), 67-77.

Gupta, A.K., Raj, S.P., and Wilemon, D. (1986)."A Model for Studying the R&D – Marketing Interface in the Product Innovation Process," *Journal of Marketing* (50), April , 7-17.

Henderson, J.C. and Venkatraman, N.(1990). "Strategic Alignment: A Model for Organizational Transformation via Information Technology," *Working Paper #217,* Center for Information Systems Research, Massachusetts Institute of Technology, Boston, MA.

Henderson, J.C. and Venkatraman, N.(1993). "Strategic Alignment: Leveraging information technology for transforming organizations," *IBM Systems Journal* 32(1), 4-16.

Henderson, J.C., Venkatraman, N., and Oldach, S.(1996). "Aligning Business and IT Strategies," in *Competing in the Information Age: Strategic Alignment in Practice,* Ed. J.N. Luftman (ed.), Oxford University Press, Inc., New York, NY, 21-42.

Hitt, M.A., Hoskisson, R.E., and Nixon, R.D. "A mid-range theory of cross-functional integration, its antecedents and outcomes," *Journal of Engineering and Technology Management* (10:1-2), June 1993, pp. 161-185.

Hutt, M.D., and Speh, T.W.(1984). "The Marketing Strategy Center: Diagnosing the Industrial Marketer's Interdisciplinary Role," *Journal of Marketing* (48), Fall , 53-61.

Kalakota, R., and Robinson, M. (1999). *e-Business: Roadmap for Success,* Addison Wesley, Reading, MA.

Kaplan, R.S., and Norton, D.P.(1992). "The Balanced Scorecard – Measures that Drive Performance," *Harvard Business Review,* September-October, 134-142.

Kaplan, R.S., and Norton, D.P.(1993). "Putting the Balanced Scorecard to Work," *Harvard Business Review,* January-February 71-79.

Kaplan, R.S., and Norton, D.P.(1996A). "Using the Balanced Scorecard as a Strategic Management System," *Harvard Business Review,* January-February 1996a, pp.

75-85.

Kaplan, R.S., and Norton, D.P.(1996B). *The Balanced Scorecard*. Boston, MA: Harvard Business School Press.

King, W.R.(1978). "Strategic planning for management information systems," *MIS Quarterly*, 2(1), 27-37.

King, W.R., and Teo, T.S.H. (1997)."Integration Between Business Planning and Information Systems Planing: Validating a Stage Hypothesis," *Decision Sciences*, 28(2), 279-308.

Lawrence, P.R., and Lorsch, J.W.(1967). "Differentiation and Integration in Complex Organizations," *Administrative Science Quarterly*, 12(1), 1-47.

Lawrence, P.R., and Lorsch, J.W.(1969). *Organization and Environment: Managing Differentiation and Integration*, Irwin, Homewood, IL.

Lederer, A.L., and Mendelow, A.L.(1989). "Coordination of Information Systems Plans with Business Plans," *Journal of Management Information Systems*, 6(2), 5-19.

Li, E.Y.(1995). "Marketing information systems in the top U.S. companies: a longitudinal analysis," *Information & Management*, 28(1), 13-31.

Lim, J., and Reid, D.A.(1992). "Vital Cross-Functional Linkages with Marketing," *Industrial Marketing Management*, 21(2), 159-165.

Luftman, J.N.(1996). "Applying the Strategic Alignment Model," in *Competing in the Information Age: Strategic Alignment in Practice*, J. N. Luftman (ed.), Oxford University Press, New York, NY, 43-69.

Miller, D., and Friesen, P.H.(1982). "Innovation in conservative and entrepreneurial firms: Two models of strategic momentum," *Strategic Management Journal* (3), 1-25.

Miller, J.(1993). "Measuring and aligning information systems with the organization: A case study," *Information & Management*, 25(4), 217-228.

Olve, N., Roy, J., and Wetter, M.(1999). *Performance Drivers: A Practical Guide to Using the Balanced Scorecard*. Chichester, UK: John Wiley & Sons, Ltd.

Rockart, J.F., and Short, J.E. (1989)."IT in the 1990s: Managing Organizational Interdependence," *Sloan Management Review*, 30(2), 7-17.

Rothwell R., and Whiston, T.G.(1990). "Design, innovation and corporate integration," *R&D Management*, 20(3), 193-201.

Ruekert, R.W., and Walker, O.C., Jr.(1987). "Marketing's Interaction with Other Functional Units: A Conceptual Framework and Empirical Evidence," *Journal of Marketing* (51), January,1-19.

Sabherwal, R.(1999). "The Relationship Between Information System Planning Sophistication and Information System Success: An Empirical Assessment," *Decision Sciences*, 30(1), 137-167.

Sashittal, H.C. and Wilemon, D. (1994)."Integrating technology and marketing: implications for improving customer responsiveness," *International Journal of Technology Management*, 9(5-7),691-708.

Slater, S.F., and Narver, J.C. (1994)."Market Orientation, Customer Value, and Superior Performance," *Business Horizons*, 37(2), 22-28.

Stone, M.A. and Clarkson, A.H.(1989). "MIS and the Strategic Development of Financial Institutions," *Marketing Intelligence and Planning*, 7(1/2), 22-30.

Talvinen, J.M. and Saarinen, T. (1995). "MkIS support for the marketing management process: perceived improvements for marketing management," *Marketing*

Intelligence and Planning, 13(1), 18-27.

Whiston, T.G.(1981). *Managerial and Organisational Integration*, Springer-Verlag, London, UK.

Williams, A.J., Giunipero, L.C., and Henthorne, T.L. (1994). "The Cross-Functional Imperative: The Case of Marketing and Purchasing," *International Journal of Purchasing and Materials Management*, 30(3), 29-33.

Woolfe, R.(1993). "The Path to Strategic Alignment," *Information Strategy: The Executive's Journal*, 9(2), 13-23.

Chapter IV

Information Systems Strategy, Structure and Alignment

Yolande E. Chan
Queen's University, Canada

ABSTRACT

A study sponsored primarily by the Advanced Practices Council of the Society for Information Management (SIM) International is briefly described. The research involved a mail survey in which data were gathered from insurance companies and manufacturing firms in the US and Canada. Sixty-seven CEOs and 67 CIOs responded to questions on business and information systems strategy, structure, alignment, and performance without knowing what their business unit counterparts were saying. Their views were compared and used to 1) examine the importance of strategic and structural alignment, 2) highlight difficulties experienced in achieving this alignment, and 3) document approaches used to improve alignment.

INTRODUCTION

What constitutes business and information systems (IS) alignment? Are strategic alignment and structural alignment equally important to IS performance and business performance? How do we measure these and other forms of business and IS alignment? How important is IS performance to business performance? What particularly difficult alignment issues are companies grappling with today? What strategies and tactics are companies using to increase alignment? What key measures are companies using to assess the overall performance of the IS department?

In order to address these questions, a study sponsored by the Advanced Practices Council of the Society for Information Management (SIM APC) and by the Social Sciences and Humanities Research Council of Canada was conducted. IS alignment was modeled as having two primary dimensions: IS strategic alignment (i.e., the fit between business strategy and IS strategy) and IS structural alignment (i.e., the fit between business structure and IS structure). These alignment dimensions are related to those discussed by Henderson and Venkatraman (1993), Luftman (1996) and Papp (1998). In the Strategic Alignment Model discussed by these authors, 'functional integration' is the term used to describe the fit between business strategy and IT strategy, and also between organizational infrastructure and IT infrastructure. The term 'strategic fit' is reserved for the congruence of business strategy with organizational infrastructure, and also for the congruence of IT strategy with IT infrastructure. These authors therefore also examine strategic and structural issues. However, their terminology is somewhat different. In the current study, the focus is on 'functional integration'. However, providing two distinct terms, 'strategic alignment' and 'structural alignment,' for the two separate components of 'functional integration' was thought to be helpful.

Appendix I and Appendix II provide details of this study's alignment model and measurement approach. Increased IS alignment was expected to be related to increased IS performance. For companies in information-intensive industries, increased IS performance was expected to lead to improved business performance.

In order to test these propositions, a survey of US and Canadian manufacturing and financial services firms was conducted. A focus on more than one industry was expected to increase the generalizability of the research findings. Extensive pretesting (Dillman, 1978) and multiple revisions of the research instruments occurred prior to the mailing of the questionnaires. The pretesting involved academic reviews, questionnaire item sorting exercises (Moore and Benbasat, 1991), interviews with IS executives and consultants, and pilot testing the questionnaires with appropriate senior executives in multiple organizations.

Dun and Bradstreet directories were used to compile lists of North American firms operating in financial services (insurance/SIC 6321) and manufacturing (pharmaceutical preparations/SIC 2834 and auto parts/SIC 3714), with more than 100 employees. Because the survey involved senior executives and multiple respondents, response rates were expected to be low (Raghunathan and King, 1988; Venkatraman, 1989), so a large number of firms needed to be contacted. Approximately 1,000 firms were randomly selected from the Dun and Bradstreet lists. The mail correspondence sent to each of these firms included a cover letter from the primary research sponsor (SIM APC), an article describing the results of an earlier study by the researcher, a letter of invitation to participate in the research, and two research questionnaires. (The questionnaires were designed to be 'practitioner friendly' and were presented, and referred to in the study, as workbooks.) The first questionnaire was to be completed by the CEO or a senior non-IS vice-president. The second was to be completed by the CIO or the executive in charge of information systems in the business unit. Later that month, reminder postcards were sent to each of these firms. Finally, firms were sent a second set of research questionnaires and invited again to participate in the research, if they had not already done so.

Sixty-seven sets of completed, matched research questionnaires were received. (Unfortunately many other questionnaires had to be discarded when only one company questionnaire was received.) This represented a matched pair success/response rate of 7%. Although the author uncovered limited evidence of systematic response bias (i.e., the firms responding generally appeared to be typical of the firms surveyed), the low response rate meant that research findings had to be interpreted cautiously.

Executives responding to the business questionnaire ranged from Presidents to managers. Executives responding to the IS questionnaire ranged from Vice-presidents to superintendents. Total personnel in the business units studied ranged from under 300 employees to 3,000 employees. Annual business unit revenues ranged from under 100 million US dollars to 2 billion US dollars. Most annual business unit profits were under 100 million US dollars. Business units ranged in age from under 15 years old to over 150 years old.

IS personnel in the business units ranged from under 15 IS employees to 135 IS employees. The annual IS budget ranged from under $10 million to over $100 million and, in most cases, amounted to no more than 3% of revenues. The percentage of IS-related expenditures in the business unit that were under the direct control of the IS department ranged from less than 10% to 100%. The percentage of capital projects in the business units that were IS projects ranged from less than 10% to just under 90%.

STUDY RESULTS

The study's findings are presented in two sections below. First, bivariate relationships among business and IS strategy, structure, alignment, and performance are discussed[1]. Second, sample comments provided by executives in response to questions in the business and IS workbooks (i.e., the questionnaires) are listed. These comments illustrate the range of IS alignment and performance issues that were being grappled with in the companies surveyed. Strategies and tactics for addressing these issues are also listed. Finally, several measures used by survey participants to assess IS departmental performance are provided.

Before reviewing the findings, it is important to note that the results apply mainly to business units with somewhat centralized, internal IS departments. They are less applicable to firms that rely primarily on outsourcing arrangements.

Relationships Among Strategy, Structure, Alignment and Performance

The workbooks assessed strategy, structure, alignment and performance (the research constructs). As Appendix I and II illustrate, *business and IS strategy* were assessed in two primary ways:
1. Business and IS "strategic orientation" (Venkatraman, 1989; Chan et al., 1997). The strategic orientation construct assesses management actions in terms of their emphasis on market aggressiveness, analysis, external/internal orientation, future orientation, innovativeness, proactiveness and risk aversion.
2. Other business and IS strategy factors (e.g., strategy formulation processes).
   Business and IS structure were measured using a single approach only. Factors such as the degree of centralization, the use of matrix structures, the use of teams, and the use of human resource incentive mechanisms were assessed. Note that in this study, business unit structure refers to the ways in which the organization's

labor is divided into distinct tasks and these tasks are coordinated (Mintzberg, 1983)[2]. IS structure refers to the ways in which the IS department's labor is divided into distinct tasks which are coordinated.

IS strategic alignment was measured in three ways (see Appendix II):

1. The synergy between business and IS strategic orientation.
2. The match between business and IS strategic orientation.
3. The match between other business and IS strategy factors.

IS structural alignment was measured as the match between business and IS structure factors. The term 'match' is meant to suggest similarity, parallelism and mirroring. A high matching strategy score for a business unit suggests that the business unit strategy and the IS strategy have much in common. A low matching score suggests that they differ in several respects. A high matching structure score suggests that responsibilities are handled similarly (e.g., the amount of centralization and specialization of tasks is roughly the same for the IS department as it is for the rest of the business unit).

The term 'synergy' is meant to suggest complementarity, interaction, combination and reinforcement. A high synergy score suggests that the business unit and IS strategies complement each other well. Perceived weaknesses in one area may be offset in part by perceived strengths in the other. Also, strengths in the business unit (e.g., with respect to market aggressiveness) may be combined synergistically with strengths in the IS area (e.g., tools to support market aggressiveness) to create opportunities for competitive advantage. (See Chan et al. (1997) for a fuller discussion of matching and synergy models of alignment.)

SPSS was the statistical package used to analyze the data. Statistically significant bivariate relationships discovered between the constructs, as they were measured in this study, are described below. Italics are used to highlight associated management implications.

Business performance and business strategic orientation

- Financial performance was generally not significantly related to individual strategic orientations. Having an external orientation was an exception to this rule. *All other things being equal, an emphasis in the business unit on external stakeholders (e.g., customers, suppliers, competitors) was associated with better business performance. This suggests that, in the industries studied, an external focus (vs. an internal, efficiency focus) yielded superior results and was to be advocated.*
- Innovativeness was also associated with better performance. *This suggests that a strategic emphasis on innovation could also be strongly advocated.*
- However, aggressiveness and analysis were not associated with performance gains. Chan et al. (1997), in their study of the strategy and performance of firms in finance and manufacturing industries also found that a management emphasis on analysis was not associated with superior performance. *Organizations can become stuck in an analysis mode. In fast changing industries, an insistence on completing thorough analyses before acting can prove limiting because problems may keep changing before they can be solved. 'Guesstimate' decision-making may be necessary at times.*

Business performance and IS strategic orientation

- *Reputation was influenced positively by increased IS resources to support the various strategic orientations (with the exception of IS resources to support aggressiveness).* This suggests that firms that are known to be investing in information systems/technology may find their company reputations enhanced. In this study, IS investment tended to result in positive reputational impacts. Managers should not underestimate the symbolic value of technology investments.
- *Financial performance was also positively influenced by increased IS resources to support an external orientation.* This study found that technology investments to provide support for an external (e.g., customer or competitor) company focus were particularly clearly associated with improved financial performance, and were to be recommended.

Business performance and other business strategy factors

- *Of all the business strategy factors investigated, having a well-defined, participative business strategy formulation process and managing business change smoothly were the factors found to be associated with better business performance.* This study underscores the importance for firms competing in the finance and manufacturing industries, of having cross-functional team-based development of company strategy. The study also highlighted the importance of devoting substantial attention to change management.
- Having a frequently changing business strategy was associated with negative market growth.

Business performance and other IS strategy factors

- *Changing IS strategy frequently and managing IS-related changes were associated with increased market growth and an improved business reputation.* This study draws attention to the rapid rate of technological change in the industries studied, and the need for ongoing flexibility and experimentation. The ability to shift technological direction successfully, and manage technological change, was linked in this study with improved business performance.

Business performance and matching strategy factors

- *A correspondence in business and IS strategy factors was at times surprisingly negatively linked to business performance.* This suggested that having the IS department simply mirror what the rest of the business is doing is not always helpful. There are times when the IS department may need to take the lead or depart from traditional company approaches to doing business. *Having both IS and the rest of the business formulate strategy using well-defined processes was slightly negatively linked to market growth.* Bureaucratic structures and processes were not rewarded in this study. *However, having both business and IS personnel participate in the development of business strategy was once again positively linked to innovation.*
- A match between the level of IS participation in the development of business strategy and line participation in the development of IS strategy was associated negatively with market growth and financial performance. Note, how-

ever, that a match simply indicates 'mirroring' or similarity in behavior. It does not imply that both line and IS are heavily involved in the development of strategy. It could mean that they were both somewhat involved or were both minimally involved. The match simply suggests that IS was following the 'tune played by the piper', i.e., the rest of the business.

- *Having similarly changing business and IS strategies, and matching abilities of line and IS personnel to manage change, were associated positively with business performance. This suggests that although innovation was necessary, business and IS strategies were frequently realigned. This in turn has implications for the skillsets of both line and IS personnel. Realignment requires shared knowledge, communication and cooperation.*

Business performance and business structure
- The key finding here was that people more so than other aspects of the organization impact the bottom line. *An emphasis on human resources and the use of incentive mechanisms (e.g., annual reviews, bonuses) were both markedly associated with improved business performance, even in difficult economic times.*
- The use of teams and other cross-functional arrangements was also positively associated with performance. *These findings suggest once again that cross-functional teamwork should be encouraged.*

Business performance and IS structure
- The formal structure of the IS organization did not appear to be tightly linked with business performance. *Alternative IS organization structures may be equally effective. However, an emphasis in the IS department on its human resources was consistently associated with increased innovation. Successful IS departments invested in training and motivating their personnel.* Having IS (not line) planning of the IS infrastructure and applications portfolio was positively associated with both financial performance and company reputation.

Business performance and IS performance
- When links could be detected statistically between IS performance and business performance, they were always positive. *The quality of the information product had particular importance for financial performance and company reputation. The IS departments studied benefited from focusing on improving the timeliness, accuracy and usefulness of management information available to company personnel.* IS contributions to management effectiveness, IS contributions to the development of external market ties, and IS contributions to the development of new products and services were all positively linked with innovation. *In this study, contributions made by the IS department were linked clearly to innovation and other important aspects of firm performance.*

Business performance and IS alignment
- The different measures of IS alignment used in this study were related somewhat differently to business performance. *Structural alignment was related positively to business reputation. Overall strategic alignment was related to improved innovation. Alignment and performance were clearly linked.* However, a

high "match" alignment score was negatively linked to innovation. This was perhaps to be expected. If everyone was doing the same thing, innovation was not expected to be the primary result.

IS performance and IS strategic orientation

- Increased IS resources to support an external orientation were linked with the business's perception of an improved information product, and also with improved IS contributions to the establishment of market links, and the development of new products and services. Increased IS resources to support proactiveness were associated positively with these dimensions of IS performance also.
- IS resources to support an internal orientation (i.e., an emphasis on efficiency) and innovativeness were linked with better perceptions of the information product, and improved contributions made by IS to the establishment of market ties. IS resources to support business aggressiveness were associated with perceptions of better contributions made by IS to the development of new products and services and the establishment of market ties.
- *These findings suggest that the allocation of scarce IS resources is critical. The overall IS budget is not an adequate indicator of IS effectiveness. While important, it does not reveal important choices and tradeoffs between competing IS investments, and does not highlight the likely consequences of alternative investments. It is important to be familiar with the IS portfolio of existing and planned systems, and to understand the support that individual systems provide for business operations. The nature and impacts of planned investments, and not just their dollar totals, should be understood.*

IS performance and other IS strategy factors

- Well-defined IS strategy formulation processes were associated with an improved information product. Being perceived to be a critical or important part of the business was associated with better IS contributions. *This study suggests that the more valuable the IS groups are perceived to be, the more likely they are to be invested in and heeded, and the more valuable they are actually likely to become. The reverse is also true: historically marginalized IS groups can get stuck in negative cycles and may need to be radically rearranged or even dismantled.*

IS performance and matching strategy factors

- Once again, having both line and IS executives participate in the development of business strategy was positively related to IS contributions to market ties and the development of products and services.
- A match between the level of IS participation in the development of business strategy and line participation in the development of IS strategy was associated positively with IS contributions to the establishment of market links or ties. *Line personnel should be involved in the development of IS strategy.*

IS performance and business structure

- A number of structural facets of the business were generally associated with improved perceptions of IS performance. These included an emphasis on people (i.e., human resources), the use of human resource incentive mechanisms, the use of teams and the use of cross-functional arrangements.

IS performance and IS structure

- A number of structural facets of the IS organization were associated with IS performance. *The reliance on IS-only (i.e., non-cross functional) teams was negatively associated with the performance of the IS function. However, an emphasis in IS on its people (e.g., skill development), the use of chargeback mechanisms, the use of IS department performance metrics, and flexibility in the IS structure were associated positively with the various aspects of IS performance. High performers appeared to combine flexibility and investment in people with tough expectations of performance and cost control.*

IS performance and matching structure factors

- Having matching structural practices within the IS organization and the rest of the business in general did not seem to be related to IS performance. Whereas similar use of TQM teams was somewhat positively linked to increased IS contributions to market links, the use of similar human resource incentive mechanisms was actually somewhat negatively associated with IS performance. *The study's findings suggest that in order to retain and motivate top IS personnel, the IS department may need to depart from standard company compensation packages and norms, and offer innovative, uniquely tailored incentives.*

IS performance and IS alignment

- It was encouraging to note that wherever links could be detected statistically between IS alignment and IS performance, these links were positive. *Improved IS strategic alignment and IS structural alignment (according to the CEO) were consistently related to better IS performance.* Increased IS "synergy" was consistently related to better IS performance. However, no links could be detected between IS "match" and IS performance. This would suggest that IS "synergy" was a better predictor of performance than was IS "match" (the simple mirroring by IS of the practices observed in the rest of the business; please see Appendix II). *It may be more important for the IS department to influence/leverage business strategy than to simply mirror/implement it.*

IS alignment and business strategy factors

- A well-defined business strategy formulation process, changes in business strategy, and the ability to manage business change smoothly were all associated with improved strategic alignment. The first of these factors was also associated with improved structural alignment. *The management of change is critical for successful, ongoing strategic alignment.*

IS alignment and IS strategy factors

- *A well-defined IS strategy formulation process and the ability to manage IS change were associated with overall strategic alignment and overall structural alignment, according to the CIO.*

IS alignment and business structure
- A number of business structure factors were positively linked with increased strategic and structural alignment according to the information provided by the CEO. *Increased emphasis on human resources, increased use of personnel incentive mechanisms, increased use of teams, and increased use of cross-functional arrangements were all associated with improved alignment.*

IS alignment and IS structure
- A number of IS structure factors were positively linked with increased strategic and structural alignment according to the CIO. These factors included having a flexible or changing IS structure, having positive IS-line working relationships, having an emphasis on human resources in the IS function, having IS use several personnel incentive mechanisms, having IS recruit and supervise completely its own personnel (i.e., with minimal line assistance), using IS cross-functional arrangements, using IS teams, using IS subcontracting arrangements and chargeback mechanisms, and finally, having IS manage the main databases in the business unit. *Achieving IS alignment is an ongoing challenge ('a journey, not a destination,' as Dr. John Henderson of Boston University has been known to state). It is a complex task as is shown by the many factors that influence alignment. These factors will constantly be changing, and realignment will be needed frequently. IS departments should periodically review their levels of alignment ('doing the right things') and performance ('doing the right things right'). The workbooks used in the current study are useful tools for managers seeking to periodically assess their IS alignment and performance.*

Business Workbook Comments

Whereas in the discussion above, the focus was on statistical analysis of numerical Likert-scale data provided by survey participants, below the spotlight shifts to qualitative comments that were provided by executives in response to open-ended questions. Several of the more helpful and informative business workbook responses are presented below.

IS Workbook Comments

Comments provided by executives in response to questions in the information systems workbook are provided below. Whereas the comments presented above were generally provided by senior line (i.e., non-IS) executives, the comments below were generally provided by senior IS executives.

SUMMARY

Before closing, let us directly address the questions that were raised at the very start of this chapter. In order to do so, we draw on the quantitative and qualitative evidence presented above.

Are there any particularly difficult IS strategic alignment issues that you are currently grappling with?
Business Workbook Comments
We have 3 relatively autonomous business units that interface with a single corporate IS group. Business units are allocated IS charges on a usage/support basis and are responsible for ensuring that the cost allocations are competitive with external support costs. The concern relates to managing systems development and consistency in interfaces/upgrades to ensure the overall corporation is at the same level. The risk is that as each business unit sets its own standards, overall systems support costs rise because different timing on upgrades, etc. cause interface and complexity problems.
Our company has made a strategic decision that we will be an all-electronic company with all records being kept electronically without hard copy. Problem is to get executives like me familiar and comfortable with using the computer.
There are pressures to reduce costs throughout the company. Operating units look to IS to provide greater automation so they can reduce their costs, plus IS is expected to provide this service at a reduced cost as well.
We have spent the last 2 years completely rewriting all of our information systems. We were able to complete this successfully in large part by ensuring that MIS was aligned completely with business priorities and requirements. Our problem now is that key MIS staff are integral in not only running the business but also completing any new functionality. Some of our business people are in fact "abdicating" their responsibility too completely to MIS. Therefore, on the one hand, MIS is responsible for completing priorities identified by the business, but MIS appears to be driving the business with less support than would be optimal.
The IS function is an integral part of executive management decision making.
Inability for many MIS employees to think like business managers.

Are there any strategies, tactics or techniques that you are using to increase IS strategic alignment?
Business Workbook Comments
We have made a concerted effort to move IS activity into the business units (forces less central control although guidance continues).
We do not track and measure it as such. Our practices are as follows: (1) MIS staff attend the business unit's planning sessions and provide input to the prioritized divisional objectives, (2) MIS staff are also involved in the consolidation of these divisional goals into corporate level objectives, (3) The VP of MIS ensures that no MIS objectives are on the list without an identified business sponsor, (4) Bi-weekly business staff meetings are attended by MIS personnel,

(5) Bi-weekly MIS meetings are attended by business personnel,
(6) MIS management are encouraged to rigorously force the business to make tradeoffs at the divisional/corporate objective level to ensure allocation of resources to only those projects that support the objectives.

We have recently developed a technology strategy that focuses the organization on the premise that technology exists to support and add value to the business.

(1) The IS products are determined primarily by business needs,
(2) Functions are developed using cross-departmental teams,
(3) Systems are developed one chunk at a time (no project takes >1 year), and there is a process of continuous improvement.

We are using formal IS strategic planning for operating units.

What key measures do you use to assess the overall performance of your IS department?

Business Workbook Comments

(1) User surveys,

(2) Cost as a percentage of sales, benchmarking, plus "help desk" cause analysis,

(3) Management board level "check-ins",

(4) Review IS portfolio with management teams.

(1) Feedback from the community,

(2) Meeting budget reduction targets,

(3) Implementing the established direction.

Achievement of strategic business unit goals and objectives.

(1) Response time to problems or system enhancements,

(2) Availability to help,

(3) Training,

(4) Participation as a team player.

We are developing service agreements within the organization. We use benchmarking comparisons.

Operational effectiveness = Reliability + Availability + Responsiveness. Objective for production systems is 100% R+A+R for the 12 hour period 8am to 8pm. Objective for systems development is to meet all mandated requirements on-time, and to add new business functions to meet competitive deadlines.

(1) Productivity,
(2) Efficiency,
(3) Accuracy,
(4) Development,
(5) Control,
(6) Future planning,
(7) Disaster recovery,
(8) Department support.

Are there any particularly difficult IS strategic alignment issues that you are currently grappling with?
IS Workbook Comments
Older line management are generally reluctant to accept the advances of IT and focus more on cost than value. The view of integrating IT into all work functions is not common. Younger management personnel and "high achievers" are aggressive in their exploitation of IT. This creates political stress between the previous and current generations of management.
In the second year of a 3 year financial reduction program requiring an overall reduction of 21% in budget. To accomplish this while also focusing on quality and service requires platforms of new cooperation and openness in realigning remaining resources for efficiency. Surmounting resistance to change continues to be a strategic challenge.
(1) Alignment of Canadian business IS technology with global business IS technology,   (2) Transition from Canadian or regional or "country" coding systems (product, customer, supplier etc.) to global coding conventions,   (3) How to best leverage global IS resources for the business and reduce the number of similar systems that exist?
Part of our IS function is centralized making plant vs. overall planning difficult. Also the timing of our strategic planning leaves little time for IS to adjust their planning to meet local manufacturing goals.
Getting Strategic Business Units to include IS as part of their planning and operational agenda.
Advancing newer technologies while minimizing costs and determining actual business value.
(1) The degree of structural fit between IS and the rest of the business — e.g., (de)centralization of IS services and infrastructure and the role of cross-functional teams,   (2) Managing reductions in IS positions with the objectives of reducing IS staffing costs, dealing adequately with a large development workload and providing a level of service satisfactory to the customers of IS.
ROI/Payback of technology.

What metrics or indicators help you assess the degree of IS strategic alignment in your business unit?
IS Workbook Comments
The performance measurements of the business processes themselves.
(1) Chargeback system,   (2) An Activity-Based Costing system with performance measures portraying "value-for-money",   (3) Business unit's measures are mainly financial therefore IT's detailed contributions to making coordination, control, cycle times and so forth cost less are highly prized.
Open communication is the key ingredient in getting IS in alignment with the operating units.
(1) Direct detailed chargeback system for all IS services by product line,   (2) IS/User Steering Committees (monthly) to review project priorities/ status and discuss new directions by business unit,   (3) Corporate Executive Committee must approve the "business case" prior to start of all IS projects - NOT business unit priority driven; projects are company wide policy/priority/bottom line driven,   (4) Monthly IS/User Manager operational review meeting re: prioritization of day-to-day improvements/enhancements and legislative requirements,   (5) 3 year rolling IS strategic plan synchronized to 3 year business plans (this exercise has recently lost some focus as new parent company integration opportunities prevail).
IS plans and activities are dictated by business unit's priorities. IS plans are subject to the approval of the user community. Strategic IS plans are approved by senior management with full end-user participation.
Balanced Score Card (BSC) prioritization process for IS projects. Rates 6 factors of business importance. Business objective translated to IS plans to IS Manager Objectives. Objectives vs. results used to evaluate management/employee performance.

Are there any strategies, tactics or techniques that you are using to increase IS strategic alignment?
IS Workbook Comments
We are working on a model which identifies our company's critical success factors. First we assign a weighting to each CSF. Then each IS project is rated against the CSFs. The weighting is multiplied by the rating to equal total project points. This helps us to prioritize projects and eliminate those projects that should not be on the list. However, it doesn't by itself stimulate discussion about what other projects should be considered. However, I'm also a firm believer in the more education you do, the higher the payoff will be in the long-run... eventually everyone will be asking for IS input in planning, instead of IS asking to be included.
Examine business strategies that have an IS "component"; record them as a "matrix" item; define IS strategy that will help achieve the business strategy (on the same matrix); record operational tactics to implement each IS strategy (on the same matrix); review frequently to keep "evergreen"; have the business include an IS section in their strategic plans.
Applied education in the form of: (1) MRP II philosophy and training,   (2) Continuous improvement techniques,   (3) Outside technical consultants,   (4) Line management experience of IS managers.
ABC (activity-based costing) system and "IS a business" paradigm are very effective.
Used IS applications reengineering as the vehicle to force senior management to formulate a corporate strategic plan.
We have an internally developed index (PCI - Plant Computing Index) that looks at business functions, their importance, and how well they are being supported by systems. We also use this as a planning/strategic direction tool to show areas where there are low systems support or ineffective support which may need higher priority.
We have undertaken a formal "Information Strategic Planning" exercise. This initiative, while initiated by IS, is very much business driven. It is being facilitated by an external consulting organization for expertise and methodology application and mentorship. IS and line business people are intimately and significantly involved. Objectives include: (1) clear articulation of IS vision aligned with business vision, (2) current situation assessment and actionable plan forward, (3) knowledge transference in strategic planning and implementation.

Are there any particularly difficult issues that you are currently grappling with regarding the appropriate structure (i.e. organization) of the IS function?
IS Workbook Comments
(1) How do we best leverage IS resources globally? (2) How do we effectively network business integrated IS resources with the central IS unit? (3) How do we get a higher percentage of our IS resources out of operate & maintain-type systems into strategic business systems?
The current structure consists of a centralized unit, a matrix unit to support semi-centralized matrix teams, and business unit departments. The coordination of all these activities is both time and cost consuming. The organization also runs two separate sets of hardware and concomitant applications. Developing communications between the two has been a major challenge. At the business unit level, we also run a union and a non-union IS shop which has created some conflict.
Developing skills of people in a migrating context (e.g., mainframe —> client-server).
Who should the IS personnel report to?
We have attempted to structure our MIS organization in such a way that MIS staff are both technologists and business analysts. We have found several people that can effectively operate in this capacity. However, these people are consultants and our full-time staff are not capable of making this leap. This leaves an awkward "reporting" relationship internally and places excessive strain on "scarce" resources.
(1) The degree of structured fit between IS and the rest of the business — e.g., (de)centralization of IS services and infrastructure and the role of cross-functional teams, (2) Managing reductions in IS positions with the objectives of reducing IS staffing costs, dealing adequately with a large development workload and providing a level of service satisfactory to the customers of IS, (3) What are the "appropriate" (efficient and effective from corporate and business unit needs/points of view) models or options we should be considering for managing the new information technology which we are now in the course of implementing in a distributed client-server environment, enterprise-wide?
Resolving the balance between functional expertise and business alignment. We're moving to a hybrid: business systems analysts aligned with the business; other IS specialists organized functionally.

Please describe what led to the last significant change in the organization of the IS department, and how you were able to assess whether the new IS structure was effective.
IS Workbook Comments
Fiscal restraint has reduced the IS staff complement by some 70 positions in the last 6 years. The IS department is on its 4th director and the management layer has been reduced from 18 to 4. The department has reorganized roughly every 2 years to accommodate these reductions.
(1) Management of operations and technology (systems programming) was split. The result was a much more effective management of both areas because it allowed focus. (2) Desktop computer programming was centralized in one development team. This provided a critical mass of skills but limited business knowledge. The short term trade-off was positive.
Moved from partly decentralized to centralized structure to squeeze out redundancies and create flexibility in assigning resources to projects (i.e., regardless of strategic business unit). Evaluation of resourcing of projects clearly demonstrates that a positive shift has occurred.
The last MIS organizational change further aligned MIS staff with the business. The change was driven primarily by a manager leaving and being replaced by another manager. Assessment of effectiveness was completed in two ways. First, that the group affected continued to perform at or above the level of performance prior to the move. Second, that the business unit which they support continued to be satisfied with the group's performance.
The change was caused by increased workload in the Systems and Programming area which caused us to realign this area under functional project teams. The results showed that the change was very effective.
We merged a systems development group which supported research together with an unofficial "shadow group" in research doing similar work. Inefficiencies, overlaps, and gaps in coverage were eliminated by combining the two groups. They now report jointly to IS and to research — a first in the company.

What key measures do you rely on to assess the overall performance of your IS department?
IS Workbook Comments
(1) Completion of projects, (2) On-time, (3) Under-budget, (4) To the satisfaction of the user group.
Education (applied), background, leadership, peer confirmation.
(1) Meeting deadlines, (2) Accuracy of the information, (3) Presentation of the information, i.e. format.
(1) Schedule — ready on time, (2) Quality of the development, (3) Partnership with end-users and IS staff.
(1) Availability, stability and reliability of production services and business applications (includes the availability, reliability and stability of the platform on which they are delivered), (2) Cost containment ("actuals" year over year), (3) Staff morale.
(1) Percentage of total systems costs to sales, (2) Percentage of systems activities in each of 4 or 5 categories: (a) operation & maintenance, (b) legislative & mandated changes, (c) environmental & safety requirements, (d) strategic initiatives, (3) Value of new capital expenditures for computing equipment — are we renewing our hardware on a frequent enough basis? (4) Satisfaction survey of end users.
(1) Cost/benefit studies, (2) Customer feedback, (3) Benchmarking with other companies (real decisions), (4) Auditing of our processes.

What constitutes business and IS alignment?

This study suggests that alignment is more than a simple parallelism between what IS does and what the rest of the business is doing. That is, it involves more than a simple "match" between IS and the rest of the business. It involves using IS resources to influence, leverage and execute business strategy. There are both strategic and structural dimensions of IS alignment. The two dimensions are distinct although related.

Are strategic alignment and structural alignment equally important to business and IS performance?

From a business performance point of view, strategic alignment was linked with business innovation and with business reputation. Structural alignment was linked primarily with business reputation. From an IS performance point of view, both IS strategic alignment and IS structural alignment were very important to every aspect of performance; neither aspect of alignment eclipsed the other in importance.

How do we measure IS alignment?

This study has highlighted a set of strategic alignment and structural alignment factors to be aware of and to monitor. (See Appendix I and Appendix II.) Some of these factors appear to be more strongly linked with performance than others. For instance, aspects of IS strategy to focus on include the IS strategy formulation process, changes in IS strategy, and the ability to manage these changes. Aspects of IS structure to monitor closely include personnel skillsets, the use of human resources incentive mechanisms, and the use of cross-functional teams. For IS structural alignment, a great deal of emphasis should be placed on *human* (not just IS) resources.

This study directed attention to the importance of business and IS strategic orientations. It illustrated that the synergy between (i.e., reinforcement between and combination of) these orientations should be monitored more closely than their match (i.e., parallelism).

How important is IS performance to business performance?

The study's findings suggest that IS performance is particularly clearly linked to company innovation and company reputation. The availability of high quality, relevant and timely information is also strongly linked to improved financial performance.

What particularly difficult strategic and structural alignment issues are companies grappling with today?

In some organizations, executives were struggling to enable members of the senior management team to become comfortable with information technology and be willing to aggressively exploit business opportunities afforded by this technology. Other executives spoke of the challenges involved in improving IS service levels while simultaneously reducing IS budgets. Still other executives found it difficult to coordinate, develop standards for, and conduct planning for, very decentralized IS groups. Skill development, given the rapidly changing technological platforms in many organizations, was another commonly cited challenge.

What strategies and tactics are companies using to increase alignment?

Having IS attend business unit planning sessions and weekly business staff meetings was one successful approach used to increase IS alignment. Conducting formal IS strategic planning and ensuring that all IS projects had clearly identified business sponsors were other successful approaches discussed. Using cross-departmental teams, continuous improvement programs, and decentralized IS personnel were still other approaches described.

What key measures are companies using to assess the overall performance of the IS department?

Executives provided a range of measures including the following: the *business unit's* performance, benchmarking, IS cost containment and budget compliance, IS costs as a percentage of sales, adherence to service agreements within the organization, business partner surveys and feedback, timely IS project completion, IS project audits, and performance measures for individual networks/systems (e.g., response time, reliability, and availability).

This study addressed several questions concerning IS alignment and performance. A great deal of information was presented. It is hoped that each reader will find valuable "nuggets" to take away: for instance, new information regarding links between strategy, structure and alignment, or thought-provoking suggestions regarding alignment challenges. A key goal of the chapter has been to provide new insights into the detailed components of IS alignment and the complexities involved in enhancing IS alignment and performance.

REFERENCES

Chan, Y., Huff, S., Copeland, D. and Barclay, D. (1997). "Business Strategy, Information Systems Strategy, and Strategic Alignment," *Information Systems Research* 8(2), 125-150.

Daft, Richard L. (1992). *Organization Theory and Design.* West Publishing, NY.

Dillman, D. (1978). *The Total Design Method.* Wiley Interscience, NY.

Henderson, J. and Venkatraman, N. (1993). "Strategic Alignment: Leveraging Information Technology for Transforming Organizations," *IBM Systems Journal* 32(1), 4-16.

Luftman, J. (1996). *Competing in the Information Age: Practical Applications of the Strategic Alignment Model* Oxford University Press, NY.

Mintzberg, H. (1983). *Structure in Fives: Designing Effective Organizations* Prentice-Hall, Inc, Englewood Cliffs, NJ.

Moore, G. and Benbasat, I. (1991). "Development of an Instrument to Measure the Perceptions of Adopting an Information Technology Innovation," *Information Systems Research* 2(3), 192-222.

Papp, R. (1998). "Alignment of Business and Information Technology Strategy: How and Why?," *Information Management*, 11(3-4), 6-11.

Raghunathan, T. and W. King. (1988). "The Impact of Information Systems Planning on the Organization," *OMEGA International Journal of Management Science* 16(2), 85-93.

Venkatraman, N. (1989). "Strategic Orientation of Business Enterprises," *Management Science* 35(8), 942-962.

ENDNOTES

1 See Venkatraman (1989) and Chan et al. (1997) for a discussion of 'bivariate' versus 'systems' analyses. Relationships among multiple variables can be examined a pair at a time (as has been done in this chapter), or with larger

groupings (potentially all) of the variables simultaneously. Larger groupings require larger amounts of data to draw equally robust conclusions however. So the simpler bivariate approach has been used in this study.

2 Dimensions of organizational structure include (Daft, 1992): formalization (the amount of written documentation), specialization (the degree to which tasks are subdivided), standardization (the extent to which work activities are performed in a uniform manner), hierarchy of authority (who reports to whom and the span of control for each manager), complexity (the number of activities or subsystems within the organization), centralization (the hierarchical level that has authority to make a decision), professionalism (the level of formal education and training of employees), and personnel allocations (the deployment of people to various functions and departments).

APPENDIX I: DEFINITION OF TERMS

Table 1—Key Aspects of Strategy, Structure, Alignment and Performance

STRATEGIC ORIENTATION OF BUSINESS ENTERPRISES
(i.e., Business Strategy)

Business Aggressiveness	Push to dominate (i.e., increase market share) even if this means reduced prices and cash flow.
Business Analysis	Reliance on detailed, numerically oriented studies prior to action.
Business External Orientation	Forming tight marketplace alliances (e.g., with customers, suppliers, and competitors).
Business Future Orientation	Having a forward-looking, long-term focus.
Business Innovativeness	Creativity and experimentation are strengths.
Business Internal Orientation	Emphasis on cost cutting and efficiency; internally "lean and mean".
Business Proactiveness	First to introduce new products and services; a step ahead of the competition.
Business Risk Aversion	Reluctance to embark on risky projects.

STRATEGIC ORIENTATION OF INFORMATION SYSTEMS
(i.e., IS Strategy)

IS Resources to Support Aggressiveness	IS deployments used by the business unit when pursuing aggressive marketplace action.
IS Resources to Support Analysis	IS deployments used by the business unit when conducting analyses of business situations.
IS Resources to Support External Orientation	IS deployments used by the business unit to strengthen marketplace links.
IS Resources to Support Future Orientation	IS deployments used by the business unit for planning and projection purposes.
IS Resources to Support Innovativeness	IS deployments used by the business unit to facilitate creativity and exploration.
IS Resources to Support Internal Orientation	IS deployments used by the business unit to improve the efficiency of company operations.
IS Resources to Support Proactiveness	IS deployments used by the business unit to expedite the introduction of products and services.
IS Resources to Support Risk Aversion	IS deployments used by the business unit to make business risk assessments.

IS STRATEGIC ALIGNMENT

Business Strategy Factors

Business Strategy Formulation	E.g., The business unit has a well-defined business planning process.
Business Strategy Changes	E.g., The business unit's strategy has changed substantially during the past three years.
Managing Business Change	E.g., Compared to its competitors, the business unit has been able to respond and adapt smoothly to change as it has arisen over the past three years.

IS Strategy Factors

IS Strategy Formulation	E.g., The IS strategy is well-defined and agreed upon.
IS Strategy Changes	E.g., The IS strategy has substantially changed over the past three years.
Managing IS Change	E.g., Compared to other departments, the IS function has been able to respond and adapt smoothly to change as it has arisen over the past three years.
IS-Line Relationships	E.g., Senior IS personnel sit on line management committees.
Importance of IS to the Organization	E.g., Information technology is critical to the business unit's operations and success.
Overall IS Strategic Alignment	E.g., Business and IS are strategically well aligned.

IS STRUCTURAL ALIGNMENT

Business Structure Factors

Business Unit Centralization	E.g., The structure of the business unit is currently highly centralized.
Business Structure Changes	E.g., The business unit's structure has changed significantly during the past three years.
Business Use of Cross-Functional Arrangements	E.g., Line managers work in different departments to gain a variety of business skills.
Business Use of Teams	E.g., The business unit often utilizes total quality management (TQM) teams and/or process improvement teams.
Business Emphasis on HR	E.g., The business unit provides a lot of on-the-job training to maintain and upgrade the skillsets of their employees.

Business HR Incentive Mechanisms	E.g., Personnel in the business unit regularly compete for recognition awards and pay bonuses.

IS Structure Factors

IS Centralization	E.g., The structure of the IS function is currently highly centralized.
IS Structure Changes	E.g., The structure of the IS function has changed significantly over the last three years.
IS Use of Cross-Functional Arrangements	E.g., IS personnel report to both IS and line management.
IS Use of Teams	E.g., The IS function often utilizes self-managed teams that establish their own objectives, work allocation mechanisms, and evaluation systems.
IS Emphasis on HR	E.g., IS personnel have the technical and business skills they need.
IS HR Incentive Mechanisms	E.g., The IS function regularly monitors IS project outputs, budgets, and schedules.
Use of IS Department Metrics	E.g., Objective measures are used to demonstrate the performance and contributions of the IS department.
Use of IS Chargeback Mechanisms	E.g., Chargeback systems are used to recover development costs for new IS.
Use of IS Subcontracting Arrangements	E.g., Cooperative arrangements are used to contract out IS development activities.
IS Infrastructure and Portfolio Planning	E.g., Infrastructure planning & portfolio planning are carried out completely by IS personnel.
IS Purchasing	E.g., Personal computer purchasing is completely managed by IS personnel.
IS Database Management	E.g., Databases in the business unit are completed managed by IS personnel.
IS Training of End Users	E.g., Systems-related training of end users is completely managed by IS personnel.
IS LAN Management	E.g., Local area network management is completely carried out by IS personnel.
IS Systems Development and Maintenance	E.g., Systems development and maintenance are completely managed by IS personnel.
Supervision of IS Personnel	E.g., IS (not line) personnel are responsible for the recruitment and supervision of IS personnel.
Location of IS Personnel	E.g., Systems support (e.g., help desk) personnel are primarily located in the IS department.
Overall IS Structural Alignment	E.g., The structure/organization of the IS function is appropriate and effective.

IS PERFORMANCE
(i.e., IS Contributions to Business Performance)

Satisfaction with IS Staff and Services	E.g., with respect to cooperation received from, and communication with, IS personnel.
Satisfaction with the Information Product	E.g., with the quality of on-line information and reports available.
Satisfaction with End User Involvement and Knowledge	E.g., with respect to IS development in the organization.
IS Contributions to Operational Efficiency	E.g., improvements in the efficiency of internal company operations attributed to IS services.
IS Contributions to Management Effectiveness	E.g., improvements in management decision making, planning and span of control attributed to company IS.
IS Contributions to the Establishment of Market Links	E.g., the creation of electronic ties to customers, suppliers and competitors.
IS Contributions to the Creation/ Enhancement of Products and Services	E.g., via changing the information content of existing products and services.

BUSINESS PERFORMANCE

Market Growth	E.g., market share gains, sales growth, revenue growth.
Financial Performance	E.g., return on investment, return on sales, liquidity, cash flow, profitability.
Product-Service Innovation	E.g., improvements in business operations, products and services.
Company Reputation	E.g., reputation among major customer segments.

APPENDIX II:
MEASUREMENT GUIDE

This guide is designed to be used in conjunction with the workbooks entitled 1) Business Strategy, Structure and Performance, and 2) Information Systems Strategy, Structure, and Performance. Please contact the author if you would like more information about these workbooks. Note that all constructs were measured using 5-point Likert scales. Note also that a comprehensive list of terms used in this guide (e.g., Company Aggressiveness) is provided in Table 1 in Appendix I.

Business Strategic Orientation, Information Systems Strategic Orientation, and Information Systems Strategic Alignment (Synergy Component)

In information-intensive industries, information systems strategy is capable of moderating (i.e., influencing) the relationship between overall business strategy and business performance; similarly, overall business strategy can moderate the relationship between information systems strategy and information systems performance (i.e., the same information systems strategy is likely to have different results, given different business strategies). Obviously, this ability to moderate can be either positive (i.e., having a reinforcing effect upon performance), negative (i.e., having a mitigating effect upon performance) or neutral (i.e., having no effect upon performance).

In order to quantify strategy, the underlying orientation of the business (i.e., its priorities and culture) is assessed. The dimensions of strategic orientation studied are Aggressiveness, Analysis, External Orientation, Future Orientation, Innovativeness, Internal Orientation, Proactiveness, and Risk Aversion.

In order to quantify the information systems synergy or moderation effect, the mean (i.e., average) value for each of the eight dimensions of business strategy (e.g., Company Aggressiveness) is multiplied by the mean value for the corresponding information systems strategy dimension (e.g., Information Systems Aggressiveness).

Information Systems Strategic Alignment (Match Component)

This examines the extent of the disparity, if any, between the strategies employed by the information systems function and the overall organization. Within each strategy dimension (e.g., Aggressiveness), information systems and line executives are asked essentially the same questions; however, the questions are tailored in order to examine unique information systems and business priorities and activities.

The degree of match is calculated by subtracting the mean value of the scores received for the information systems strategy dimension from the mean value of the scores received for the corresponding business strategy dimension.

Information Systems Strategic Match (Other Components)

This investigates the fit between the information systems function and the overall business unit with regard to a different set of strategy dimensions from those which were just examined. Please see the dimensions illustrated in Table 1 in

Appendix I. The scores for these dimensions are calculated in the same fashion and use the same rationale as those discussed in the immediately preceding category (i.e., Match Component).

Business Structure, Information Systems Structure, and Information Systems Structural Match

This category explores the disparity, if any, between information systems and the overall business unit with regard to a set of structural dimensions. Please see the dimensions illustrated in Table 1 in Appendix I. The scores for these structural dimensions are calculated in the same fashion and use the same rationale as those in the Information Systems Match category (see above).

Information Systems Performance

This category evaluates dimensions of information systems performance (i.e., Satisfaction with IS Staff and Services through IS Contribution to Product-Service Enhancement). Please see Table I in Appendix I. An average information systems performance score (the average response received to several related workbook items) is produced for each dimension.

Business Performance

This category examines four dimensions of business performance (i.e., Market Growth to Company Reputation). Please see Table I in Appendix I. An average score is produced for each dimension.

Chapter V

Communicating Strategic IT Vision to Organization Members: A Conceptual Framework

Mary Elizabeth Brabston, University of Manitoba, Canada
Robert W. Zmud, University of Oklahoma, USA
John R. Carlson, Baylor University, USA

ABSTRACT

The development, communication, use, and benefits of organizational strategic visions have been well documented. Visions focus the enterprise on achieving their strategic goals. Little research has been done to date on the development, communication, and benefits of strategic visions for information technology. Based on a review of the strategic management, information systems, organizational theory, and change management literature, we present a conceptual framework for the development, communication, and potential benefits of a strategic vision for information technology and its alignment with the overall organizational strategic vision.

INTRODUCTION

Today's dispersal of information technology (IT) decision making across many organizational members offers the promise of greatly increasing the extent to which IT is applied to managerial and operational work systems (Boynton & Zmud, 1987; Jarvenpaa & Ives, 1990). Along with the advantages of such distributed action come the potential disadvantages of inappropriate allocations of effort and resources and associated outcomes — chiefly poor investment decisions, lost opportunities, duplicated efforts, and incompatible platforms and applications. One strategy for minimizing these disadvantages lies in the development of a common understanding among an organization's members concerning the primary roles to be served by information and by IT throughout the organization. One tactic for achieving this common understanding is through the development, articulation, and dissemination of a *strategic IT vision* (SVIT) (Collins & Porras, 1991; Nanus, 1992; Parker, 1995; Parker & Benson, 1991; Robbins & Duncan, 1988).

The value of developing and effectively communicating an organization's overall strategic vision to its members is well-recognized (Nanus, 1992; Robbins & Duncan, 1988; Locke, Kirkpatrick, Wheeler, et al., 1991). By sharing a common strategic vision, organizational members will better understand how their individual roles contribute to their organization's strategic mission and will be more likely to act in an appropriate and consistent manner when faced with uncertain or ill-defined situations. Similar benefits are believed to arise when an SVIT is shared by an organization's members (Parker, 1995; Parker & Benson, 1991). If an organization's members are aware of the organization's SVIT, more effective IT decision making and information use are likely to occur.

In order for an organization's members to understand an SVIT, the vision must be effectively communicated to them. Effective communication occurs "when the transfer of an idea from a source to a receiver results in a change in knowledge, attitude or overt behavior on the part of the receiver" (Rogers & Bhowmik, 1970-1971, p. 529). Understanding the IT vision (i.e., change in knowledge) is the first step in recognizing an effectively communicated IT vision. Understanding is followed by a change in attitude and changes in overt behavior, consisting of specific actions taken to implement the vision.

Little prior research has been directed toward the communication process by which organizational members may come to understand the SVIT. While Jarvenpaa and Ives (1990) did propose that annual report letters to stockholders "... can effectively serve as rough surrogates for CEOs' views and the status of IT in the organization" (p. 356), their research did not examine how effective this specific channel was in communicating an SVIT. A review of the strategic and organizational communication literature did not reveal any other findings regarding the process of communicating an SVIT throughout an organization.

The process by which an SVIT is developed is clearly important. If the process produces an appropriate, aligned IT vision, then the IT vision may become reality. We begin by first discussing the nature of an SVIT and its importance to organizations; then a conceptual framework for creating, aligning, and communicating an SVIT is presented. The final part of the framework is the acceptance of the IT vision. Finally, the framework's limitations and implications for information systems research and practice are discussed.

THE NATURE OF A STRATEGIC IT VISION

An organization's overall strategic vision is a shared, realistic, yet idealistic and attractive view of the organization that inspires and motivates others, through their individual and collective efforts, to move toward the vision (Nanus, 1992; Collins & Porras, 1991; Kouzes & Posner, 1996). Figure 1A graphically represents how an organizational strategic vision can serve as the stimulus for all organizational planning. Figure 1B depicts a similar role for the SVIT. The intent is similar but with a narrower scope involving only the organizational role of information and IT. As shown by the dashed lines, the IT strategic vision must be aligned with the organizational strategic vision (Venkatraman, Henderson and Oldach, 1993; Parker, 1995; Parker & Benson, 1991).

Figure 1 models the relationship between an organization's strategic vision and its subsequent planning and goal setting and those of the IT strategic vision. The typical process at the organizational level is that a group of individuals develop the organization's enterprise-wide strategic vision (e.g., Gerber's vision that "Babies are our most important product"). This vision is then communicated to others in the organization, resulting in the setting of other goals. Each of these goal sets should be aligned with the enterprise-wide strategic vision.

In the same way, a group of individuals would develop the IT vision, communicate it, and set goals. At each stage of the IT strategic vision process, the SVIT and goals should be aligned with the vision and goals of the enterprise-wide strategic vision, as indicated by the dashed lines.

If appropriately developed, articulated, and disseminated, an SVIT should both formally and informally influence the many IT-related decisions made throughout an organization so that these decisions, taken together, help to achieve the organization's overall strategic vision. In the absence of an enterprise-wide SVIT, information and IT decision making will most likely be framed by the numerous (and potentially conflicting) mental models that are maintained in the minds of individuals, as well as those that are collectively developed by formal and informal groups throughout the organization (Boland & Tenkasi, 1995).

Figure 1A. A model of Organizational Strategic Vision and Planning. Figure 1. Model of Relationship Between Organizational Strategic Vision and Planning and Information Technology Strategic Vision and Planning.

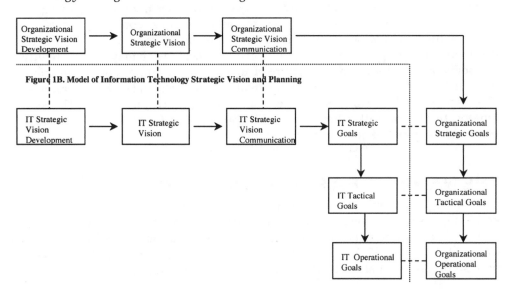

We need to distinguish between an SVIT, the focus of this chapter, and a strategic vision for an organization's IT function. The IT function's strategic vision articulates the organizational role of the IT function as well as the dominating values applied in carrying out these roles (c.f., Nanus, 1992). It may be valuable, but not necessary, that the strategic vision of the IT function be communicated across an organization; it is only necessary that it be communicated to those organizational members who significantly affect the IT function's efforts in carrying out that area's mission, e.g., IT departmental employees, IT vendors, etc.

An SVIT can be explicitly or implicitly developed. With an explicit vision, a formal vision statement is articulated and disseminated throughout the organization. With an implicit vision, the top management group evokes the vision through its on-going decision making processes, communication activities, and behaviors. Although we are unaware of any objective supporting data, our experience strongly suggests that, while few organizations have developed explicit SVITs, many organizations have evolved implicit SVITs. Current research (Brabston, Zmud, & Carlson, 1999) indicates that most organizations only develop an IT function vision. This is one of the reasons IT so frequently does not add its expected value. The lack of an SVIT results in a shotgun or unplanned approach to IT management and investment. Without a vision of what IT should be in the organization, development of a plan to manage IT has no foundation on which to build (c.f., James, 1985; Nanus, 1992; Wilson, 1992; Knorr, 1993; Taylor, 1994).

ALIGNMENT OF ORGANIZATIONAL AND IT STRATEGIC VISIONS

As Figure 1 illustrates, in an ideal model of strategic vision, the organization's strategic vision and their strategic information technology vision are completely aligned at every level. Unfortunately, in the real world, IT visions do not necessarily keep up with the organization's strategic vision.

For example, in a study of financial holding companies, the impact of newer information and communication technologies had influenced a change in the companies' culture, vision, and policies. They now espouse cross-selling, indicating that their customer contact employees should have access to information about their customers' banking services. Yet their information systems were still focused on the old culture, vision, and policies of confidentiality, so that information was provided on a "need-to-know" basis only. For example, if a customer made a large checking account deposit with a teller, the teller could not access the customer's records (other than the checking account) to determine if the customer had other accounts with the bank. The teller could not then suggest to the customer that a new savings account or certificate of deposit might be a better type of account for the deposit. This sort of cross-selling is possible today in myriad types of businesses, yet many information systems still segregate information and keep it from those who may need access based on their new organizational vision.

Another pair of examples illustrates the difference made by alignment of SVITs. Parsons Technology was founded over a dozen years ago and has since been acquired by Quicken. Their vision was to offer simple, user-friendly, bug-free software for personal use (e.g., MoneyCounts) at an extremely reasonable price. As part of their vision, they wanted to develop a loyal customer base. Their SVIT aligned with their organizational vision by using a single customer database to maintain all customer records, including every Parsons product bought, down to the version number. When a customer calls in, whether for customer support or to purchase something from their catalogue, the sales or technical representative is presented with not only the customer's database record, but also a customized list of "specials" to cross-sell the customer.

Microsoft, on the other hand, has a different database for each product. If a customer owns both Microsoft Windows and Microsoft Office, that customer's record is in two unrelated databases. A customer cannot ask a sales or technical representative about any other product or be offered "specials" or cross-selling techniques. Microsoft's vision is to have their customers using only Microsoft products, essentially the same vision as Parsons. It is, of course, ironic that Microsoft would not have aligned its SVIT with its organizational strategic vision.

This type of "blinder effect" is but one reason why organizational and IT visions should be aligned and regularly reviewed to ensure that they are still aligned. The framework presented in this chapter is an ongoing, iterative process; once the vision, whether organizational or IT, is developed, it must be communicated and implemented, and then the process starts again.

DEVELOPMENT OF THE IT VISION

A vision is created during an envisioning process (Nadler & Tushman, 1990; Collins & Porras, 1992; Robbins & Duncan, 1988; Bryman, 1992). The vision created is the guiding philosophy. However, it is not sufficient to simply create a vision. A tangible "image" must be communicated throughout the organizational levels affected by the vision (Nanus, 1992; Bennis & Nanus, 1985; Nadler & Tushman, 1990; Bryman, 1992; Bennis, 1994, 1995). In the case of an information-intensive organization, the IT vision must be communicated throughout the organization because information affects the entire organization (Tapscott & Caston, 1993).

While many authors (Nanus, 1992; Bryman, 1992; Collins & Porras, 1991; Robbins & Duncan, 1988; Sibbet & O'Hara-Devereaux, 1991) have discussed organizational vision, few have discussed the need for an SVIT (Frohman, 1985; Ferreira & Harris, 1985; Fagan, 1987; Martinsons, 1994; Radding & Maglitta, 1993; Tapscott & Caston, 1993; Wang, 1995; Rockart & Hofman, 1992). Because SVIT is important to IT planning, it is important to determine the factors influencing the development of the SVIT, and its alignment and communication throughout the organization. To date, little work has been published which elucidates these factors and the communication of the SVIT (c.f., Jarvenpaa & Ives, 1990).

Our conceptual framework develops these factors, defines the characteristics of SVIT, and shows how SVIT is aligned and communicated throughout the organization. The development of such a model can help managers to understand this important new area of IT management and to be able to develop, align, and communicate an SVIT. A thorough study of the strategic, information systems, organizational communication, and change management literature resulted in the development of Figures 1 and 2.

Figure 2 shows that our conceptual framework is a model of two processes which together create a widespread IT vision (Nanus, 1992). The first process is the envisioning process, composed of three factors, wherein the vision is developed, refined, aligned, and agreed upon by those creating it. The second process is the communication process wherein the IT vision is communicated throughout the organization. The outcome of these two processes is the organization members' acceptance of a common vision (Koehler, 1989). The model also includes a delineation of the characteristics of the vision; this delineation has not been previously developed but is important to understanding the envisioning and communication processes. Figure 2 further explains the model, separating out the envisioning process from the communication process and its outcome.

The Envisioning Process

In an information-intensive organization (or one that could become so), the top management team should include the chief information officer (CIO) or the individual whose duties include those of CIO. One of the CIO's top management team responsibilities should be the development and articulation of an SVIT (Paul, 1998). The CIO should form a working group to develop the IT vision. The envisioning process is constrained by environmental and organizational factors discussed next. A review of the envisioning team characteristics follows the discussion of these constraints.

Figure 2. Theoretical Model for IT Envisioning, Alignment, and Communication

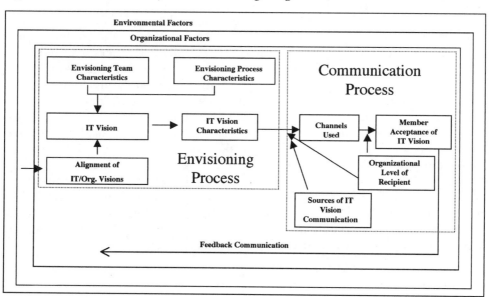

The Environment

The envisioning and communication processes and the vision itself are presented with opportunities and constrained by the organization's environment (Pearson, 1989; Locke, et al., 1991; Nanus, 1992). An organization may find that it has unprecedented opportunities, is greatly constrained, or faces a period of flux in which it must adapt rapidly to a changing environment. Many of these variables are economy or industry specific (Dess, Ireland & Hitt, 1990; Larwood, Falbe, Kriger & Miesing, 1995) and are primarily a result of the industry's structure, markets, mission, and economy (global, national, local) in which the organization is situated. Taken together, these variables influence not only the envisioning process but also the communication process. These environmental variables are:

- Economic/financial status
- Technological status, and
- Potential strategic value for IT.

Economic/Financial Status. This variable is defined as the speed and degree of change expected in the organization's economic marketplace, both in financial terms and in terms of market share. A dynamic economic and industry market environment may make the creation and/or re-creation of an IT vision more urgent than a less volatile environment because the IT vision may need to change to meet the changing environment. In addition, in an economy that is in a downturn, an IT vision can help to give the organization an advantage over other organizations which have no IT vision by helping to focus the organization on the potential impact of IT to help them recover.

Technological Status. This is the level of technology currently available. Technological advances in the industry or in the global marketplace also represent constraints or opportunities to organizations. As technological advances are made, not only may the IT vision need to change, there may be more communication channels available to communicate the IT vision, due to cost reduction or communication hardware and software advances.

Potential Strategic Value for IT. Depending on the organization's niche in its industry and marketplace, IT may or may not have strategic value for the organization. For example, the potential to use IT strategically will differ for a "mom and pop" grocery store and a large grocery chain. For information-intensive organizations that depend on large volumes of information for their survival, the value of IT can usually enhance performance at almost every functional and hierarchical level of the organization (Johnston & Vitale, 1988; Porter & Millar, 1985). Because such an organization is dependent on information, it should be more likely to have a formal envisioning process for IT and to take formal steps to communicate the IT vision throughout the organization in order to reach all its members, thereby adding to the value of IT to the organization (c.f., Nanus, 1992; Martinsons & Schindler, 1995; Barrett, 1994). Where an organization does not rely on IT for strategic value, its IT vision may be much less formal and may be communicated less formally and less broadly in the organization. Even the view that information and, therefore, IT are not important is a form of IT vision.

The Organizational Context

An SVIT is also a direct result of organization-specific forces that constrain and present opportunities for a variety of organizational processes, e.g., organizational communication, top management processes and outcomes, and interfunctional collaboration. These organizational elements include:

- Organization size
- Formalization of IT planning
- Centralization/structure
- Culture
- IT management success to date.

Organization size. Organization size has been shown to be positively associated with innovativeness (Cohen & Mowery, 1985; Rothwell & Zegveld, 1985; Bantel & Jackson, 1989; Ettlie, Bridges & O'Keefe, 1984; Haveman, 1993). A larger organization has more resources to devote to issues such as planning and envisioning. Size also influences the individual subunits' innovativeness as well. A larger organization would be more likely to have an individual subunit such as the Information Systems Department that would promote the creation of an SVIT in the organization. Organization size should also influence the number and types of communication channels available to top management to communicate the IT vision, as well as changing scope needed to align and communicate the vision.

Formalization of IT Planning. An organization with formal planning mechanisms may be more likely to engage in an envisioning process. Such an organization should be more likely to follow a step-by-step methodology in IT planning, beginning with the envisioning process.

Centralization/Structure. Much of the way in which an organization operates and carries out its functions, including envisioning and organizational communication, is determined by its hierarchical structure and degree of centralization. Decision-making, planning, authorization and delegation processes are all affected by the organization's structure.

Culture. Alvesson and Berg (1992) refer to the cultural or symbolic use of internal corporate communication as "one of the more important tools for the internal legitimation of strategic actions... By 'framing' the company and its context, and by communicating the mission to the employees, a framework for action is created" (p. 163). Organizational culture is a factor in the envisioning and communication processes because culture in and of itself may facilitate, restrict, or prevent a vision from being developed, aligned, communicated, or accepted by organization members. Culture influences the number and variety of channels available and accessible to organization members. Culture also influences communication patterns between organization members at the same and differing levels.

IT management success to date. Prior IT management success is an indicator of future IT management success (Bantel & Jackson, 1989) and is a variable influencing the background, or starting point, for envisioning, aligning, and communicating. Organizations that have been successful in managing IT to date recognize that IT management is important and presumably pay close attention to IT management activities, including IT vision processes. Prior IT management success may be an indicator that an SVIT already exists and has been successfully communicated and accepted.

Envisioning Team Characteristics

Those individuals who develop the vision form an "envisioning team." They may be all or some of the top management team, the CEO, the CIO, or any other individual or group, one of whose tasks is the development of an SVIT. These individuals bring to the envisioning process their own set(s) of personal biases, perceptions, and motivations. These personal influences play a part in the envisioning process and in the content of the resulting IT vision (Bantel & Jackson, 1989; Hambrick & Mason, 1984; Bantel, 1994). To a large degree, these biases, perceptions and motivations are the result of their background and demographic characteristics. Personal characteristics of envisioners (like decision-makers) may influence both the envisioning and communication processes, but most theory and research relates to the effects of personal characteristics during the phases of problem identification and problem solving (Bantel & Jackson, 1989; Bantel, 1994), which are analogous to envisioning.

Both individual and group or team characteristics are important to the envisioning process. They represent filters through which each team member "sees" the IT vision and can respond to others in negotiating the content of the IT vision (Nadler & Tushman, 1990; Hambrick & Mason, 1984).

Envisioning team individual characteristics. Demographic and other personal characteristics can be used as indicators of the psychological characteristics of managers (Hambrick & Mason, 1984; Bantel & Jackson, 1989; Bantel, 1994). Background variables have been linked before to values and beliefs as well as preferences and behaviors (Mills & Bohannon, 1980; Boscarino, 1979; Hambrick & Mason, 1984). In addition, top management team demography has been shown to be directly and indirectly (through process) related to organizational performance (Smith, Smith, Olian & Sims, 1994) and to corporate change (Wiersema & Bantel, 1992). Individual envisioning team characteristics are:

- Age
- Gender
- Race
- Educational level
- Tenure in the organization and on the envisioning team
- Functional background (past and present)
- IT interest, knowledge and bias
- Perceptions of the organization and the role of IT in the organization

Bantel and Jackson (1989) used age, educational level and area of study, tenure in the organization and on the top management team, and functional background as variables in their study of the effects of top management team characteristics on organizational innovation in the banking industry. Frohman (1982) found that "top management orientation" toward technology is important to an organization's ability to use technology competitively. The values of the top management team influence the level of organizational innovation (Hage & Dewar, 1973). This values orientation is essentially the same as the IT knowledge, interest and bias mentioned above. It is important to add race and gender to these characteristics as these, like age, may also influence the actions of the envisioning team by acting as additional filters through which management actions and processes occur.

Because the CEO is the top executive, one should segregate out his/her characteristics and pay close attention to those characteristics as well as team process characteristics involving the CEO. Generally, the CEO is the organizational vision setter (Bennis & Nanus, 1985; Nanus, 1992; Bryman, 1992; Ranhunathan, 1992; Coulson-Thomas, 1992). CEO support for IT is essential for SVIT (Jarvenpaa & Ives, 1990). Therefore, the CEO's demographic and other personal characteristics should have more influence on the envisioning team than those of any other individuals.

Also recognizing that the presence of an IT champion or the CIO may influence the actions of the envisioning team (Howell & Higgins, 1990; Yellen, 1993; Martinsons, 1993; Beatty, 1992; Day, 1994), his/her characteristics must also be given special attention. Because such a champion is more interested in IT (Beath, 1991; Martinsons, 1993), he/she should presumably focus more of the envisioning team's attention on IT issues than would otherwise occur. Another assumption is that the envisioning team would rely more on the IT champion for information regarding IT issues.

It is important that these individual characteristics be considered in determining the makeup of the envisioning team. One financial holding company studied by the authors had an informal envisioning team composed only of IT managers, with the chief financial officer who did not even use a computer as the head of the envisioning team. Their IT vision was more focused on the present than the future and was not competitive in nature. Another holding company's team was headed by their CEO, a technophile who used three computers, and composed of those who had expressed an interest in furthering the company's IT strategy. A survey of IT vendors who dealt with these two companies revealed that the CEO-led team's company was more advanced in fulfilling their mission through IT than the other company.

Envisioning team group characteristics. In addition to individual characteristics, group characteristics of the envisioning team also operate to influence the processes and actions of the envisioning team (Bantel & Jackson, 1989). These include:

- The size of the envisioning team (which may be a result of organization size)
- The formality of the envisioning team
- The degree of influence of the CEO, the CIO and/or the IT and other area champions
- Group heterogeneity on all of the individual characteristics, and
- The group's IT interest, knowledge and bias and IT motivations taken at the aggregated group level (since the influence of the group process may result in the aggregate level of these variables being different from a simple sum of the individual levels of these factors).

Bantel and Jackson (1989) found that the size of the top management team influences organizational innovation. The larger the team, the more innovative the organization. This is probably a result of increasing heterogeneity and the diversity of ideas on the team and might also influence its desire to create and communicate an IT vision.

The degree of influence of the CEO, the CIO, the IT champion and other area champions should also be investigated to determine to what extent these individuals' characteristics shape the processes and actions of the envisioning team (Beath,

1991; Bantel & Jackson, 1989; Howell & Higgins, 1990; Martinsons, 1993; Day, 1994; Beatty, 1992; Buckholtz, 1994). It is possible that these individuals could have so much influence that the characteristics of the rest of the team are not nearly as important as they are on a more balanced team.

The interest and knowledge of technology, and of IT in particular, of the envisioning team taken as a whole is also important. The group's interest and knowledge may be more or less than the simple sum of the interests and knowledge of its individual members. It is important to measure the interest and knowledge aggregated at the group level as well in order to take into account the possibility of group influences on the individual levels of these variables. The same is true for technology bias and for motivation.

Heterogeneity of the envisioning team is another important component (Hambrick & Mason, 1984; Bantel & Jackson, 1989; Elder, 1975; Pfeffer, 1983; Katz, 1982; Wagner, Pfeffer & O'Reilly, 1984). Heterogeneity of the demographic and other characteristics may enable an envisioning team to broaden its interests and perspectives as well as to open its processes so that they include more input from a broader constituency (Elder, 1975; Katz, 1982; Wagner, Pfeffer & O'Reilly, 1984). However, heterogeneity might lead to increased conflict over differing values and beliefs and to communication problems (Pfeffer, 1983). Thus heterogeneity can lead to dysfunctional conflict. It is, therefore, important to consider heterogeneity to determine what influence, if any, it has on the envisioning process.

Envisioning Process Characteristics

The process of envisioning presents constraints and opportunities for the creation of the vision and affects the characteristics as well as the content of the IT vision. Envisioning process characteristics are:

- Formality
- Responsibility
- Consensus
- Simultaneity with organizational envisioning
- Urgency.

The Formality of the Envisioning Process. A formal process is one in which specific steps occur in a specific order with forethought as to the process. This may include a place for the envisioning process on the top management team's agenda, formal meetings to discuss the IT vision, and requested input from others outside the envisioning team. Otherwise, the envisioning process might simply consist of one or more persons deciding on the vision. An envisioning process undertaken with a formal planning approach will probably have formal communication methods as well. In addition, the more formal the envisioning process, the more likely it is that attention will be paid to this process and to its outcome.

Responsibility for the envisioning process. If no one is responsible for the envisioning process, that process may not be viewed as important to the organization. The hierarchical level of the individual or group responsible for creating the vision serves as an indicator of the degree of importance and urgency attached to the vision and its outcome (Schiemann, 1992; Coulson-Thomas, 1992). The higher the level of the responsible party, the more likely acceptance will be achieved because of the greater influence of the higher members in an organization (Shimp & DeLozier, 1986; Feeny, Edwards & Simpson, 1992). The higher the level of the individual responsible for the IT vision, the more likely it is that he or she can enforce alignment of the SVIT with the organization's strategic vision. Again, in the case of the two holding companies, the CEO who led the envisioning team ensured that alignment occurred at all levels while the CFO led envisioning team never really aligned their IT vision at all.

Consensus about the IT Vision. Consensus about the SVIT among the members of the envisioning team should alleviate conflict in the group's envisioning process and should focus the group on the outcome (Alderson, 1993). Consensus should also help communication as well because the envisioning team members will be more likely to communicate their agreement with the IT vision down through the organizational hierarchy. Consensus will also help to ensure that the SVIT is properly aligned with the organization's vision.

Simultaneity with organizational strategic envisioning. Simultaneity is a characteristic of the envisioning process. Conducting the IT envisioning simultaneously with the organizational envisioning process may aid the IT envisioning process in several ways, among them consensus, alignment with organizational strategic vision, and future communication (c.f., Parker & Benson, 1991).

Urgency. If the need for the IT vision is perceived as being urgent, the IT envisioning process should receive a high priority on the group's agenda, and more of the envisioning team's attention should be paid to ensure its success. Urgency is influenced by the environment, current technological status, the potential strategic value of IT, and IT management success to date.

Implicit in the preceding discussion of factors influencing the development of the IT vision is that these influence each other. For example, if there is an urgent need for the IT vision to be developed, the formality of the envisioning process may well vary, depending on whether the decision maker decides to use a formal process and also depending on the makeup of the envisioning team (both individual and group characteristics). The team may prefer to use a formal process, but the decision maker (presumably the CIO) may deem the need so urgent as to bypass formality in order to meet the urgency by using a less formal, presumably shorter process.

VISION CHARACTERISTICS

As a result of the constraints and opportunities presented above, the SVIT has certain characteristics that influence the way in which the vision is communicated throughout the organization. The six characteristics of IT vision are:
- Stage of development
- Degree of change implied
- Alignment with organizational strategic vision
- Degree of formality, and
- Source Legitimacy.

Stage of Development

IT vision may be in one of several developmental stages that should be viewed as a continuum proceeding from "not yet developed at all" through "in the envisioning process", to "about to be communicated" to "partially communicated" to "institutionally communicated" to the re-envisioning process wherein a current vision is being redefined and then will be re-communicated (Nanus, 1992; Locke et al., 1991). The process of communication depends on the stage of development of the IT vision. A vision that has not yet been developed cannot be communicated; a vision that has been previously partially communicated may be communicated in different ways from one that has never been communicated before.

Degree of Change Implied

The degree of change between the current future situations implied by the IT vision will cause a similar degree of uncertainty (c.f., Brabston, 1993a; Ettlie et al., 1984; Henderson and Clark, 1990). For example, a radical degree of change implied by the IT vision between the present situation (roles, functions, budgets, etc.) and a future situation described in the IT vision will cause a high degree of uncertainty in those who receive the vision message. The degree of change implied may also influence the effectiveness of vision communication as evidenced by member acceptance of the IT vision (c.f., Schiemann, 1992; Brabston, 1993a).

Alignment with Organizational Strategic Vision

Business strategy should drive technology strategy (Davenport, Hammer & Metsisto, 1989; Radding & Maglitta, 1993; Tapscott & Caston, 1993; Zahra & Covin, 1993; Fink, 1994). Therefore, strategic IT vision should be aligned with the overall organizational strategic vision (Lewis & Linden, 1990; Fagan, 1987; Henderson & Sifonis, 1988; Mulloy, 1990). Alignment ensures that the IT vision is not at odds with organizational strategy. Improper alignment diminishes the members' understanding of the vision due to expectancy effects.

Degree of Formality

Formality forces the envisioning team to articulate their vision and to arrive at a negotiated group vision (James, 1985; Nadler & Tushman, 1990). An IT vision that exhibits features of formality, such as an IT mission statement, will influence the choice of channels used to communicate the IT vision.

Legitimacy of the Source

Legitimacy of the source of communication of the IT vision will affect the channels used for communication and the effectiveness of its subsequent communication. Legitimacy is comprised of three sub-elements: the perceived status/power of the owner or sender (or both), the perceived expertise of the owner or sender, and the perceived credibility or trustworthiness of the owner or sender (Shimp & Delozier, 1986). The higher in the organizational hierarchy the party responsible for communicating the IT vision is, the more influence the responsible individual has and the more attention should be paid to the IT vision communication. For example, if the CEO is perceived as "owning" the IT vision, the vision has greater legitimacy than if the assistant IT department head is perceived as the owner. Organization members will pay more attention and communication will be more effective when it is received from higher levels in the organization (Huber, 1982) as well as when it has urgency or importance (Shimp & DeLozier, 1986).

Communication from an expert in the topic is also perceived to have legitimacy and will be more likely to be accepted (Harrison & Spoth, 1992; Wilson & Sherrell, 1993; Chawla, Dave & Barr, 1994). Finally, communication coming from a source perceived to be trustworthy or credible — whether because of past associations, personal relationships, or a lack of self-interest in the outcome of the communication — will be perceived to have more legitimacy and will be more likely to be accepted (Shrimp & DeLozier, 1986; Chawla et al., 1994; Harrison & Spoth, 1992). Legitimacy of the communication can also be increased by increasing the number of sources (Shrimp & DeLozier, 1986).

THE COMMUNICATION PROCESS

Once the vision has been developed during the envisioning process, it must be communicated to all organization members affected by the vision (Nanus, 1992, James, 1985; Locke et al., 1991; Wilhelm, 1992; Bennis, 1995, 1994). The purpose of communication is to "share" the vision, to motivate organization members to help to achieve the vision, and to help organization members to believe in the vision (Nanus, 1992; Bryman, 1992; Bennis & Nanus, 1985; James, 1985; Collins & Porras, 1991; Nadler & Tushman, 1990; Robbins & Duncan, 1988; Locke et al., 1991; Wilhelm, 1992; Knorr, 1993). Communication gives "employees a guide to acceptable and legitimate behavior and helps put the corporate strategy in action. Communication must permeate throughout the entire organization and include customers and suppliers" (Wilhelm, 1992, p. 74). The communication process is composed of the channels used for IT vision communication, moderated by the organizational level of the organization member, and finally, the outcome of the communication, member acceptance of the IT vision. Feedback is systemic and influences both the envisioning and communication processes.

Channels Used

The communication channels used to communicate a message are extremely important (Trevino, Daft & Lengel, 1990; Saunders & Jones, 1990; Zmud, Lind & Young, 1990; O'Reilly, 1982; Jones & McLeod, 1986). Each channel carries its own hidden message as well as the intended message (Trevino et al., 1990). For purposes of this framework, these hidden messages are "assumed away." Each channel is assumed to have "generic" characteristics. It is proposed here that certain channels are used to enhance member acceptance of the vision. Specific channels are used to communicate the vision message based on vision characteristics, generic channel characteristics and the moderating influence of the message recipient's organizational level. Each channel is assumed to have an objective degree of richness. The potential for use of multiple channels and repeated use of single channels are also important.

The Number of Channels Used. Organization members have differential access to different channels and pay different channels varying amounts of attention. Use of a variety of channels for communication should enhance the likelihood of all members becoming aware of the vision. Use of multiple channels, even of the same type, will also permit more detail to be communicated. This is also true regarding the repeated use of one channel, such as the sending of several memoranda. Frequent and repetitive communication that carries a simple vision message is beneficial (Wilhelm, 1992). The repetitive nature of using multiple channels should also ensure that the employees see the importance of the vision which is being communicated.

Richness of Channels Used. Depending on the richness and detail involved in communicating the IT vision, different channels may be chosen (Trevino et al., 1990; Saunders & Jones, 1990; O'Reilly, 1982). Richness is a composite of four factors: cue variety, immediate feedback, message personalization and naturalness of language (Daft & Lengel, 1986). Studies have shown that certain types of media are generally considered to be richer while others are generally considered to be leaner (Trevino et al., 1990; Saunders & Jones, 1990). In addition, the capacity of diverse media to convey detail varies, e.g., from verbal conversations to lengthy written memoranda (O'Reilly, 1982). Other studies have shown that the appropriateness of the media for the intended use is another factor affecting effectiveness (Trevino et al., 1990; Culnan & Markus, 1987; Zmud, Lind & Young, 1990; Fulk, Schmitz, & Steinfield, 1990). Examining the types of channels used in an organization to communicate the IT vision may determine which types of channels are better than others for communicating IT vision to specific segments of the organization.

There is a caveat to the use of objective measures of channel richness. It may be that a more hermeneutic, qualitative method may be needed to judge how rich a channel is in a particular context. Several studies have shown that it is as much the specific use of the channel as the channel itself that determines its richness and detail capacity (Sproull & Kiesler, 1986; Finholt & Sproull, 1989; Carlson & Zmud, 1994; Lee, 1993; Markus, 1994).

Organizational Level of Recipient

Organizational relationships, particularly distance in the hierarchical structure, influence communication patterns and perceptions (Zahn, 1991; Nicoll, 1993; Brabston, 1993b). O'Reilly and Roberts (1974) found that significant distortion occurs as a message moves through an organization. Allen and Cohen (1969) found that more information is communicated within status levels than across levels. Hambrick (1981) found a decline in strategy awareness in descending levels of the managerial hierarchy. Hierarchical distance, therefore, influences the perception of communication and the reception of a message in downward communication.

Organizational level moderates both the choice of channels used to communicate the IT vision and the relationship between these channels and the members' acceptance of the IT vision. Organization members may receive different IT vision messages depending on their level in the organizational hierarchy. It seems intuitive that a member of senior management would receive different communication, probably even on a different communication channel, than would a department head or clerical worker. Channels used to communicate the IT vision to different levels in the hierarchy may, therefore, vary depending on the targeted level. Attitudes and opinions vary depending on the organizational level of the organization member. Therefore, those closer in organizational level to those who created the IT vision should more readily agree with the IT vision created by those close to them. Certainly, the organization member's perception of the message will be different depending on the member's hierarchical level.

ORGANIZATION MEMBERS' ACCEPTANCE OF THE IT VISION

The outcome of all of these factors and processes is the acceptance by organization members of the IT vision. Acceptance of change, represented by acceptance of the IT vision, is one of the most important factors in IS implementation (Ginzberg, 1981). IT implementations represent changes that are a direct result of the SVIT. If an organization can positively influence the acceptance of its IT vision by its organization members, implementation of the IT vision should be more successful.

An effective communication occurs "when the transfer of an idea from a source to a receiver results in a change in knowledge, attitude or overt behavior on the part of the receiver" (Rogers & Bhowmik, 1970-71, p. 529). If IT vision communication is completely effective, those organization members who were sent the vision message should be aware of the IT vision, they should agree with it, and they should work toward its achievement. These three elements correspond with knowledge (awareness), attitude (convergence of understanding or agreement), and overt behaviors (actions). Where fewer than three of these elements are present, the communication is only partially effective and acceptance is not complete. Where none of these factors is present, the communication is completely ineffective, and no acceptance exists.

Awareness of the IT Vision

If an organization member is aware of the IT vision, communication has at least reached the organization member. Awareness may not be an overt recognition that there is an IT vision and what that vision is but may rather be an implicit recognition of procedures, attitudes, budgeting and other less formal manifestations of the vision. Awareness may be simply the individual's overall perception of the role of IT in the organization; the individual may not even be aware that this perception is held until asked to describe the role of IT in the organization.

Convergence of Understanding Between the Organization Member and the Envisioning Team Regarding the IT Vision

According to Lind and Zmud (1991), convergence of understanding is the "tendency of two or more individuals to move toward one point, or for individuals to move toward others and unite in a common interest or focus" (p. 197). This view emphasizes the importance of information exchange so that individuals can achieve "understanding, consensus, and collective actions" (p. 197). Where such an understanding exists, it is most likely the result of effective communication rather than chance circumstance. An organization member who agrees with management regarding the IT vision will be more likely to act in creative ways to implement the vision (Nanus, 1992; Bennis & Nanus, 1985). The organization member does not need to be aware that there is a vision in order to converge with the substance of the vision and to take actions consistent with the vision.

Actions to Achieve the IT Vision

If an organization member takes action to achieve the IT vision, he or she may be operating under procedural orders without regard to the existence of a vision. Even so, communication has been somewhat effective, or else such rote procedures would not exist. Actions taken to achieve the IT vision that were taken as a result of vision awareness and convergence of understanding represent more effective communication than do actions taken as a result of rote procedures. It is through organization members' actions that the organization will receive benefits from its SVIT. This then is the most desired outcome of IT vision communication. If all three effects are present, communication has been fully effective for the current IT vision, and it can be inferred that the organization member accepts the IT vision.

FEEDBACK

While the theoretical framework appears to read from right to left with little or no feedback, this is not the case in theory or reality. Feedback is an important part of the framework, but one which is indigenous and ubiquitous. As each step is taken in developing and communicating an SVIT, opportunities for feedback exist throughout the framework.

CONCLUSION

This chapter has presented a theoretical framework representing the envisioning, alignment, and organizational communication of a strategic vision for information technology. This framework also takes into account informal as well as formal communication channels (Johnson, Donohue, Atkin & Johnson, 1994). The model can be used by both practitioners and academic researchers to examine and describe these two important parts of the IT planning process.

Using a properly developed, aligned, and communicated IT vision, employees located throughout an organization should be able to align their work, purchases, and decision making with the IT vision, thus also aligning their work with the organizational vision. This alignment should improve organizational performance.

For academic researchers, each of the constructs presented here carries with it a set of research questions. For example, does mere awareness of the IT vision influence organizational performance, or is convergence of understanding required for this to happen? Does the use of multiple, varied channels result in greater IT vision awareness than the multiple uses of a single channel?

This research is theory based and does not take into account differences in organizational size beyond the organizational context. It may be, for example, that organizational size influences the communication process. This might mean that IT vision communication is so filtered that awareness of the IT vision becomes meaningless. A further limitation is the possibility that all organizational members do not, in fact, need to be aware of the IT vision and agree with it. It may be that only those in the IT area and those in the top management areas of the organization need to be aware of and agree with the IT vision.

This work developed a theoretical framework for IT vision that may help top managers to better understand the IT management process and to better develop, align, and communicate their IT strategic vision. This understanding and actions derived therefrom should help organizational performance since communication and concurrence with the vision should motivate employees to accomplish the goals set by such a vision.

REFERENCES

Alderson, S. (1993). Reframing management competence: Focusing on the top management team. *Personnel Review, 22*(6), 53-62.

Allen, T. J., & Cohen, S. I. (1969). Information flow in research and development laboratories. *Administrative Science Quarterly, 14*, 12-20.

Alvesson, M., & Berg, P. O. (1992). *Corporate culture and organizational symbolism.* New York: Walter de Gruyter.

Bantel, K. A. (1994). Strategic planning openness: The role of top team demography. *Group and Organization Management, 19*(4), 406-424.

Bantel, K. A., & Jackson, S. E. (1989). Top management and innovations in banking: Does the composition of the top team make a difference? *Strategic Management Journal, 10*, 107-124.

Barrett, J. L. (1994). Process visualization. *Information Systems Management, 11*(2), 14-23.

Beath, C. M. (1991). Supporting the information technology champion. *MIS Quarterly, 15*, 354-372.

Beatty, C. A. (1992). Implementing advanced manufacturing technologies: Rules of the road. *Sloan Management Review, 33*(4), 49-60.

Bennis, W. (1995). Leading change. *Executive Excellence, 12*(2), 6.

Bennis, W. (1994). Introducing change. *Executive Excellence, 11*(11), 9-10.

Bennis, W., & Nanus, B. (1985). *Leadership: Strategies for taking charge.* New York: Harper and Row.

Boland, R. J., Jr., & Tenkasi, R. V. (1995). Perspective making and perspective taking in communities of knowing. *Organization Science, 6*(4), 350-373.

Boscarino, J. (1979). Alcohol abuse among veterans: The importance of demographic factors. *Addictive Behaviors, 4*, 323-330.

Boynton, A., & Zmud, R. W. (1987). Information technology planning in the 1990's: Directions for practice and research. *MIS Quarterly, 11*, 59-72.

Brabston, M. E. (1993a). Categorizing IT innovation by extent of change and location of impact: A contextual approach. *Journal of Computing and Information Technology, 1*, 133-144.

Brabston, M. E. (1993b). Effectiveness of channel use for communication of strategic vision for information technology to organization members. *Proceedings of the 24th Annual Meeting of the Decision Sciences Institute*. Washington, D.C.

Brabston, M. E., Zmud, R. W., & Carlson, J. R. (1999). Communicating IT vision to organization members: An assessment of channel usage behaviors. Under revision for *MIS Quarterly*.

Bryman, A. (1992). *Charisma and leadership in organizations*. Newbury, CT: Sage.

Buckholtz, T. J. (1994). Identity crisis. *CIO, 7*(15), 26,28.

Carlson, J. R., & Zmud, R. W. (1994). Channel expansion theory: A dynamic view of media and information richness Perceptions. *Proceedings of the Annual Meeting of the Academy of Management*: Dallas, TX.

Chawla, S. K., Dave, D. S. & Barr, P. B. (1994). Role of physical attractiveness in endorsement: An empirical study. *Journal of Professional Services Marketing, 10*(2), 203-215.

Clark, K. B. (1989). What strategy can do for technology. *Harvard Business Review, 67*(6), 94-98.

Cohen, W., & Mowery, D. (1984). Firm heterogeneity and R&D: An agenda for research. In B. Bozeman, M. Crow & A. Link (Eds.), *Strategic management of industrial R&D* (107-120). Lexington, NY: Lexington Books.

Collins, J. C., & Porras, J. I. (1991). Organizational vision and visionary organizations. *California Management Review, 34*, 30-52.

Coulson-Thomas, C. (1992). Strategic vision or strategic con? Rhetoric or reality? *Long Range Planning, 25*(1), 81-89.

Culnan, M. J., & Markus, M. L. (1987). Information technologies: Electronic media and intraorganizational communication. In F. M. Jablin, L. L. Putnam, K. H. Roberts, & L. W. Porter (Eds.), *Handbook on organizational communication* (420-443). Newbury Park: Sage.

Daft, R. L., & Lengel, R. H. (1986). Organizational information requirements, media richness and structural design. *Management Science, 32*, 554-571.

Davenport, T. H., Hammer, M., & Metsisto, T. J. (1989). How executives can shape their company's information systems. *Harvard Business Review, 67*, 130-134.

Day, D.L. (1994). Raising radicals: Different processes for championing innovative corporate ventures. *Organization Science, 5*(2), 148-172.

Dess, G. G., Ireland, R. D., & Hitt, M. A. (1990). Industry effects and strategic management research. *Journal of Management, 16*, 7-27.

Elder, G. H., Jr. (1976). Age differentiation and life course. *Annual Review of Sociology*, 165-190.

Ettlie, J. E., Bridges, W. P., & O'Keefe, R. D. (1984). Organization strategy and structural differences for radical versus incremental innovation. *Management Science, 30*, 682-695.

Fagan, R. J. (1987, September). Active control and better organization curtail costs. *Savings Institutions*, S20-S24.

Feeny, D. F., Edwards, B. R., & Simpson, K. M. (1992). Understanding the CEO/CIO relationship. *MIS Quarterly, 16*(4), 435-448.

Ferreira, J. & Harris, P. R. (1985, Fall). The changing role of IRM professionals. *Information Strategy: The Executive's Journal*, 18-22.

Finholt, T., & Sproull, L. S. (1989). Electronic groups at work. *Organization Science, 1*, 41-64.

Fink, D. (1994). Information systems planning in a volatile environment. *Long Range Planning, 27*(6), 108-114.

Frohman, A. L. (1982). Technology as a competitive weapon. *Harvard Business Review, 60* (1), 97-104.

Frohman, A. L. (1985). Putting technology into strategic planning. *California Management Review, 27*(2), 48-59.

Fulk, J., Schmitz, J., & Steinfield, C. W. (1990). A social influence model of technology use. In J. Fulk & C. Steinfield (Eds.), *Organizations and communication technology* (117-141). Newbury Park: Sage.

Ginzberg, M. J. (1981). Early diagnosis of MIS implementation failure: Promising results and unanswered questions. *Management Science, 27*, 459-478.

Hage, J., & Dewar, R. (1973). Elite values versus organizational structure in predicting innovations. *Administrative Science Quarterly, 18*, 279-290.

Hambrick, D. C. (1981). Strategic awareness within top management teams. *Strategic Management Journal, 2*, 263-279.

Hambrick, D. C., & Mason, P. A. (1984). Upper echelons: The organization as a reflection of its top managers. *Academy of Management Review, 9*, 193-206.

Harrison, R. & Spoth, J. (1992). Matching change interventions to organizational realities. *Industrial and Commercial Training, 24*(2), 3-8.

Haveman, J. A. (1993). Organizational size and change: Diversification in the savings and loan industry after deregulation. *Administrative Science Quarterly, 38*(1), 20-50.

Henderson, R. M., & Clark, K. B. (1990). Architectural innovation: The reconfiguration of existing product technologies and the failure of established firms. *Administrative Science Quarterly, 35*, 9-30.

Henderson, J. C., & Sifonis, J. G. (1988). The value of strategic IS planning: Consistency, validity and IS markets. *MIS Quarterly, 12*, 186-200.

Howell, J. M., & Higgins, C. A. (1990). Champions of technological innovation. *Administrative Science Quarterly, 35*, 317-341.

Huber, G. P. (1982). Organizational information systems: Determinants of their performance and behavior. *Management Science, 28*, 138-155.

James, P. N. (1985, Fall). A framework for strategic and long-range information resource planning. *Information Strategy: The Executive's Journal*, 4-12.

Jarvenpaa, S., & Ives, B. (1990). Information technology and corporate strategy: A view from the top. *Information Systems Research, 1*, 351-376.

Johnson, J.D., Donohue, W. A., & Atkin, C. K. (1994). Differences between formal and informal communication channels. *The Journal Of Business Communication, 31*(2), 111-123.

Johnston, H. R., & Vitale, M. R. (1988). Creating competitive advantage with interorganizational information systems. *MIS Quarterly, 12*, 152-165.

Jones, J. W., & McLeod, R. M. (1986). The structure of executive information systems. *Decision Sciences, 17*, 220-249.

Katz, R. (1982). The effects of group longevity on project communication and performance. *Administrative Science Quarterly, 27*, 81-104.

Kettinger, W. K. & Teng, J. T. C. (1998). Aligning BPR to strategy: A framework for analysis. *Long Range Planning, 31*(1), 93-107.

Knorr, R. O. (1993). A strategy for communicating change. *Journal of Business Strategy, 14*(4), 18-20.

Koehler, K. G. (1989, August). Turn strategic vision into reality. *Small Business Reports*, 15-17.

Kouzes, J. M. & Posner, B. A. (1996). Envisioning your future: Imagining ideal scenarios. *Futurist, 30*(3), 14-19.

Larwood, L., Falbe, C. M., Kriger, M. P., & Miesing, P. (1995). Structure and meaning of organizational vision. *Academy of Management Journal, 38*(3), 740-769.

Lee, A. S. (1993). Electronic mail as a medium for rich communication: An empirical investigation using hermeneutic interpretation. *Proceedings of the Fourteenth International Conference on Information Systems*, December 5-8, 1993. Orlando, FL.

Lewis, W. W., & Linden, L. H. (1990). A new mission for corporate technology. *Sloan Management Review, 31*(4), 57-67.

Lind, M., & Zmud, R. W. (1991). The influence of a convergence in understanding between technology providers and users on information technology innovativeness. *Organization Science, 2*, 195-217.

Locke, E. A., Kirkpatrick, S., Wheeler, J. K., Schneider, J., Niles, K., & Goldstein, H. (1991). *The essence of leadership*. New York: Lexington.

Markus, M. L. (1994). Electronic mail as the medium of managerial choice. *Organization Science, 5*(4), 502-527.

Martinsons, M. (1994). A strategic vision for managing business intelligence. *Information Strategy: The Executive's Journal, 10*(3), 17-30.

Martinsons, M. (1993). Cultivating the champions for strategic information systems. *Journal of Systems Management, 44*(8), 31-34.

Martinsons, M. & Schindler, F. R. (1995). Organizational visions for technology assimilation: The strategic roads to knowledge-based systems success. *IEEE Transactions on Engineering Management, 42*(1), 9-19.

Mills, C. J. & Bohannon, W. E. (1980). Personality Characteristics of Effective State Police Officers. *Journal of Applied Psychology, 65*(6), 680.

Mulloy, M. (1990). IS execs need to actively shape corporate strategy. *Network World, 7*(38), 23-24.

Nadler, D. A., & Tushman, M. L. (1990). Beyond the charismatic leader: Leadership and organizational change. *California Management Review, 32*(2), 77-97.

Nanus, B. (1992). *Visionary leadership*. San Francisco: Jossey-Bass.

Nicoll, D. (1993). Corporate value statements and employee communications. *Management Decision, 31*(8), 34-40.

O'Reilly, C. A., III. (1982). Variations in decision-makers' use of information sources: The impact of quality and accessibility of information. *Academy of Management Journal, 25*, 756-771.

O'Reilly, C. A., III, & Roberts, K. H. (1974). Empirical findings and suggestions for future research on organizational communication. Tech Rep. No. 6. Arlington,

VA: Office of Naval Research, Contract No. N000314-69-A-0200-1054, as referenced in R. V. Farace, J. A. Taylor, & J. P. Stewart (1978), Criteria for evaluation of organizational communication effectiveness: Review and synthesis. *Communication Yearbook, 2,* 271-332.

Parker, M. M. (1995). *Strategic transformation and information technology: Paradigms for performing while transforming.* Upper Saddle River, NJ: Prentice Hall.

Parker, M. M., & Benson, R. J. (1991). Why business strategy should not follow financial systems. *Financial and Accounting Systems, 6*(4), 20-29.

Paul, L. G. (1998). A separate piece. *CIO, 12*(2), 50-60.

Pearson, A. E. (1989). Six basics for general managers. *Harvard Business Review, 68*(3), 94-101.

Pfeffer, J. (1983). Organizational demography. In L. L. Cummings & B. M. Staw (Eds.), *Research in organizational behavior* (299-357). Greenwich, CT: JAI Press.

Porter, M. E., & Millar, V. E. (1985). How information gives you competitive advantage. *Harvard Business Review, 63*(4), 149-160.

Radding, A. & Maglitta, J. (1993). Techno renaissance. *Computerworld, 27*(17), 67-72.

Raghunathan, T.S. (1992). Impact of the CEO's participation on information systems steering committees. *Journal of Management Information Systems, 8*(4), 83-96.

Robbins, S. R., & Duncan, R. B. (1988). The role of the CEO and top management in the creation and implementation of strategic vision. In D. C. Hambrick (Ed.), *The executive effect: Concepts and methods for studying top managers* (205-233). Greenwich, CT: JAI Press.

Rockart, J. F. & Hofman, J. D. (1992). Systems delivery: Evolving new strategies. *Sloan Management Review, 33*(4), 21-31.

Rogers, E. M., & Bhowmik, D. P. (1970-1971). Homophily-heterophily: Relational concepts for communication research. *Public Opinion Quarterly, 34*(4), 523-538.

Rothwell, R., & Zegveld, W. (1985). *Reindustrialization and technology.* Essex, UK: Longman.

Saunders, C., & Jones, J. W. (1990). Temporal sequences in information acquisition for decision-making: a focus on source and medium. *Academy of Management Review, 15,* 29-46.

Schiemann, W. A. (1992). Why change fails. *Across the Board, 29*(4), 53-54.

Shimp, T. A., & DeLozier, M. W. (1986). *Promotion management and marketing communications.* Chicago: Dryden Press.

Sibbet, D., & O'Hara-Devereaux, M. (1991). The language of teamwork. *Healthcare Forum Journal, 34*(3), 27-30.

Smith, K.G., Smith, K. A., Olian, J. D., Sims, H. P., Jr. et al. (1994). Top management team demography and process: The role of social integration and communication. *Administrative Science Quarterly, 39*(3), 412-438.

Sproull, L., & Kiesler, S. (1986). Reducing social context cues: electronic mail in organizational communication. *Management Science, 32,* 1492-1512.

Tapscott, D. & Caston, A. (1993). The demise of the IT strategic plan. *IT Magazine, 25*(1), 28-35.

Taylor, G. (1994). The challenge of the 90's. *Inform, 8*(5), 39, 42.

Trevino, L. K., Daft, R. L., & Lengel, R. H. (1990). Understanding managers' media choices: A symbolic interactionist perspective. In J. Fulk & C. Steinfield (Eds.), *Organizations and communication technology* (71-94). Newbury Park: Sage.

Venkatraman, N., Henderson, J. C., & Oldach, S. (1993). Continuous strategic alignment: Exploiting information technology capabilities for competitive success. *European Management Journal, 11*(2), 139-150.

Wagner, W. G., Pfeffer, J., & O'Reilly, C. C., III. (1984). Organizational demography and turnover in top management groups. *Administrative Science Quarterly, 29*, 74-92.

Wang, C. (1995). *TechnoVision: The Executive's Survival Guide to Understanding and Managing Information Technology*.

Wiersema, M. F. & Bantel, K. A. (1992). Top management team demography and corporate strategic change. *Academy of Management Journal, 35*(1), 91-121.

Wilhelm, W. (1992). Changing corporate culture — or corporate behavior? How to change your company. *Academy of Management Executive, 6*(4), 72-77.

Wilson, E. J. & Sherrell, D. L. (1993). Source effects in communication and persuasion research: A meta-analysis of effect size. *Journal of the Academy of Marketing Science, 21*(2), 101-112.

Wilson, I. (1992). Realizing the power of strategic vision. *Long Range Planning, 25*(5), 18-28.

Yellen, R. E. (1993). Introducing group decision support software (GDSS) in an organization. *Journal of Systems Management, 44*(10), 6-8.

Zahn, G. L. (1991). Face-to-face communication in an office setting. *Communication Research, 18*, 737-754.

Zahra, S.A. & Covin, J.G. (1993). Business strategy, technology policy and firm performance. *Strategic Management Journal, 14*(6), 451-478.

Zmud, R. W., Lind, M. R., & Young, F. W. (1990). An attribute space for organizational communication channels. *Information Systems Research, 1*, 440-457

Chapter VI

Assessing Business-IT Alignment Maturity

Jerry N. Luftman
Stevens Institute of Technology, USA

ABSTRACT

Business and IT practitioners, researchers, and consultants have been asking for an effective tool to assess IT-business alignment. Until now, none was available. This chapter introduces the strategic alignment maturity assessment. This assessment tool is based on the authors' research and consulting experience that identified the major enablers and inhibitors in the achievement of business-IT alignment and the methodology that leverages the most important enablers and inhibitors. Alignment focuses on the activities that management performs to achieve cohesive goals across the IT (information technology) and other functional (e.g., finance, marketing, H/R, manufacturing) organizations. Therefore, alignment addresses both how IT is in harmony with the business, and how the business should/could be in harmony with IT. Alignment evolves to a relationship where IT and business adapt their strategies together. Achieving alignment is evolutionary and dynamic. IT requires strong support from senior management, good working relationships, strong leadership, appropriate prioritization, trust, and effective communication, as well as a thorough understanding of the business and technical environments. Achieving and sustaining alignment demands focusing on maximizing the enablers and minimizing the inhibitors. The purpose of this chapter is to discuss an approach for assessing the maturity of the business-IT alignment. Once the maturity is understood, an organization can identify opportunities for enhancing the harmonious relationship of business and IT.

INTRODUCTION

Decades have passed. Billions of dollars have been invested on information technology (IT). Today, every organization is in the information business. Alignment — applying IT in an appropriate and timely way, in harmony with business strategies, goals and needs — remains a key concern of business executives. This definition addresses both how IT is aligned with the business, and how the business should/could be aligned with IT. Alignment must evolve to a relationship where IT and business adapt their strategies together. Frustratingly, organizations seem to find it difficult or impossible to harness the power of information technology (IT) for their own long-term benefit, even though there is worldwide evidence that IT has the power to transform whole industries and markets.[1] How can companies achieve alignment? How can companies assess alignment? There are known enablers and inhibitors that help and hinder alignment. Executives experience them daily. Anecdotal publications have described them.[1]

The purpose of this chapter is to present a tool for assessing the maturity of a firm's business–IT alignment. Until now, no tool was available. This alignment maturity assessment provides a comprehensive vehicle for organizations to evaluate business–IT alignment with regard to where they are and what could be done to improve the harmony. The maturity assessment applies the authors' previous research that identified enablers/inhibitors to achieving alignment as building blocks for the evaluation. It is based on the popular work done by the Software Engineering Institute[2], Keen's reach and range[3], and an evolution of the Nolan and Gibson stages of growth.[4]

THEORETICAL PERSPECTIVES AND PREVIOUS RESEARCH

Alignment's importance has been well known and documented since the late 1970s.[5] It has persisted among the top ranked concerns by business executives. Alignment seems to grow in importance as companies strive to link technology and business in light of dynamic business strategies and continuously evolving technologies.[6] Importance aside, what is not clear is how to achieve and sustain this harmony relating business and IT, how to assess the maturity of alignment, and what the impact of misalignment might be on the firm.[7] The ability to achieve and sustain this synergistic relationship is anything but easy. Identifying an organizations alignment maturity provides an excellent vehicle for understanding and growing the business-IT relationship. For years, firms have been channeling billions of dollars into technology in an attempt to successfully incorporate technology into their processes and long-term plans. Many of these efforts have failed despite overwhelming evidence of IT's ability to transform both individual firms and entire industries. Frustrated, executives have asked for help in how they can better understand and improve alignment, given this seemingly difficult interrelationship. This is especially true as executives realize that every organization is in the business of information.

The strategic alignment model, suggested by Henderson and Venkatraman,[8] was applied throughout a five-year research project. The components of the modifications of their model are shown in Figure 1. It is the relationships that exist among the 12 components of this model that define business-IT alignment. The components of this model in concert with the enablers/inhibitors research form the building blocks for the strategic alignment maturity assessment. Once the maturity is understood, an organization can identify opportunities for enhancing the harmonious relationship of business and IT.

The alignment of information technology (IT) and business strategy to leverage the capabilities of IT and to transform the business has increased in importance over the past few years, as firms strive for competitive advantage in a diverse and changing marketplace.[10] In light of this, there has been a great deal of research and insight into the linkages between Business and IT,[11] the role of partnerships between IT and business management,[12] as well as the need to understand the transformation of business strategies resulting from the competitive use of IT.[13] Firms have been able to change not only their business scope, but also their infrastructure (see Figure 1) as a result of innovation regarding IT.[14]

Several frameworks have been proposed to assess the strategic issues regarding the role of IT as a competitive weapon. They have not, however, yielded

Figure 1. The Twelve Components of Alignment[9]

I. BUSINESS STRATEGY

1. **Business Scope** – Includes the markets, products, services, groups of customers/clients, and locations where an enterprise competes as well as the competitors and potential competitors that affect the business environment.
2. **Distinctive Competencies** – The critical success factors and core competencies that provide a firm with a potential competitive edge. This includes brand, research, manufacturing and product development, cost and pricing structure, and sales and distribution channels.
3. **Business Governance** – How companies set the relationship between management, stockholders, and the board of directors. Also included are how the company is affected by government regulations, and how the firm manages its relationships and alliances with strategic partners.

II. ORGANIZATION INFRASTRUCTURE & PROCESSES

4. **Administrative Structure** – The way the firm organizes its businesses. Examples include central, decentral, matrix, horizontal, vertical, geographic, federal, and functional.
5. **Processes** - How the firm's business activities (the work performed by employees) operate or flow. Major issues include value added activities and process improvement.
6. **Skills** – H/R considerations such as how to hire/fire, motivate, train/educate, and culture.

III. IT STRATEGY

7. **Technology Scope** - The important information applications and technologies.
8. **Systemic Competencies** - Those capabilities (e.g., access to information that is important to the creation/achievement of a company's strategies) that distinguishes the IT services.
9. **IT Governance** - How the authority for resources, risk, conflict resolution, and responsibility for IT is shared among business partners, IT management, and service providers. Project selection and prioritization issues are included here.

IV. IT INFRASTRUCTURE AND PROCESSES

10. **Architecture** -The technology priorities, policies, and choices that allow applications, software, networks, hardware, and data management to be integrated into a cohesive platform.
11. **Processes** - Those practices and activities carried out to develop and maintain applications and manage IT infrastructure.
12. **Skills** – IT human resource considerations such as how to hire/fire, motivate, train/educate, and culture.

empirical evidence nor have they provided a roadmap to assess and enhance alignment. There have also been numerous studies that focus on business process redesign and reengineering[15] as a means to achieve competitive advantage with IT. This advantage comes from the appropriate application of IT as a driver or enabler of business strategy.

Research underway since 1992[2] has identified trends and established benchmarks against exemplar organizations. Analysis of the research data shows that the six most important enablers and inhibitors, in rank order are:

ENABLERS	INHIBITORS
Senior executive support for IT	IT/business lack close relationships
IT involved in strategy development	IT does not prioritize well
IT understands the business	IT fails to meet commitments
Business - IT partnership	IT does not understand business
Well-prioritized IT projects	Senior executives do not support IT
IT demonstrates leadership	IT management lacks leadership

What is striking about these lists is that the same set of topics (executive support, understanding the business, IT-business relations, and leadership) show up in both. Previous papers presented the detailed findings of the enablers-inhibitors study[3] and presented the methodology applied to leverage the enablers and inhibitors[4]. The purpose of this chapter is to discuss an approach for assessing the maturity of business-IT alignment. Until now, none was available. Maturity assessment provides a comprehensive vehicle for organizations to evaluate business-IT alignment with regards to where they are and what could be done to improve the harmony. The maturity assessment applies these enablers/inhibitors as building blocks for the evaluation.

Alignment of IT strategy with the organization's business strategy is a fundamental principle that has been advocated for over a decade.[16] IT investment has been on the rise for years and managers are looking for ways in which this vital resource can be successfully managed and integrated into the organization's strategies. IT managers must be knowledgeable about how these new technologies can be integrated into the business (in addition to the integration among the different technologies and architectures) and must be privy to senior management's tactical and strategic plans. IT and business executives must be present when corporate strategies are discussed. IT executives must be able to delineate the strengths and weaknesses of the technologies in question and understand the corporate-wide implications.[17] While alignment is discussed extensively from a theoretical standpoint in the literature, there is scant empirical evidence regarding the appropriate route to take for aligning business and IT strategies.

THE STRATEGIC ALIGNMENT MATURITY MODEL LEVELS

As Figure 3 illustrates, there are five levels of Strategic Alignment Maturity. They are:

1. Initial/Ad Hoc Process
2. Committed Process
3. Established Focused Process
4. Improved/Managed Process
5. Optimized Process

This maturity assessment is based on the popular work done by the Software Engineering Institute,[18] Keen's reach and range[19], and an evolution of the Nolan and Gibson stages of growth.[20] Each of the levels of alignment maturity focuses on six building blocks or criteria derived from the enablers/inhibitors research (described in the introduction) and the strategic alignment components (described in Figure 1). The criteria are listed (see Figure 2) and later explained in alphabetical order because each is equally important to the assessment of alignment maturity. Hence, having a low evaluation for any one of the criteria would bring the entire maturity assessment level down.

An essential part of the assessment process is recognizing that it must be done with a team of business and IT executives. The convergence on a consensus of the

Figure 2

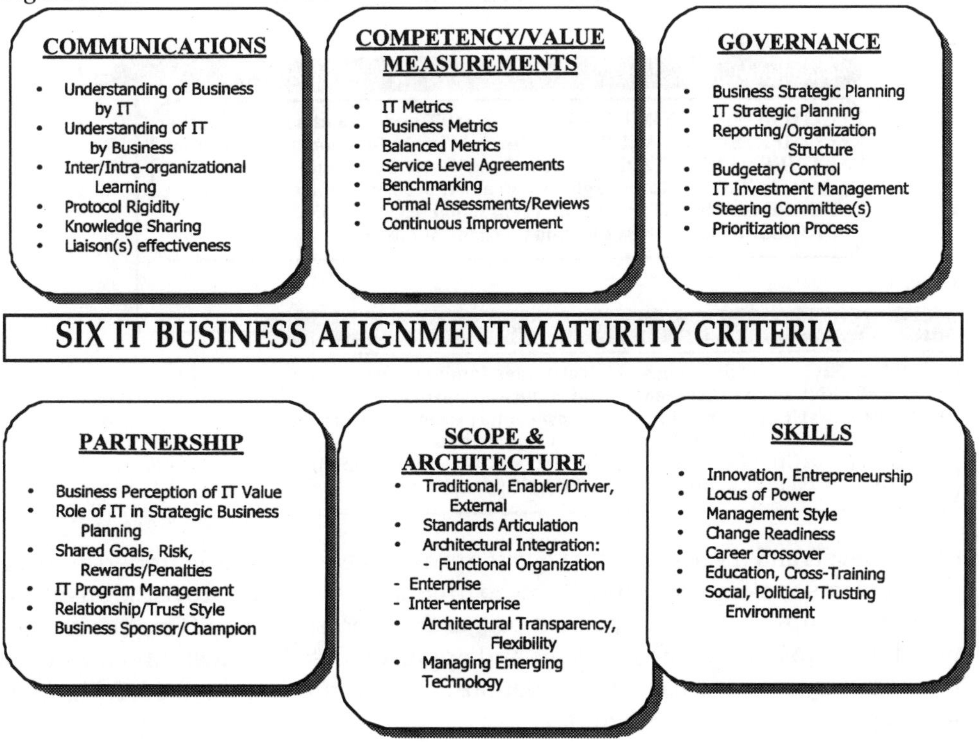

COMMUNICATIONS

- Understanding of Business by IT
- Understanding of IT by Business
- Inter/Intra-organizational Learning
- Protocol Rigidity
- Knowledge Sharing
- Liaison(s) effectiveness

COMPETENCY/VALUE MEASUREMENTS

- IT Metrics
- Business Metrics
- Balanced Metrics
- Service Level Agreements
- Benchmarking
- Formal Assessments/Reviews
- Continuous Improvement

GOVERNANCE

- Business Strategic Planning
- IT Strategic Planning
- Reporting/Organization Structure
- Budgetary Control
- IT Investment Management
- Steering Committee(s)
- Prioritization Process

SIX IT BUSINESS ALIGNMENT MATURITY CRITERIA

PARTNERSHIP

- Business Perception of IT Value
- Role of IT in Strategic Business Planning
- Shared Goals, Risk, Rewards/Penalties
- IT Program Management
- Relationship/Trust Style
- Business Sponsor/Champion

SCOPE & ARCHITECTURE

- Traditional, Enabler/Driver, External
- Standards Articulation
- Architectural Integration:
  - Functional Organization
  - Enterprise
  - Inter-enterprise
- Architectural Transparency, Flexibility
- Managing Emerging Technology

SKILLS

- Innovation, Entrepreneurship
- Locus of Power
- Management Style
- Change Readiness
- Career crossover
- Education, Cross-Training
- Social, Political, Trusting Environment

Figure 3: Strategic Alignment Maturity Summary

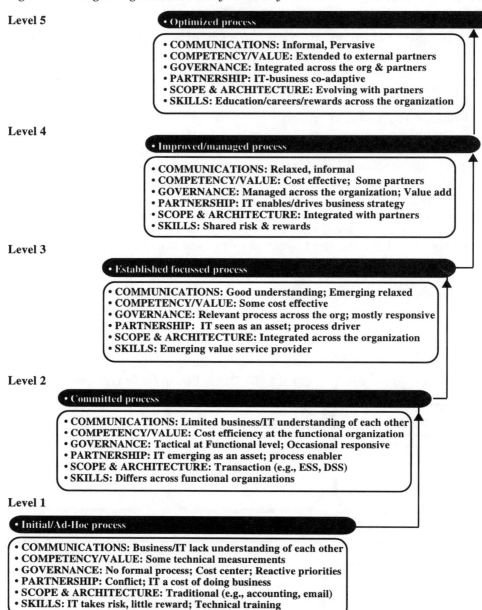

Level 5

• Optimized process

- **COMMUNICATIONS: Informal, Pervasive**
- **COMPETENCY/VALUE: Extended to external partners**
- **GOVERNANCE: Integrated across the org & partners**
- **PARTNERSHIP: IT-business co-adaptive**
- **SCOPE & ARCHITECTURE: Evolving with partners**
- **SKILLS: Education/careers/rewards across the organization**

Level 4

• Improved/managed process

- **COMMUNICATIONS: Relaxed, informal**
- **COMPETENCY/VALUE: Cost effective; Some partners**
- **GOVERNANCE: Managed across the organization; Value add**
- **PARTNERSHIP: IT enables/drives business strategy**
- **SCOPE & ARCHITECTURE: Integrated with partners**
- **SKILLS: Shared risk & rewards**

Level 3

• Established focussed process

- **COMMUNICATIONS: Good understanding; Emerging relaxed**
- **COMPETENCY/VALUE: Some cost effective**
- **GOVERNANCE: Relevant process across the org; mostly responsive**
- **PARTNERSHIP: IT seen as an asset; process driver**
- **SCOPE & ARCHITECTURE: Integrated across the organization**
- **SKILLS: Emerging value service provider**

Level 2

• Committed process

- **COMMUNICATIONS: Limited business/IT understanding of each other**
- **COMPETENCY/VALUE: Cost efficiency at the functional organization**
- **GOVERNANCE: Tactical at Functional level; Occasional responsive**
- **PARTNERSHIP: IT emerging as an asset; process enabler**
- **SCOPE & ARCHITECTURE: Transaction (e.g., ESS, DSS)**
- **SKILLS: Differs across functional organizations**

Level 1

• Initial/Ad-Hoc process

- **COMMUNICATIONS: Business/IT lack understanding of each other**
- **COMPETENCY/VALUE: Some technical measurements**
- **GOVERNANCE: No formal process; Cost center; Reactive priorities**
- **PARTNERSHIP: Conflict; IT a cost of doing business**
- **SCOPE & ARCHITECTURE: Traditional (e.g., accounting, email)**
- **SKILLS: IT takes risk, little reward; Technical training**

criteria levels and discussions that ensue are extremely valuable in understanding the problems and opportunities that need to be addressed to improve the business-IT relationship. The most important part of the process is identifying the recommendations to address the problems and opportunities. The most difficult step is actually carrying out the recommendations. The six criteria, described in Figure 2, to be applied in the assessment are:

1 Communications Maturity
2 Competency/Value Measurement Maturity
3 Governance Maturity
4 Partnership Maturity
5 Scope & Architecture Maturity
6 Skills Maturity

Each of the six criteria described in Figure 2 are assessed based on five levels of Strategic Alignment Maturity. The five levels of maturity are attained through the assessment of the qualities of the attributes associated with each of the criteria. This conceptual framework (qualities and attributes) is described in the following pages for each of the Strategic Alignment Maturity Levels. A summary of the five levels of maturity is illustrated in Figure 3. The six criteria are expanded for each of the five levels following the summary figure (Figure 3). After the discussion of the criteria for each of the five levels, Figures 4A – 4F look at each of the six criteria independently by reviewing the results of actual assessments. This last section ties the respective assessment metrics together with examples.

SIX CRITERIA FOR EACH OF THE FIVE LEVELS OF MATURITY

LEVEL 1 – INITIAL/AD HOC PROCESS

Organizations that meet many of the characteristics of the attributes in the six Strategic Alignment Maturity criteria for Level 1 can be characterized as having the lowest level of Strategic Alignment Maturity. It is highly improbable that these organizations will be able to achieve an aligned IT business strategy, leaving their investment in IT significantly unleveraged. The journey has just begun.

COMMUNICATIONS

ATTRIBUTE	CHARACTERISTICS
Understanding of Business by IT	Minimum
Understanding of IT by Business	Minimum
Inter/Intra-organizational learning	Casual, ad-hoc
Protocol Rigidity	Command and Control
Knowledge Sharing	Ad-hoc
Liaison(s) Breadth/Effectiveness	None or Ad-hoc

COMPETENCY/VALUE MEASUREMENTS

ATTRIBUTE	CHARACTERISTICS
IT Metrics	Technical; Not related to business
Business Metrics	Ad-hoc; Not related to IT
Balanced Metrics	Ad-hoc unlinked
Service Level Agreements	Sporadically present
Benchmarking	Not generally practiced
Formal Assessments/Reviews	None
Continuous Improvement	None

GOVERNANCE

ATTRIBUTE	CHARACTERISTICS
• Business Strategic Planning	Ad-hoc
• IT Strategic Planning	Ad-hoc
• Reporting/Organization Structure	Central/Decentral; CIO reports to CFO
• Budgetary Control	Cost Center; Erratic spending
• IT Investment Management	Cost based; Erratic spending
• Steering Committee(s)	Not formal/regular
• Prioritization Process	Reactive

PARTNERSHIP

ATTRIBUTE	CHARACTERISTICS
• Business Perception of IT Value	IT Perceived as a cost of business
• Role of IT in Strategic Business Planning	No seat at the business table
• Shared Goals, Risk, Rewards/Penalties	IT takes risk with little reward
• IT Program Management	Ad-hoc
• Relationship/Trust Style	Conflict/Minimum
• Business Sponsor/Champion	None

SCOPE & ARCHITECTURE

ATTRIBUTE	CHARACTERISTICS
• Traditional, Enabler/Driver, External accounting, email)	Traditional (e.g.,
• Standards Articulation	None or ad-hoc
• Architectural Integration: - Functional Organization	No formal integration
- Enterprise	
- Inter-enterprise	
• Architectural Transparency, Flexibility	None

SKILLS

ATTRIBUTE	CHARACTERISTICS
• Innovation, Entrepreneurship	Discouraged
• Locus of Power	In the business
• Management Style	Command and control
• Change Readiness	Resistant to change
• Career crossover	None
• Education, Cross-Training	None
• Social, Political, Trusting Environment	Minimum

LEVEL 2 – COMMITTED PROCESS

Organizations that meet many of the characteristics of the attributes in the six Strategic Alignment Maturity criteria for Level 2 can be characterized as having committed to begin the process for Strategic Alignment Maturity. This level of Strategic Alignment Maturity tends to be directed at local situations or functional organizations (e.g., Marketing, Finance, Manufacturing, H/R) within the overall enterprise. However, due to limited awareness by the business and IT communities of the different functional organizations use of IT, alignment can be difficult to achieve. Any business-IT alignment at the local level is typically not leveraged by the enterprise. However, the potential opportunities are beginning to be recognized.

COMMUNICATIONS

ATTRIBUTE	CHARACTERISTICS
• Understanding of Business by IT	Limited IT awareness
• Understanding of IT by Business	Limited Business awareness
• Inter/Intra-organizational learning	Informal
• Protocol Rigidity	Limited relaxed
• Knowledge Sharing	Semi structured
• Liaison(s) Breadth/Effectiveness	Limited tactical technology based

COMPETENCY/VALUE MEASUREMENTS

ATTRIBUTE	CHARACTERISTICS
• IT Metrics	Cost efficiency
• Business Metrics	At the functional organization
• Balanced Metrics	Business and IT metrics unlinked
• Service Level Agreements	Technical at the functional level
• Benchmarking	Informal
• Formal Assessments/Reviews	Some, typically for problems
• Continuous Improvement	Minimum

GOVERNANCE

ATTRIBUTE	CHARACTERISTICS
• Business Strategic Planning	Basic planning at the functional level
• IT Strategic Planning	Functional tactical planning
• Reporting/Organization Structure	Central/Decentral, some co-location; CIO reports to CFO
• Budgetary Control	Cost Center by functional organization
• IT Investment Management	Cost based; Operations & maintenance focus
• Steering Committee(s)	Periodic organized communication
• Prioritization Process	Occasional responsive

LEVEL 2 (continued)

PARTNERSHIP

ATTRIBUTE	CHARACTERISTICS
• Business Perception of IT Value	IT emerging as an asset
• Role of IT in Strategic Business Planning	Business process enabler
• Shared Goals, Risk, Rewards/Penalties	IT takes most of the risk with little reward
• IT Program Management	Standards defined
• Relationship/Trust Style	Primarily transactional
• Business Sponsor/Champion	Limited at the functional organization

SCOPE & ARCHITECTURE

ATTRIBUTE	CHARACTERISTICS
• Traditional, Enabler/Driver, External	Transaction (e.g., ESS, DSS)
• Standards Articulation	Standards defined
• Architectural Integration:	
- Functional Organization	Early attempts at integration
- Enterprise	Early attempts at integration
- Inter-enterprise	Early concept testing
• Architectural Transparency, Flexibility	Limited

SKILLS

ATTRIBUTE	CHARACTERISTICS
• Innovation, Entrepreneurship	Dependent on functional organization
• Locus of Power	Functional organization
• Management Style	Consensus-based
• Change Readiness	Dependent on functional organization
• Career crossover	Minimum
• Education, Cross-Training	Minimum
• Social, Political, Trusting Environment	Primarily transactional

LEVEL 3 – ESTABLISHED FOCUSSED PROCESS

Organizations that meet many of the characteristics of the attributes in the six Strategic Alignment Maturity criteria for Level 3 can be characterized as having established a focussed Strategic Alignment Maturity. This level of Strategic Alignment Maturity concentrates governance, processes and communications towards specific business objectives. Level 3 leverages IT assets on an enterprise-wide basis and applications systems demonstrate planned, managed direction away from traditional transaction processing to systems that use information to make business decisions.

COMMUNICATIONS

ATTRIBUTE	CHARACTERISTICS
• Understanding of Business by IT	Senior and mid-management
• Understanding of IT by Business	Emerging business awareness
• Inter/Intra-organizational learning	Regular, clear
• Protocol Rigidity	Emerging relaxed
• Knowledge Sharing	Structured around key processes
• Liaison(s) Breadth/Effectiveness	Formalized, regular meetings

COMPETENCY/VALUE MEASUREMENTS

ATTRIBUTE	CHARACTERISTICS
• IT Metrics	Traditional Financial
• Business Metrics	Traditional Financial
• Balanced Metrics	Emerging business and IT metrics linked
• Service Level Agreements	Emerging across the enterprise
• Benchmarking	Emerging
• Formal Assessments/Reviews	Emerging formality
• Continuous Improvement	Emerging

GOVERNANCE

ATTRIBUTE	CHARACTERISTICS
• Business Strategic Planning	Some inter-organizational planning
• IT Strategic Planning	Focused planning, some inter-organizational
• Reporting/Organization Structure	Central/ Decentral, some federation; CIO reports to COO
• Budgetary Control	Cost Center; some investments
• IT Investment Management	Traditional; Process enabler
• Steering Committee(s)	Regular clear communication
• Prioritization Process	Mostly responsive

LEVEL 3 (continued)

PARTNERSHIP

ATTRIBUTE	CHARACTERISTICS
• Business Perception of IT Value	IT seen as an asset
• Role of IT in Strategic Business Planning	Business process enabler
• Shared Goals, Risk, Rewards/Penalties	Risk tolerant; IT some reward
• IT Program Management	Standards adhered
• Relationship/Trust Style	Emerging valued service provider
• Business Sponsor/Champion	At the functional organization

SCOPE & ARCHITECTURE

ATTRIBUTE	CHARACTERISTICS
• Traditional, Enabler/Driver, External	Expanded scope (e.g., business process enabler)
• Standards Articulation	Emerging enterprise standards
• Architectural Integration:	Integrated across the organization
- Functional Organization	Integrated for key processes
- Enterprise	Emerging enterprise architecture
- Inter-enterprise	Emerging with key partners
• Architectural Transparency, Flexibility	Focused on communications

SKILLS

ATTRIBUTE	CHARACTERISTICS
• Innovation, Entrepreneurship	Risk tolerant
• Locus of Power	Emerging across the organization
• Management Style	Results based
• Change Readiness	Recognized need for change
• Career crossover	Dependent on functional organization
• Education, Cross-Training	Dependent on functional organization
• Social, Political, Trusting Environment	Emerging valued service provider

LEVEL 4 – IMPROVED/MANAGED PROCESS

Organizations that meet many of the characteristics of the attributes in the six Strategic Alignment Maturity criteria for Level 4 can be characterized as having a managed Strategic Alignment Maturity. This level of Strategic Alignment Maturity demonstrates effective governance and services that reinforce the concept of IT as a value center. Organizations at Level 4 leverage IT assets on an enterprise-wide basis and the focus of applications systems is on driving business process enhancements to obtain sustainable competitive advantage. A Level 4 organization views IT as a strategic contributor to success.

COMMUNICATIONS

ATTRIBUTE	CHARACTERISTICS
• Understanding of Business by IT	Pushed down through organization
• Understanding of IT by Business	Business aware of potential
• Inter/Intra-organizational learning	Unified, bonded
• Protocol Rigidity	Relaxed, informal
• Knowledge Sharing	Institutionalized
• Liaison(s) Breadth/Effectiveness	Bonded, effective at all internal levels

COMPETENCY/VALUE MEASUREMENTS

ATTRIBUTE	CHARACTERISTICS
• IT Metrics	Cost effectiveness
• Business Metrics	Customer based
• Balanced Metrics	Business and IT metrics linked
• Service Level Agreements	Enterprise wide
• Benchmarking	Routinely performed
• Formal Assessments/Reviews	Formally performed
• Continuous Improvement	Frequently

GOVERNANCE

ATTRIBUTE	CHARACTERISTICS
• Business Strategic Planning	Managed across the enterprise
• IT Strategic Planning	Managed across the enterprise
• Organizational Reporting Structure	Federated; CIO reports to COO or CEO
• Budgetary Control	Investment Center
• IT Investment Management	Cost effectiveness; Process driver
• Steering Committee(s)	Formal, effective committees
• Prioritization Process	Value add, responsive

LEVEL 4 (continued):

PARTNERSHIP

ATTRIBUTE	CHARACTERISTICS
• Business Perception of IT Value	IT is seen as a driver/enabler
• Role of IT in Strategic Business Planning	Business strategy enabler/driver
• Shared Goals, Risk, Rewards/Penalties	Risk acceptance & rewards shared
• IT Program Management	Standards evolve
• Relationship/Trust Style	Valued service provider
• Business Sponsor/Champion	At the HQ level

SCOPE & ARCHITECURE

ATTRIBUTE	CHARACTERISTICS
• Traditional, Enabler/Driver, External driver)	Redefined scope (business process
• Standards Articulation	Enterprise standards
• Architectural Integration:	Integrated with partners
- Functional Organization	Integrated
- Enterprise	Standard enterprise architecture
- Inter-enterprise	With key partners
• Architectural Transparency, Flexibility	Emerging across the organizations

SKILLS

ATTRIBUTE	CHARACTERISTICS
• Innovation, Entrepreneurship	Enterprise, partners, and IT managers
• Locus of Power	Across the organization
• Management Style	Profit/value based
• Change Readiness	High, focussed
• Career crossover	Across the functional organization
• Education, Cross-Training	At the functional organization
• Social, Political, Trusting Environment	Valued service provider

LEVEL 5 – OPTIMIZED PROCESS

Organizations that meet the characteristics of the attributes in the six Strategic Alignment Maturity criteria for Level 5 can be characterized as having an optimally aligned Strategic Alignment Maturity. A sustained governance process integrates the IT strategic planning process with the strategic business process. Organizations at Level 5 leverage IT assets on an enterprise-wide basis to extend the reach of the organization into the supply chains of customers and suppliers.

COMMUNICATIONS

ATTRIBUTE	CHARACTERISTICS
Understanding of Business by IT	Pervasive
Understanding of IT by Business	Pervasive
Inter/Intra-organizational learning	Strong and structured
Protocol Rigidity	Informal
Knowledge Sharing	Extra-enterprise
Liaison(s) Breadth/Effectiveness	Extra-enterprise

COMPETENCY/VALUE MEASUREMENTS

ATTRIBUTE	CHARACTERISTICS
IT Metrics	Extended to external partners
Business Metrics	Extended to external partners
Balanced Metrics	Business, partner, & IT metrics
Service Level Agreements	Extended to external partners
Benchmarking	Routinely performed with partners
Formal Assessments/Reviews	Routinely performed
Continuous Improvement	Routinely performed

GOVERNANCE

ATTRIBUTE	CHARACTERISTICS
Business Strategic Planning	Integrated across & outside the enterprise
IT Strategic Planning	Integrated across & outside the enterprise
Organizational Reporting Structure	Federated; CIO reports to CEO
Budgetary Control	Investment Center; Profit Center
IT Investment Management	Business value; Extended to business partners
Steering Committee(s)	Partnership
Prioritization Process	Value added partner

LEVEL 5 (continued):

PARTNERSHIP

ATTRIBUTE	CHARACTERISTICS
• Business Perception of IT Value	IT co-adapts with the business
• Role of IT in Strategic Business Planning	Co-adaptive with the business
• Shared Goals, Risk, Rewards/Penalties	Risk & rewards shared
• IT Program Management	Continuous improvement
• Relationship/Trust Style	Valued Partnership
• Business Sponsor/Champion	At the CEO level

SCOPE & ARCHITECTURE

ATTRIBUTE	CHARACTERISTICS
• Traditional, Enabler/Driver, External strategy	External scope; Business driver/enabler
• Standards Articulation	Inter-Enterprise standards
• Architectural Integration:	Evolve with partners
- Functional Organization	Integrated
- Enterprise	Standard enterprise architecture
- Inter-enterprise	With all partners

SKILLS

ATTRIBUTE	CHARACTERISTICS
• Innovation, Entrepreneurship	The norm
• Locus of Power	All executives, including CIO & partners
• Management Style	Relationship based
• Change Readiness	High, focussed
• Career crossover	Across the enterprise
• Education, Cross-Training	Across the enterprise
• Social, Political, Trusting Environment	Valued Partnership

HOW TO USE THE MODEL

Each of the criteria and levels has been described by a set of attributes that will allow a particular dimension to be assessed using a Likert scale along a continuum of 1 to 5, where:

1 = this does not fit the organization, or the organization is very ineffective
2 = low level of fit for the organization
3 = moderate fit for the organization, or the organization is moderately effective
4 = this fits most of the organization
5 = strong level of fit throughout the organization, or the organization is very effective

Different scales can be applied to perform the assessment (e.g., good, fair, poor; 1, 2, 3). However, it is very important to evaluate each of the six criteria individually in detail with both business and IT executives to get an accurate assessment. The intent is to have the team of IT and business executives converge on a maturity level. Typically, the initial review will produce divergent results. This is indicative of the problem that you are trying to address.

Using a Delphi approach with a Group Decision Support Tool often helps in attaining the convergence. However, the author's experience suggests that having "discussions" among the different team members helps to ensure a clearer understanding of the problems and opportunities that need to be addressed. Keep in mind, the primary objective of the assessment is to identify specific recommendations to improve the alignment of IT and the business. A trained facilitator is typically needed for these sessions.

As of this writing, experience with 25 Fortune 500 companies indicates that over 80% of the organizations are at Level 2 maturity with some characteristics of Level 3 maturity. Figure 4 (A, B, C, D, E, F) illustrates the "average" results of the Strategic Alignment Maturity assessments for these companies. Figure 4 (without the average numbers) can be used as the basis for determining an organization's maturity level. It shows the maturity attributes for each of the six maturity components. The following section describes summaries of six actual assessments of Fortune 200 companies from different industries. Keep in mind that it is not the results of the maturity assessment that matters. It is what the organization does to improve the maturity level, hence improving IT-business strategic alignment.

Strategic Alignment Maturity Assessment Examples

The following are summaries of six actual assessments of Fortune 200 companies and a large university.

1. **A large aerospace company** assesses its alignment maturity as a 2:
   Communications (2): Business-IT understanding is sporadic. The relationship between IT and the business function could be improved. Improving communication should focus on how to make IT be viewed more as a strategic business partner by the businesses it supports versus being solely a service provider. The CIO made the comment that there is "no constructive partnership". Whereas in an interview with the Director of Engineering & Infrastruc-

Figure 4A

COMMUNICATIONS

		AVERAGE
•	**Understanding of Business by IT**	
	1. IT Management not aware	2
	2. Limited IT awareness	4
	3. Senior and mid-management	3
	4. Pushed down through organization	1
	5. Pervasive	1
•	**Understanding of IT by Business**	
	1. Business Management not aware	3
	2. Limited Business awareness	4
	3. Emerging business awareness	1
	4. Business aware of potential	1
	5. Pervasive	
•	**Inter/Intra-organizational learning**	
	1. Casual, ad-hoc	4
	2. Informal	4
	3. Regular, clear	1
	4. Unified, bonded	1
	5. Strong and structured	
•	**Protocol Rigidity**	
	1. Command and Control	4
	2. Limited relaxed	3
	3. Emerging relaxed	1
	4. Relaxed, informal	1
	5. Informal	
•	**Knowledge Sharing**	
	1. Ad-hoc	1
	2. Semi structured	5
	3. Structured around key processes	3
	4. Institutionalized	1
	5. Extra-enterprise	
•	**Liaison(s) Breadth/Effectiveness**	
	1. None or Ad-hoc	2
	2. Limited tactical technology based	4
	3. Formalized, regular meetings	3
	4. Bonded, effective at all internal levels	1
	5. Extra-enterprise	

MATURITY LEVEL   *2+*

Figure 4B

COMPETENCY/VALUE MEASUREMENTS

	AVERAGE
• **IT Metrics**	
1. Technical; not related to business	5
2. Cost efficiency	4
3. Traditional Financial	3
4. Cost effectiveness	2
5. Extended to external partners	1
• **Business Metrics**	
1. Ad-hoc; not related to IT	4
2. At the functional organization	4
3. Traditional Financial	4
4. Customer based	3
5. Extended to external partners	2
• **Balanced Metrics**	
1. Ad-hoc metrics unlinked	3
2. Business and IT metrics unlinked	4
3. Emerging business and IT metrics linked	3
4. Business and IT metrics linked	1
5. Business, partners, & IT metrics linked	1
• **Service Level Agreements**	
1. Sporadically present	3
2. Technical at the functional level	4
3. Emerging across the enterprise	2
4. Enterprise wide	1
5. Extended to external partners	1
• **Benchmarking**	
1. Not generally practiced	2
2. Informal	4
3. Focussed on specific processes	3
4. Routinely performed	2
5. Routinely performed with partners	1
• **Formal Assessments/Reviews**	
1. None	2
2. Some; typically for problems	4
3. Emerging formality	2
4. Formally performed	1
5. Routinely performed	
• **Continuous Improvement**	
1. None	2
2. Minimum	3
3. Emerging	3
4. Frequently	2
5. Routinely performed	1
MATURITY LEVEL	**2+**

Figure 4C

GOVERNANCE

	AVERAGE
• **Business Strategic Planning**	
1. Ad-hoc	3
2. Basic planning at the functional level	5
3. Some inter-organizational planning	2
4. Managed across the enterprise	1
5. Integrated across & outside the enterprise	
• **IT Strategic Planning**	
1. Ad-hoc	3
2. Functional tactical planning	4
3. Focused planning, some inter-organizational	4
4. Managed across the enterprise	1
5. Integrated across & outside the enterprise	
• **Reporting/Organization Structure**	
1. Central/Decentral; CIO reports to CFO	4
2. Central/Decentral, some co-location; CIO reports to CFO	4
3. Central/Decentral, some federation; CIO reports to COO	3
4. Federated; CIO reports to COO or CEO	2
5. Federated; CIO reports to CEO	2
• **Budgetary Control**	
1. Cost Center, Erratic spending	3
2. Cost Center by functional organization	5
3. Cost Center; some investments	3
4. Investment Center	1
5. Investment Center; Profit Center	1
• **IT Investment Management**	
1. Cost based, Erratic spending	4
2. Cost based; Operations & maintenance focus	5
3. Traditional; Process enabler	3
4. Cost effectiveness; Process driver	1
5. Business value; Extended to business partners	
• **Steering Committee(s)**	
1. Not formal/regular	2
2. Periodic organized communication	4
3. Regular clear communication	1
4. Formal, effective committees	1
5. Partnership	
• **Prioritization Process**	
1. Reactive	4
2. Occasional responsive	4
3. Mostly Responsive	3
4. Value add, Responsive	1
5. Value added partner	
MATURITY LEVEL	***2+***

Figure 4D

PARTNERSHIP

	AVERAGE
• **Business Perception of IT Value**	
1. IT perceived as a cost of business	4
2. IT emerging as an asset	5
3. IT is seen as an asset	2
4. IT is part of the business strategy	1
5. IT-business co-adaptive	
• **Role of IT in Strategic Business Planning**	
1. No seat at the business table	4
2. Business process enabler	5
3. Business process driver	1
4. Business strategy enabler/driver	
5. Co-adaptive with the business	
• **Shared Goals, Risk, Rewards/Penalties**	
1. IT takes risk with little reward	4
2. IT takes most of the risk with little reward	5
3. Risk tolerant; IT some reward	1
4. Risk acceptance & rewards shared	
5. Risk & rewards shared	
• **IT Program Management**	
1. Ad-hoc	2
2. Standards defined	4
3. Standards adhered	2
4. Standards evolve	2
5. Continuous improvement	
• **Relationship/Trust Style**	
1. Conflict/Minimum	3
2. Primarily transactional	4
3. Emerging valued service provider	2
4. Valued service provider	
5. Valued Partnership	
• **Business Sponsor/Champion**	
1. None	4
2. Limited at the functional organization	4
3. At the functional organization	3
4. At the HQ level	1
5. At the CEO level	

MATURITY LEVEL   **_2+_**

Figure 4E

SCOPE & ARCHITECTURE

AVERAGE

- **Traditional, Enabler/Driver, External**
  1. Traditional (e.g., accounting, email) — 2
  2. Transaction (e.g., ESS, DSS) — 3
  3. Expanded scope (e.g., business process enabler) — 4
  4. Redefined scope (business process driver) — 1
  5. External scope; Business strategy driver/enabler

- **Standards Articulation**
  1. None or ad-hoc — 2
  2. Standards defined — 4
  3. Emerging enterprise standards — 3
  4. Enterprise standards — 1
  5. Inter-Enterprise standards

- **Architectural Integration:**
  - **Functional Organization**
    1. No formal integration — 2
    2. Early attempts at integration — 5
    3. Integrated across the organization — 1
    4. Integrated with partners
    5. Evolving with partners

- **Enterprise**
  1. No formal integration — 3
  2. Early attempts at integration — 4
  3. Standard enterprise architecture — 3
  4. Standard inter-enterprise architecture
  5. Evolving with partners

- **Inter-enterprise**
  1. No formal integration — 3
  2. Early concept testing — 3
  3. Emerging with key partners — 2
  4. With partners — 1
  5. Evolving with partners

- **Architectural Transparency, Flexibility**
  1. None — 4
  2. Limited — 4
  3. Focussed on communications — 3
  4. Emerging — 2
  5. Across the infrastructure

MATURITY LEVEL   **2+**

Figure 4F

SKILLS

AVERAGE

- **Innovation, Entrepreneurship**
    1. Discouraged — 4
    2. Dependent on functional organization — 3
    3. Risk tolerant — 2
    4. Enterprise, partners, and IT managers — 1
    5. The norm
- **Locus of Power**
    1. In the business — 3
    2. Functional organization — 4
    3. Emerging across the organization — 2
    4. Across the organization — 1
    5. All executives, including CIO & partners
- **Management Style**
    1. Command and control — 4
    2. Consensus-based — 3
    3. Results based — 2
    4. Profit/value based — 1
    5. Relationship based
- **Change Readiness**
    1. Resistant to change — 4
    2. Dependent on functional organization — 4
    3. Recognized need for change — 2
    4. High, focussed
    5. High, focussed
- **Career crossover**
    1. None — 3
    2. Minimum — 4
    3. Dependent on functional organization — 2
    4. Across the functional organization
    5. Across the enterprise
- **Education, Cross-Training**
    1. None — 3
    2. Minimum — 4
    3. Dependent on functional organization — 3
    4. At the functional organization — 1
    5. Across the organization
- **Social, Political, Trusting Environment**
    1. Minimum — 4
    2. Primarily transactional — 3
    3. Emerging valued service provider — 3
    4. Valued service provider — 1
    5. Valued Partnership

MATURITY LEVEL   **2**

ture, he stated that he views his organization as a "strategic business partner". One way to possibly improve communication and more importantly understanding would be to establish business function/IT liaisons.

Competency/Value (2): IT operates as cost center. IT metrics are focused at the functional level, and Service Level Agreements (SLAs) are technical in nature. One area that could help to improve maturity would be to add more business related metrics to SLAs to help form more of a partnership between IT and the businesses. Periodic formal assessments and reviews in support of continuous improvement would also be beneficial.

Governance (2): IT governance is tactical at the core business level and not consistent across the enterprise. IT can be characterized as reactive to CEO direction. Developing an integrated enterprise-wide strategic business plan for IT would facilitate better partnering within the firm and would lay the ground work to partner with external partners including customers and suppliers.

Partnership (2): Some businesses don't view IT as a business partnership. IT is an imposed expensive service. Making IT more of a business enabler helping to drive business strategy rather than being seen as just a business cost is what the company should be striving for.

Scope and Architecture (3): IT has had architectural integration success and adheres to enterprise standards. Integrating IT systems and strategies in the current business climate of e-commerce, business-to-business and business-to-customer scenarios is an essential item for the company to address to improve maturity.

Skills (2): A definite command and control management style exists within IT and the businesses. Power resides at certain operating companies. Diverse business cultures abound. Getting to a non-political trusting environment between the businesses and IT where risks are shared and innovation and entrepreneurship thrive is essential to achieve improvements in each of the other maturity tenets.

2. **A large software development company** assesses their maturity as a level 2.

Communications: There is very little contact between the IT function and other parts of the business, both from physical perspective, and through job-related activities. IT is rarely involved in decisions by the business functions and is isolated from the day-to-day concerns of the business users. The only significant contact between IT and business is during the application development process, such as the Knowledge Management project. This is the only reason that this criterion is rated at a 2 instead of a 1.

Competency/Value: IT would be rated at level 3 for this criterion, because there are metrics established for the level of service provided to the business functions. These metrics go beyond basic service availability and help desk responsiveness, into such areas as end-user satisfaction and application development effectiveness. The metrics are consolidated on to an overall dashboard. However, there are no formal feedback mechanisms in place to react to a metric, therefore the dashboard cannot be considered to be managed.

Governance: This criterion can be considered at a level 3 because IT priorities are decided at the enterprise level. Although the CIO is not a member of the Leadership Council, he does report directly to them.

Partnership: The IT function is mainly an enabler of the company. It does not have a seat at the business table, be it the enterprise or the business function that is making the decision. There are no shared risks in that only the business will fail in the majority of cases. There are signs that this criterion may rise from a level 2 to 3 as top management sees IT as an asset, and that there is a very high enforcement of standards at the company.

Scope and Architecture: This is another area where the company is moving from a level 2 to a level 3. ERP systems have been installed and all projects are monitored at an enterprise level. There are integrated standards across the organization and there is a standard enterprise architecture. It is only in the area of Inter-enterprise that there is no formal integration.

Skills: In the area of skills, the company is a solid 2 across the board. Much depends on the functional organization in which the employee works. Few people switch functions, and there is little cross-fertilization across the enterprise.

3. **A large financial services company** belongs to level 2 with some attributes of level 1

Communications (2): Business awareness within IT is through specialized IT business analysts, who understand and translate the business needs to other IT staff. So there is limited awareness of business by general IT staff. There is limited awareness of IT by business, however senior and mid-level management is aware of IT potential. Further communications are through bi-weekly priority meetings that the senior and middle level management from both sides attend to discuss requirements, priorities and IT implementation.

Competency/Value (2): IT is measured using the cost efficiency methods at the business and functional organizations. Balanced metrics are emerging with business and IT metrics links, and a balanced scorecard for senior management. Service level agreements are technical at the functional level. Benchmarking is not generally practiced and is informal in the few areas where it is practiced. Formal assessments are done typically for problems and minimum measures are taken after the assessment of failures.

Governance (2): Business and IT strategic planning are at the functional level. The CIO reports to the CFO. IT investments are cost based with focus on operations and maintenance. IT is occasionally responsive.

Partnership (2): IT is emerging as an asset. IT is seen as a business process enabler. IT takes most of the risks with little rewards. Initiatives are being taken to share risks, rewards and penalties with business, subsequent to decentralization.

Scope & Architecture (1): Defined standards, transactional, no formal integration, across the enterprise. Functional integration exists.

Skills (1): Career crossover between Business and IT is a recognized need for change. Innovation is dependent on the functional organization and the locus of power is in the business. The management style is top down, and education and cross-training are improving at the functional organization level.

4. For one of the **largest communications manufacturing companies**, the overall maturity assessment is a level 2 with some characteristics of 1. The assessment highlighted the lack of relationship between IT and business organizations.
Communications (2): There is very limited understanding of IT and Business within the company. The business units are focused on reducing IT costs and do not look upon IT as an enabler to business initiatives.
Competency/Value (2): IT metrics are technically focused on reducing cost such as telecommunications and help desk. These metrics are not linked to the business metrics that determine the health of the organization.
Governance (1 or 2): As a cost center, in which priorities are to reduce costs for the organization, there is not much IT strategy planning. In addition, priorities are reactive to business needs as business managers request them.
Partnership (1): IT is perceived as cost of being in the communications business. There is little value placed on the IT function. The perception of IT is only as help desk support and network maintenance.
Scope & Architecture (1): There is a lack of systemic competencies to drive and enable the business. The scope of the architecture is traditional email, accounting systems.
Skills (2): There is little career cross-over and not much effort in sharing risks and rewards between IT and the business units.

5. A **large computing services company** assesses itself between a level 1 and 2.
Communication (2): Learning is mostly informal. IT training has been expanding recently into courses such as "Know your Business" and basic payroll. These classes are small and held infrequently. Twice a Year "President's Update" is presented to employees. Clients have little interface with changes until delivery.
Competency/Value Measurements (2): Metrics are based on cost and Quality Surveys which are transactional and looking for cost efficiencies. SLAs are non-existent or technical only. Benchmarking is done on very few business processes only. Assessment/Reviews are done only when problems arise. Successful projects are not reviewed. Business and IT metrics are not closely linked. Continuous improvement of processes is at a minimum.
Governance (1): A strategic planning committee meets twice a year. The committee consists of corporate top management with regional representation. Topics or results are not discussed or published to all the employees. The reporting structure is federated with the CIO reporting to COO. IT investments are traditionally on operations and maintenance. Regional or Corporate sponsors are involved with some projects. Prioritization is occasional responsive.
Partnership (2): IT is a business process enabler as demonstrated by the Web development, since the business executives have pursued the project. Unfortunately business is now leaving IT with the risks of the project. Most IT projects have an IT sponsor.
Scope & Architecture (1): Some standards have been established but an impor-

tant project stopped before any major impact was realized. Also management does not enforce these standards. There is little or no early concept testing until it is too late to change. There are no expert or knowledge-based systems. *Skills (1):* Crossover is not encouraged outside of Top Management. Innovation is dependent on the organization but in general frowned upon. Management style is dependent on the organization, but usually command and control. Training is encouraged but left up to the employee.

6. **A large university** assesses its alignment maturity as a 2:
   Communications (2): IT understands the goals, needs and expectations of the college very well. However, learning is informal, protocol is rigid, sharing is only semi-structured and effectiveness is limited.
   Competency (2): Business metrics are functional and not linked to IT, and most benchmarking is informal.
   Governance (2): Functional and tactical planning, focused in operation and maintenance, funding is difficult. The university received a grant to facilitate recent changes, fundraising is tied in with IT growth, but since grants are not "guaranteed" it is hard to budget when relying on grants.
   Partnership (2): Ad-hoc planning, in some cases partnership is not quite at level 2 (business perception and IT program management), however, in other areas, partnerships are stronger (business partner/champion).
   Skills (2-3): Ready for change and risk tolerant, but management style at the college is based on consensus, cross training is minimal.

Strategic Alignment as a Process

The approach applied to attain and sustain business-IT alignment focuses on understanding the alignment maturity, and maximizing alignment enablers and minimizing inhibitors. The process[21] uses the following six steps:
1. Set the goals and establish a team
2. Understand the business-IT linkage
3. Analyze and prioritize gaps
4. Specify the actions (project management)
5. Choose and evaluate success criteria
6. Sustain alignment

The Strategic Alignment Maturity assessment is an important tool in understanding the business-IT linkage (step 2) and in sustaining alignment (step 6). Naturally, knowing where the organization is with regards to alignment maturity will drive what specific actions (step 4) are appropriate to enhance IT-business alignment.

The research to derive the business-IT alignment maturity assessment has just begun. The author would appreciate hearing from practitioners, researchers, and consultants, as the strategic alignment process and the alignment maturity assessment are applied. The intent is to enhance the alignment assessment tool and provide a vehicle to benchmark exemplar organizations.

CONCLUSIONS

Achieving and sustaining IT-business alignment continues to be a major issue. Experience has shown that there is no single activity that will enable a firm to attain and sustain alignment. There are too many variables. The technology and business environments are too dynamic.

The strategic alignment maturity assessment provides a vehicle to evaluate and compare where an organization is and where they need to go with regards to attaining and sustaining business-IT alignment. The careful assessment of a firm's alignment maturity is an important step in identifying the specific actions necessary to ensure IT is being used to appropriately enable or drive the business strategy.

REFERENCES

1   King, J. (1995) "Re-engineering Focus Slips," *Computerworld,* (March 13), 6; and Henderson, J., & Venkatraman, N. (1990). "Strategic Alignment: A model For Organizational Transformation Via Information Technology," Working Paper 3223-90, Sloan School of Management, Massachusetts Institute of Technology; and Henderson, J., & Venkatraman, N. (1996). "Aligning Business and IT Strategies," Competing in the Information Age, Luftman, New York, Oxford University Press; and Earl, Michael J (1993). "Experience in Strategic Information Systems Planning," MIS Quarterly, 17(1), 1-24; and Luftman, J. (1996). Competing in the Information Age: Practical Applications of the Strategic Alignment Model, New York: Oxford University Press; and Luftman, J., Lewis, P., & Oldach, S. (1993). "Transforming the Enterprise: The Alignment of Business and Information Technology Strategies," IBM Systems Journal, 32(1), 198-221; and Goff, L. (1993). "You Say Tomayto, I Say Tomahto," Computerworld, (Nov. 1), 129; and Liebs, S. (1992). "We're All In This Together," Information Week, (October 26), 8; and Watson, R., & Brancheau, J. (1991). "Key Issues In Information Systems Management: An International Perspective," Information & Management, 20, 213-23; and Robson, W. (1994). Strategic Management and Information Systems: An Integrated Approach, London, Pitman Publishing.

2   Wang, C. (1997). Techno Vision II, New York, McGraw-Hill.

3   Luftman, J., Papp, R. Brier, T. "Enablers and Inhibitors of Business-IT Alignment," Communications of the Association for Information Systems, Volume 1, Article 11, (1999). Luftman, J., Papp, R., & Brier. T. (1995). " The Strategic Alignment Model: Assessment and Validation," In Proceedings of the Information Technology Management Group of the Association of Management (AoM) 13th Annual International Conference, Vancouver, British Columbia, Canada, August 2-5, 1995, 57-66.

3   Luftman, J., Papp, R. Brier, T. "Enablers and Inhibitors of Business-IT Alignment," Communications of the Association for Information Systems, Volume 1, Article 11, (1999).

4   Luftman, J., & Brier, T., "Achieving and Sustaining Business-IT Alignment," California Management Review, Third Quarter 1999.

5   McLean, E., & Soden, J., (1977). *Strategic Planning for MIS*, New York, John Wiley & Sons; and IBM (1981). *Business Systems Planning, Planning Guide*, GE20-0527, IBM Corporation, 1133 Westchester Ave, White Plains, New York; and Mills, P., (1986), *Managing Service Industries*, New York Ballinger; and Parker, M., & Benson, R., (1988). *Information Economics*, Englewood Cliffs, New Jersey, Prentice-Hall; Brancheau, J., & Wetherbe, J. (1987). "Issues In Information Systems Management," MIS Quarterly, 11(1), 23-45; and Dixon, P., & John, D. (1989). "Technology Issues Facing Corporate Management in the 1990s," MIS Quarterly, 13(3), 247-55; and Niederman, F., Brancheau, J., & Wetherbe, J. (1991). "Information Systems Management Issues For the 1990s," MIS Quarterly, 15(4), 475-95.

6   Papp, R. (1995). *Determinants of Strategically Aligned Organizations: A Multi-industry, Multi-perspective Analysis*, (Dissertation), Stevens Institute of Technology, Hoboken, New Jersey; and Luftman, J. (1996). *Competing in the Information Age: Practical Applications of the Strategic Alignment Model*, New York: Oxford University Press

7   Papp, R., & Luftman, J. (1995). "Business and IT Strategic Alignment: New Perspectives and Assessments," In *Proceedings of the Association for Information Systems, Inaugural Americas Conference on Information Systems*, Pittsburgh, PA, August 25-27, 1995.

8   Henderson, J., & Venkatraman, N. (1990). "Strategic Alignment: A model For Organizational Transformation Via Information Technology," Working Paper 3223-90, Sloan School of Management, Massachusetts Institute of Technology; and Henderson, J., & Venkatraman, N. (1996). "Aligning Business and IT Strategies," *Competing in the Information Age*, Luftman, New York, Oxford University Press; and Luftman, J. (1996). *Competing in the Information Age: Practical Applications of the Strategic Alignment Model*, New York: Oxford University Press.

9   Luftman, J. (1996). *Competing in the Information Age: Practical Applications of the Strategic Alignment Model*, New York: Oxford University Press.

10 Faltermayer, E. (1994). "Competitiveness: How US Companies Stack Up Now," Fortune, 129(8), (April 18), 52-64; and Adcock, K., Helms, M., & Wen-Jang, K. (1993). "Information Technology: Can it provide a sustainable competitive advantage?" Information Strategy: The Executive's Journal, (Spring), 10-15; and Cardinali, R. (1992). "Information Systems—A Key Ingredient To Achieving Organizational Competitive Strategy," Computers in Industry, 18, 241-45.

11 Chan, Y., & Huff, S. (1993). "Strategic Information Systems Alignment," Business Quarterly, 58(1), 51-56; and Luftman, J. (1996). *Competing in the Information Age: Practical Applications of the Strategic Alignment Model*, New York: Oxford University Press; and Earl, Michael J. (1983). *Corporate Information Systems Management*, Homewood, Illinois, Richard D. Irwin, Inc.; and Henderson, J., Thomas, J., & Venkatraman, N. (1992). "Making Sense Of IT: Strategic Alignment and Organizational Context," Working Paper 3475-92 BPS, Sloan School of Management, Massachusetts Institute of Technology.

12 Keen, P. (1996). "Do You Need An IT Strategy?" *Competing in the Information Age*, Luftman, New York, Oxford University Press; and Ives, B., Jarvenpaa, S., &

Mason, R. (1993). "Global Business Drivers: Aligning Information Technology To Global Business Strategy," IBM Systems Journal, 32(1), 143-161.

13 Boynton, A., Victor, B., & Pine II, B. (1996). "Aligning IT With New Competitive Strategies", *Competing in the Information Age*, Luftman, New York, Oxford University Press; and Davidson, W. (1993). "Managing the Business Transformation Process," *Competing in the Information Age*, Luftman, New York, Oxford University Press.

14 Keen, P. (1991). *Shaping the Future*, Boston, MA: Harvard Business School Press; and Foster, R. (1986). *Innovation: The Attacker's Advantage*. New York: Summit Books.

15 Rockart, J., & Short, J. (1989). "IT in the 1990s: Managing Organizational Interdependence," Sloan Management Review, 30(2), 7-17; and Davenport, T., & Short, J. (1990). "The New Industrial Engineering: Information Technology and Business Process Redesign," Sloan Management Review, 11-27; and Hammer, M., & Champy, J. (1993). *Reengineering the Corporation: A Manifesto For Business Revolution*, New York: Harper Business; and Hammer, M., & Stanton, S. (1995). *The Reengineering Revolution*, New York: Harper Business.

16 Robson, W. (1994). *Strategic Management and Information Systems: An Integrated Approach*, London, Pitman Publishing. Rogers, L. (1997). Alignment Revisited. *CIO Magazine*, May 15, 1997. Rockart, J., Earl, M., and Ross, J. (1996). Eight Imperatives for the New IT Organization. *Sloan Management Review*, Fall 1996, 43-55.

17 Rockart, J., Earl, M., Ross, J. (1996). "Eight Imperatives for the New IT Organization", Sloan Management Review, Fall.

18 Humphrey, W. S., "Characterizing the Software Process: A Maturity Framework," IEEE, 1988.

19 Keen, P. (1996). "Do You Need An IT Strategy?" *Competing in the Information Age*, Luftman, New York, Oxford University Press.

20 Nolan, R.L., "Managing the crises in data processing," Harvard Business Review March-April 1979.

21 Luftman, J., & Brier, T. (1999). "Achieving and Sustaining Business-IT Alignment," *California Management Review*, Third Quarter.

Chapter VII

Outsourcing Decisions: Using Porter's Model

Anne L. Powell
Southern Illinois University-Edwardsville, USA

ABSTRACT

It is no longer questioned that the management of information systems (MIS) is an important variable when studying organizational effectiveness and competitiveness. There have been numerous studies on how information systems (IS) can be used by organizations for strategic purposes, yet actual experiences of an organization's use of IS have often been less than satisfactory. Problems with cost, quality, and IS performance, as well as unfavorable end-user – IS relations are frequently reported. Partially because of these problems, the outsourcing of IS functions has become increasingly common. Outsourcing IS functions provides advantages to an organization but it may also create a new set of problems if the impact of the outsourcing decision to the organization as a whole is not fully considered. This chapter reviews the strategic use of IS in organizations, discusses the growing popularity of outsourcing IS functions, and uses Porter's model of five competitive forces to provide a different viewpoint on the decision to outsource.

INTRODUCTION

In the last dozen years, the use of information systems (IS) in organizations has expanded exponentially. IS has gone from a supportive role in organizations to becoming an integral part of corporate strategy. In the mid 1980s, academic journals published numerous articles about the growing relevance of IS as a strategic weapon. Several of these articles built on Porter's (1980) descriptions of five competitive forces and three generic strategies used by organizations. By the late 1980s, researchers were acknowledging that IS could be used for strategic and competitive reasons and were turning their focus to how to select and implement an IS strategy that would align with the corporate strategy.

In the 1990s, questions about the sustainability of IS competitiveness dominated IS strategy literature. Outsourcing became one strategy organizations used to deal with difficulties in sustaining competitive advantage over rivals. Outsourcing can be defined as a "make-versus-buy" decision facing an organization. Some or all aspects of the IS area can be outsourced including, but not limited to, hardware, software application development, and management functions (Loh and Venkatraman, 1992). Simply stated, outsourcing has become increasingly popular in both small and large firms as competition and other external pressures increase.

Porter (1980) stated that all organizations had strategic plans, whether explicit or implicit. He emphasized the importance of explicit strategic planning for all organizations. He created a framework to "help a firm analyze its industry as a whole and predict the industry's future evolution, to understand its competitors and its own position, and to translate this analysis into a competitive strategy for a particular business" (Porter, 1980, p. xiv). The basis of the framework is the analysis of five competitive forces (rivals, new entrants, suppliers, buyers, and substitute products) and their impact and strategic implications on the organization and the industry as a whole. Porter defined three generic strategies implemented by organizations: low-cost, differentiation, and niche, and discussed how the five forces affect the chosen strategy. Porter acknowledged that all five forces may not be crucial to a particular organization and that managers should use the framework to determine which factors are crucial and how they can be analyzed.

The goal of this chapter is to illustrate how Porter's five forces model can be used to determine when an organization is most likely to successfully outsource IS functions and whether certain forces are more important than others in the decision. Outsourcing's reported advantages of cost cutting and higher system quality have been questioned by researchers and practitioners as more data becomes available to study the long-term effects of IS outsourcing. This chapter suggests the use of Porter's framework when formulating strategic IS plans to determine whether an organization should outsource IS functions or keep them in-house for optimal success and satisfaction.

The chapter is divided into four further sections. The second section reviews IS literature and the history of the strategic use of IS within an organization. The next section defines outsourcing, reviews management information systems (MIS) literature on outsourcing, and describes advantages and disadvantages commonly associated with outsourcing. Next, Porter's framework is reviewed in more detail, outsourcing questions are fit into Porter's framework, and suggestions/proposals are given for organizations making an outsourcing decision. The final section applies theory to practice and reinforces the usefulness of the strategic alignment model of business and information technology.

IS AS A STRATEGIC WEAPON

In the early 1980s, academic articles began promoting IS as a competitive weapon that could enhance an organization's corporate strategy. Several frameworks were developed to assist managers in developing their organization's IS into a strategic advantage. Earl (1987) summarized and compared the early frameworks, categorizing them into awareness, opportunity, and positioning frameworks. Awareness frameworks helped executives determine where strategic opportunities for IS applications existed and answered such questions as 'How do I assess the current and potential impact of IS on my business?' and 'When do I know they exist?' (McFarlan, 1984; Parsons, 1983). Opportunity frameworks were more prescriptive than awareness frameworks and examined the 'what' issues rather than 'when' issues, i.e., What specific applications should be developed? and what strategies should an organization pursue to exploit technology? (Ives and Learmoth, 1984; Porter and Millar, 1985). Finally, positioning frameworks strove to increase understanding of how the IS function should be managed by helping executives assess the strategic importance of IS in their business. Positioning frameworks were created with the belief that no one methodology was likely to fit all the needs of an organization or that there would always be one preferred strategic approach for any organization (Earl, 1987). In the positioning framework, IS is depicted as supporting an organization's overall strategy and structure. Earl (1987) emphasized the need to create a more formalized method of planning IS strategy and the need to align IS strategy with corporate strategy with his framework.

In the mid 1980s, research focused on aligning the IS strategy with the business strategy. Aligning IS planning with the organizations' strategy was not new in the 1980s; earlier articles addressed the importance of linking organizational strategies to IS planning efforts (Zani, 1970), established the importance of linking IS planning to an organization's strategic direction (King, 1978), and focused on the development of an IS plan within the context of existing organizational strategies (Cash, McFarlan, and McKenney, 1983). However, rather than viewing IS as leading organization strategy or IS strategy coming from an organization's strategic direction, research began addressing the need to develop the two strategies together rather than one following the other. Henderson and Sifonis (1988) argued that there must be internal consistency between the strategic business plan and the strategic IS plan. To further investigate the interrelationship between business and IS, Henderson and Venkatraman (1990) developed the Strategic Alignment Model; it was then expanded and empirically validated using Fortune 1000 companies by Papp (1995). Earl (1993) found organizations' dominant objective for strategic IS planning was alignment of IS with business needs; nearly 70 percent of executive respondents to his study ranked it as most important, and 93.7 percent ranked it in their top five objectives.

While using IS as a strategic resource was widely accepted, less widely recognized or understood was how IS could be a source of sustainable competitive advantage. As early as 1986, Vitale warned that competitors could easily copy strategic applications of IS giving limited advantages to the innovator. Other early work on strategic sustainability included Clemons (1986) who noted the importance of imposing switching costs on customers to ensure sustainability. Clemons and Knez (1988) noted that a particular application may be necessary but not sustainable, so they described developing an application in association with competitors rather than always developing applications independently. Feeny and Ives (1990) created a framework for determining sustainability of a strategic system. Finally, Kettinger, Grover, and Segars (1995) reviewed several famous strategic systems in business to find factors that enhanced sustainability and then created a diagnostic tool for ranking and selecting systems within the corporate IS portfolio.

Recognizing IS as strategic, aligning IS strategy with corporate strategy, and sustaining IS competitive advantage have all received attention in MIS research. Both the desire to use IS as a competitive weapon and to achieve sustainable competitive advantage contributed to an increase in outsourcing. Outsourcing was seen by many as a viable strategic alternative in managing increasingly complex IS functions (Teng, Cheon, and Grover, 1995). After Eastman Kodak Company (the first major and visible company to outsource all of its IS functions) suggested that information was critical, but how it was produced was not, many organizations began to consider their IS functions as commodity services rather than strategic functions of the organization. A Massachusetts Institute of Technology study concluded that technology rarely gave businesses a competitive advantage; rather, it only reduced the cost of doing business (Benko, 1993). Many business executives came to believe that the best strategy might be to have outside vendors do all or at least some portion of their IS work rather than internal IS departments. Outsourcing, a trend of the 1990s, is discussed more fully in the next section.

OUTSOURCING THE IS FUNCTIONS

Outsourcing is broadly defined as the practice of turning over part or all of an organization's IS functions to external service provider(s). More recently, there has been a trend toward selective sourcing, where only a portion of IS functions are outsourced to outside vendors, with a substantial internal IS department retained (Lacity, Willcocks, and Feeney, 1996). Rising IS costs, rapidly changing technology, and inadequate customer service by the current IS department are some reasons executives have chosen to outsource IS functions (Benko, 1992; Bryce and Useem, 1998; McFarlan and Nolan, 1995). IS tasks that might be turned over to an outside vendor include applications development and maintenance, systems operation, networks/telecommunications management, end-user computing support, systems planning and management, and purchase of application software (Grover, Cheon and Teng, 1994).

The focus of this chapter is on outsourcing of applications development and maintenance – widely outsourced functions. Arnett and Jones (1994) found two thirds of respondents indicated that contract programming and maintenance were major types of outsourcing. In another study, respondents indicated that 30 percent of the increase in outsourcing would be concentrated in applications development and maintenance, only systems operations, with a 36 percent increase, was higher (Grover et al., 1994).

There are several reasons an organization chooses to outsource some or all of its IS functions. Several popular reasons for outsourcing are given by Bryce and Useem (1998), Palvia (1995), and Wagner (1994). One consistent reason given for outsourcing is reduction of cost. Vendors are able to utilize economies of scale to achieve lower costs and make a profit. Another major advantage of outsourcing is the transfer of risk. Some of the risks associated with IS (large capital investments, quickly changing technology, obsolete hardware and software) are shifted from the organization to the vendor with outsourcing. In addition, IS quality is expected to improve since the vendor will have employees who are knowledgeable about current and leading-edge technologies. Improved IS service as a goal of outsourcing is expected because the vendor is not dealing with the other aspects of the organization's business, and instead concentrates only on IS needs. Another popular reason for making the outsourcing choice is the belief that it will be advantageous for an organization to concentrate on the core business of the firm. Teng et al. (1995), who used resource-based theories and resource dependence theories, showed that difficulties in providing good information outputs and IS support services were the primary factors in the decision to outsource.

Although many advantages and great successes in outsourcing can be found, disadvantages have also surfaced. Early reports of outsourcing outcomes found 60-70% of organizations with outsourcing contracts were unsatisfied, although the success rate for organizations using selective sourcing was higher (Lacity, Willcocks, and Feeney, 1995). Many of the disadvantages and failures in outsourcing occur because of insufficient and/or poorly chosen vendors and written contracts. As companies (and vendors) learn more about potential pitfalls in outsourcing relationships, many of these disadvantages can be eliminated, or at least controlled. Vendor success for outsourcing is in providing daily task efficiency, not in developing new and strategic uses of technology for an organization. So, if a new technology could give an organization a competitive advantage, the organization may be less likely to realize it with outsourcing. Further, a vendor may emphasize economies of scale over providing more appropriate technology for a particular organization. Although improved service is considered to be an advantage of outsourcing, an organization is only one of many customers to the vendor and the needs of any one organization are not necessarily top priority for the vendor. Therefore, improved service promised by the vendor may not materialize after the contract is signed. As far as allowing managers to concentrate on core functions, a long-range vision for the organization (including IS) is needed for an organization to be successful. Breaking off all or a portion of IS so managers can concentrate on the core business can imply that managers do not need to consider the IS function in planning for the business as a whole (Sampler and Short, 1998; Wagner, 1994). In addition, organizational learning about new IS technology and how existing IS can be improved may be lost with outsourcing (Chesbrough and Teece, 1996; King, 1994; Slywotsky and Morrison, 1998). One of the most negative and visible effects of outsourcing is the decrease in employee morale and an increase in job uncertainty for existing IS personnel. During the outsourcing process, productivity may decline and superior employees may seek jobs elsewhere (Bryce and Useem, 1998; Due, 1992; Molloy, 1993). Finally, the advantage of having better technically trained IS personnel may not be realized through outsourcing; an organization's own IS employees (or those who have not yet left for another job) are often absorbed by the vendor resulting in no change in IS personnel for the organization (Lacity, Hirscheim, and Willcocks, 1994), although the attitudes of personnel moved to the vendor organization may suffer (Lacity et al., 1996).

Yet, despite potential disadvantages being uncovered about outsourcing, it continues to be a popular alternative for organizations. Research evidence is showing that well-designed and well-managed outsourcing agreements can provide a strategic advantage through reduced costs, enhanced competitive strategy and increased shareholder value. Expenditures for outsourcing contracts are expected to continue to increase, with organization expenditures expected to reach $300 billion by 2001. Research on outsourcing in the 1990s has consisted of empirical studies evaluating the outcome of outsourcing decisions or conceptual pieces describing pros and cons of outsourcing. Research is also needed to analyze and evaluate the decision process. The next section shows how Porter's five competitive forces and three generic competitive strategies can aid organizations who are deciding whether or not to outsource IS application development.

INTEGRATING PORTER AND THE OUTSOURCING DECISION

Questions about he decision process have come to the forefront as more organizations realize that their outsourcing decision has not led to the desired benefits. Cost benefits, the reason for outsourcing for 70% of organizations, did not materialize for half of them (Dugan, 1999), and in fact, the cost to the company in decreased organizational learning is now being said to offset dollar cost benefits a company might have realized (Chesbrough and Teece, 1996; Palvia, 1995; Slywotsky and Morrison, 1998). In addition, it is also being reported that vendors are not the strategic partners they were once thought to be because vendors do not share the same profit motive as the organization hiring them. It has also been argued that internal IS departments can often provide the same services as the vendor at the same price, if given the chance to compete (Lacity and Hirscheim, 1993).

Some researchers contend that strategic decision making by managers does not always follow a rational-comprehensive model (Lindblom, 1959; Quinn, 1980). Lindblom focused on cognitive limits (e.g., limited intellectual capacity) that prevent a rational/comprehensive process, while Quinn focused on process limits (e.g., time needed to overcome political and informational barriers, build comfort levels for risk taking, etc.). Schwenk (1984) examined the cognitive simplification processes that are likely to be operating at various stages of the decision making process. These cognitive simplification processes contribute to an individual's "cognitive bias" which (along with the individual's values) can filter and distort the decision maker's perceptions and thus influence strategic decisions. Part of the cognitive bias toward outsourcing may be a result of early media reports that were nearly unanimous in claims of outsourcing benefits. However, it should be recognized by managers faced with an outsourcing decision that these reports may be biased themselves because they are coming from outsourcing vendors, consultants, senior executives, and individuals who were instrumental in a successful outsourcing decision.

To reduce cognitive bias and decision-making limitations, a broad overview of outsourcing variables must be examined. Porter's framework encompasses the industry the organization competes in, their competitors, and their own strategic decision. Looking broadly at all these issues, rather than focusing on a single reported advantage, will assist managers in the outsourcing decision-making process. The basis of the framework is the analysis of five competitive forces (rivals, new entrants, suppliers, buyers, and substitute products). The following sections concentrate on each of Porter's five forces. Within each section, proposals for an organization to consider when making the outsourcing decision are given. Because the importance of each of the five forces may be different for different firms, three generic strategies defined by Porter are also taken into account when presenting some of the proposals.

Rivalry

Rivalry among existing organizations in an industry occurs because of several reasons (i.e., numerous competitors, slow industry growth, lack of differentiation, diverse competitors, high strategic stakes, and high exit barriers) (Porter, 1980). One step in the outsourcing decision is an evaluation of the organization's software productivity rate, software efficiency, time to market with new software-related products, and quality level of software when compared to competitors' levels (Jones, 1994). In industries with a high intensity of rivalry, the risks of outsourcing to the organization should be recognized. In outsourcing, the organization is more likely to lose control of the direction and quality of its IS and this could result in poor service to the organization's customers. In addition, critical information, which could be leaked to competitors, is entrusted to outside vendors who may not have the loyalty to the organization that internal personnel would have (Lowell, 1992). Questions to be asked when evaluating intensity of rivalry and the outsourcing decision include: 1) does the organization's IS provide a competitive or strategic advantage to the company?, 2) can IS provide the organization with components that differentiate the company in the marketplace?, and 3) is IS simply a "commodity" service? (Benko, 1992).

Because organizations following a low-cost strategy are generally producing standardized products (Porter, 1980), IS is less likely to provide a competitive or strategic advantage and more likely to be a commodity service in the organization. For organizations operating in the niche or differentiation strategies, IS is more likely to provide products that will differentiate them in the marketplace and products are more likely to depend on proprietary software. The loss of control of software quality and direction is also more likely to negatively impact organizations with these strategies. Therefore, the first strategic proposal is as follows.

> 1: *When intensity of rivalry is high, outsourcing of IS application development will be more successful for organizations operating with low-cost strategies than for organizations operating with niche or differentiation strategies.*

New Entrants

The threat of entry into an industry depends on the barriers to entry that are present (Porter, 1980). Economies of scale and experience are both entrance barriers that can be circumvented by outsourcing. Vendors are able to utilize economies of scale in order to achieve lower costs and make a profit (Wagner, 1994). Porter (1980) advocates gaining experience to create an entrance barrier by purchasing know-how from consultants. However, if an organization is in an industry that is changing rapidly, outsourcing may prevent them from overcoming further barriers that arise when they encounter a need to change to meet new demands. An organization whose business runs on a vendor's IS cannot easily change vendors. In the same way, if an organization decided a new IS architecture would better suit their needs the change is difficult, *if not impossible*, if the vendor resists the change (James, 1993). When outsourcing, a change in business practices even in a modest way requires cooperation and help from the vendor (Lowell, 1992). While more and more organizations (and vendors themselves) are recognizing the need for shorter, more flexible contracts, if the vendor insists on a long-term contract it can inhibit flexibility in an organization (Meyer, 1994). Organizations planning to move into a new market or facing potential changes in an existing market are more likely to require IS changes best handled by in-house IS departments (Lacity et al., 1995). The following three strategic proposals address the entry barrier issue in outsourcing.

> 2: *The know-how and economies of scale provided by vendors through outsourcing of application development will enable organizations who outsource to more effectively create entry barriers.*
>
> 3: *Organizations that have outsourced their IS application development will have more difficulty overcoming entrance barriers created by rivals than those organizations with internal IS departments.*
>
> 4: *Organizations choosing to outsource application development who expect significant changes in business practice or technology needs should ensure the vendor contract includes provisions for changes.*

Substitute Products

"Identifying substitute products is a matter of searching for other products that can perform the same function as the product of the industry" (Porter, 1980, pg. 23). Within the outsourcing decision, substitute products will be defined as the commonality of systems that vendors support and that organizations are currently using. Basic systems, common to many organizations that record history rather than manage day-to-day operations are better candidates for outsourcing (Benko, 1993). Critical, strategic systems, even those considered a commodity, are not substitutable and should not be outsourced (Grover and Teng, 1993; Lacity et al., 1995). Vendors offer customized but similar systems for multiple organizations, some of whom might be direct competitors, so concern over data security might adversely affect the decision to outsource for certain systems (Grover and Teng, 1993). It is disadvantageous to outsource systems that contain critical and or proprietary information on such topics as trade secrets, competitors, specific customers, employee appraisals, or pending or active litigation. If the decision is to outsource, special consideration must then be taken to ensure the data is carefully protected under the outsource agreement (Jones, 1994; Lowell, 1992). The more significant the system is to the firm's competitive advantage, the less likely the desire for outsourcing. Moreover, this significance must be evaluated for both the short run and the long run. Too often managers look only at short term goals and short term IS capabilities, but the critical question is "Does IS have the potential to be of critical importance?" (Grover and Teng, 1993; King, 1994).

> 5: *Outsourcing development of common, basic systems rather than critical, strategic systems ensures greater outsourcing success.*

Power of Buyers

In the typical analysis using Porter's framework, the buyer refers to the organization's customer. But the outsourcing decision is transparent to the organization's customer with the exception of possible interruptions in product quality and service that were noted in the rivalry section. Therefore, for the purpose of applying Porter's model to the outsourcing decision, the power of buyers refers to the power of end-users and business managers. The acceptance of outsourcing by these people is a critical success factor because they are the ones who deal directly with products of the vendor(s) (James, 1993).

Based on current MIS literature, it would seem that most end-users would be favorable to outsourcing because of prevalent problems with IS (such as quality, responsiveness, and cost). However, there are also many reasons why end-users might feel threatened by outsourcing. Outsourcing can be perceived as a loss of control over both the quality of software and the timetable of a project. Since system users have a huge stake in the quality of the systems, most want a good deal of control over their systems. Use of a vendor reduces that control—or at least can feel like it does. Communicating and coordinating with people who are strangers, are potentially geographically separated, and who report to a different organization can be difficult (Grover and Teng, 1993; Lowell, 1992).

End-user computing is potentially hampered by outsourcing. During the mid-1980s end-user computing (EUC) began increasing in importance in organizations. EUC was seen as a way to more efficiently use technology available in the organization by having end-users develop software applications in support of their own organizational tasks. EUC was seen as a way to reduce applications development backlog, receive ad hoc queries and reports in a more timely manner, and overcome the shortage of qualified professionals. In some organizations end-users have access to corporate data so they can retrieve ad-hoc queries and reports quickly. This function can be reduced or eliminated with outsourcing which leaves end-users relying on others (vendors) to create reports for them, reducing their sense of control over the IS process.

In the 1970s, most information systems (IS) departments were centralized. As companies felt the need for the IS department to be more responsive to end-user needs and to give end-users more control over their IS processes, many IS departments were decentralized into their business functions (Zmud, 1984; Hodgkinson, 1992). The degree of centralization/decentralization of an IS department is important when considering outsourcing. Greater decentralization gives business units more control and access to IT tools and increases end-user computing. A centralized IS unit provides greater control to the IS department and more standards and policies on hardware and software decisions. Because of the potential for loss of control and reduced EUC, it seems that end-users in decentralized organizations will be more likely to be dissatisfied with removal of the internal IS department. Strategic proposals related to the buyer force follow.

6: *System users in decentralized organizations will be less satisfied with a decision to outsource application development than system users in centralized organizations.*

7: *Outsourcing of application development will be less successful and less satisfactory in organizations where EUC is widespread than in firms where EUC is limited.*

8: *If an organization decides to outsource application development, any limits or changes to EUC access should be discussed and spelled out in the contract to ensure greater outsourcing success.*

Suppliers

Suppliers in the outsourcing decision are defined as not only the vendor groups that can provide outsourcing to organizations, but also includes the current internal IS department. The primary reason for the move toward outsourcing is attributed to strengths of the vendors/suppliers and weaknesses of the internal IS personnel. Literature on outsourcing has proposed that outsourcing gives organizations a chance to have the world's best working on their IS problems, that it offers higher quality and greater flexibility than internal IS groups can provide (Benko, 1993; Quinn, Doorley and Paquette, 1990), and that outsourcing also eliminates the need for never-ending training to keep IS employees' skills up to date (Wagner, 1994).

Recently, more focus has been on why the internal IS department should be reevaluated as the supplier of an organization's IS. Organizations are now finding that, if given the chance, their internal IS department can be as efficient and cost competitive as a vendor (Benko, 1992; Palvia, 1995). One good reason for reevaluating the internal IS department is that organizational learning may be lost with outsourcing. Organizational learning and innovativeness are potentially reduced if the organization has outsourced its IS services (Chesbrouth and Teece, 1996; Earl, 1996; Slywotsky and Morrison, 1998). Management tends to learn the value of IT applications by using them and seeing further opportunities for development. Many strategic information systems were discovered through evolution within the organization, and this possibility is eliminated with outsourcing (Earl, 1996). Even when a system is not strategic, an organization risks being unable to keep up to date with the latest technological opportunities when they outsource because they have lost many IS personnel who have an intimate knowledge of technology (King, 1994). A case example was provided by Earl (1996) when he looked at an organization that outsourced much of its IS after suffering losses. Once the business was profitable again, growth strategies were stymied because the organization had sold out most of their creative, relevant people. Vendors are more likely to rotate employees among several organizations, so there is no guarantee of continuity among personnel working for the client who has outsourced (Meyer, 1994). An organization loses control and flexibility in assigning people to different projects. So, even if the same employees are working for the vendor, the client organization no longer has control over who will work on what project (James, 1993). The argument that vendors are able to provide specialists that one organization cannot, might also be questioned. In many instances, the client company's IS personnel go to work for the vendors, so administrative details are transferred to the vendor, but quality of the personnel remains the same (Earl, 1996).

Another argument has been that outsourcing may not mesh well with established organizational culture. Outsourcing introduces insecurity to the work force. Employees can be terminated, transferred to other jobs, or employed by the outsourcing vendor. All these alternatives can have negative impacts on morale of both IS personnel and end-users (Molloy, 1993).

A final dimension in evaluating the outsourcing decision with consideration toward the suppliers is the realization that hardware and software vendors quickly stop calling on organizations who have outsourced IS. Although these salespeople are often considered irritants by IS executives, their absence reduces an organization's knowledge about new developments in the IS world (King, 1994).

The above discussion is not intended to disregard the value of outsourcing, only to emphasize advantages of keeping an internal IS department that many managers, in their hurry to join the outsourcing trend, have overlooked. An argument for an outsourcing decision is the increased view of a "partnership" relationship with vendors as opposed to a "vendor/client" relationship (Greco, 1997). Partnership quality has been found to positively affect the outcomes of IS outsourcing (Lee and Kim, 1999; Saunders, Gebalt, and Hu, 1997).

It is important that measures be in place to evaluate both the current IS operation and any vendor considered. The following strategic proposals stem from the above discussion.

9:   *Organizations with a strong culture for retaining employees will tend to experience less success and less satisfaction with a decision to outsource application development.*

10: *Organizations need to evaluate potential consequences to long term organizational learning when making an outsourcing decision.*

11: *If an organization's goal is to simply improve IS personnel quality, a decision to outsource will not necessarily fulfill this goal.*

APPLYING THEORY TO PRACTICE

An overarching recommendation in the outsourcing decision is that the decision not be based solely on a single factor that predominates at the time, such as a reaction to a competitor, a response to a temporal down cycle in the economy, or a need to retain control over the IT infrastructure (Grover and Teng, 1993), but that it be made after fully considering all of the competitive forces. It is likely that, as Porter predicted, different forces will be stronger determinants of the outsourcing decision for different organizations and that different organizations will experience greater or lesser outsourcing success depending on their overall corporate strategy.

Many of the issues for outsourcing decisions raised by the application of Porter's five forces map nicely into the strategic alignment model (SAM) which is the focus of this book. Assessment of both Porter's model and the SAM includes analyses of both overall strengths and weaknesses of an organization. By identifying these areas, a decision can be made on how best to align the organization for competitive advantage. Furthermore, the alignment model perspective when combined with the Porter-based analysis of this chapter provides additional structure to the decision making process that managers considering outsourcing should undertake:

When *rivalry* is high and IS is a nonstrategic organizational function, an organizational strategy of low cost suggests the possibility of lowering IS costs by outsourcing. The anchor on organizational strategy pivots on a change in IS strategy to one of outsourcing with a resulting impact on the delivery of information services from an internal IS department to an external vendor. Conversely, if the organizational strategy is one of differentiation and internal provision of information services is critical to creating and maintaining differentiation, then a change to outsourcing would be an inappropriate realignment and should be avoided.

When an organization pursues a strategy of *barriers to entry*, IS outsourcing may help create barriers through vendor economies of scale and vendor expertise. Again, the alignment to the organizational strategy anchor pivots on a change in IS strategy to one of outsourcing with a resulting impact on the way in which IS services are delivered.

Substitutes in the context of this chapter mean basic transaction processing systems capabilities, which many vendors offer and are capable of supporting. When a system need is characterized by high substitutability, it is a candidate for outsourcing. The move to outsourcing is the impact on IS processes of an alignment on an organizational strategy of low cost. In contrast to the notion of substitutes, IS processes that involve strategic systems align through IS strategy with an overall corporate strategy of differentiation. Given the possible loss of control and compromise in information privacy that outsourcing entails, it is usually inappropriate to outsource these systems.

When internal *customers* of IS services have considerable power and importance, outsourcing should be discouraged. Internal customers are the workers in an organization who undertake end-user computing in decentralized computing environments. Outsourcing often reduces flexibility and constrains end-user computing activity. Therefore, an anchor on an organizational strategy of decentralization pivots through decentralized businesses processes and encouragement of end-user computing to an impact or requirement that delivery of IS services be correspondingly decentralized and flexible – something that outsourcing may not provide. And an organization in which end-user computing spontaneously grows and anchors as part of its business processes would do well to align and pivot on the delivery of IS services in a flexible manner which requires that the corresponding IS strategy be one of insourcing, not outsourcing.

Finally, the *supplier* of an information service is either an outsourcing vendor or an internal IS function. When supply of information services through outsourcing entails risks of vendor staff churning, loss of organizational learning capability or a compromise in the ability to adjust to changes in business conditions or new technology, outsourcing is inappropriate. In the context of the alignment model, these negative consequences of outsourcing represent a diminished organizational ability to align – either at the level of strategy or the level of processes.

The proposals in this chapter have not been tested. Given the nuance and complexity of strategy and alignment issues, preliminary data gathering and analysis might best be conducted through case studies of organizations that have successfully and unsuccessfully undertaken outsourcing with appropriate variation in the characteristics of organizational strategy, systems outsourced and organizational structure introduced in the analysis above. A case study approach provides opportunity for elaboration and refinement of the basic framework of this chapter and its related proposals, as well as a test of the proposals themselves.

CONCLUSION

This chapter shows that there are still many questions to be answered before managers can evaluate and make the best outsourcing decision for their organization. Research supports the positive impact of an outsourcing decision; however, it is important that managers question whether expectations of outsourcing are feasible given their organization's current competitive strengths and strategic goals. The potential for failure exists if the outsourcing decision is made without considering both internal *and* external factors of the organization and how these factors align with business strategies and goals. Assessing Porter's model will enable a manager to make an outsourcing decision that effectively aligns IS goals and business strategies.

The increasing complexity of IS in organizations and its continued importance in relationship to the overall corporate strategy makes the development of application systems a vital component of an organization - whether the development is done in-house or outsourced. Porter's competitive forces framework, along with the SAM, can assist organizations in making the correct outsourcing decision.

REFERENCES

Arnett, K. and Jones, M. (1994). Firms that choose outsourcing: A profile. *Information & Management, 26,* 179-188.

Benko, C. (1992). If information system outsourcing is the solution, what is the problem? *Journal of Systems Management, 43,* 32-35.

Benko, C. (1993). Outsourcing evaluation. *Information Systems Management, 10,* 45-50.

Bryce, D. and Useem, M. (1998). The impact of corporate outsourcing on company value. *European Management Journal, 16,* 635-643.

Cash, J., McFarlan, F., and McKenney, J. (1983). *Corporate information systems management: Text and cases.* Homewood, IL: Richard D. Irwin, Inc.

Chesbrough, H. and Teece, D. (1996). When is virtual virtuous? Organizing for innovation. *Harvard Business Review, 74,* 65-73.

Clemons, E. (1986). Information systems for sustainable competitive advantage. *Information & Management, 18,* 131-136.

Clemons, E. and Knez, M. (1988). Competition and cooperation in information systems innovation. *Information & Management, 20,* 25-35.

Due, R. (1992). The real costs of outsourcing. *Information Systems Management, 9,* 78-81.

Dugan, S. (1999). The myth of saving money by outsourcing. *InfoWorld, 21,* 21.

Earl, M. (1987). Formulation of information systems strategies: A practical framework. In *The Role of Information Management in Competitive Success,* Pergamon-Infotech ltd.

Earl, M. (1993). Experiences in strategic information systems planning. *MIS Quarterly, 17,* 1-24.

Earl, M. (1996). The risks of outsourcing IT. *Sloan Management Review, 37,* 26-32.

Feeney, D. And Ives, B. (1990). In search of sustainability: Reaping long-term advantage from investments in information technology. *Journal of Management Information Systems, 7,* 27-45.

Greco, J. (1997). Outsourcing: The new partnership. *Journal of Business Strategy, 18,* 48-54.

Grover, V. and Teng, J. (1993). The decision to outsource information systems functions. *Journal of Systems Management, 44,* 34-38.

Grover, V., Cheon, M. and Teng, J. (1994). A descriptive study on the outsourcing of information systems functions. *Information & Management, 27,* 33-44.

Henderson, J. And Sifonis, J. (1988). The value of strategic IS planning: Understanding consistency, validity, and IS markets. *MIS Quarterly, 12,* 187-200.

Henderson, J. and Venkatraman, N. (1990). "Strategic alignment: A model for organization transformation via information technology." Working Paper 3223-90, Sloan School of Management, Massachusetts Institute of Technology.

Hodgkinson, S. (1992). IT structures for the 1990s: Organization of IT functions in large companies: A survey. *Information & Management, 22,* 161-175.

Ives, B. and Learmoth, G. (1984). The information system as a competitive weapon. *Communications of the ACM, 27,* 1193-1201.

James, P. (1993). Wendall Jones: On outsourcing. *Information Systems Management, 10,* 72-77.

Jones, C. (1994). Evaluating software outsourcing options. *Information Systems Management, 11,* 28-33.

Kettinger, W., Grover, V., and Segars, A. (1995). Do strategic systems really pay off? *Information Systems Management, 12,* 35-43.

King, W. (1978). Strategic planning for management information systems. *MIS Quarterly, 2,* 27-37.

King, W. (1994). Strategic outsourcing decision. *Information Systems Management, 11,* 58-61.

Lacity, M., and Hirscheim, R. (1993). *Information systems outsourcing: Myths, metaphors, and realities.* Chichester UK: John Wiley & Sons.

Lacity, M., Hirscheim, R., and Willcocks, L. (1994). Realizing outsourcing expectations. *Information Systems Management, 11,* 7-18.

Lacity, M., Willcocks, L, and Feeny, D. (1995). IT outsourcing: Maximize flexibility and control. *Harvard Business Review, 73,* 84-93.

Lacity, M., Willcocks, L., and Feeny, D. (1996). The value of selective IT sourcing. *Sloan Management Review, 37,* 13-25.

Lee, J. and Kim, Y. (1999). Effect of partnership quality on IS outsourcing success: Conceptual framework and empirical validation. *Journal of Management Information Systems, 15,* 29-61.

Lindblom, C. (1959). The science of 'muddling through'. *Public Administration Review, 19,* 79-88.

Loh, L. And Venkatraman, N. (1992). Determinants of information technology outsourcing: A cross-sectional analysis. *Journal of Management Information Systems, 9,* 7-24.

Lowell, M. (1992). Managing your outsourcing vendor in the financial services industry. *Journal of Systems Management, 43,* 23-27.

McFarlan, F. (1984). Information technology changes the way you compete. *Harvard Business Review, 62,* 98-101.

McFarlan, F. And Nolan, R. (1995). How to manage an IT outsourcing alliance. *Sloan Management Review, 36,* 9-23.

Meyer, N. (1994). A sensible approach to outsourcing. *Information Systems Management, 11,* 23-27.

Molloy, J. (1993). The outsourcing source book. *Journal of Business Strategy, 14,* 53-54.

Palvia, P. (1995). A dialectic view of information systems outsourcing: Pros and cons. *Information & Management, 29,* 265-275.

Papp, R. (1995). *Determinants of strategically aligned organizations: A multi-industry, multi-perspective analysis,* (Dissertation), Stevens Institute of Technology, Hoboken, New Jersey.

Parsons, G. (1983). Information technology: A new competitive weapon. *Sloan Management Review, 25,* 3-15.

Porter, M. (1980). *Competitive Strategy: Techniques for Analyzing Industries and Competitors.* New York: Free Press.

Porter, M. And Millar, V. (1985). How information gives you competitive advantage. *Harvard Business Review, 63,* 149-160.

Quinn, J. (1980). *Strategies for change: Logical incrementalism.* Homewood, IL: R.D. Irwin.

Quinn, J., Doorley, T., and Paquette, P. (1990). Beyond products: Services-based strategy. *Harvard Business Review, 68,* 58-67.

Sampler, J. and Short, J. (1998). Strategy in dynamic information-intensive environments. *Journal of Management Studies, 35,* 429-436.

Saunders, C., Gebelt, M., and Hu, Q. (1997). Achieving success in information systems outsourcing. *California Management Review, 107,* 63-79.

Schwenk, C. (1984). Cognitive simplification processes in strategic decision-making. *Strategic Management Journal, 5,* 111-128.

Slywotsky, A. and Morrison, D., with Andelman, B. (1998). *The Profit Zone: How Strategic Business Design Will Lead You to Tomorrow's Profits.* New York: Times Books/Random House.

Teng, J., Cheon, M., and Grover, V. (1995). Decisions to outsource information systems functions: Testing a strategy-theoretic discrepancy model. *Decision Sciences, 26,* 75-103.

Vitale, M. (1986). The growing risks of information systems success. *MIS Quarterly, 10,* 327-334.

Wagner, J. (1994). Factors in the outsourcing decision. *Journal of End User Computing, 6,* 27-31.

Zani, W. (1970). Blueprint for MIS. *Harvard Business Review, 48,* 95-100.

Zmud, R. (1984). Design alternatives for organizing information systems activities. *MIS Quarterly, 8,* 79-93.

Chapter VIII

The Changing Roles
of IT Leaders

Petter Gottschalk
Norwegian School of Management

ABSTRACT

Information technology (IT) leadership has undergone fundamental changes over the past decade. Despite increased interest in recent years, little empirical research on IS/IT leadership has been done. To better understand the changes, this study compares leadership roles, individual characteristics and position characteristics of newly appointed IS/IT executives (who have been in their position for two years or less) with established IS/IT executives based on a survey in Norway. Survey results indicate that new leaders spent more time in the informational role and in the change leader role than established leaders. New leaders had worked shorter in the organization and shorter in IS/IT than established leaders. New leaders had less responsibility for computer operations, communication networks and technical infrastructure than established leaders. New leaders had more responsibility for strategic alignment between IT and business.

INTRODUCTION

Information systems (IS)/information technology (IT) leadership has undergone fundamental changes over the past decade (Cross et al., 1997; CSC, 1996; Stephens et al., 1995). Despite increased interest in recent years (e.g., Armstrong and Sambamurthy, 1995; Brown et al., 1996; Earl and Feeny, 1994; Rockart et al., 1996), little empirical research on IS leadership has been done.

This research was motivated by Applegate and Elam (1992), who conducted a study of newly appointed IS executives. In their study, a new senior IS executive was defined as one who had been in the position for two years or less, while an old/established IS executive was defined as one who had been in the position for five years or more. This research applied the same definitions.

RESEARCH QUESTIONS

The study addressed the following questions:

1. What are the main leadership roles of new IS executives? Do they differ from those of established IS executives?
2. What are the individual characteristics of new IS executives? Do they differ from those of established IS executives?
3. What are the characteristics of new IS executives' positions? Do they differ from those of established IS executives?
4. How does the importance of strategic alignment influence IS/IT leadership roles?

LEADERSHIP ROLES

Managers undertake activities to achieve the objectives of the organization. Mintzberg (1994) notes a number of different and sometimes conflicting views of the manager's role. He finds that it is a curiosity of the management literature that its best-known writers all seem to emphasize one particular part of the manager's job to the exclusion of the others. Together, perhaps, they cover all the parts, but even that does not describe the whole job of managing. Mintzberg's role typology is frequently used in studies of managerial work (e.g., Pinsonneault and Rivard, 1998).

Describing the manager's work has been an ongoing pursuit of researchers and practitioners. The manager's work is characterized by brevity, variety, and fragmentation of tasks, a preference for action (as opposed to reflection), and a preference for verbal communication over formal reports (Mintzberg, 1994). Managers in organizations are continuously confronted by an array of ambiguous data and vaguely felt stimuli which they must somehow order, explicate and imbue with meaning before they decide on how to respond (Kuvaas, 1998). A number of models describing the manager's work have been proposed including functional descriptions such as planning, organizing, directing, controlling, coordinating, and innovating. Similarly, frameworks based on the methods used to accomplish these functions, for example, Mintzberg's role typology, have been proposed. According to Mintzberg (1990), the manager's job can be described in terms of various roles:

1. **Informational Roles**. By virtue of interpersonal contacts, both with subordinates and with a network of contacts, the manager emerges as the nerve center of the organizational unit. The manager may not know everything but typically knows more than subordinates do. Processing information is a key part of the manager's job. As monitor, the manager is perpetually scanning the environment for information, interrogating liaison contacts and subordinates, and receiving unsolicited information, much of it as a result of the network of personal contacts. As a disseminator, the manager passes some privileged information directly to subordinates, who would otherwise have no access to it. As spokesperson, the manager sends some information to people outside the unit.

2. **Decisional Roles**. Information is not an end in itself; it is the basic input to decision making. The manager plays the major role in a unit's decision-making system. As its formal authority, only the manager can commit the unit to important new courses of action; and as its nerve center, only the manager has full and current information to make the set of decisions that determines the unit's strategy. As entrepreneur, the manager seeks to improve the unit, to adapt it to changing conditions in the environment. As disturbance handler, the manager responds to pressures from situations. As resource allocater, the manager is responsible for deciding who will get what. As negotiator, the manager commits organizational resources in real time.

3. **Interpersonal Roles**. As figurehead, every manager must perform some ceremonial duties. As leader, managers are responsible for the work of the people of their unit. As liaison, the manager makes contacts outside the vertical chain of command.

Kotter (1999) discusses what effective general managers really do, and defined key issues in management work depending on short term, medium term and long term perspectives. He defined two fundamental roles: agenda setting and execution. Agenda setting is concerned with figuring out what to do despite uncertainty and an enormous amount of potentially relevant information. Execution is concerned with getting things done through a large and diverse group of people despite having little direct control over most of them.

IT LEADERS

The role of the chief information officer (CIO) emerged in the 1970s as a result of increased importance placed on IT. As a manager of people, the CIO faces the usual human resource roles of recruiting, staff training and retention, and the financial roles of budget determination, forecasting and authorization. As the provider of technological services to user departments, there remains a significant amount of work in publicity, promotion, and internal relations with user management (Brown et al., 1996). As a manager of an often virtual information organization, the CIO has to coordinate sources of information services spread throughout and beyond the boundaries of the firm (Heckman, 1998). The CIO is thus concerned with a wider group of issues than are most managers (Jordan, 1993). Earl and Feeny (1994) concluded that the IT director's ability to add value is the biggest single factor in determining whether the organization views IT as an asset or a liability.

The earliest scientifically conducted research on the CIO position (Brumm, 1988) examined 43 of the 50 top-ranked Fortune 500 service organizations and noted that 23 (58%) of these organizations had the CIO position. Brumm (1990) examined the 200 largest Fortune 500 industrial and service organizations and found that 77% of the industrials had a CIO position as compared with 64% of the service organizations. It is likely that this number has increased in recent years (Stephens et al., 1995).

Few studies have examined the reasons behind creation of the CIO position in firms. Creation of the position effectively increases the accountability by making a single executive responsible for corporate information processing needs (Arnett and Jones, 1994). In a sample of stable Fortune 500 firms, i.e., appearing on the list for four consecutive years, Karake (1995) compared 287 firms with CIOs to firms without CIOs on a number of variables hypothesized to predict creation of the position. She observed that a number of characteristics of the corporate board, including the number of outside directors and equity ownership of the directors, predicted the existence of the CIO position. A firm's information intensity is also positively related to the creation of the CIO position. Information intensive industries such as banking were among the earliest to establish the CIO position (Boyle, 1994). This study of 14 Fortune 1000 firms also noted the information intensity as a determining factor and showed that the CIO position is most likely to exist when IS functions are decentralized, and the CEO appreciates the strategic value and importance of IT.

Several studies have been devoted to examining the nature of the information system executive's work in the U.S. (Applegate and Elam, 1992; Stephens et al., 1992), in Australia (Watson, 1990; Broadbent et al., 1994), and in the UK (Feeny et al., 1992). While information systems executives share several similarities with the general manager, notable differences are apparent. The information systems manager is not only concerned with a wider group of issues than most managers (Jordan, 1993), but also, as the chief information systems strategist, has a set of responsibilities that must constantly evolve with the corporate information needs and with information technology itself.

The CIO title itself has become a source of confusion. The CIO label actually denotes a function rather than a title in the U.S. The actual title of the individuals filling the CIO position is generally a vice president with very few bearing the title of CIO (Brumm, 1988). Other common titles include executive vice president, senior vice president, and director of information services. The CIO label itself has been met with resistance, and some firms have replaced the title with alternative labels such as knowledge manager or chief technology officer. CSC (1998b) has suggested the role of chief knowledge officer (CKO) which is not so much to provide knowledge management facilities and services as to enable the organization to innovate. Earl and Scott (1999) found that CKOs have to discover and develop the CEO's implicit vision of how knowledge management would make a difference.

A field study of the two largest law firms in Norway illustrates the difference between the traditional IT manager and a CKO (Gottschalk, 1999). Both TKGL Law (see Table 1a) and Schjødt (see table 1b) had newspaper advertisements on November 28 and December 22, 1998, respectively. While TKGL received 53 applications, out of which 10 were very well qualified, Schjødt received only 11 applications, none of which were really qualified (OR, 1999). When comparing the two advertisements, some explanations emerge. First, the title "Knowledge Manager" created curiosity. Second, TKGL focused on the CIO responsibilities, while Schjødt focused on technical competencies of candidates. While TKGL ended up recruiting a CIO as planned, Schjødt changed its mind and used head-hunting to find a CIO and an IT support person. The CIO hired by TKGL was 37 years old and has a Master's of Science degree in computer and information science from Ohio State University in the U.S. She has worked with Norsk Data, IBM and Sybase. The CIO hired by Schjødt was 30 years old and has a Master of Science degree in information systems from Norway. He has worked with a local municipality and with a consulting firm.

Creation of the CIO role was driven in part by two organizational needs. First, accountability is increased making a single executive responsible for the organization's information processing needs (Arnett and Jones, 1994). Second, creation of the CIO position facilitates the closing of the "gap" between organizational and IT strategies which has long been cited as primary business concern (Stephens et al., 1992). Alignment of business and IT objectives is not only a matter of achieving competitive advantage (Stephens and Loughman, 1994), but is essential for the firm's very survival. Though the importance of IT in creating competi-

Table 1a: Main Text in TKGL Newspaper Advertisement

CIO - Knowledge Manager
The CIO will be responsible for our information systems and for enhancing these systems in accordance with our business strategy. With three capable IT-persons, your management responsibility will include:
- Development and implementation of IT strategy and information architecture for knowledge management
- Improvement of technical infrastructure
- Enhancement of access to databases
- Applications procurement
- User training and support
- You should have higher IT-education or IT-related education from university or college, experience from management of IT projects, preferably from a knowledge firm, experience from office support systems and databases, and you should have creative and pedagogical abilities.

Table 1b: Main Text in Schjødt Newspaper Advertisement

IT coordinator
You will be responsible for improving our IT strategy, enhancing database access, network operations, etc. You should have higher education and experience from IT-related projects. Other desired qualifications include:
- Experience from operations of NT network
- Good knowledge of Office applications such as Word, Excel, PowerPoint and Access
- Knowledge of routers and datacom generally
- Ability to work structured and independent
- Creative and pedagogical abilities.

tive advantage has been widely noted, achieving these gains has proven elusive. Sustained competitive advantage requires not the development of a single system, but the ability to consistently deploy IT faster, cheaper, and more strategically than one's competitors (Ross et al., 1996). IS organizations play a critical role in realizing the potential of information technology. The performance of IS organizations, in turn, often centers on the quality of IS leadership (Prattipati and Mensah, 1997).

The CIO's pivotal responsibility of aligning business and technology direction presents a number of problems. "It is a common problem for the CIOs: they dream of creating innovative business applications to help the company gain competitive advantage but end up stuck, spending most of their time putting out fires and grappling with legacy system maintenance" (Hoffman, 1998, p. 10). Moreover, rapid changes in business and information environments have resulted in corresponding changes in the IS function helm (Applegate and Elam, 1992). This role has become increasingly complex, causing many firms to look outside the organization for the right qualifications (Applegate and Elam, 1992). Characteristics such as professional background, educational background, and current length of tenure have been examined in previous research (e.g., Applegate and Elam, 1992; Stephens et al., 1992).

In addition, some firms have sought to redefine the role itself. The nature of the CEO/CIO relationship is also seen as a major determinant of the CIO's strategic focus (Jones et al., 1995; Peppard, 1999). Issues in management also affect the role of managers, forcing them to prioritize activities and to set agendas based on these priorities (Mintzberg, 1994). Likewise, issues in information systems management are important determinants of the CIO role, representing a guidance for his/her work. As a result, CIOs vary greatly in terms of the information systems spending, organizational structure, and number of directly managed in order to achieve IS goals.

IT LEADERSHIP ROLES

Changes in both information technology and competition continue to change the role of the information systems executive. CSC (1996) has suggested six new IS leadership roles which are required to execute IS's future agenda: chief architect, change leader, product developer, technology provocateur, coach and chief operating strategist. These roles are described in Table 2. Although these roles were produced by the CSC consultancy firm without any scientific approach, they seem very well tailored for scientific investigation into IS leadership roles. People who fill these roles do not necessarily head up new departments or processes, but they exert influence and provide leadership across the organizational structure.

Brown et al. (1996) discuss four IS leadership roles—technologist, enabler, innovator and strategist—which have similar role descriptions to the six roles suggested by CSC (1996). Brown et al. (1996) developed a model for IS leadership roles. Earl and Scott (1999) discuss four leadership roles for the chief knowledge officer (CKO) - Technologist, Environmentalist, Entrepreneur, and Consultant. As a technologist, the CKO has to understand which technologies contribute to capturing, storing, exploring, and, in particular, sharing knowledge. Several of

Table 2: Six IS Leadership Roles (CSC, 1996)

1. ***Chief architect.*** The chief architect designs future possibilities for the business. The primary work of the chief architect is to design and evolve the IT infrastructure so that it will expand the range of future possibilities for the business, not define specific business outcomes. The infrastructure should provide not just today's technical services, such as networking, databases and desktop operating systems, but an increasing range of business-level services, such as workflow, portfolio management, scheduling, and specific business components or objects.

2. ***Change leader.*** The change leader orchestrates resources to achieve optimal implementation of the future. The essential role of the change leader is to orchestrate all those resources that will be needed to execute the change program. This includes providing new IT tools, but it also involves putting in place teams of people who can redesign roles, jobs and workflow, who can change beliefs about the company and the work people do, and who understand human nature and can develop incentive systems to coax people into new and different behaviors.

3. ***Product developer.*** The product developer helps define the company's place in the emerging digital economy. For example, a product developer might recognize the potential for performing key business processes (perhaps order fulfillment, purchasing or delivering customer support) over electronic linkages such as the Internet. The product developer must "sell" the idea to a business partner, and together they can set up and evaluate business experiments, which are initially operated out of IS. Whether the new methods are adopted or not, the company will learn from the experiments and so move closer to commercial success in emerging digital markets.

4. ***Technology provocateur.*** The technology provocateur embeds IT into the business strategy. The technology provocateur works with senior business executives to bring IT and realities of the IT marketplace to bear on the formation of strategy for the business. The technology provocateur is a senior business executive who understands both the business and IT at a deep enough level to integrate the two perspectives in discussions about the future course of the business. Technology provocateurs have a wealth of experience in IS disciplines, so they understand at a fundamental level the capabilities of IT and how IT impacts the business.

5. ***Coach.*** The coach teaches people to acquire the skillsets they will need for the future. Coaches have two basic responsibilities: teaching people how to learn, so that they can become self-sufficient, and providing team leaders with staff able to do the IT-related work of the business. A mechanism that assists both is the center of excellence - a small group of people with a particular competence or skill, with a coach responsible for their growth and development. Coaches are solid practitioners of the competence that they will be coaching, but need not be the best at it in the company.

6. ***Chief operating strategist.*** The chief operating strategist invents the future with senior management. The chief operating strategist is the top IS executive who is focused on the future agenda of the IS organization. The strategist has parallel responsibilities related to helping the business design the future, and then delivering it. The most important, and least understood, parts of the role have to do with the interpretation of new technologies and the IT marketplace, and the bringing of this understanding into the development of the digital business strategy for the organization.

these are emerging technologies. As an environmentalist, the CKO has to design office and relaxation areas, and acquire and furnish retreats and learning centers. It includes bringing together communities with common interest who rarely interact with each other. As an entrepreneur, the CKO has to have a spirit of newness, adventure and risk taking. A critical attribute of such entrepreneurship is being a strategist who can grapple with the implications of using knowledge management as a tool for corporate transformation. As a consultant, the CKO has to bring in ideas and seed them and listen to other people's ideas and back them if they make sense and fit the knowledge vision.

Andrews and Carlson (1997) suggest that we are now in the 4th CIO wave. The first wave consisted of glorified DP managers, the second wave consisted of technocrats, the third wave consisted of business executives and the fourth wave consists of executives that combine the skills of technocrats and business executives. For example, in the field of knowledge management technocrats will focus on data warehouses, Internet, intranet, workflow tools and groupware, while business executives will focus on data mining, managing intellectual capital and introducing new knowledge-based processes.

The magazine *CIO* surveyed 3,000 high-level IS executives in the U.S. for their opinions of innovative IS organizations (Hildebrand, 1997). Respondents could nominate up to five companies, including their own, and were asked to rate their choices in each of five best practices categories: infrastructure management, internal customer support, internal operations, IT and business alignment, and innovation and learning. Based on the survey responses, the magazine produced their list of the top 100 CIOs.

CIOs are less frequently replaced in Europe than in North America and Asia/ Pacific (CSC, 1998a). While European companies had replaced 26% of their CIOs in the past two years, North American companies had replaced 36% and Asia/Pacific companies had replaced 44%. Only 28% of the CIO replacements in Europe were recruited from outside the company, while the figures were 56% and 37% for North America and Asia/Pacific respectively.

When Stephens et al. (1992) selected CIOs for observation, they applied the following criteria:

- Highest ranking information technology executive
- Reports no more than two levels from CEO, i.e., either reports to the CEO or reports to one of the CEO's direct reports
- Areas of responsibility include information systems, computer operations, telecommunications, office automation, end-user computing/information center
- Responsibility for strategic planning of information resources.

As originally conceived, the chief information officer's responsibility would include all corporate information, not just information on computers. Historically, however, the focus of the CIO's job was predominantly information technology. This involves a number of roles including strategic information system roles, the most critical of these being strategic information systems planning (Stephens et al., 1992), strategic management through participation in top management planning teams (Stephens et al., 1995), strategic alignment of business and information systems plans (Rockart et al., 1996), and interpretation of external IT success stories for potential applicability for the organization (Earl and Feeny, 1994). In addition to strategic planning, the CIO's responsibilities also include a number of tactical IT roles. These include architecture planning, development, and management; fostering relationships between the information systems department and including the superiors (Feeny et al., 1992), functional units/line managers (Stephens et al., 1992), vendors (Rockart et al., 1996) and end users; and technology champion - gaining support and commitment of top management during the implementation of new technology. In this research, we will use the same selection criteria as Stephens et al. (1992): the highest ranking information technology executive, areas of responsibility include information systems and computer operations, and responsibility for strategic planning of information resources.

The guiding theoretical framework for this research is based on Mintzberg (1990, 1994). It is assumed that information systems executives' jobs can be described in terms of various roles. According to Yin (1994, p. 30), this is an application of individual theory for predictions of individual behaviors.

STUDY METHODOLOGY

Data were collected through a survey in Norway. In Norway, IT leadership roles are frequently debated. The top ranked IT leader or CIO as defined by Stephens et al. (1992) is typically called "IT-direktør" (IT director), "IT-sjef" (IT-manager) or "IS-leder" (IS-leader) in Norway. The survey sample consisted of 168 private and public member firms of the Norwegian Computing Society (NCS). This sample is biased towards organizations interested in IT issues in general. The informants in this research were IT managers who reported their own perceptions of roles and possible explanations of roles.

For each of Mintzberg's (1994) three leadership roles, respondents were asked to indicate how much time they spent in each role. An extent response of one indicated that they spent little time in that role, while an extent response of six indicated that a great deal of time is spent in that role.

For each of CSC's (1996) six leadership roles, respondents were asked to indicate the extent to which that role characterizes their job. For example, an extent response of one for chief architect implies that this role does not characterize at all the job, while an extent response of six indicates that the chief architect characterizes the job really well.

Variables in the research model were operationalized by both single-item measures and multiple-item measures. For example, responsibility which is one of the position characteristics, was measured by ten items. The item questions were concerned with responsibility for information systems, computer operations, communication networks, strategic IS/IT planning, bridging IS/IT and business strategy, benefits realization, information architecture, technical infrastructure, IS/IT budget, and IS/IT personnel (Applegate and Elam, 1992; Boynton et al., 1992; Cross et al., 1997; CSC, 1996; Earl and Feeny, 1994; Rockart et al., 1996; Stephens et al., 1995).

RESULTS

Of the 168 mailed questionnaires, 101 were returned, providing a response rate of 60%. The sample included organizations from a broad range of industries as listed in Table 3.

Out of 101 responses, 41 IS executives had been in the current position for two years or less, while 60 IS executives had been in the current position for more than two years. These two groups are used in the following and labeled new and old respectively.

While Mintzberg (1994) defined three general leadership roles, CSC (1996) defined six IS/IT leadership roles. A Likert scale from 1 to 6 was used to measure the extent of each role as listed in Table 4.

Substantial differences between new and old IS/IT leaders were found in the informational role and the change leader role. While the change leader role is the highest scoring role among new IS/IT leaders, it is a relatively modest role among old IS/IT leaders. According to CSC (1996), a change leader orchestrates resources

Table 3: Sample Breakdown by Industry

Primary Activity	Percent
Manufacturing	39
Service	21
Public administration	21
Trade	12
Finance	7
TOTAL	100

Table 4: Leadership Roles

Leadership role	New IS/IT leaders	Old IS/IT leaders	t-statistic for difference
Informational Role	4.35	3.98	1.547*
Decisional Role	4.43	4.58	-.793
Interpersonal Role	4.38	4.42	-.207
Chief architect	4.27	4.28	-.027
Change leader	4.61	4.24	1.490*
Product developer	3.27	3.57	-1.252
Technology provocateur	4.29	4.26	.140
Coach	4.12	4.22	-.487
Chief operating strategist	4.27	4.31	-.159

Note: * if p<.10, ** if p<.05, *** if p<.01

Table 5: Individual Characteristics

Characteristics	New IS/IT leaders	Old IS/IT leaders	t-statistic for difference
Years worked in the organization	6.42	10.81	-2.922***
Years worked in IS/IT	12.55	17.15	-2.910***
Years worked in current position	1.36	6.01	-8.077***
Years of higher education	4.47	4.52	-.093
Internal hires	44%	30%	-
Extent of IS/IT use	5.54	5.69	-1.106
Relationship with chief executive	1.59	1.59	-.097

Note: * if p<.10, ** if p<.05, *** if p<.01

to achieve optimal implementation of the future. The essential role of the change leader is to orchestrate all those resources that will be needed to execute the change program. This includes providing new IT tools, but it also involves putting in place teams of people who can redesign roles, jobs and workflow, who can change beliefs about the company and the work people do, and who understand human nature and can develop incentive systems to coax people into new and different behaviors.

Information on individual characteristics of IS/IT leaders was collected through the survey and is listed in Table 5.

New IS/IT leaders have worked significantly fewer years in the organization and in IS/IT than established IS/IT leaders. Concerning characteristics such as education level, personal technology use and relationship with chief executive, new and old IS/IT leaders report similar characteristics.

IS leaders were classified as internal hires if they had been with the company for more than five years at the time they had assumed the IS leadership position. Individuals were classified as external hires if they had been with the company for five years or less. Five years was chosen as the cutoff because individuals are typically considered to be part of the corporate establishment after five years of employment (Applegate and Elam, 1992). The results of this survey show that internal hires have increased.

Information on characteristics of the IS/IT leadership position was collected through the survey and is listed in Table 6.

Reporting level was measured as the number of management levels between the IS/IT executive and the chief executive. It may seem surprising that new IS/IT leaders are lower in the hierarchy than old IS/IT leaders. This finding differs from earlier research where Applegate and Elam (1992) found that an increasing number of new IS executives reported directly to the CEO. Five dimensions of responsibility show some differences between new and old leaders. Typically, strategic IS/IT

Table 6: Characteristics of Position

Characteristics	New IS/IT leaders	Old IS/IT leaders	t-statistic for difference
Persons reporting to leader	18.05	20.93	-.350
Reporting level	1.05	0.82	1.508*
Responsibility for information systems	4.73	4.90	-.634
Responsibility for computer operations	4.29	5.10	-2.355**
Responsibility for communication networks	4.32	5.03	-2.026**
Responsibility for strategic IS/IT planning	5.34	5.15	0.976
Responsibility for bridging strategy	4.80	4.52	1.122
Responsibility for benefits realization	3.61	3.44	0.597
Responsibility for information architecture	4.37	4.66	-1.113
Responsibility for technical infrastructure	4.41	5.20	-2.835***
Responsibility for IS/IT budget	5.07	5.44	-1.611*
Responsibility for IS/IT personnel	4.76	5.41	-2.241**

Note: * if p<.10, ** if p<.05, *** if p<.01

planning, bridging IS/IT planning and benefits realization represent strategic responsibilities. These responsibilities have a higher score among new IS/IT leaders, but the differences are not statistically significant. Typically, computer operations and communication networks represent operating responsibilities. These responsibilities have a significantly lower score among new IS/IT leaders.

The analyses so far has treated experience (years worked in current position) as a dichotomous variable. When experience is treated as a continuous measure in regression analyses, results as listed in Table 7 emerge.

Regression analysis confirms the decreasing change leader role as the years in current position increase. For other predicted variables, regression analysis provides slightly different results. For example, while decreasing responsibility for computer operations among new leaders was not confirmed, there is a significant positive relationship between the number of years in current position and the extent to which the leader has responsibility for IS/IT personnel.

Table 7: Regression Analysis Using Experience as Predictor

Dependent variable	Adjusted R-square	Regression F-statistic	Beta coefficient	Coefficient t-statistic
Informational role	.070	1.723	-.132	-1.313
Decisional role	.001	1.090	.105	1.044
Interpersonal role	.006	1.603	.127	1.266
Chief architect	-.010	0.064	.026	0.253
Change leader	.041	5.230**	-.226	-2.287**
Product developer	.002	1.226	.112	1.107
Technology provocateur	.004	1.437	-.121	-1.199
Coach	-.008	0.234	-.049	-0.484
Chief operating strategist	-.010	0.076	-.028	-0.276
Years worked in the organization	.270	37.542***	.526	6.127***
Years worked in IS/IT	.167	20.583***	.418	4.537***
Years of higher education	.001	1.105	-.107	-1.051
Internal hires	-.006	0.380	.062	0.616
Extent of IS/IT use	-.010	0.006	-.008	-0.079
Relationship with chief executive	-.010	0.000	-.001	-0.012
Persons reporting to leader	-.010	0.086	-.030	-0.293
Reporting level	-.008	0.179	-.043	-0.423
Responsibility for information systems	-.001	0.944	.098	0.972
Responsibility for computer operations	-.002	0.827	.091	0.909
Responsibility for communication networks	.012	2.246	.150	1.499
Responsibility for strategic IS/IT planning	.013	2.301	-.151	-1.517
Responsibility for bridging IS/IT and business strategy	.028	3.894*	-.195	-1.973*
Responsibility for benefits realization	.006	1.570	-.126	-1.253
Responsibility for information architecture	-.010	0.042	.021	0.205
Responsibility for technical infrastructure	.015	2.492	.157	1.579
Responsibility for IS/IT budget	.008	1.792	.134	1.339
Responsibility for IS/IT personnel	.046	5.818**	.237	2.412**

Note: * if p<.10, ** if p<.05, *** if p<.01

STRATEGIC ALIGNMENT

Strategic alignment is concerned with the appropriate use of information technology in the integration and development of business strategies and corporate goals (Henderson and Venkatraman, 1993; Luftman et al., 1999). Luftman et al. (1999) have identified both enablers and inhibitors of alignment. Several of the top ranked enablers and inhibitors are dependent on IS/IT leadership. Out of the four domains of the strategic alignment model (Henderson and Venkatraman, 1993), the research presented in this chapter is mainly concerned with the IT strategy domain. This section investigates the extent to which collected survey data can shed light on the changing role of IS/IT leaders concerning strategic alignment.

First, the chief operating strategist invents the future with senior management by aligning IT and business. Although not statistically significant, new IS/IT leaders report that they spend less time in this role than old leaders (see Table 4). This is quite a surprising result.

Second, among the items measuring responsibility, the relevant issue is concerned with bridging IS/IT strategy with business strategy. Although not statistically significant, new IS/IT leaders report that they have more responsibility for this activity than old leaders (see Table 6).

Overall, there are several indications that new IS/IT leaders are more concerned with strategic alignment than old leaders. Their focus on information and change, combined with responsibilities for alignment and benefits realization, indicate a more strategic orientation. However, the change in roles seems to progress in a low-speed fashion.

COMPARISON OF SURVEY RESULTS

Among all the 101 respondents, 44 percent reported to the managing director (CEO), while 23 percent reported to the financial director, and 33 percent reported to others (technical director, staff director, or other). As illustrated in Table 8, these results are in line with recent previous studies.

The conducted survey collected data on the three roles defined by Mintzberg (1990). Stephens found that the five CIOs which she studied, spent most of their time in the decisional roles (60%), less of their time in the informational roles (36%)

Table 8: Information Systems Executive Reporting Relationship

Reporting Relationship of Respondents	Applegate & Elam (1992)	CSC (1997)	Gott-schalk (1998)	This study (1999)
Reports directly to managing director (CEO)	27%	43%	48%	44%
Reports to financial director (CFO)	44%	32%	21%	23%
Reports to other officer	29%	25%	31%	33%

and very little time in the interpersonal roles (4%). This research suggests that Norwegian CIOs, on a scale from 1 (little extent) to 6 (great extent), have the same decision roles ranked on top (4.5), but they spend much more time on interpersonal roles (4.4) and informational roles (4.1) than the CIOs in the Stephens' study.

In this survey, respondents had been in the current position for the last 4.1 years. This is slightly less than the results obtained by CSC (1997) who found that the average reported tenure of a company's senior IS professional was 4,7 years worldwide, ranging from 5.0 years in North America to 4.9 years in Europe to 4.0 years in Asia Pacific.

Seven years ago, Boynton et al. (1992) posed the question: Whose responsibility is IT management? They claimed that line managers were increasingly assuming responsibility for planning, building, and running information systems that affect their operations. In this perspective, it is interesting to study results from this survey. For example, realization of benefits is not a large responsibility of IS leaders as illustrated in Table 6. A possible explanation is that this responsibility is assumed by line managers.

Applegate and Elam (1992) found that 53% of new IS leaders were internal hires, while 94% of old IS leaders were internal hires. In this survey, 44% and 45% respectively were internal hires. The fraction of internal hires in this survey was lower, and there was no difference between new and old IS leaders.

MANAGEMENT IMPLICATIONS

The CIO function is a continuously evolving role (Stephens, 1993). The present research provides a snapshot in this progression. Identifying these trends in information systems leadership has implications for both research and practice. First, educators can use this information to develop management programs. Second, these roles and trends represent important guidelines for practicing CIOs. The senior IS executives must be able to bring both a business and IT perspective to the position. More definitive role expectations could also aid in career planning (Applegate and Elam, 1992). Finally, clarifying the CIO role also has implications for office technology design and use. Studies continue to show the executives' preference toward verbal communications (Stephens, 1993). These studies also point to relatively limited use of the technologies that these managers purvey. One possibility is that this limited technology use is due in part to limitations in the technologies themselves. Identifying these limitations could improve executive acceptance of these systems. However, the survey data do not show us what technology the CIOs use.

Of general interest is which findings from previous research (if any) are still applicable in this volatile environment. Previous research on the role of the CIO has either focused on the "micro" level—examining the executive's activities and contacts, or at a "macro" level—analyzing the issues, strategies and objectives of these executives. Micro-level activities can further be divided into desk work and coordination activities (Applegate and Elam, 1992; Stephens et al., 1992). Deskwork includes activities performed in relative isolation such as resume reviews, environmental scanning, and email (Jordan 1993; Watson 1990). Coordination activities include activities conducted with one or more other individuals by means such as phone calls, scheduled meetings, unscheduled meetings, or tours (Stephens and Loughman, 1993). The second aspect of coordination activities are the activities completed by interfacing with a number of groups including superiors (corporate), subordinates (IS group), clients (business units), suppliers (consultants, vendors, etc.), and peers (other information system executives). At the macro level, there exists a need to look at strategies that distinguish higher and lower performing firms, organizational structures used to achieve strategic goals, and issues associated with these strategies and the technologies used to achieve these goals.

Individual characteristics are also potential areas of future research. Individual characteristics such as CIO educational and career backgrounds and relationship with the CEO have been shown to influence perceptions (Stephens et al., 1992) which in turn affect strategy. CEOs often do not understand the CIO's contribution well enough to properly evaluate the IS function's performance (Earl and Feeny, 1994). An essential element to a good CEO/CIO relationship is a common understanding of business critical success factors and the role and importance of IT in the organization (Feeny et al., 1992). The CIO's perception of key issues are influenced by the relationship with the CEO (Watson, 1990). National culture may also prove to have a bearing on issue perceptions. Future research may concentrate on further clarifying the role of the CIO.

Table 8 compares four studies which include samples from very different organizational and cultural backgrounds. IS leadership roles in the Norwegian culture may be different from other studies done in the U.S. and UK or around the globe. For example, Norwegian organizations tend to be much smaller than surveyed organizations in the U.S., and hierarchies in Norway tend to be flatter than in most other countries. Such aspects can lead to implications for management practice and future research. According to the Scandinavian research on information systems development, Scandinavia has high living standards and educational levels, an advanced technology infrastructure, an open community and key innovative leaders (Boland, 1999). This research tradition seems different from research in other countries such as the UK with control structures (Towell et al., 1998) and Mexico with economic development (Mejias et al., 1999), which may imply different IS leadership roles. In future research, eight cultural dimensions can be investigated: power distance, uncertainty avoidance, individualism, masculinity, time orientation, monocrony and polychrony, context, and polymorphic and monomorphic (Hasan and Ditsa, 1999).

One would expect the role of the IT manager to be changing with the changing role of IT as discussed in this book. This is a nice avenue for future research.

CONCLUSIONS

The main point of this research is the changing face of IT management. The empirical analysis indicated that operational responsibilities are decreasing among IS/IT leaders. They spend much of their time as change leaders, and they are more concerned with strategic alignment of IT with business. Strategic alignment is not a major issue in this chapter. However, one is tempted to conclude that the role of

IT leaders is changing due to the increasing impact of IT and increased understanding of the significance of alignment, however this research does not prove that idea.

The data provided in this research will hopefully stimulate similar research in other nations and regions. Just like key IS management issues research has enabled global comparisons (Watson et al., 1997), future IS leadership research may gain from global comparisons as indicated in the section on survey comparisons. Practicing IS/IT leaders will gain from this research by balancing leadership roles according to individual characteristics, organizational characteristics and stages of growth.

REFERENCES

Andrews, P. and T. Carlson (1997). The CIO IS The CEO Of The Future. *CIO Conference*, Naples, Florida, http://www.cio.com/conferences/eds/sld018.htm.

Applegate, L.M. and J.J. Elam (1992). New Information Systems Leaders: A Changing Role in a Changing World. *MIS Quarterly*, 16 (4), 469-490.

Armstrong, C.P. and Sambamurthy, V. (1995). Creating business value through information technology: The effects of chief information officer and top management team characteristics. *Proceedings of the International Conference on Information Systems*, Netherlands.

Arnett, K.P. and C.J. Jones (1994). Firms that chose outsourcing: A profile. *Information & Management*, 26 (4), 179-188.

Boland, R.J. (1999). Some Sources of the Unity in Plurality of Scandinavian Research on Information Systems Development, *Scandinavian Journal of Information Systems*, 10(1&2), 187-192.

Boyle, R.D. (1994). Critical success factors for establishing and maintaining the position of CIO. *Information Strategy: The Executive's Journal*, 10, 29-38.

Boynton, A.C.; Jacobs, G.C. and R.W. Zmud (1992). Whose responsibility is IT management? *Sloan Management Review*, 33 (4), 32-38.

Broadbent, M.; Butler, C. and A. Hansell (1994). Business and technology agenda for information systems executives. *International Journal of Information Management*, 14 (6), 411-423.

Brown, C.V.; McLean, E.R. and D.W. Straub (1996). Partnering Roles of the IS Executive, *Information Systems Management*, Spring.

Brumm, E.K. (1988). Chief information officers in service and industrial organizations: A survey. *Information Management Review*, 3, 17-30.

Brumm, E.K. (1990). Chief information officers in service and industrial organizations. *Information Management Review*, 5, 31-45

Cross, J.; Earl, M.J. and J.L. Sampler (1997). Transformation of the IT function at British Petroleum. *MIS Quarterly*, 21 (4), 401-423.

CSC (1996). *New IS leaders*, CSC Index Research, UK: London.

CSC (1997). *Critical Issues of Information Systems Management - 10th Annual Survey*, Computer Sciences Corporation, USA: El Segundo, California.

CSC (1998a). *Critical Issues of Information Systems Management - 11th Annual Survey*, Computer Sciences Corporation, USA: El Segundo, California.

CSC (1998b). *Explicit Management of the Knowledge Asset*, Computer Sciences Corporation, UK: London.

Earl, M.J. and D.F. Feeny (1994). Is your CIO adding value? *Sloan Management Review*, 35 (3), 11-20.

Earl, M.J. and I.A. Scott (1999). What is a Chief Knowledge Officer? *Sloan Management Review*, Winter.

Feeny, D.F.; Edwards, B.R. and K.M. Simpson (1992). Understanding the CEO/CIO Relationship. *MIS Quarterly*, December, 435-448.

Gottschalk, P (1998). *Content Characteristics of Formal Information Technology Strategy as Implementation Predictors*, Tano Aschehoug Publishing, Norway: Oslo.

Gottschalk, P (1999). Knowledge management in the professions: lessons learned from Norwegian law firms. *Journal of Knowledge Management*, vol. 3 (3), pp. 203-211.

Hasan, H. and G. Ditsa (1999). The Impact of Culture on the Adoption of IT: An Interpretive Study, *Journal of Global Information Management*, vol. 7 (1), pp. 5-15.

Heckman, R. (1998). Planning to Solve the "Skills Problem" in the Virtual Information Management Organization, *International Journal of Information Management*, vol. 18 (1), pp. 3-16.

Henderson, J.C. and N. Venkatraman (1993). Strategic alignment: Leveraging information technology for transforming organizations, *IBM Systems Journal*, vol. 32 (1), pp. 4-16.

Hildebrand, C. (1997). 10th Annual CIO 100 Top I.T. Performers, *CIO*, August.

Hoffman, T. (1998). Too many IT duties? Hire a second CIO. *Computerworld*, March 16, 32 (11), 10.

Jones, M.C.; Tayllor, G.S. and B.A. Spencer (1995). The CEO/CIO relationship revisited: An empirical assessment of satisfaction with IS. *Information & Management*, 29 (3), 123-130.

Jordan, E. (1993). Executive information systems for the chief information officer. *International Journal of Information Management*, 13 (4), 249-259.

Karake, Z.A. (1995). The management of information technology, governance, and managerial characteristics. *Information Systems Journal*, 5, 271-284.

Kotter, J.P. (1999). What effective general managers really do, Harvard Business Review, March-April, pp. 145-159.

Kuvaas, B. (1998). *Strategic issue diagnosis: The roles of organizational scanning, information processing structure of top management teams, and managers' cognitive complexity*, Unpublished doctoral dissertation, Norway: Norwegian School of Economics and Business Administration.

Luftman, J.N.; Papp, R. and T. Brier (1999). Enablers and Inhibitors of Business-IT Alignment, *Communications of AIS*, vol. 1, article 11.
http://cais.aisnet.org/articles/

Mejias, R.J.; Palmer, J.W. and M.G. Harvey (1999). Emerging Technologies, IT Infrastructure, and Economic Development in Mexico, *Journal of Global Information Technology Management (JGITM)*, vol. 2 (1), pp. 31-54.

Mintzberg, H. (1990). The Manager's Job: Folklore and Fact. *Harvard Business Review*, March-April.

Mintzberg, H. (1994). Rounding out the manager's job. *Sloan Management Review*, 36 (1), 11-26.

Peppard, J. (1999). Bridging the gap between IT organization and the rest of the business: plotting a route. *Proceedings of the 7th European Conference on Information Systems* (ECIS), June 23-25, Copenhagen, Denmark, vol. II, pp. 542-558.

Pinsonneault, A. and S. Rivard (1998). Information Technology and the Nature of Managerial Work: From the Productivity Paradox to the Icarus Paradox?, *MIS Quarterly*, September, 287-311.

Prattipati, S.N. and M.O. Mensah (1997). Information systems variables and management productivity. *Information & Management*, 33 (1), 33-43.

Rockart, J.F.; Earl, M.J. and J.W. Ross (1996). Eight Imperatives for the New IT Organization. *Sloan Management Review*, 38 (1), 43-55.

Ross, J.W.; BEeath, C.M. and D.L. Goodhue (1996). Develop Long-Term Competitiveness through IT Assets. *Sloan Management Review*, 38 (1), 31-42.

Stephens, C.S. (1993). Five CIO's At Work: Folklore and Facts Revisited. *Journal of Systems Management*, 44 (3), 34-40.

Stephens, C.S.; Ledbetter, W.N.; Mitra, A. and F.N. FOord (1992). Executive or Functional Manager? The Nature of the CIO's Job. *MIS Quarterly*, 16 (4), 449-467.

Stephens, C.S.; and T. Loughman (1994). The CIO's chief concern: Communication. *Information & Management*, 27 (2), 129-137.

Stephens, C.S.; Mitra, A., Ford, F.N. and W.N. Ledbetter (1995). The CIO's Dilemma: Participating in Strategic Planning. *Information Strategy*, 11 (3), 13-17.

Towell, R.E; McFadden, K.L. and J. Lauer (1998). ISO 9000 Certification in the U.K.: A Study of the Role Played by the Information Systems Organization, *Journal of Global Information Technology Management (JGITM)*, vol. 1 (4), pp. 3-16.

Watson, R.T. (1990). Influences on the IS manager's perceptions of key issues: Information scanning and the relationship with the CEO. *MIS Quarterly*, 14 (2), 217-231.

Yin, RK (1994). *Case study research: design and methods*, 2nd edition, USA: SAGE Publications.

Chapter IX

Strategic Information Systems for Competitive Advantage: Planning, Sustainability and Implementation

Gareth Griffiths and Ray Hackney
Manchester Metropolitan University, UK

INTRODUCTION

This chapter describes **three** critically important features for the planning, sustainability and implementation of strategic information systems (SIS). The literature identifies a consistent lack of success by organisations in achieving business benefits from their SIS investments and in particular the difficulties of obtaining a sustained competitive advantage over rivals. There appears to be little evidence that this record has improved as organisations increasingly rely on SIS to support their business strategy. The chapter focuses upon the need for appropriate SIS planning, the role of unique, causally ambiguous 'isolating mechanisms' in order to sustain SIS-derived competitive advantages and concludes by summarising the implementation factors deemed to be of real practical importance for the success of large-scale SIS projects based upon recent empirical research. The high failure rate of SIS applications in business is deemed to be largely of a managerial rather than a technical causation (Earl, 1989;Burn, 1993; Galliers et al., 1994;Barnett and Burgelman, 1996; Powell and Dent-Micallef 1997; Willcocks and Lester 1999; Watson et al., 2000). This chapter identifies and considers three components which are critical in this respect to enable an IT strategy fusion with the rest of the business (Papp, 1998).

Earlier studies, for example Long (1987) found that 90 per cent of the failures in office applications were due to organisational problems (poor planning, poor management, lack of training) and only 10 per cent due to technical difficulty. Kearney (1990) reports that following a study of 400 British and Irish companies, only 11 per cent had been successful in their SIS applications when based upon criteria of scope of applications and benefits achieved, project completion on time and return on investment. Morley (1991) claimed that more than a quarter of major SIS projects greatly exceeded budget and were well behind schedule. Clegg et al. (1996) found that 80-90% of IT investments fail to meet their performance objectives, 80% of systems were delivered late and over budget, 40% of developments fail or are abandoned completely, under 40% fully address training and skills requirements, less than 25% properly integrate business and technology objectives and only 10-20% meet all their success criteria. SIS developments have also been difficult to analyse in terms of ROI or on any other accounting basis. The resultant factors may be identified as relating, at least in part, to the planning, sustainability and implementation of SIS. This chapter will consider each factor in turn and consequently attempt to provide practical guidelines for successful IT strategy fusion, as shown in Figure 1.

SIS PLANNING

Surveys throughout the 1980s consistently identified SIS planning as a major concern for both user and management (Brancheau and Wetherbe, 1987). SIS planning is the process of identifying the computer-based applications that will assist an organisation in executing its business plans and realising its business goals. The planning focuses upon the sequencing and implementation of SIS applications, as well as the investigation of existing and proposed SIS applications (Sambamurthy

Figure 1. Strategic Information Systems - strategic fusion

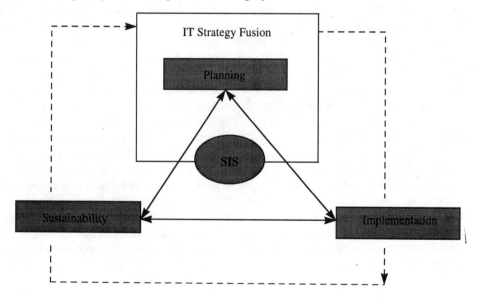

et al., 1994). The plans must be rigid enough to allow for large projects but also flexible in order to adjust to environmental change (Lederer and Mendelow 1993). McBride (1998) emphasises the dynamic nature of organisations and the need for strategies that adapt. He defines SIS planning as the "continuous review of computer technology, applications and management structure to ensure that the current and anticipated information and process needs of the organisation are met in a way that provides an acceptable return on investment, is sensitive to the dynamic politics and culture of the organisation and is aware of the sociological environment within which the organisation exists". The literature shows that SIS planning, in some form, is common in many organisations.

Earl's (1990) research, for example, recognises that issues with SIS occur across method, process and implementation. He claims that much of the existing research focuses only on the specific issues with respect to planning. While Earl examined method, process and implementation issues he does not deal with them in detail. Earl only provides indications as to where potential issues may occur without rigorously analysing them. As issues in SIS are complex and dynamic a structure is needed to analyse them; the various planning frameworks available provide this structure. They assist organisations in understanding and classifying the relationship between business strategy and information technology. Most frameworks assess the impact of SIS or search for opportunities and reorient the thinking and raise awareness of the SIS strategy relationship.

Awareness Frameworks

As models, they are helpful in increasing senior management understanding but tend to be less useful in searching for and identifying strategic uses for SIS. They can be used as tools to persuade senior management of the strategic nature of SIS rather than guide them in the identification of specific strategic opportunities. These frameworks are not detailed enough to provide a detailed strategic plan but may be useful in the planning process.

Positioning Frameworks

Models are required to enable organisations to develop systems with higher value-adding potential. Nolan (1979) provides a six stage maturity model based on actual use of SIS by large U.S. companies. Wiseman (1985) criticised the attention given to operational systems (traditional DP) to the detriment of progression to the third era, namely SIS, aimed at improving competitiveness by changing the way organisations conduct their business. He developed his 'Extended Application Portfolio Model' which combines the functions and objectives of applications systems on one matri.. This model must be extended to include the impact of expert and image-based systems. It is clearly important that organisations should have information systems to support these stages of the information life cycle. Also development should take into account the value-adding potential of each of the stages and there should be increasing consideration of SIS that can improve the way the organisation competes.

In acknowledgment of the need to support existing applications while progressively moving into the SIS era. McFarlan (1984) proposed an 'applications portfolio management matrix'. It is concerned with four categories of system (strategic, turnaround, factory and support) and with the need to balance the applications mix so that efforts can be directed into obtaining maximum overall business leverage through its SIS. Organisations attempt to balance the potential high return systems with supporting systems.

Opportunity Frameworks

McFarlan's (1984) framework is useful in identifying the types of application that may have a strategic significance. Ward & Griffiths (1996) studied 150 systems that 'claimed' strategic success and arrived at the following classification:

i)   Those that linked the organisation via technology-based systems to its customers or suppliers. Besides well documented cases (Ford, Nissan, American Hospital Supplies. etc.), this could also include jumping parts of the value system itself, e.g., using IS to remove the need for middlemen in the transformation of raw materials through production to finished product (e.g. Directline Insurance).

ii) Those that produce more effective integration of the use of information in the organisation's value adding process

iii) Those that enable the organisation to develop, produce, market and deliver new or enhanced products or services based on information

iv) Those that provide executive management with information to support the development and implementation of strategy

(i), (ii) & (iii) support conditions for SIS with (iv) being an additional type of system that aids strategic planning. By specifically addressing these four types of system, an organisation stands the best chance of developing systems which could genuinely be called SIS. Sullivan's (1985) model is another example where he investigated the planning experiences of 37 major US organisations to identify the factors that correlated with planning success. The two main factors identified, which determine the position of any organisation within his model were the degree of systems dispersion (diffusion) and the degree of impact of systems (infusion):

i.   Diffusion: This factor was defined as the extent of the deployment of IS throughout the organisation. The deployment refers to the extent of the physical deployment of IS and the extent of any devolution of the control and responsibility of the management and decision making aspect of SIS throughout the organisation.

ii. Infusion: This factor was defined as the degree of impact that the organisation perceived that SIS systems have on the business. A low level of infusion was defined as one where the impact of SIS was of a tactical nature. A high level of infusion was defined as one where the impact of SIS was of strategic significance. SIS was important to the organisations' achievement of its business objectives and therefore the organisation was dependent on SIS for its ultimate success.

Multiple Frameworks

Earl (1989) argued that no single method provides the full answer and suggested a multiple approach to IS planning. Earl (1990) later found that firms over time use a number of planning techniques, this seemed to support his multiple method approach. The likelihood of any one particular approach being predominant depends, according to Earl, on the nature of the organisation and its industry at a particular point in time. In general no one technique is necessarily better than any other. Each framework has its place depending on the preference of the particular managers, the culture and experience of the organisation and the industry dynamics faced by the firm.

Without appropriate planning, organisations may fail to realise the anticipated benefits of their SIS investments (Clemons and Weber, 1990). Lederer and Mendelow (1990) also demonstrated that excessive delays in the execution of SIS investments resulted from poor planning, changes in business direction and changes in project priorities. Organisations function within a dynamic business environment where there is frequently environmental turbulence. These unpredictable environmental changes can radically impact SIS strategy planning (Vitale et al. , 1986). While comprehensive SIS planning has been demonstrated to have merit, it is suggested that less rigorous SIS planning is advantageous in turbulent environments. Change occurs so frequently that plans become obsolete before they can be followed (Lederer and Mendelow, 1990). Vitale et al. (1986) found the planning process susceptible to wasted efforts, low morale and misdirected investments. Recent work by Salmela et al. (1997) noted that in turbulent business environments, the more meticulous and comprehensive the SIS planning was, the more likely it would enable the organisation to be flexible and engage the support of those involved.

SUSTAINABILITY OF SIS

There has been much debate as to what distinguishes sustainability from ephemeral SIS-derived advantage. (Hackney, 1996; Hackney et al, 1999). Clemons and Kimbrough (1987) differentiate between strategic necessity and sustained competitive advantage. SIS that is a strategic necessity must be present for an organisation to operate effectively (e.g., the IT used by large supermarket chains), but it can lead to damaging effects on the industry. SIS purchased by all firms in an industry in order to lower production costs may well result in higher profits for all, providing prices can be maintained and all firms purchase similar technology. On the other hand, when it is necessary for all competitors to purchase technology, equal savings can be obtained by all which may lead to a price war. Smaller margins occur, with the benefit being passed to the customers but the industry might well wish that SIS had never being introduced (Cragg and Finlay 1991). Beinhocker (1997) describes companies being "locked in an arms race from which they obtain no benefit to their profits".

Ephemeral Advantages

Much field work has focused upon the use of SIS as a competitive weapon (Sillince, 1995; Hackney et al., 1999). Studies indicate that an SIS competitive advantage is probably only sustainable in the short term (Neumann, 1994; Eardley et al., 1995). Very often organisations try to gain a competitive edge simply by adopting new technology more quickly than competitors. Clearly this advantage can rarely be maintained for long, unless the cost of acquiring similar technology is prohibitive. Although competitors will shortly 'catch up' with the SIS, the gain that has been derived might well have caused the organisation to 'jump' ahead in terms of market share, profitability, reducing costs etc. which could have much more long term benefits.

Internally focused SIS, internally developed SIS or SIS that are aimed at 'soft' areas (e.g., involving aspects of company culture) will usually prove to be the most sustainable, simply because it is much more difficult for competitors to gain knowledge about the system and will therefore create the longer lasting advantages. However the key to successful searches for SIS is the organisation's ability to think of *innovative* uses for SIS, and this is most likely to be the route to any really sustainable advantages i.e., by out-thinking the competitors. To maintain an SIS-based competitive edge, organisations must continually look to improve and redesign their SIS applications, or to ensure that there is a constant stream of new SIS's following on behind its existing ones. Lee and Adams (1990) investigated ways in which changes may be sustained for longer periods through 'mobility barriers'. Cecil and Goldstein (1990) describe three basic reasons why SIS in itself is increasingly less likely to deliver sustainable advantage:

i) Market competitors often have comparable knowledge and skills to develop particular applications;
ii) The differences in application knowledge and skills is often evened out by vendors;
iii) Large scale developments rarely translate into cost advantage.

Zmud and Apple (1988), basing their work on supermarket optical scanning systems, distinguish between the *routinisation* of an innovation, defined as the accommodation of an organisation's governance system to the innovation, and its *institutionalisation*, defined as the organisation's achievement of higher levels of use and benefits from the innovation. Routinisation being necessary for institutionalisation, but institutionalisation is not certain to occur when an innovation is routinised. Clemons and Row (1991) also discuss how SIS innovators can defend the economic value of their development:

i) Barriers to duplication via patents, trade secrets, government legislation, monopoly situation or lack of technical expertise (not common with IS);
ii) High financial or emotional switching costs, helped by being the 'first-mover'——examples include AHS and AA's SABRE reservation system (Vitale, 1986);
iii) The innovation changes the underlying industry characteristics (e.g. customer preferences or the IS used in the industry) that influence costs to favour the innovator

Clemons and Row (1991) further claim that one of the best ways to achieve sustainable competitive advantage is when SIS leverages differences in an organisation's strategic resources and that this underlies all of the above factors to a greater or lesser extent. As these resources are unique to that organisation then it will be difficult and expensive for another to copy and obtain similar benefit from the SIS innovation. SIS can change the value of key resources by reducing the cost of integrating and coordinating economic activities. This increases the potential production economies (e.g,. scale, scope and specialisation) that can be exploited. The way SIS aids unstructured activities may lead to a more sustainable advantage as these situations are unique, and organisation specific which makes them difficult to copy (Cragg and Finlay, 1991). It is the use of the information that is clearly important here and not the IT itself. Computerising the routine structured tasks of order processing and stock control will never lead to a sustained gain as rivals have access to similar technology and skills. It is important to reiterate that the unique, company specific synergy situations will be difficult for rivals to duplicate as they will not have access to the same diverse resources.

Mata et al. (1995) examined a range of factors and concluded that only SIS management skills were likely to be the source of sustained competitive advantage. These skills were identified as the ability to understand and appreciate business needs, their ability to work with functional managers; ability to coordinate SIS activities in ways that support other functional managers and ability to anticipate future needs. They recommended that organisations should focus more on the process of organising and managing SIS within an organisation. Dvorak et al. (1997), Silver et al. (1998) and Skok and Hackney (1999) support this view and suggest that the distinguishing feature as to what separates companies that achieved a sustained competitive advantage from those that do not is not technical superiority but training and the way they handle their organisational SIS activities. The types of organisations that can benefit from SIS depends upon the impact that information has on its industry and the way it conducts its business. Apart from the early models presented which are useful tools, Broadbent (1991) suggests eight features present in companies which had already achieved some information-based advantage over their competitors;

i)   Strong well-established planning approach which involved staff at all levels;
ii)   Strategic processes which were well documented;
iii)   A consensus between senior managers and IS managers;
iv)   A concern for information content;
v)   Alignment of IS with organisational infrastructure;
vi)   Maximum interaction between IS and business managers;
vii)   IS literate business managers;
viii) Business literate IS managers

Many authors have promoted the contributions offered by resource-based theory (Rumelt, 1987; Barney, 1991) and some go as far as stating that it is a potential integrating paradigm for strategy research (Mahoney and Pandian, 1992; Peteraf, 1993). Resource-based theory is related to the premise of heterogeneous resource portfolios—whether by history, accident or design. According to Peteraf, (1993), this resource heterogeneity is responsible for observed variability in financial returns across firms. However, firms that manage to achieve sustained perfor-mance advantages by accumulating resource portfolios that produce economic value, are relatively scarce, and can sustain competitive attempts at imitation, acquisition, or substitution (Barney, 1986). Traditional strategy research was driven more by IS-oriented strategic planning focused on advantages derived from industry and competitive positioning whereas resource based research has focused on advantages stemming from firm-specific, intangible resources such as organisation culture, learning, and capabilities (Hall, 1993).

Henderson and Venkatraman (1993) conclude that companies must use SIS to leverage or exploit firm-specific, intangible resources such as organisational leadership, culture, and business processes. Keen (1988) divided resources into human, business, and technology and developed a *fusion* framework that strongly parallels resource-based theory arguing that the key to SIS success lies in the capacity of organisations to fuse technology with latent, difficult-to-imitate, firm-specific advantages embodied in existing human and business resources. A variety of alternative resource typologies exist (Black and Boal, 1994), but Keen's theory arose primarily in an SIS context. The use of *isolating mechanisms* to promote sustainability in the resource-based framework has been explored by Reed and DeFillippi (1990). The idea of isolating mechanisms, at the firm level of analysis has been described as analogous to entry barriers at the industry level, and mobility barriers at the strategic group level (Caves and Ghemawat 1992). Lippman and Rumelt (1982) ascertained that apart from legislation, isolating mechanisms exist because of the *rich connections between uniqueness and casual ambiguity.* A number of academics, most notably Teece (1990), have stated that it is intangible (and therefore often invisible) assets and organisational capabilities that are the most likely to be unique and casually ambiguous.

IMPLEMENTATION OF SIS

The final section refers to those factors that have been found to be relevant to the successful implementation of SIS developments. A number of research studies have examined the implementation approaches of organisations to identify the main issues. The research literature suggests the following as being the main causes of failure:

i)   Lack of top management support and understanding (Earl and Feeney, 1994; Mata et al.1995; Ross et al. 1996; Venkatraman 1997; Peppard and Ward,1998);

ii)   A lack of user commitment to projects (Tait and Vessey ,1988; Whyte et al, 1997);

iii) A poor level of communication between users and IS staff (Taylor-Cummings and Feeney, 1997);

iv)   Over optimistic estimates which lead to systems being delivered late (Keen, 1987; Galliers et al 1994);

v)   Serious cost budget overruns due to insufficient understanding of the work necessary to deliver the project (Henderson and Venkatraman 1993; Ward and Griffiths 1996; Willcocks and Lester, 1999);

vi)   Poorly defined business objectives caused by inadequate appreciation of the business's needs (Keen, 1987).

Wilson (1989) found that difficulties in recruiting appropriate staff, the lack of resources to engage in user education, the nature of the business and difficulties with measuring the benefits of SIS were significant implementation issues. He argued that implementation issues cannot be separated from the strategic planning process. The implementation of SIS strategies is itself a strategic, not a tactical, issue. The main conclusion was that the examples of failure were not due to ill-conceived systems at the planning stage, but poor implementation. In every instance, the failure to implement the system successfully was due to organisational, not technological, causes. Successful examples, using the McKinsey 7S model, suggest that companies succeeded in balancing the 7S carefully, while unsuccessful companies fail to manage at least four of the seven S's, as follows:

i)   Strategy: The champion of the strategic system was a senior executive in the business unit in which the system was used. The senior strategic decision makers led the implementation. Strategic systems were developed through a phased, adaptive, evolutionary approach.

ii)   Structure: The most appropriate project structure was one where the team members had overlapping roles on the project.

iii)   Skills: Project members had good business acumen as well as technical skills.

iv)   Systems: Successful implementations involved a change in the company's risk/renewal structure.

v)   Style: Team members were flexible, willing to accept change and cope with uncertainty.

vi)   Staff: An effective management champion was crucial to successful implementation.

vii)   Shared values: Team members must have a belief in the value of their efforts and share a common, well communicated vision of the project's outcome.

Consequently, a number of specific implementation issues can be identified, as follows:

Lack of Top Management Commitment

The lack of top management commitment to the implementation is identified as a general issue in the empirical studies reviewed above. Addressing the issue is recognised as a prerequisite to successful SIS implementation (Yap and Thong, 1997; Enns and Huff, 1997; Peppard and Ward, 1998).

Change Issues

The failure to take account of, and understand, the business change issues at the implementation stage is a common issue in the literature (Benjamin and Levinson,1993; Korunka et al, 1993; Hackney, 1996; Dhillon and Hackney, 2000). They all provide their variant of a change management based model which recognises that people are the core of organisations and that human related issues must be recognised and managed during a technical implementation.

Role of the Project Champion

The literature highlights the potential impact that project champions have on the success of a project: the existence of a project champion is a key factor determining the success of IS projects. A number of authors have identified the importance of the role of a project champion (Prager and Overholt, 1994;

Chesher, 1997). The literature argues that the project champion should be a senior manager from the business.

Financial Reserves

Management has to be willing to invest substantial financial resources in order to develop an SIS as most developments require an abundance of resources (Reich and Benbasat, 1990). A strong financial position of the firm has therefore been identified as a major enabling factor for the development of SIS, while budgeting constraints act as an inhibitor (King et al., 1989).

Project Structure

The traditional approach to organising an SIS project involves the appointment of a project manager, often with SIS experience, to manage the delivery of the technical solution. The role of business resources is often limited to the provision of business requirements and user testing and acceptance. There is a growing body of literature which argues that the traditional project structure is inappropriate for the successful implementation of SIS. McKersie and Walton (1991) recommend a project structure based on the definition of the main roles necessary for effective implementation of SIS:

• *the role of the senior manager:*

There is a clear and necessary role for a senior manager who has responsibility for SIS. The main role is to provide the vision and delineate the steps necessary for realising the vision. The specific roles include: setting the policy regarding the introduction of SIS; have a reasonable understanding of the capabilities and limitations of SIS; understand the interplay of the technical and social aspects of the system, ensure that the human resource aspects are carefully managed; exhibit a strong commitment to the successful introduction of the project, and address middle management concerns concerning displacement by SIS.

This view supports that of other researchers (Earl and Feeney (1994) and Ross et al. (1996). The general view is that not only do senior managers need to be involved but the quality of their involvement has to be sufficient to guide the project over organisational objectives.

• *the role of middle management:*

McKersie and Walton (1991) claim that the stakeholder group most at risk from SIS developments is the group which is most crucial to its success. As a result, it is important that the group members are well educated and supportive towards IS. The specific roles of this group include: understanding the interplay between the technical and social aspects, promoting an environment of continuous learning and involving users.

• *the role of users:*

User participation is recognised as a key facilitator in successful implementation. Their main role is to provide assistance in the selecting, introduction and assessment of systems. This view is supported by other studies which also show that lack of user involvement throughout the implementation phase will lead to a greater likelihood of project failure (Taylor-Cummings and Feeney, 1997; Yap and Thong, 1997).

These implementation factors are clearly linked to the resources, capabilities and knowledge within the organization, as McKee and Varadarajan (1995) note: "Competitive advantage is the cornerstone of strategy, and enacted knowledge is the essence of competitive advantage".

CONCLUSION

Organisations may only have two possible options for achieving an SIS-based advantage. Firstly to continually reinvent leading-edge SIS innovations and using the opportunity to set up unassailable first mover advantages. Secondly to embed SIS in such a way as to produce sustainable resource complementarity. Perpetual innovation may hypothetically produce advantages, but these advantages vanish if innovation stops. Very few firms manage to be continuously innovative. The rate of technological change is ever increasing (Sarker and Lee, 1999) making this constant struggle more problematic. First mover SIS advantages seem more promising particularly when they can harness proprietary systems customised to exploit firm specific strengths or opportunities. Such systems frequently come down to resource complimentarities: they produce advantage by merging with skills, relationships, or strategic positions, but even then the empirical research (Kettinger et al, 1994; Powell and Dent-Micallef, 1997) suggests that such advantages rarely endure. However the proponents of resource based theory still maintain that complementary resources are the most likely way of achieving long term gains; a practical framework for these features is shown in Figure 2.

On this practical level traditional systems development, which is based on a structured and inflexible method-orientated approach, may not be the most appropriate for exploiting SIS. SIS by their nature require flexibility as the business may change constantly (McBride, 1998, Dhillon and Hackney, 2000) and the nature of the strategic opportunity may be difficult to define in the detail expected from traditional

Figure 2: A Practical Framework for SIS

	Planning	Sustainability	Implementation
FEATURES			
DISTINCTORS	awareness	ephemeral	senior support
	positioning	processes	user commitments
	opportunity	innovation	project champion
	multiple	uniqueness	objectives
CRITICAL FACTORS	1) continually relevant leading-edge SIS applications and innovations 2) embedded SIS to produce sutainability resource complementarity		

methods (Hackney and Little, 1999). The claim is that newer ways, which are based upon working closely and iteratively with the business users and utilising such techniques as prototyping, are better approaches for SIS. The literature also argues that traditional systems development approaches can be counter productive because they focus attention on technological factors at the expense of human and organisational factors. In implementing SIS the requirement is for constant adaptation, indeed the nature of these systems is often that requirements cannot be specified in sufficient detail in advance. Another criticism of traditional methods is that they do not encourage communication between the SIS function and the business. The real challenge in the future will be for the strategic development of systems for 'virtual' organisations and the demands of e-commerce strategies (Burn and Hackney, 2000).

The findings of these studies suggest that competitive advantage and the potential for its sustainability arise from complex, causally ambiguous, intangible resources and it is here that organisations should focus their efforts.

REFERENCES

Barnett, W.P. and Burgelman, R.A. (1996) Evolutionary perspectives on strategy, *Strategic Management Journal*, 17, p5-19

Barney, J. B. (1991) Firm Resources and Sustained Competitive Advantage, *Journal of Management, 17(1)*, 99-120

Beinhocker, E.D. (1997) Strategy on the edge of chaos, The McKinsey Quarterly, 1, 24-39

Benjamin, R. and E. Levinson (1993). A framework for managing IT-enabled change, *Sloan Management Review*, Summer, pp. 23-33.

Black, J. and Boal, K. (1994) Strategic Resources: Traits, Configurations, and Paths to Sustainable Competitive Advantage, *Strategic Management Journal*, Summer Special Issue, 15, 131-148

Brancheau, J.C. and Wetherbe, J.C. (1987) Key Issues in Information Systems Management, *MIS Quarterly*, March, 23-45

Broadbent, M. (1991) *Information Management: strategies and alliances*, Aslib Proceedings (Jan),1-11

Burn, J. (1993) Information Systems Strategies and the Management of Organisational Change – a strategic alignment model, *Journal of Information Technology*, 8, 205-216

Burn J and Hackney R A (2000) Strategic Planning for E-Commerce Systems (SPECS), AMCIS Mini-Track Proceedings (forthcoming)

Burton, J. (1995) Composite Strategy: the combination of collaboration and competition, *Journal of General Management'*, 21(1).

Caves, R.E. and Ghemawat, P. (1992) Identifying Mobility Barriers, *Strategic Management Journal*, 13 (1), 1-12

Cecil, J. and Goldstein, M. (1990) Sustaining Competitive Advantage from IT, *The McKinsey Quarterly*, Vol. 4, 74-89

Checkland P.B. (1981) Systems Thinking, Systems Practice Wiley, Chichester

Chesher, M. (1997) Impact of Emerging Technologies on Companies in Sustaining

Competitive Advantage, 7th Annual BIT Conference, Nov

Clegg, C.W., Axtell, C., Damodaran, L., Farbey, B., Hull, R., Lloyd-Jones, R., Nicholls, J., Sell, R., Tomlinson, C., Ainger, A. and Stewart, T. (1996). 'The Performance of Information Technology and the Role of Human and Organisational Factors, Report to the Economic and Social Research Council, United Kingdom, January

Clemons, E.K., and Kimbrough, S.O. (1987). Information Systems and Business Strategy: a review of strategic necessity, Report 87-01-04, Department of Decision Sciences, The Warton School, University of Pennsylvania

Clemons, E.K. and Row, M.C. (1991). Sustaining IT Advantage: the role of structural differences, *MIS Quarterly*, September, 275-292

Clemons, E.K. and Weber, B.W. (1990). Strategic Information Technology Investments: guidelines for decision making, *Journal of Management Information Systems*, 7(2), 9-28

Cragg, P.B. and Finlay, P.N. (1991). IT: running fast and standing still? *Information and Management*, 21, pp193-200

Dhillon, G and Hackney R A (2000) IS/IT and Dynamic Business Change, *HICSS Proceedings*, Hawaii, Jan

Dutta, S. and Doz, Y. (1995). Linking Information Technology to Business Strategy at Banco comercial portugues', *Journal of Strategic Information Systems*, 4, 89-110

Dvorak, R.E., Holen, E., Mark, D. and Meehan, W.F. (1997). Six Principles of High-Performance IT, *The McKinsey Quarterly*, No. 3, 164-177.

Eardley, A., Avison, D. and Powell, P. (1995) How Strategic Systems are Strategic Information', *International Journal of Technology Management*, Special Issue on the 5th International Forum on Technology Management, 11(3/4). 395-411

Earl, M.J. (1989). Management Strategies for Information Technology, Prentice Hall, New York

Earl, M.J. (1990). Approaches to Strategic Information Systems Planning: experience in twenty-one UK companies, *Proceedings of the International Conference on Information Systems*, Copenhagen.

Earl, M.J. and Feeney, D.F. (1994). Is your CIO adding value?, *Sloan Management Review*, Spring, 11-20

Enns, H.G. and Huff, S.L. (1997). CIOs' influence on business strategy formulation and realization', *2nd AIS Conference*, Indianapolis, Indiana, Aug 15-17th

Galliers, R.D., Merali, Y. and Spearing, L. (1994) Coping with Information Technology? how british executives perceive the key issues in the mid 1990s, *Journal of Information Technology*, 9, 223-238

Grant, R. (1991). The Resource-based Theory of Competitive Advantage, *California Management Review* 33(3), pp.114-135

Hackney, R A (1996) Sustaining an Information Systems Strategy: a congruence of agenda model within UK local authorities, *UKAIS Proceedings*, Cranfield, April

Hackney R A and Little, S (1999) Opportunistic Strategy Creation: challenging IS planning, *European Journal of Information Systems*, 8(2), 119-126

Hackney, R A, Griffiths, G H and Burn, J. (1999) Strategic Information Systems Planning: Towards the Sustainability of Competitiveness, *BAM Proceedings*,September, 334-350.

Hall, R. (1993) A Framework Linking Intangible Resources and Capabilities to Sustain Competitive Advantage', *Strategic Management Journal*, 14 (8), 607-618

Henderson, J.C. and Venkatraman, N. (1993) Strategic Alignment: leveraging information technology for transforming organisations, *IBM Systems Journal*, 32, 4-16

Kearney, A.T. (1990) Barriers to the Successful Application of Information Technology, Department of Trade and Industry and CIMA, London

Keen, P.G.W. (1988) Competing in Time, Cambridge

Kettinger, W., Grover, V., Guha, S. and Segars, A. (1994) Strategic Information Systems Revisited: a study in sustainability and performance, *MIS Quarterly*, 31-58

King, W.R., Grover, V. and Hufnagel, E. H. (1989) Using Information and Information Technology for Sustainable Competitive Advantage', *Information and Management*, 17(2), 87-93

King, W.R. (1998) IT-Enhanced Productivity and Profitability, *Information Systems Management*, Winter, 64-66

Korunka, C., Weiss, A. and Karetta, B. (1993) Effects of New Technologies with Special Regard for the Implementation Process per-se, Journal of Organizational Behaviour, Vol. 14(4), 331-348

Lederer, A.L. and Mendelow, A.L. (1993). Information Systems Planning and the Challenge of Shifting Priorities, *Information and Management*, 24(6), 319-328

Lederer, A.L. and Salmela, H. (1996) Toward a Theory of Strategic Information Systems Planning, *Journal of Strategic Information Systems*, 5, 237-253

Lee, M.C.S. and Adams, D.A. (1990) A Manager's Guide to the Strategic Potential of Information Systems', *Information and Management* (Oct.) 169-182

Lieberman, M.B. and Montgomery, D.B. (1988) First Mover Advantages', *Strategic Management Journal*, Summer Special Issue, 9, 41-58

Lippman, S.A. and Rumelt, R.P. (1982) Uncertain Imitability: an analysis of inter-firm differences in efficiency under competition, *Bell Journal of Economics*, 13, Autumn, 418-438

Long, R. (1987) Human and Managerial Implications, New Office Information Technology, Croom Helm, London

Mahoney, J.T. and Pandian, J.R. (1992) The Resource-Based View Within the Conversation of Strategic Management, *Strategic Management Journal*, 13 (5), pp363-380

Mata, F.J., Fuerst, W.L. and Barney, J. (1995) Information Technology and Sustained Competitive Advantage: a resource-based analysis, *MIS Quarterly*, Dec., 487-505

McBride, N. (1998) Towards a Dynamic Theory of Strategic IS Planning, *UKAIS Proceedings*, Lincoln University, 15-17 April

McFarlan, F.W. (1984) Information Technology Changes the Way You Compete, *Harvard Business Review* Vol 62:3 (May-June), 98-103

McKee, D.O. and Varadarajan, P.R. (1995) Special Issue on Sustaining Competitive Advantage – introduction, *Journal of Business Research*, 33(2), 77-79

McKersie, R.B. and Walton, R.E. (1991) Organisational Change' In Scott-Morton (ed.) (1991) 'The Corporation of the 1990s: Information Technology and Organizational Transformation', OUP

Morley, L. (1991) Expense Account, *Computing*, 2 May, 18-19

Neumann, S. (1994) Strategic Information Systems, Macmillan College Publishing Company

Nolan, R. (1979), Managing the Crisis in Data Processing, *Harvard Business Review*, (Mar-April)

Papp, R (1999) Alignment of Business and Information Technology Strategy: How and why?, *Information Management*, Fall, 12(3/4).

Peppard, J. and Ward, J. (1998) Mind the Gap: diagnosing the relationship between the IT organisation and the rest of the business, *Journal of Strategic Information Systems*, 8(1), 29-60

Peteraf, P. (1993) The Cornerstones of Competitive Advantage: a resource-based view, *Strategic Management Journal*, 14(3), 179-191

Powell, T.C. and Dent-Micallef, A. (1997) Information Technology as Competitive Advantage: the role of human, business and technology resources', *Strategic Management Journal*, Vol. 18 (5), 375-405

Reed, R. and DeFillippi, R. (1990) Causal Ambiguity: barriers to imitation, and sustainable competitive advantage', *Academy of Management Review*, 15, 88-102

Reich, B.H. and Benbasat, I. (1990) An Empirical Investigation of Factors Influencing the Success of Customer-oriented Strategic Systems, *Information Systems Research*, 1(3), 325-347

Ross, J.W., Beath, C.M.and Goodhue, D. (1996) Develop Long-Term Competitiveness Through IT Assets', *Sloan Management Review*, Fall, 31-42

Rumelt, R.P. (1987) Theory, Strategy and Entrepreneurship'. In Teece, D. (ed.), The Competitive Challenge, Ballinger, Cambridge, MA, 137-158

Salmela, H., Lederer, A.L. and Reponen, T. (1997) Prescriptions for Information Systems in a Turbulent Environment, *ICIS 97 Conference Proceedings*, 356-368

Sambamurthy, V., Zmud, R.W. and Byrd, T.A. (1994) The Comprehensiveness of IT Planning Processes: a contingency approach, *Journal of Information Technology Management*, 5(1),1-10

Schmalensee, R. (1988) Industrial Economics: an overview, *Economic Journal*, 98, 643-681

Skok, W and Hackney R A (1999) Managing the Integration of Information Technology and Systems: reflections on the 'hybrid' debate, *Journal of Failures & Lessons Learned in IT Management*, 2(3), 59-65

Sillince, J.A.A. and Frost, C.E.B. (1995) Operational, Environmental and Managerial Factors in Non-alignment of Business Strategies and IS strategies for the Police Service in England and Wales, *European Journal of Information Systems*, 4, 103-115

Silver, M.S., Markus, M.L. and Beath, C. M. (1995) The IT Interaction Model: a foundation for the MBA core course', *MIS Quarterly*, 19(3), 361-390

Sullivan, C.H. (1985) Systems Planning in the Information Age, *Sloan Management Review* (Winter)

Tait, P. and Vessey, I. (1988) The Effect of User Involvement on System Success', MIS Quarterly, 12(1), 91-110

Taylor-Cummings, A. and Feeney, D.F. (1997) The Development and Implementation of Systems: bridging the user-IS gap'. In Willcocks, L., Feeney, D.F. and Islei,

G. (1997) *Managing IT as a Strategic Resource*, McGraw-Hill, 171-202 .

Teece, D (1990) Contributions and Impediments of Economic Analysis to the Study of Strategic management, in Fredrickson F (Eds) *Perspectives on Strategic Management*, Harper Business, Grand Rapidsm, MI, 185-219.

Venkatraman, N. (1997) Beyond Outsourcing: managing IT resources as a value centre', *Sloan Management Review*, Spring, 51-64.

Vitale, M.R. (1986) The Growing Risks of Information Systems Success, *MIS Quarterly* (10:4), December, 327-334.

Vitale, M.R., Ives,B. and Beath C.M. (1986) Linking Information Technology and Corporate Strategy: an organizational view'. In Maggi, L., Zmud, R. and Wetherbe, J. (eds.) (1986) *Proceedings of the Seventh International Conference on Information Systems*, San Diego, California, December 15-17.

Ward, J., Griffiths, P. (1996) Strategic Planning for Information Systems, John Wiley

Willcocks, L.P. and Lester, S. (1999) (Eds) *Beyond the IT Productivity Paradox*, Wiley

Wilson, T.D. (1989) The Implementation of Information Systems Strategies in UK Companies: aims and barriers to success, *International Journal of Information Management*, 9 (4), 245-258.

Wiseman, C. (1985) Strategy and Computers: Information Systems as Competitive Weapons Dow-Jones Irwin, Illinois.

Watson, R Hackney R A and McBride, N (2000) Out of Tune Out of Time: hermeneutics of strategic information systems planning, *UKAIS Proceedings*, Cardiff, April.

Whyte G, Bytheway A and Edwards C (1997) Understanding User Perceptions of Information Systems Success, *Journal of Strategic Information Systems*, Vol 6, 35-68.

Yap, C. and Thong, J.Y.L. (1997), Programme Evaluation of a Government Information Technology Programme for Small Businesses, *Journal of Information Technology*, 12, 107-120.

Zmud, R.W. and Apple,L.E. (1988) Measuring the Infusion of a Multi-Business Unit Innovation, Unpublished Working Paper, Florida State University.

Chapter X

Aligning IT Resources for E-Commerce

Makoto Nakayama
DePaul University, USA

ABSTRACT

The era of e-commerce requires firms to have a more sophisticated IT alignment model. Now IT strategy and business strategy (r)evolve together while firms' operating environments change more rapidly. In addition, the use of Web-based systems necessitates more frequent interaction both between IT management and IT users and between firms and their trading partners and customers. Consequently, firms must skillfully strike a balance between current and future business capabilities. They also must constantly readjust business and IT objectives considering their organizational needs and environmental needs. From the perspective of organizational learning loops, this chapter introduces a framework of IT resource alignment model to enable dynamic processes of IT alignment.

INTRODUCTION

Traditionally IT alignment was considered from the perspective of strategy and organizational structure. For example, McKenny et al. (1997) provide an historical account on how Bank of America (BoA) strived to become an industry leader by crafting its IT strategy when BoA was faced with operational crises. Their study illustrates how operational necessity leads a company to devise a new strategy followed by the adoption of IT innovations. Similarly, Baets (1996) describes a sequence where a new industry situation leads to a renewed corporate strategy triggering the alignment of IT strategy in the banking industry as a whole.

Those previous studies note that IT alignment used to follow business strategy, which had adapted to environmental changes. In other words, previous studies tend to assume that IT strategy and business strategy are given, separate entities.

However, such IT alignment perspective needs to be reconsidered in the e-commerce era when business and IT strategies intricately intertwine with each other and must adapt quickly to market changes. First, IT strategy may now shape a firm's business strategy rather than the other way around, because the IT function can drive a firm's value chain management, as information plays a critical role in the e-commerce era (Rayport & Sviokla, 1994, 1995). Notable examples are seen in financial brokerage (e.g., www.etrade.com, fundevaluator.fidelity.com), automobile distribution (e.g., www.carsdirect.com, www.carorders.com) and online customer service functions (e.g., product inquiry, technical support, complaints).

Second, we need to realize alignment must be done more dynamically because of the increased velocity of change in the market, business management and IT. In the 1970s and 1980s, companies had a few years for IT strategy implementation to react with anticipated business requirements. Now, in a period of six months contingencies occur where companies must realign IT strategy.

Third, the past view of alignment processes lacks the perspective of organizational capability that is enhanced through *organizational learning*, although Venkatraman et al. (1993) noted earlier the importance of IT capability in aligning IT strategy with business strategy. When a brick-and-mortar retailer realizes it should engage in e-commerce, it does not go far on just its initial ambition. To build an effective Web site, for example, the retailer must learn how to provide information, deliver service and manage the site at the corporate, business unit and individual levels. In other words, it needs the capability—a set of skills and resources at the organizational, functional and individual levels—to deploy a Web site successfully *and* sustain competitive advantage by continuously adjusting itself to rapid environmental changes. A key challenge is how to manage such process of IT capability enhancement while the organization attempts to align IT resources for moving targets.

Applying the double loop model of organizational learning (Argyris, 1977) and self-regulation theory (as referenced by Brett et al., 1999), this chapter introduces a framework that enables managers to focus on dynamically aligning four key foci of IT resources with firm strategy. The next section introduces what these four foci are and why they are important. The following section applies the framework in the context of supply chain management (SCM) and Web-based consumer transaction applications.

TOWARD A NEW MANAGERIAL FRAMEWORK FOR IT ALIGNMENT

Business models must change as the environment changes. We have seen successful companies with their successful business models struggle to renew their strategy and organization to adapt for a new environment. In the late 1980s and early 1990s, IBM went through a long corporate renewal process in which it has repositioned itself from a mainframe vendor to a solution provider for the client-server era.

What is different with the era of e-commerce is the accelerated pace of business environment changes and the increased velocity in which strategies must change.

For example, Hewlett-Packard (HP) recently recognized that it had been behind in so-called "Internet strategy" to exploit the e-commerce boom. This resulted in major business model reconfigurations including the replacement of its CEO and its divesture of the Test-and-Measurement Division. The change process undertaken by HP is much shorter than that of the previously mentioned IBM. A similar challenge is seen in SAP, the market leader of enterprise resource planning (ERP) system software. Recent reports indicate that SAP has also been caught behind in exploiting the Internet Revolution, and is investing heavily in catching up (Boudette, 2000).

E-commerce, in particular, is susceptible to quick environmental changes because changes in corporate Web sites—be they information publication or transaction procedures—are instantly seen by customers. With the ambition of exploiting the first-mover advantage, Amazon.com has aggressively formed alliances and/or had a majority/minority interest during the past few years with leading online retailers in different retailing sectors such as Drugstore.com (online drugstore), Gear.com (sporting goods), Pets.com (pet products and services), HomeGrocer.com (grocery retailing) and Della.com (gift registry and services). In the context of SCM, forming such interorganizational relationships usually adds complexity in managing the governance process of IT deployment (cf. Venkatraman et al., 1993).

When the firm's critical success factor lies in its ability to study the market quickly and to deliver products and services accordingly, how should the firm quickly realign its IT resources to new strategies and tactics?

The primary IT implication of this time-sensitive competitive environment is that a firm must nimbly manage the linkage between its *current* and *near-future* business operational needs so that it handles both its current operations while positioning itself for known or anticipated market changes.

For a technology company, the key decision is how to allocate resources between research & development (R&D) and development & engineering (D&E). R&D aims at long-term outcomes whereas D&E handles short-term product development issues. Once R&D sees a certain outcome, R&D transfers it to business units occasionally with R&D staff members in charge. Thus, R&D operations are generally "protected" from D&E operations.

On the other hand, IT alignment involves the investment (or dis-investment) decisions on both short-term and long-term resources. Moreover, it also concerns organizational IT skill capability, which influences how successful an IS implementation would be. The time when IT functions were exclusively assigned to an MIS department is long past. Now, new IT functions such as Web-based transaction processing and Web site management require active involvement of non-IS personnel (e.g., sales, marketing, logistics) who also have responsibility for other tasks.

When the IT function in the new era requires more coordination between the IS unit and non-IT units, the linkage between the current and future IT operations is not so clearly separated as it is in the relationship between R&D and D&E. This implies that the adoption of a new IT must involve more organizational processes at various managerial levels than before. As a result, the enhancement of organizational IT capability needs to be planned ahead and continuously readjusted at the organizational level as IT capability is actually used.

In addition, a firm must manage IT alignment not only internally but also *externally*. This is especially so with its trading partners. For example, EDI technology, be it traditional, objective-oriented or XML-based EDI systems, usually requires detailed coordination – what EDI standard(s) to use, how these standards are to be implemented, what and how product codes are used for EDI, what systems requirements and operator skills should be, and how they are to be maintained. Similarly, the success of extranet systems demands continuous collaboration between the firm and its trading partners at both technical and business process levels. Web-based consumer transactions require "collaboration" with consumers in the sense that a firm must know consumer profiles (demographics and their "Net" usage patterns) and establish "dialogue" processes with its customers.

This leads us to consider IT resource alignment strategy in terms of what firms currently *do* (operations) and what they *are* or *can be* (capability) for their internal and external business operations. In other words, IT resource alignment needs to be considered with four foci in two key dimensions: (1) operational vs. capability domain; and (2) external vs. internal domain (Table 1).

The upper left quadrant of Table 1 shows that one focus of IT alignment is how a firm aligns IT resources with its strategy for the current business operations *within*

Table 1: Four Key Foci of IT Resource Alignment

	Internal domain	External domain
Operational domain	*Internal Operational Focus* • aligning IT resources for the current business operations within the firm • alignment examples: short-term data/ information integration across business units, making IS interoperable among different business units	*External Operational Focus* • aligning IT resources for the current business operation across the organizational boundary • alignment examples: short-term implementation of SCM and web site (e.g., reducing bottlenecks of operational information flows with trading partners, collecting customer information)
Capability domain	*Internal Capability Focus* • aligning IT resources for building and maintaining the firm's capability in business operations within the firm to respond market changes • alignment examples: planning and implementing a new corporatewide IT infrastructure, integrating database systems corporatewide, coordinating IT skills between IS and other business units	*External Capability Focus* • aligning IT resources for building and maintaining units maintaining the firm's capability in business operations across its organizational boundary to respond to market changes • alignment examples: long-term implementation of SCM & web site (e.g., planning & implementing enterprise/customer relationship management programs), coordinating IT capability with trading partners, being ready for potential alliances (partner search, potential partner information)

the organization. At the same time, the firm also needs to manage IT alignment for the current operations *across* its organizational borders (the upper right quadrant in Table 1). Together, the two upper quadrants in Table 1 indicate that a firm must focus on IT alignment to realize effective outcomes from its business processes in the short term (e.g., 2 to 6 months).

The firm also manages its IT capability for the future business operations (e.g., 6 months and beyond), because IT capability gives the firm the flexibility to implement whatever strategy it decides to enact in the future. This IT capability is the sum total of its IT resources and skills that enable the firm to respond to market changes. Similar to the operational domain, the capability domain is managed both internally (the lower left quadrant in Table 1) and externally (the lower right quadrant). Building IT capability just internally is not sufficient, because business operations now inevitably involve IT linkages on external transactions with business partners and customers. These two additional IT alignment foci jointly play a critical role to determine how much strategic flexibility the firm will have down the road.

Altogether these four foci determine the parameters for managing a firm's IT alignment. How is IT alignment done within each focus?

For each focus, the firm must manage IT alignment by using a corresponding *alignment feedback (or control) loop*. A feedback loop is a continuous process of (1)

Figure 1: Four IT Resource Alignment Loops

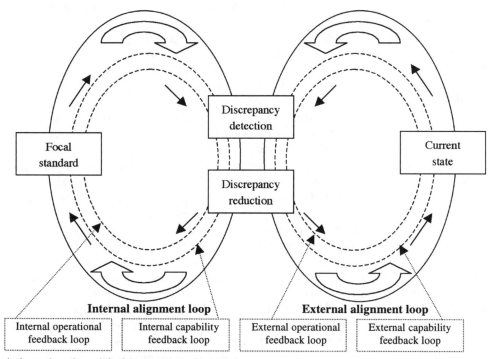

(adopted and modified in Brett et al., 1999)

discrepancy detection between what an IT alignment is supposed to be (focal standard) and what it actually is, and (2) subsequent act of *discrepancy reduction* to minimize harmful consequences and to make future IT alignment easier (Figure 1).

First, a firm needs to constantly scan its operating environment to know what its IT resources and strategy must be for effective *current external* business operations (external operational feedback loop). At the same time, a firm adjusts its IT resources and strategy to meet its *near-future external* operational needs (external capability feedback loop). Second, a firm must frequently reevaluate its IT resources and strategy to maximize the efficiency of *current internal* business operations (internal operational feedback loop) while managing IT resources and strategy for what its *near-future internal* business operations will likely require in the near future (internal capability feedback loop).

In Figure 1, two inner concentric loops in the left side (internal operational and internal capability feedback loops) enable—or constrain—what is done internally (operations) and what can be internally (capability) with IT resources for a firm's internal business operations. In the right side, the two inner loops similarly enable (or constrain) a firm' external operations and its organizational external capabilities.

The concept of two outer loops (internal and external alignment loops) is rooted in Argyris's (1977) double loop model of organizational learning. Argyris analyzed why firms often fail to change their management practice when it is not working. For example, although a firm recognizes that one of its main product lines is or will soon be failing, it may continue to depend on that product line because of its dysfunctional organizational behaviors. Such dysfunctional behaviors are often attributed to CEO's emotional attachment to the product line and/or organizational culture that abhors any deviations from the existing management practices.

Argyris suggests that a successful firm uses two loops of organizational learning, which is a process of detecting and correcting error. Such a firm questions not only how a product line should be manufactured and sold (single-loop learning) but also whether or nor it should have the product line in the first place (double-loop learning). Thus, a successful firm, for instance, questions not only how its current operations are done without using Web-based transactions but also what would be the consequences of not preparing for Web-based transactions.

Furthermore, self-regulation theory (as referenced by Brett et al., 1999) provides a rationale on the managerial effectiveness of feedback loops. For example, using adaptive self-regulation framework (Tsui & Ashford, 1994), Tsui et al. (1995) reported that the perceived effectiveness of managers is higher when they minimize the gap between their actions and stakeholders' expectations. Although the scope of such empirical studies is limited to expectation or "impression" management at this point, the theory gives a positive support for the utility of double-loop organizational learning.

Looking at the operational-capability dimension, the resource-based view (e.g., Barney, 1986) supplies a theoretical foundation for the concept of "capability." The resource-based view (RVB) considers that the variances in firm performance are based on variances in resources applied (what enables capability) and in capabilities (the potential of what the firm can do using those resources). Such resources and capabilities, for example, can be categorized into four domains: *financial* (e.g., equity capital, retained earnings), *physical resources* (e.g., machines, factories), *human resources* (e.g., experience, intelligence, wisdom of individuals) and *organizational* (team work, firm reputation) (Barney & Hesterly, 1996).

An important implication is that a firm is not likely to implement a strategy successfully unless it has sufficient capabilities to do so. For instance, although a brick-and-mortar firm devises an e-commerce strategy, the lack of capabilities will hamper its successful execution of such strategy; however, e-commerce becomes the norm.

Because of the increasing velocity and uncertainty of environmental change, it is critical for firms to properly manage a balance between what the firm's current business processes do and what organizational resources and skills could handle in some likely market scenarios.

APPLYING THE FRAMEWORK

This chapter considers how a firm can use the framework for supply chain management (SCM) and Web-based consumer transaction systems. Table 1 places both SCM and Web-based consumer transaction systems in the right-side column –that is, in the external domain. However, we will see that their successful implementation also depends on how IT strategy alignment is done in the internal domain.

IT alignment for SCM. SCM aims to streamline the total process of product/ service delivery with trading partners. For example, Cisco Systems now conducts 70-80% of its business online by leveraging its business operations with SCM (Sweeney, 1999).

The initial scope of SCM was geared toward simplifying logistics typically by using EDI technology. While logistics-based SCM shows improvements using such new technologies as Internet-based and XML-based EDI systems, recently SCM has broadened its scope to include sales, marketing and customer service. In particular, this trend is driven by major vendors of enterprise resource planning (ERP) systems such as SAP, People Soft and Oracle. These vendors started providing integrated cross-functional solutions by combining their ERP systems with EDI systems and (enterprise-level) knowledge-based systems.

Notwithstanding this technology advancement, technology alone rarely guarantees business success. Cisco's success was realized because it aligned its internal IT strategy by streamlining internal operations and managing its IT capabilities.[1] The total throughput of transactional information processing between two parties depends on how efficiently transactional information is processed not only between the parties but also within each firm. Without the smooth internal flows of management information, SCM information does not efficiently flow between two firms.

Using the framework, Table 2 summarizes how firms can fully exploit potentials of IT for SCM with the proposed managerial framework.

For the current internal operations, there are two critical issues a firm needs to handle before it can successfully implement SCM. First, a firm should cut the number of steps and shorten the lead-time for various operations that involve different

Table 2: IT Resource Alignment for Supply Chain Management

	Internal domain	External domain
Operational domain	• streamline operational processes across functional areas • make data/information exchanges interoperable across different functional units • enable IS to interoperate across functional areas (e.g., accounting IS, sales IS, warehouse IS, etc.)	• remove bottlenecks of data/ information flows in cross-organizational operational processes • modify IT infrastructure (e.g., platforms) to minimize IT costs for the firm and its partner
Capability domain	• adopt or enhance the firm's intranet to increase its operational efficiency within the organization • integrate IT platforms • integrate databases	• coordinate partner IT skill building • adopt extranet systems • manage (potential or existing) channel conflicts • conduct feasibility studies on new IT tools (e.g., XML-EDI)

functional areas such as inbound logistics, manufacturing, sales, and accounting. An initiation of business process reengineering (BPR) is certainly an excellent way to accomplish such an objective. However, given the high levels of required commitment and risk with BPR, a firm may elect to start making interoperable internal managerial data (e.g., part inventory, product inventory, account receivables). At the very least, a firm can initiate a feasibility study on the current status of internal data flows and their formats, and aim towards their standardization.

This leads to the second issue: a firm must enable their internal IS to interoperate across different functional areas. In other words, the firm should not only make data exchanges between different systems interoperable but also coordinate or consolidate two or more systems. Priority should be given to a few critical operational areas. If a firm's core competency lies in manufacturing, the firm should start out with IS interoperation between inbound logistics and manufacturing.

Closely related efforts must be made for the firm's near-future operational needs, or the firm's capability building. To streamline a firm's operations, the adoption of an intranet may be helpful. For organizing the flow of managerial information, a firm will also want to manage a portfolio of hardware platforms and major software systems. One successful method is reducing the number of major hardware and software platforms. Similarly, a firm will want to centralize important managerial data into one or a few database systems. The crucial dilemma often lies in a trade-off between legacy system integration and its costs.

Operational and capability domains are not independent. They are interdependent managerial foci in which management allocates resources for the current and future operations. The importance of the proposed framework lies in its role to guide management's focus onto a few most important strategic decisions—that is, to focus on striking a balance between the present and the future.

While aligning IT strategy internally is one challenge for SCM, aligning IT strategy externally is equally important and challenging.

The first task is to establish the flows of trading information (e.g., order, order inquiry, account payables) between trading partners. Whereas the purchaser is the final user in the business-to-consumer (B2C) transactions, business-to-business (B2B) transactions involve more functional units: information exchanged between buyer's inbound logistics and seller's sales/marketing department, between buyer's inbound logistics and accounting department, between buyer's and seller's accounting departments, and so forth.

The more complicated the exchanges, the higher the number of products traded, and the higher the frequency of orders, the more critical the buyer and the seller streamline their cross-organizational operational processes. It is important to note that this streamlining process must first examine how entire business processes can be simplified (i.e., BPR) rather than which part of trade exchanges can be done electronically.

Another external operational issue is to optimize IT infrastructure between the buyer and seller sides. For a firm that uses EDI systems with its buyers, a critical IT management decision considers what is the best way to minimize the current transactional costs given the variances of EDI capability among its buyers. For example, is it best to enforce traditional EDI with all partners, or to use traditional EDI with larger, IT-capable partners and browser-based or fax-based EDI for smaller, less IT-capable partners?

Moreover, the firm that wants to leverage SCM must build its IT capabilities not just for the present but also for the near future. For starters, this firm will want to map IT-skills of all its trading partners and to coordinate partner IT skill building with them. The firm also can adopt an extranet solution if it recognizes a disparity of IT skills among its business partners. For emerging technologies such as XML, it needs to review the technologies and conduct feasibility studies in case some technologies appear to become a major force. Finally, the firm must manage existing or potential channel conflicts that arise from the use of IT. Indeed, an industry-wide study on IT-enabled grocery retail distribution notes that one of the biggest challenges for such an effort is building trust-based relationships between partners partly because SCM involves sharing of sensitive information (Joint Industry Project on ECR, 1995). The issues of channel conflict are discussed further in the following section on Web-based consumer transaction applications.

As in the internal domain, the external operational focus and the external capability focus are closely related to each other. They are also closely interrelated with the internal operational focus and the internal capability focus.

Today's pace of new technology introductions requires IS managers to learn constantly new technologies and manage often confusing interrelationships between old and new systems. Such complex situations can easily distract management and cause difficulty in setting the right priorities. The proposed framework aims to direct managers' attention to the most critical aspect of IT strategy alignment – striking a balance between four foci.

One example of SCM is seen in the history of Efficient Consumer Response (ECR), an industry-wide SCM initiative in retail grocery distribution channels. Although ECR predated today's e-commerce hype, the experience of ECR gives useful insights on how the four foci of IT alignment may differentiate successful from less successful firms.

In the early 1990s, the industry welcomed ECR with high hopes that it would drastically reduce channel excess inventories and increase product sales by utilizing storefront marketing information that EDI systems provide. ECR's positive impacts are well documented in firms such as H. E. Butt (HEB) Grocery Company (Clark & Croson, 1994), Campbell Soup (Clark, 1994), and Proctor & Gamble (Clark, 1995). However, these studies also show that ECR requires complex coordination both within a firm and between trading partners at operational, managerial and technical levels. For example, HEB led an effort of internal IS upgrading and integration slightly ahead of its external IS integration efforts (cf. Clark & Croson, 1994). More important, HEB's internal and external IS developments evolved together as HEB crafted its business strategy on ECR. Also HEB managed its growth by balancing the current IT operations and IT capability building for the near future.

We can see a similar evolution pattern of IT use in apparel distribution channels with another industry-wide initiative called Quick Response (QR) in the late 1980s. Implementation of a new IT-enabled SCM strategy required interorganizational, interfunctional and intra-functional coordination (cf. Hammond, 1992).

The key lesson learned from ECR and QR is that the growth of business must be based on a right business strategy supported by the well-balanced IT implementation in the four key foci of IT strategy alignment.

IT alignment for Web-based consumer transaction systems. Today, "going online" is the mantra for many retailers. The proportion of online purchasers, indeed, has steadily increased across a variety of product items; it is estimated that 17 million U.S. households will be shopping online by the end of 1999 (Zellner et al., 1999).

Setting up a Web site seems easier, as a number of retailers have already established their Web presence, be it a one-page Web site or a sophisticated database-driven Web site. Nevertheless, recent reports indicate that many commercial Web sites are noted for unreliable information and the lack of service or follow-up (e.g., Webber, 1999). The causes of such system implementations are not just the result of poor Web site designs but rather inadequate managerial attention to the four key foci of IT strategy alignment (Table 3).

When a firm wants to initiate a Web-based customer transaction system, the first obvious task is to institute a Web infrastructure. The firm can either build the Web infrastructure in-house or outsource it entirely. Regardless, this infrastructure must be scalable not only because Web access is instant once the Web is set up but also because the firm must be prepared for a rapid growth in Web site use provided that the site design attracts a sufficient number of visitors. At the same time, it is crucial that the Web development team in charge coordinate key functional areas (e.g., marketing, marketing communications, sales) to prepare them for handling customer inquiries, especially via email. Furthermore, this Web development team should create and distribute an initial milestone plan to the key managers in the firm. Lastly, information exchanges must become interchangeable across different business functional units. Top IS management needs to be aware of what information exchanges must be standardized across the firm and start planning on how the standardization may be accomplished.

While the above tasks are geared toward the current internal business operations, the firm must also examine how it can enhance its internal capability to scale up and take advantage of the Web-based online customer transaction systems.

The adoption of an intranet facilitates the processing of online customer transactions, because it makes easier to handle customer inquiries and orders across different functional units. Moreover, intranet adoption would create a synergy for IS development and management between intranet and extranet systems. With or without an intranet, the firm must integrate those database systems that act as the engine of these intranet and extranet systems. In addition, it is advisable that the firm start organizing its computing platforms such as Web servers, network servers, database systems, Web authorization tools all across business units early on.

Another important issue for internal capability enhancement is the education of key functional personnel, especially sales and marketing. The Web as a medium differs from other media such as paper-based product documentation, radio and television. Customers can seek out companies and products much more easily. The Web can dynamically interact with customers by using Web personalization technology; depending on customer profiles, the firm can present tailor-made information to customers according to the preferences set by the firm and/or its customers. Sales and marketing personnel can instantly publish and modify the content of the Web site by using text, graphic, 3-D and sound elements. At the same time, the Web has limitations especially in its communication bandwidths regarding graphic resolution and downloading speed. It takes organizational learning to understand the nature of Web medium, to create effective Web content, and to be able to update it with reasonable frequency before customers feel the Web site is not providing up-to-date, useful information. This learning process is organizational not only because the Web content depends on the joint work of different functional units but also because the support and follow-up of customer transactions require multi-functionally coordinated efforts.

Unlike traditional IS, Web-based customer transaction systems are externally oriented. Their impact first appears outside the organization if at all. Therefore, the firm must examine IT strategy alignment with its Web system from the standpoint of the external domain.

It is vital that a firm collects information on its current customer profiles. While the firm can trace site visitors' page access sequence using "cookies," the firm can also collect more detailed information (e.g., address, profession, user needs) from customers who purchase something from the site when they fill out purchase order form online. This information collection, nonetheless, must be fairly selective;

otherwise, customers feel that their privacy is invaded and that they are forced to participate in a survey. Finally, a firm should poll current customers to find out how satisfied they are with the Web service the firm offers.

The information collected must be organized, analyzed and *used* to make the Web site more effective. Here, we are getting into a new era where the line between IS management and other business functions is blurred. Unlike the previous era, part of Web-based IT strategy alignment is "marketing" of what IS (i.e., Web site) can do for customers. Yet, customers do not distinguish between how IT *functions* and how the *content* of the Web site serves them (or doesn't).

The last area that needs our attention is how to build the firm's capability in the external domain. There are two key tasks to be done with this IT alignment focus. First, the firm must plan and implement customer relationship management (CRM) programs. Once the firm starts collecting customer information in a systematic manner, it is imperative to transform that information into customer knowledge by using data warehousing software tools.

The use of a Frequently-Asked-Questions (FAQs) page is particularly effective for Web-based customer transaction systems. Many customers usually have similar questions which may comprise the majority of customer inquiries. Microsoft, for example, is a sophisticated user of customer technical support knowledge bases to manage a potentially very large number of customer inquiries (*cf.* msdn.microsoft.com).

Customers have found that Internet searches are frequently a time-consuming and frustrating experience. Companies such as Dell Computers and Office Depot apply Ask Jeeves' natural-language approach (Sweeny, 1999). CRM may also be effectively done with a combination of their Web site, telephone hotlines and face-to-face communication with customers.

In short, CRM is a key driver for organizational learning to enable dynamic IT strategy alignment with the four foci, because it makes the feedback loops work.

Second, the firm needs to anticipate the issue of channel conflict. Web-based transaction systems can enable companies in the upper stream of marketing channels to sell their products to end-users by bypassing their down-stream channel partners. For example, Home Depot recently planned to sell its product online. Having found that its suppliers also planned to go online, Home Depot sent them letters to warn them of the consequences of selling online (Nathan, 1999). Another example of "conflict" is the relationship between Avon Products and its sales reps with their Web page use. Avon asked its entrepreneurial reps, who set up their own Web sites to sell Avon products, to stop selling Avon products from their personal Web sites, because Avon wanted to control its corporate image (Kalin, 1998).

Other firms with similar situations take different approaches. While HP (www.hp.com) sells its product online, it also gives Web site visitors a directory of local retailers. Nordstrom.com encourages their suppliers to set up Web pages that specifically relate to the merchandise on Nordstrom.com (Nathan, 1999).

While there is no one "right" way to solve channel conflicts, the firm must anticipate potential destructive conflicts and take appropriate measures before they surface. As is the case of SCM, it is imperative that the firm work out the "soft

Table 3: IT Resource Alignment for Web-Based Customer Transaction Systems

	Internal domain	External domain
Operational domain	• create an initial mile-stone plan • set up & maintain a (scalable) web infrastructure for commerce • organize key functional areas for handling online transactions • make information exchanges interoperable across different functional units	• work with service providers to speed up implementation and to contain costs • collect online customer information • poll customer satisfaction information
Capability domain	• adopt or enhance the firm's intranet to facilitate web-based customer purchase • educate sales/marketing personnel • integrate databases	• plan & implement customer relationship management (CRM) programs • manage (potential or existing) sales channel conflicts

issues" such as commitment, trust and cultural differences with its channel partners. A failure to do so can jeopardize long-term success even though the other actors are positive. Also the firm must constantly scan its operating environment, and it should be willing to change, if appropriate, its organizational goals and strategy.

Therefore, the double-loop feedback approach in which the firm manages itself by evaluating both its own organizational and environmental situations is particularly relevant for putting channel conflicts under control.

In summary, Table 3 suggests to the firm that it manage IT resource alignment by striking a balance between external and internal operational needs as well as between current and future operational needs. To do so, the firm needs to utilize the four feedback loops: the internal operational, internal capability, external operational and external capability feedback loops.

CONCLUSION

Aligning IT resources with strategy and firm operation is not a one-time task but a continuous learning process. To cope with the rapidly changing e-commerce environment, a firm needs to scan its environment, learn the changing trends quickly and modify its organizational goals, if necessary, for current and/or future business operations. At the same time, it must examine its own organizational capability to fully exploit the potential of IT.

To effectively counter or even leverage these changes, the firm must plan ahead and build organizational IT capability for strategic business applications from short-term and/or long-term perspectives. To do so, the suggested framework helps managers to keep striking the right balance between current and future organizational needs as well as between internal and external organizational requirements. Thereby, the framework enables the firm to dynamically respond to such environmental changes and thrive by leveraging IT.

For IT researchers, the framework provides useful research foci. One focus would be how successful firms align IT resources and strategy by looking at what they do and what will they need to do in the future. Another focus would be how these successful firms dynamically manage their internal and external situations.

ENDNOTES

1. In fact, Cisco Systems has been noted for its effective Intranet use (*cf.* CIO *Web Business Magazine* 1997, 1998, 1999).

REFERENCES

Argyris, C. (1977). Double Loop Learning in Organizations. *Harvard Business Review*, 55 (5): 115-124.

Baets, W. R. J. (1996). Some empirical evidence on IS strategy alignment in banking. *Information & Management*, 30(4): 155-177.

Barney, J. B. (1986). Strategic factor markets: expectations, luck, and business strategy. *Management Science*, 42: 1231-41.

Barney, J. B., & Hesterly, W. (1996). Organizational Economics: Understanding the Relationship between Organizations and Economic Analysis. in *Handbook of Organization Studies*, S. R. Clegg, C. Hardy and W. R. Nord (eds.): 115-147. Thousand Oaks, CA: SAGE Publications.

Boudette, N. E. (2000, January 18). How a Software Titan Missed the Internet Revoluition. *Wall Street Journal*.

Brett, J. F., Northcraft, G. B., & Pinkley, R. L. (1999). Stairways to heaven: An interlocking self-regulation model of negotiation. *Academy of Management Review*, 24(3): 435-451.

Chan, Y. E, Huff, S. L., Barclay, D. W., & Copeland, D. G. (1997). Business strategic orientation, information systems strategic orientation, and strategic alignment. *Information Systems Research*, 8(2): 125-150.

CIO Web Business Magazine. (1997, August). WebMaster - 50/50 Intranet Winners. Available: http://www.cio.com/archive/webbusiness/080197_intranet.html [1999, October 13].

CIO WebBusiness Magazine. (1998, July 1). Intranet Winners - WebBusiness 50/50. Available: http://www.cio.com/archive/webbusiness/070198_intranet_winners.html [1999, October 13].

CIO WebBusiness Magazine. (1999, July 1) 3rd Annual 50/50 1999 Winners. Available: http://www.cio.com/archive/webbusiness/070199_intrawinners.html [1999, October 13].

Clark, T. H. (1994). Campbell Soup Company: A Leader in Continuous Replenishment Innovations. *Harvard Business School Case* No. 9-195-124.

Clark, T. H. (1995). Proctor & Gamble: Improving Consumer Value Through Process Redesign. *Harvard Business School Case* No. 9-195-126.

Clark, T. H., & Croson, D. C. (1994). H. E. Butt Grocery Company: A Leader in ECR Implementation. *Harvard Business School Case* No. 9-195-125.

Hammond, J. (1992). Coordination as the Basis for Quick Response: A Case for "Virtual" Integration in Supply Networks. *Harvard Business School Working Paper* #92-007.

Joint Industry Project on ECR and Kurt Salmon Associates. (1995). *ECR 1994 Progress Report*. Joint Industry Project on Efficient Consumer Response.

Kalin, S. (1998, Feb. 1). Conflict Resolution. *CIO WebBusiness Magazine*, Available: http://www.cio.com/archive/webbusiness/020198_sales.html [1999, October 13].

Nathan, S. (1999, August 26). Defining the seller in on-line market. *USA Today*.

Rayport, J. F., & Sviokla, J. J. (1994). Managing in the Marketspace. *Harvard Business Review*, 72(6): 141-150.

Rayport, J. F., and J. J. Sviokla. (1995) Exploiting the Virtual Value Chain. *Harvard Business Review*, 73(6): 75-85.

Sweeny, D. (1999, Sept. 1). Calling All Web Sites. *CIO WebBusiness Magazine*, Available: http://www.cio.com/archive/webbusiness/090199_power.html [1999, October 13].

Sweeney, S. (1999). The Road Ahead. *Business and Management Practices*, 248(7): S1-S4.

Tsui, A. S., & Ashford, S. J. (1994). Adaptive self-regulation: A process view of managerial effectiveness. *Journal of Management*, 20(1): 93-121.

Tsui, A. S., Ashford, S. J., St. Clair, L., & Xin, K. R. (1995). Dealing with discrepant expectations: Response strategies and managerial effectiveness. *Academy of Management Journal*, 38(6): 1515-1543.

Venkatraman, N., Henderson, J. C., Oldach, S. (1993) Continuous strategic alignment: Exploiting information technology capabilities for competitive success. *European Management Journal*, 11(2): 139-149.

Webber, A. (1999, Sept 21). E-commerce is almost perfect ... 'cept when it's not. *USA Today*.

Zellner, W., Forest, S. A., Morris, K., & Lee, L. (1999, Sept 6). The big guys go online. *Business Week*, 30-32.

Chapter XI

Competitive Force/ Marketing Mix (CF/MM) Framework

Brian J. Reithel, University of Mississippi, USA
Chi Hwang, California State Polytechnic University-Pomona, USA
Katherine Boswell, Univesity of Mississippi, USA

ABSTRACT

Information systems researchers continue to grapple with the development of frameworks to aid managers in the identification of opportunities for the strategic use of information technology. Many of the current frameworks have been proposed to guide the systems development process, but few have successfully dealt with the underlying business issues that drive the need to develop an information system in the first place. Because the difficulties that a particular business must cope with arise from the distinctive characteristics of the firm, its product and the particular niche in which the firm operates, this chapter presents a two-dimensional COMPETITIVE FORCE/MARKETING MIX (CF/MM) framework that can be used to recognize opportunities for strategic information systems within the firm's niche. The CF/MM framework is based on a combination of Porter's view of strategy as a response to the unique mix of the five competitive forces faced by a firm, and the firm's marketing strategy. By using the CF/MM framework, managers and researchers can identify opportunities to use emerging information technologies as part of front-line competitive strategy. After presentation of the CF/MM framework, the chapter presents a summary of the results of a CF/MM-based analysis of 150 articles related to the competitive use of information technology that have been published in both the popular press and scholarly press. Organizations that are successful in creatively focusing the use of the expanding array of modern information technologies on their particular business niche will increase their ability to survive in the dynamic business environment of the year 2000 and beyond. The CF/MM framework can also be used by IS managers to orchestrate the mix of applications held by a firm in order to maximize the strategic impact of IT investments.

INTRODUCTION

"Knowledge is Power." In the modern business environment, where "total information war" (Toffler, 1990, p. 153) rages across the world economy, the ultimate competitive edge is a result of better and wider access to information. Those organizations capable of developing better internal and/or external information systems flourish, while others fail. A strategic information system changes the basis of competition between firms; such systems either provide better support of typical organizational units (sales, purchasing, etc.) or provide new information-based services to customers. Some of the types of competitive advantage that can result from strategic information systems include short-term gains from being the market innovator, the ability to lock-in customers and/or suppliers, and the ability to change the basis of competition (Laudon and Laudon, 1991).

Many previous studies document the use of strategic information systems in large business organizations (Beath, 1986; *Business Week*, 1983; Canning, 1984; Cash and Konsynski, 1985; *Computerworld*, 1985; Copeland and McKenney, 1988; Cushman, 1989; Johnston and Vitale, 1988; McFarlan, 1984), but very few exist that offer a truly niche-driven approach to identifying opportunities for the strategic use of information technology. One of the better studies related to the strategic use of information systems offered a three-dimensional framework linking Porter's (1980) generic competitive strategies with competitive targets and organizational activities (Bergeron and Raymond, 1992). However, many of the difficulties that businesses must cope with arise from the distinctive characteristics of the firm and the particular environment in which it operates. As a result of the uniqueness associated with each firm's predicament, it may be quite difficult for managers to apply the generic strategies used in Bergeron and Raymond's (1992) framework to the task of developing competitive strategies and strategic information systems. According to Porter (1980), competitive strategy can be thought of as:

> ...taking offensive or defensive actions to create a defendable position in an industry, to cope successfully with the five competitive forces and thereby yield a superior return on investment for the firm. Firms have discovered many different approaches to this end, and *the best strategy for a given firm is ultimately a unique construction reflecting its particular circumstances* (1980, p.34; emphasis added).

Therefore, this chapter will present a two-dimensional framework that can be used to *identify opportunities* for strategic information systems based on (1) Porter's view of strategy as a response to the unique mix of the five competitive forces faced by individual firms, and (2) marketing strategy. A firm's marketing strategy is the particular mix of product, price, promotion, and place (distribution/delivery) used to respond to a specific target market. The next section of this chapter will review previous research on strategic information systems, competitive strategies, and marketing strategies. After the review, the chapter will present the Competitive Force/Marketing Mix (CF/MM) framework and a discussion of its use as an exploration and evaluation tool for identifying opportunities to use information technology in a strategic manner. After that, the chapter presents a summary of the results of a CF/MM-based analysis of published cases documenting the use of information technology for competitive advantage that have appeared in the scholarly and popular press. Finally, the chapter ends with recommendations for future use of the CF/MM framework by managers and information technology researchers.

BACKGROUND

Frameworks for the Identification of Opportunities for Strategic Use of IT: The shift toward significant use of information systems as a competitive weapon is a direct result of organizational changes in thinking about strategic planning and theory (Bakos and Treacy, 1986; Clemons, 1986; Ives and Learmonth, 1984; Johnston and Carrico, 1988; King, 1978; Lederer and Mendelow, 1988; McFarlan, 1984; Miron, Cecil, Bradcich, and Hall, 1988; Porter, 1985; Porter and Millar 1985; Rackoff, Wiseman, and Ullrich, 1985). Interest in the strategic use of IT has led to numerous frameworks for the identification of opportunities for competitive advantage. These frameworks have been used by researchers and practitioners to improve organizations' awareness of the potential uses of IT for competitive advantage, help them classify existing applications, and allow the evaluation of their strategic planning (Bergeron et al., 1991; Lee and Adams, 1990).

Among these frameworks, some provide a general conceptualization that promotes strategic thinking at an abstract level; e.g., competitive forces (Porter, 1980), strategic opportunity matrix (Benjamin et al., 1984), and strategic grid (McFarlan and McKenney, 1983). Others are more focused on a specific competitive strategy that only covers a small subset of strategic applications; e.g., strategic thrust (Wiseman, 1988), electronic integration (Benjamin and Scott Morton, 1988), and the consumer resource life cycle (Ives & Learmonth, 1984). Very few frameworks exist that offer a truly *niche-driven* approach that identifies a wide range of specific business areas in which IT can be employed to gain competitive advantage. Porter (1985) utilized the concept of the "value chain" to identify opportunities for competitive advantage by examining the entire process of product design, development, production, external logistics, marketing, and sales. Bergeron and Raymond (1992) linked Porter's (1980) generic competitive strategies (i.e., differentiation, cost, growth), Wiseman's (1988) strategic targets (i.e., suppliers, competitors, clients), and organizational activities (inventory control, production, order entry, etc.) to generate more specific IT applications in various business functions for competitive advantage. However, a recent study (Segars and Grover, 1994) indicates that traditional frameworks suffer from significant shortcomings in providing general guidelines for identifying strategic opportunities within specific industry structures.

This chapter presents an alternative framework that focuses on the linkage between a firm's marketing practices and its formulation of strategies to deal with the competitive forces in its industry. The framework is structured to offer a mechanism for identifying a reasonably wide range of opportunities for the competitive use of IT that are targeted on a specific market niche in a specific industry. The structure of the framework is built on two widely accepted concepts: Porter's (1980) five competitive forces and McCarthy's (1960) four Ps marketing mix.

Five Competitive Forces: According to Porter (1980), a firm's competitive strategy within a particular industry is driven by five primary forces: (1) threat of new entrants, (2) rivalry among existing firms in that industry, (3) threat of substitute products and/or services, (4) bargaining power of suppliers, and (5) bargaining power of buyers (customers). To create competitive advantages, firms respond to these forces in several ways. To deter new entrants from coming into an existing industry, a firm erects *barriers to entry* by cultivating proprietary, unique, or capital-intensive resources (such as information technology). In many industries, the rivalry among existing competitors is a primary driving force that firms respond to by attempting to *differentiate* their products/services from a competitor's products/services through tactics such as advertising, price competition, new product offerings, and customer service. Information technology can clearly be used to help a firm differentiate itself within its market niche.

To deal with the threat of substitute products, a firm must identify the function of its products/services and *scan the environment* for industries whose products duplicate the firm's offering in terms of *functionality*. Once a substitute has been identified, the firm must decide whether or not to compete via differentiation. Many times, competition with substitute products requires a collective response from the entire industry rather than actions by an individual firm. Once again, information technology could be employed to respond to the threat of substitution by enabling environmental scanning or supporting a change in product functionality.

In terms of the bargaining power of suppliers, a firm must strive to maintain profitability despite the downward pressure on profit from threats by suppliers to raise prices or lower quality. A firm can respond to these pressures by engaging in backward integration or *minimizing switching costs* so that the firm can move to new suppliers easily should a previous supplier attempt to abuse their relationship.

The final competitive force that a firm must deal with is the bargaining power of buyers (i.e., customers). A firm typically can best increase its strategic position by engaging in careful *buyer selection*. This refers to identifying customers who need the firm's products but possess less power to influence the profitability of the firm

Table 1: Competitive Forces and Organizational Response Summary (Porter, 1980).

Threat of new entrants:	*erect barriers to entry*
Rivalry among existing firms:	*differentiation*
Threat of substitute products:	*scan for duplicate functionality and change functionality of the firm's products/services if necessary*
Bargaining power of suppliers:	*minimize switching costs, consider backward integration*
Bargaining power of buyers:	*careful customer/buyer selection*

through unreasonable price or quality demands. The successful identification of both buyers and suppliers could also be supported/enabled through the application of information technology. A summary of the five competitive forces and the organizational response is provided in Table 1.

These five determinants of a firm's competitiveness provide a solid base upon which the firm can formulate marketing strategies. This concept has been widely understood and accepted by many managers and has been employed in the construction of many previous frameworks, such as Porter and Millar's information intensity matrix (1985), Wiseman's strategic thrust (1988), and McFarlan's strategic resource model (1984). However, the use of the five competitive forces model, by itself, would result in a decision-making framework that has an outward orientation and would thus generate strategic opportunities focused on external systems (Barrett and Konsynski, 1982; Bergeron et al., 1991; Lee and Adams, 1990). A more balanced framework needs to consider another vital dimension: an organization's internal strategic operations.

Four Ps (Marketing Mix): McCarthy's (1960) four P's marketing mix is the other polar concept of the framework developed by the current chapter. A marketing mix is a particular combination of product, price, promotion, and place designed to enhance sales to a target market. Many organizations use marketing strategy as a primary method to organize resources and respond to the firm's competitive environment (McCarthy and Perreault, 1990; Pride and Ferrell, 1989). An effective marketing strategy always identifies the target market for the firm's products or services along with a marketing mix designed to appeal to that market. The four marketing mix components are listed in Table 2.

By varying components of the marketing mix, a firm can more effectively compete in its industry, ensuring organizational survival and profitability. The embedded marketing concept is not limited merely to the selling of goods and services, but encompasses every facet of the organization's internal operations as

Table 2: Marketing Mix Components (McCarthy and Perreault, 1990, p. 37)

*	Product	physical good, service, features, quality level, accessories, installation, instructions, warranty, product lines, packaging, and branding;
*	Price	objectives, flexibility, level over product lifecycle, geographic terms, discounts, and allowances;
*	Promotion	objectives, promotion blend, salespeople (kind, number, selection, training, motivation), advertising (targets, kinds of ads, media type, copy thrust, prepared by whom), sales promotion, and publicity;
*	Place	objectives, channel type, market exposure, kinds of middlemen, kinds and locations of stores, how to handle transporting and storing, service levels, recruiting middlemen, and managing channels.

demonstrated by the detailed listing given in Table 2. Consequently, marketing strategy can be used to arrange all organizational responses in a synergistic manner to respond to the forces of the competitive environment.

Because the concept of marketing mix is one of the most fundamental ideas of marketing, it has long been used in information systems designed to support the formulation of marketing strategy (Brien and Stafford, 1988; Crissy and Mossman, 1977; Higby and Farah, 1991; Li et al., 1993; McLeod and Rogers, 1982). Obviously, information technology can be a part of, or help facilitate, the successful implementation of a firm's marketing mix.

The CF/MM Framework: The Competitive Force/Marketing Mix matrix, as shown in Figure 1, is a two-dimensional matrix linking a firm's marketing mix(es) with the competitive forces in the industry that the firm must cope with in order to succeed. Because the concept of the five competitive forces stresses a firm's *external environment* and the market mix concentrates on the firm's *internal strategy formulation*, the row/column intersections provide a *context* in which the firm can identify opportunities for the use of information technology as an integral part of the firm's competitive strategy within its particular market niche. The adaptation to a particular niche, and the application of information technology to survival within that niche, fuels the competitive advantage needed to survive the "niche economies and niche warfare" (Schwartz and Toffler, 1993, p. 64) of the late 20th and early 21st centuries.

In order to apply the CF/MM matrix to identify strategic applications for a particular organization, the responses to the competitive forces listed in Table 1 must be considered for each component of the marketing mix listed in Table 2. For example, the intersection of the competitive force "Threat of new entrants" and the marketing mix component "Price" would indicate that an effective cost management and pricing system could be used as a barrier to entry to deter potential entrants. This type of system has been used by companies such as Wal-Mart

Figure 1. Competitive Forces/Marketing Mix (CF/MM) framework.

	Product	Price	Promotion	Place
Threat of new entrants				
Rivalry among existing firms				
Threat of substitute products/services				
Bargaining power of suppliers				
Bargaining power of buyers				

(Business Week, 1992) to erect a *formidable barrier to entry* against other potential discount retailers such as Sears (Berg, 1988). In the context of the intersection between "Rivalry among existing firms" and "Place", a strategic application of IT would change the way a company's products or services are delivered in order to differentiate its offering from the competition's. One example of this type of application is that of MedExpress, a Memphis, Tennessee company that provides the results of medical testing to doctors and hospitals via electronic means rather than using the postal service or other parcel services (Elkjer, 1988). Other examples could be drawn from the exploding number of applications of the Internet (such as the World Wide Web) as a means of changing the "Place" in which a business transaction takes place.

The next section of this chapter will present a summary of the results of a study of 157 published cases documenting systems that have been used for competitive advantage. The summary includes a mapping of the strategic uses of these systems into the CF/MM framework. The case analysis demonstrates the usefulness of the framework as a means of mapping applications into the CF/MM matrix. Furthermore, the analysis results reliably reflect the differences in the patterns of strategic use of IT in different system types within different industries. Finally, the results suggest a larger pattern of the current use of IT for competitive advantage across multiple industries.

CASE ANALYSIS

In order to examine the usefulness of the CF/MM framework as a tool for identifying opportunities for IT applications for competitive advantage, an analysis of cases documenting the use of information technology as a competitive weapon was undertaken.

Case/System Profile: A total of 157 systems were drawn from articles related to the competitive use of IT and published in both popular press and the scholarly press between 1988 and 1999. Most of the selected systems represent relatively new IT applications in 141 companies. Table 3 shows that, of the 157 cases, 80 (51 percent) are in product-related industries and 77 (49 percent) are in service-related industries.

Case Review Process: During the analysis process, each application/case was summarized with a brief synopsis and was categorized into the CF/MM framework by placing an "X" into each cell of the framework that corresponded to the described competitive use of technology. For instance, Veratax Corp., a Detroit, Michigan-based distributor of medical and dental products, had developed a

Table 3. A Breakdown of Types of Industries in the Survey

Types of Industry	Number of companies	%
Product-related	80	51
Service-related	77	49
Total	157	100

neural network system to support their marketing analysis (Kestelyn, 1992). Using the patterns and interrelationships uncovered by the system, the company was able to identify customers with higher probability of placing reorders and those with a lower probability; based on the findings, the customers' buying behavior was better understood and sales promotion programs for the company's customers were designed more effectively. In this documented case, the system was used as a strategic weapon to address such competitive forces as *Threat of New Entrant*, *Rivalry Among Existing Firms*, and *Bargaining Power of Buyers* through the firm's *Promotion* market strategies. "X" can then be marked in the corresponding context cells in the CF/MM framework (see Figure 1). Thus, at the end of the analysis of the case describing Veratax's neural network system, there would be one sheet of paper that contained the synopsis of the system described in the chapter, along with a CF/MM framework with cells that contain Xs and blanks in order to map Veratax's uses of IT for competitive advantage.

RESULTS

The 157 systems were reviewed in the previously described manner, resulting in 157 summary sheets. The case descriptions captured on these 157 summary sheets were then entered into a database for further analysis. The analysis consists of two parts: the industry analysis and the system positioning analysis. The industry analysis dealt with how the CF/MM framework reflected the state of competitive uses of IT on a system typology basis. The system positioning analysis was concerned with the overall positioning patterns of types of strategic information systems in the CF/MM framework. The following subsections present some of the descriptive statistics summarized from the analysis of the cases.

Industry Analysis: The industry analysis was conducted at two levels. The first level was concerned with the database as a whole. The second level dealt with the aggregated industry types, such as product-related type and service-related type.

Level I: As shown in Table 4, there are numerous documented strategic uses of IT (marked cells) found within these 157 systems. On average, there are

Table 4: Strategic Uses of IT in the CF/MM Framework (All Systems, n=150)

	Product	Price	Promotion	Place	Total	%
Threat of new entrants	135	18	49	45	247	38.7
Rivalry among existing firms	135	20	50	46	251	39.3
Threat of substitute	30	4	9	11	54	8.5
Bargaining power of suppliers	6	7	1	1	15	2.4
Bargaining power of buyers	27	22	7	15	71	11.1
Total	333	71	116	118	638	100
%	52.2	11.1	18.2	18.5	100	

Table 5: The Distribution of the Number of Strategic Uses Per System

Number of uses	Number of systems	%
2	60	38.2
3	21	13.4
4	29	18.5
5	7	4.5
6	13	8.3
7	6	3.8
8	9	5.7
9	9	5.7
10	2	1.3
11	1	0.6
Total	157	100

approximately three strategic uses per system; for individual systems, the number of uses per system ranges from 2 to 11 (see Table 5). On the other hand, the analysis also found that a firm can use more than one IS in one strategic area. For example, American Express used an expert system to automatically process millions of credit authorizations around the clock without human involvement and an image processing system to provide digitized customer statements. Both of these systems improved the company's quality of service (i.e., Product in the 4 Ps) and would support the company's competitive strategies in building barriers for new entrants and differentiating its product from existing competitors.

Among all the strategic uses, the majority (a combined 78 percent) are used in the categories of *Threat of New Entrants* (38.7 percent) and *Rivalry among Existing Firms* (39.3 percent), followed by *Bargaining Power of Buyers* (11.1 percent), *Threat of Substitute* (8.5 percent), and *Bargaining Power of Suppliers* (2.4 percent). On the marketing-mix side, over half of the uses are in *Product* category (52.2 percent), followed by *Place* (18.5 percent), *Promotion* (18.2 percent), and *Price* (11.1 percent). These two distributions are graphically shown in Figures 2 and 3. The pattern of the overall strategic uses is graphically shown in Figure 4.

Level II: As shown in Table 6, systems in product-related and service-related industries present a similar pattern of strategic uses to that of all the systems as a whole. Thus, the strategic applications of IT were primarily used to respond to two competitive forces (*Threat of New Entrants* and *Rivalry Among Existing Firms*), followed by *Bargaining Power of Buyers*, *Threat of Substitutes*, and *Bargaining Power of Suppliers*. From the marketing-mix perspective, the majority of the strategic uses of IT concentrated in the *Product* area, followed by the *Place*, *Promotion* and *Price* areas. However, the general patterns of strategic use of IT between the two aggregated industry types shows relatively different patterns in the areas of *Threat of Substitutes*, *Bargaining Power of Suppliers*, and *Price*. For example, IT was used

Figure 2. The Distribution of all companies by Proter's Five Competitive Forces

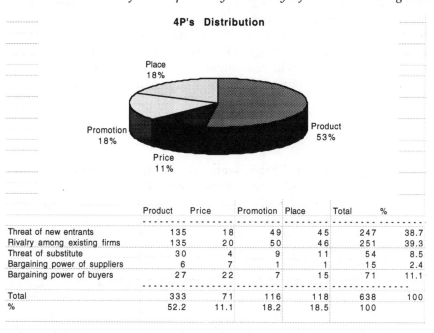

5 Forces Distribution

All Companies (150 counts)

	Product	Price	Promotion	Place	Total	%
Threat of new entrants	135	18	49	45	247	38.7
Rivalry among existing firms	135	20	50	46	251	39.3
Threat of substitute	30	4	9	11	54	8.5
Bargaining power of suppliers	6	7	1	1	15	2.4
Bargaining power of buyers	27	22	7	15	71	11.1
Total	333	71	116	118	638	100
%	52.2	11.1	18.2	18.5	100	

Figure 3. The Distribution of all companies by McCarthy's four P's marketing mix

4P's Distribution

	Product	Price	Promotion	Place	Total	%
Threat of new entrants	135	18	49	45	247	38.7
Rivalry among existing firms	135	20	50	46	251	39.3
Threat of substitute	30	4	9	11	54	8.5
Bargaining power of suppliers	6	7	1	1	15	2.4
Bargaining power of buyers	27	22	7	15	71	11.1
Total	333	71	116	118	638	100
%	52.2	11.1	18.2	18.5	100	

Figure 4. 4 P's vs. Competitive Forces

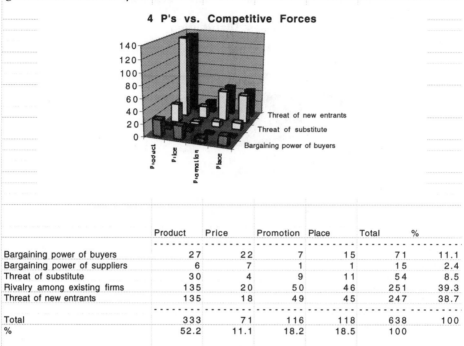

	Product	Price	Promotion	Place	Total	%
Bargaining power of buyers	27	22	7	15	71	11.1
Bargaining power of suppliers	6	7	1	1	15	2.4
Threat of substitute	30	4	9	11	54	8.5
Rivalry among existing firms	135	20	50	46	251	39.3
Threat of new entrants	135	18	49	45	247	38.7
Total	333	71	116	118	638	100
%	52.2	11.1	18.2	18.5	100	

more by product-related industries in gaining competitive advantages against the *Bargaining Power of Suppliers* and to support marketing strategy formulation in the *Price* category, by a ratio of 100:38 and 100:55 respectively. On the other hand, the service-related industries used strategic IT to deter the competitive forces of *Threat of Substitutes* more than the product-related industries by a ratio of 100:45.

In all, 48 percent of the strategic uses were in product-related companies and 52 percent were in service-related companies. The average number of uses per system in service-related industries is larger than that in service-related industries by a ratio of 100:90.

DISCUSSION

The use Of the CF/MM Framework: During the case review process, the strategic uses of the 157 published systems were effectively mapped into the framework without any major difficulty. In practice, there are two suggested steps in the use of the framework. The first step, which is essentially what the case analysis in this chapter has demonstrated, is to use the framework to map and evaluate a firm's and its competitors' current or potential uses of IT for competitive advantage in a specific industry. The rationale behind this approach is consistent with the conventional wisdom of military strategists such as Sun Tsu (Griffith, 1963), who advocated that winning always belongs to the party who better understands his enemy. This process is also analogous to the "competitor analysis" proposed by many contemporary researchers in strategic management (Ghoshal and Westney, 1991; Porter, 1980). These researchers assert the need for such an analysis in the increasingly complex and competitive environment of modern industries.

Based on the result of the competitor mapping, the firm can then identify strategic opportunities that fit the firm's market niche and choose to deploy strategic systems accordingly. Many times, the resulting strategic system will *simultaneously* deal with multiple environmental forces, and will also encompass more than one element of the marketing mix. On the other hand, several distinct strategic systems can be expected rather than a single, all-inclusive system. Hence, the resulting architecture of strategic organizational information systems can be thought of as an evolving mix or *portfolio of strategic applications* that deals with particular combinations of competitive threats across specific blends of the four elements of the marketing mix.

Furthermore, the use of the CF/MM framework has an important implication for recent IT research focusing on the assurance of *sustainability* of competitive advantage. Research has indicated that the deployment of IT may become a

Table 6: The Strategic Uses of IT by Selected Industry Types

Manufacturing (SIC: 20-39, n=57)

	PD	PR	PM	PL	Total	%
NEW	46	6	18	10	80	40
OLD	46	7	17	10	80	40
SUB	6	1	0	3	10	5
SUP	3	2	0	1	6	3
BUY	9	8	2	5	24	12
Total	110	24	37	29	200	100
%	55	12	18.5	14.5	100	

Fin, Ins, & Real Estate (SIC:60-69, n=35)

	PD	PR	PM	PL	Total	%
NEW	34	1	9	11	55	42.9
OLD	34	1	10	11	56	44.3
SUB	14	0	6	3	23	5.71
SUP	6	0	0	0	6	0
BUY	1	4	2	2	9	7.14
Total	89	6	27	27	149	100
%	59.7	4.03	18.1	18.1	100	

Retail Trade (SIC: 52-59, n=14)

	PD	PR	PM	PL	Total	%
NEW	9	5	9	4	27	42.2
OLD	9	5	9	4	27	42.2
SUB	0	1	1	1	3	4.69
SUP	1	3	0	0	4	6.25
BUY	0	1	1	1	3	4.69
Total	19	15	20	10	64	100
%	29.7	23.4	31.3	15.6	100	

Trans and Pub Utilities (SIC: 40-49, n=15)

	PD	PR	PM	PL	Total	%
NEW	13	2	5	5	25	32.9
OLD	13	2	5	6	26	34.2
SUB	4	1	1	2	8	10.5
SUP	0	1	1	0	2	2.63
BUY	5	5	2	3	15	19.7
Total	35	11	14	16	76	100
%	46.1	14.5	18.4	21.1	100	

Service (SIC: 70-89, n=9)

	PD	PR	PM	PL	Total	%
NEW	20	2	4	4	30	42.9
OLD	20	2	5	4	31	44.3
SUB	2	0	1	1	4	5.71
SUP	0	0	0	0	0	0
BUY	3	1	0	1	5	7.14
Total	45	5	10	10	70	100
%	64.3	7.14	14.3	14.3	100	

"strategic necessity" rather than a source of "competitive advantage" after the IT application is replicated by the competitors (Clemons and Row, 1988; Kettinger et al., 1994). In such an instance, a firm's current dependence on particular forms of IT and the success of its *portfolio of applications* may vary over time. Thus, sustainability may be best achieved by "leveraging unique firm attributes with information technology to realize long-term performance gain" (Kettinger et al., 1994). In order to meet the challenge of sustainability, a firm must use the CF/MM framework on a continuing basis to evaluate the dynamics of market competition resulting from the use of IT and manipulate the firm's *portfolio of applications* accordingly.

IMPLICATIONS OF THE INDUSTRY ANALYSIS

Level I: On the basis of the database as a whole, it is clear that most of strategic uses of IT fall into the areas that focus on creating barriers to deter new entrants and to compete with existing rivals by introducing new products, improving product designs and processes, reinforcing customer services, cutting prices, conducting advertising campaigns, and creating new and convenient distribution channels. One explanation for this phenomenon may be that new entrants and competitive rivalry are the two competitive forces that tend to create more direct competitive pressure than do the substitutes, suppliers, and buyers. Another explanation could be related to a firm's fear of "transaction risk" raised by the exposure to being exploited in the customer/supplier relationship through vertical integration (Clemons and Row, 1992). However, recent advances in telecommunication technologies have promoted the use of interorganizational information systems, rather than simple vertical integration, in improving customer/supplier relationships (Bakos, 1991; Clemons and Row, 1992; Stuchfield and Weber, 1992). The emergence of the commercial Internet has only accelerated this phenomenon. On the marketing-mix side, the majority of the strategic uses of IT are concentrated on the *Product* area (52 percent), followed by the areas of *Place* (19 percent), *Promotion* (18 percent), and *Price* (11 percent). This is somewhat different from the results in another relevant study about the use of marketing information systems in the *Fortune* 500 companies (Li et al., 1993), in which *Price* (39 percent) was found to be supported most by marketing information systems, followed by *Product* (32 percent), *Place* (15 percent), and *Promotion* (13 percent). This might be a result of the difference in the scope of the sampled systems. Li et al. (1993) specifically studied the area of *marketing information systems* in which a more restrictive definition of the purpose of the information system was used. Nevertheless, both the current study and the Li et al., study agree that *Place* and *Promotion* were the two areas of marketing activities that have received remarkably less emphasis in the competitive use of IT. This may be because the activities of *Promotion*, as noted by Li et al. (1993, p.181), are difficult to support on the computer due to their creative nature, and the *Place* decisions tend to be delegated to operational line staff.

In summary, the industry analysis at this level indicates that the strategic uses of IT on the industry as a whole were not equal in each strategic area of the framework. While some explanations based on logic reasoning and previous works have been proffered, it is clear that the under-emphasized areas of application deserve further study.

Level II: There are three major findings that resulted from the industry analysis on this level. First, product-related industries tended to use IT significantly more to gain competitive advantage against the *Bargaining Power of Suppliers*. This is true because most of the service-related industries do not have a large number of "suppliers." Thus, the supplier relationship in service-related industries is often less complex than that of the product-related industries. Second, the strategic uses of IT to support marketing strategies in the *Price* area received significantly more attention by product-related industries than by service-related industries. One explanation of this emphasis could be that the price structures in the product-related industries are more explicit than those in service-related industries. Thus, companies in product-related industries should certainly continue to strive to outperform their competitors in the efforts of carefully examining their price structures and better formulating their pricing strategies. Third, the service-related industries, on the other hand, tended to use IT notably more to counterattack the *Threat of Substitutes* than did the product-related industries. Again, this difference reflects a common belief that service is easier to imitate than product, because many services can be replicated with less time and capital investment than certain types of products.

Overall, service-related industries used IT in more areas than the product-related industries, by a ratio of 100 to 90. Although comfortable conclusions cannot be advanced without more evidence, this phenomenon might seem to support a common impression that the service-related industries are generally more competitive than the product-related industries.

Limitations: The nature of the sampling method chosen to select the cases analyzed by this chapter focused on articles detailing some "competitive" application of information technology during the late 1980s and 1990s. The cases studied are by no means an exhaustive set, but instead represent an attempt at capturing fairly typical applications of IT reported in the popular and scholarly literature. Furthermore, the number of articles, while representing a substantial number of similar articles, could certainly have been increased. Finally, this study did not attempt to measure the actual benefit derived by the organization from applications of IT for competitive advantage. Instead, the article focused on describing a framework that can be used to consider the portfolio of strategic applications developed by a particular firm. Within such a framework, the actual benefits (and costs) of strategic systems might certainly be considered.

CONCLUSIONS AND RECOMMENDATIONS

Many of the difficulties that businesses must cope with arise from the distinctive characteristics of the firm and the particular niche in which it operates. Because of the uniqueness associated with each firm's predicament (niche), it may be quite difficult for an organization to successfully apply the generic strategies offered by previous frameworks to the task of developing competitive strategies and strategic information systems that fit their firm's unique situation.

This chapter developed a two-dimensional framework that can be used to recognize opportunities for strategic information systems based on (1) Porter's view of strategy as a response to the *unique mix* of the five competitive forces faced by individual firms, and (2) marketing strategy (the particular mix of product, price, promotion, and distribution/ delivery mechanism used to respond to a specific target market). The COMPETITIVE FORCES/MARKETING MIX (CF/MM) IT framework can be used to assess the degree to which a particular firm is currently using information technology for competitive advantage in the areas identified by the CF/MM matrix. Furthermore, the CF/MM framework can be used to identify business-need-driven opportunities to apply information technology as part of the competitive response of a firm to the prevailing competitive forces within its market niche.

Business managers can employ the CF/MM framework to examine each application of information technology to their business's competitive needs, and to assess their entire portfolio of applications. Essentially, this assessment would consist of examining the functions provided by each individual application, mapping the functionality into the related cell(s) in the CF/MM framework (one page/table per application), and finally considering the entire portfolio (set of tables). During the consideration of the application portfolio, the manager can identify empty cells across the portfolio of CF/MM tables and identify market-driven applications of information technology to respond to the competitive force associated with that CF/MM cell.

Information technology researchers can employ the CF/MM framework to conduct studies related to each cell (or *context*) in the framework. For example, an in-depth survey could be conducted to investigate the distribution of applications of information technology across the cells within particular industries, or across industries. Additionally, researchers in systems analysis and design could examine the appropriateness of various system development methodologies for systems within each cell. Finally, researchers could consider the implications of various emerging technologies (the Internet, wireless communications, and enterprise resource planning systems) in terms of the cells in the CF/MM framework that would offer the greatest opportunities to exploit the new technologies to yield competitive advantage for firms in various industries.

The reality of the dynamic business marketplace during the early 21st century demands effective deployment of information technology to serve business needs and to counter business threats. The CF/MM framework provides a simple, coherent and useful means of organizing the search for opportunities to exploit information technology for competitive advantage. The CF/MM framework can also be used to prioritize IT spending according to the true competitive forces that a firm is required to deal with in order to successfully defend its market niche.

Knowledge is the ultimate substitute. If you have the right knowledge, you can substitute it for all the other factors of production. You reduce the amount of labor, capital, energy, raw materials and space you need to warehouse. So knowledge is not only a factor of production, it's the factor of production.
—*Alvin Toffler (Schwartz and Toffler, 1993, p. 122)*

REFERENCES

Bakos, J. Y.(1991). "Information Links and Electronic Marketplaces: The Role of Interorganizational Information Systems in Vertical Markets", *Journal of Management Information Systems* 8(2), 31-52.

Bakos, J. Y. and Treacy, M. E.(1986). "Information Technology and Corporate Strategy: A Research Perspective", *MIS Quarterly* 10(2) , 107-119.

Barrett, S. S. and Konsynski, B. R.(1982). "Inter-Organization Information Sharing Systems", *MIS Quarterly* Special issue (December), 93-105.

Beath, C. M. and Ives, B., "Competitive Information Systems in Support of Pricing", *MIS Quarterly* 10 (1) (March 1986), 85-96.

Benjamin, R. I.; Rockart, J. F.; Scott Morton, M. S. and Wyman, J.(1984)."Information Technology: A Strategic Opportunity", *Sloan Management Review*, 25(3), 3-10.

Benjamin, R. I. and Scott Morton, M. S.(1988). "Information Technology, Integration and Organizational Change", *Interfaces* 18(3), 86-98.

Berg, E. N. (1988). "Reinventing Sears: A Formidable Task", *The New York Times* (November 7) p. D1.

Bergeron, F. and Raymond, L. (1992). "Planning of Information Systems to Gain a Competitive Edge", *Journal of Small Business Management* 30 (January 1992), 21-21.

Bergeron, F.; Buteau, C. and Raymond, L.(1991). "Identification of Strategic Information Systems Opportunities: Applying and Comparing Two Methodologies", *MIS Quarterly* 15(1), 89-103.

Brien, R. H. and Stafford, J. E.(1988). "Marketing Information Systems: A New Dimension for Marketing Research", *Journal of Marketing* 23(3), 19-23.

Business Week (1983). "Business is Turning Data Into a Potent Strategic Weapon", *Business Week*, Number 2804 (August 22, 1983), 94-98.

Business Week (1992). "The New Realism in Office Systems", *Business Week* (June 15), 128-133.

Canning, R. G.(1984). "Information Systems' New Strategic Role", *EDP Analyzer* 22(1),1-12.

Cash, J. I. and Konsynski, B. R.(1985). "IS Redraws Competitive Boundaries", *Harvard Business Review* 64(2), 134-142.

Clemons, E. K.(1986)."Information Systems of Sustainable Competitive Advantage", *Information & Management* 11(3),131-136.

Clemons, E. K. and Row, M.(1988). "McKesson Drug Company: A Case Study of Economost: A Strategic Information System", *Journal of Management Information Systems* 5(1),36-50.

Clemons, E. K. and Row, M.(1992). "Information Technology and Industrial Cooperation: The Changing Economics of Coordination and Ownership", *Journal of Management Information Systems* 9(2), 9-28.

Computerworld (1985). "Technology Yields Banks Slim Return on Investment", *Computerworld* 19(18), p1.

Copeland, J. H. and McKenney, J. L.(1988). "Airline Reservations Systems: Lessons from History", *MIS Quarterly* 12(3), 353-370.

Crissy, W. J. E. and Mossman, F.(1977). "Matrix Models for Marketing Planning: An Update and Expansion", *MSU Business Topics*, 25(4) , 17-26.

Cushman, J. H. jr.(1989). "The High-Stakes Battle for Airline Reservations", *The New York Times* (June 18, 1989), F7.

Elkjer, T.(1988). "MEDEX: The 'Federal Express' of Laboratory Testing", *Computerland Magazine* (September/October 1988).

Ghoshal, S. and Westney, D. E.(1991). "Organizing Competitor Analysis Systems", 12(1), 17-31.

Griffith, S. B.(1963). *Sun Tzu: The Art of War* (London: Oxford University Press.

Higby, M. A. and Farah, B. N.(1991). "The Status of Marketing Information Systems, Decision Support Systems and Expert Systems in the Marketing Function of U.S. Firms", *Information & Management* 20(1),29-35.

Ives, B. and Learmonth, G. P.(1984). "The Information System as a Competitive Weapon", *Communications of the ACM* 27(12), 1193-1201.

Johnston, R. and Carrico, S. R.(1988). "Developing Capabilities to Use Information Strategically", *MIS Quarterly* 12(1), 37-48.

Johnston, R. and Vitale, M. R.(1988). "Creating Competitive Advantage with Interorganizational Information Systems", *MIS Quarterly* 12(2), 153-165.

Kestelyn, J.(1992). "Application Watch", *AI Expert* (January 1992), 63-64.

Kettinger, W. J.; Grover, V.; Guha, S. and Segars, A. H.(1994). "Strategic Information Systems Revisited: A Study in Sustainability and Performance", *MIS Quarterly* 8(1), 31-58.

King, W. R.(1978). "Strategic Planning for Management Information Systems", *MIS Quarterly*, 2(1),27-37.

Laudon, K. C. and Laudon, J. P.(1991). *Management Information Systems: A Contemporary Perspective*, (New York, NY: Macmillan).

Lederer, A. L. and Mendelow, A. L.(1988). "Convincing Top Management of the Strategic Potential of Information Systems", *MIS Quarterly*, 12(4), 525-534.

Lee, C. S. and Adams, D. A.(1990). "A Manager's Guide to the Strategic Potential of Information Systems", *Information & Management* 19(3), 169-182.

Li, E. Y.; McLeod, R. and Rogers, J. C.(1993). "Marketing Information Systems in the *Fortune* 500 Companies: Past, Present, and Future", *Journal of Management Information Systems* 10(1), 165-192.

McCarthy, E. J.(1960). *Basic Marketing: A Managerial Approach* (Homewood, IL: Richard D. Irwin).

McCarthy, E. J. and Perreault, jr. W. D.(1990). *Basic Marketing: A Managerial Approach* 10th ed., (Homewood, IL: Irwin).

McFarlan, F. W.(1984). "Information Technology Changes the Way You Compete", *Harvard Business Review* 62(3) , 98-103.

McFarlan, F. W. and McKenney, J. L.(1983). *Corporate Information Systems Management: The Issues Facing Senior Executives* (Homewood, IL: Richard D. Irwin).

McLeod, R., Jr. and Rogers, J. C.(1982). "Marketing Information Systems: Uses in the *Fortune* 500", *California Management Review* 25(3), 106-118.

Miron, M.; Cecil, J; Bradcich, K. and Hall, G.(1988). "The Myths and Realities of Competitive Advantage", *Datamation* 34(19), 71-82.

Porter, M.(1980). *Competitive Strategy* (New York: Free Press.

Porter, M. (1985). *Competitive Advantage* (New York: Free Press,.

Porter, M. and Millar, V. E.(1985). "How Information Gives You Competitive Advantage", *Harvard Business Review* 63(4), 149-160.

Pride, W. M. and Ferrell, O. C.(1989). *Marketing: Concepts and Strategy* 6th ed., (Boston: Houghton Mifflin Company).

Rackoff, N.; Wiseman, C. and Ullrich, W. A.(1985). "Information Systems for Competitive Advantage: Implementation of a Planning Process", *MIS Quarterly* 9(4), 285-294.

Schwartz, P. and Toffler, A.(1993). "Shock Wave (Anti) Warrior: A Conversation between Peter Schwartz and Alvin Toffler", *Wired*, 1(5), 61-65, 120-122.

Segars, A. H. and Grover, V.(1994). "Strategic Group Analysis: A Methodological Approach for Exploring the Industry Level Impact of Information Technology", *Information & Management* 22(1), 13-34.

Stuchfield, N. and Weber, B. W.(1992). "Modeling the Profitability of Customer Relationships: Development and Impact of Barclays de Zoete Wedd's BEATRICE", *Journal of Management Information Systems* 9(2), 53-76.

Toffler, A. *(1990). PowerShift* (New York: Bantam Books).

Wiseman, C.(1988). *Strategic Information Systems*, (Homewood, IL: Jones-Irwin,).

Chapter XII

The Importance of the IT-End User Relationship Paradigm in Obtaining Alignment Between IT and the Business

A.C. Leonard
University of Pretoria, South Africa

ABSTRACT

Sound relationships between IT professionals and their business counterparts (end users) could be regarded as one of many important factors playing a role during the alignment process between IT and the business. Research has, for example, shown that aligning with anything other than the customer leads to only momentary success. The chapter describes IT-end user relationships as intriguing and complex. These relationships should be seen and managed as multidimensional entities. Two such dimensions, the physical and abstract dimensions, form the basis of IT-end user relationships. These two dimensions enable one to fully describe the holistic nature of such relationships and to encapsulate the important elements of a support-oriented organization, namely mutuality, belonging and connection. The chapter describes how sound relationships can enhance alignment between the business and IT. A conceptual model for maintaining alignment is also introduced.

INTRODUCTION

International Data Corporation (CIO, 1997)) surveyed 283 top executives across three vertical industries: finance, manufacturing and retail/wholesale. They found "a strong correlation between the effectiveness of the IT department [IS organization] and the relationship between the CIO and the CEO." "We suspect that this relationship, if it is close, permits the CIO to develop the IT department [IS organization] into a service that delivers competitive advantage for the company, thus enhancing the careers of every IT professional in the organization." In other words, "a certain amount of mutual esteem will help IT [IS] function as a business partner."

In terms of alignment, sound relationships between IT and the business become even more important. Boar (1994) states that aligning with anything other than the customer leads to only momentary success. For the IT function to achieve a state of alignment with the business, it must align with the business scope, and through that business scope enable all business functions and processes to serve the customers in a superior manner.

In their research Reich & Benbasit (1999, referring to the work of Horovitz,1984), point out that there were two dimensions to strategy creation: the *intellectual dimension* and the *social dimension*. Research into the intellectual dimension is more likely to concentrate on the contents of plans and on planning methodologies. Research into the social dimension is more likely to focus on the people involved in the creation of alignment. The *social dimension* of alignment is defined as "the state in which business and IT executives within an organizational unit understand and are committed to the business and IT mission, objectives, and plans".

Another theoretical perspective supporting the concept of the social dimension of alignment is the social construction of reality. This view would suggest that, in addition to studying artifacts (such as plans and structures) to predict the presence or absence of alignment, one should investigate the contents of the players' minds: their beliefs, attitudes and understanding of these artifacts (Reich & Benbasit, 1999).

This chapter focuses on the *social dimension* in terms of the construction and nature of sound IT-end user relationships and the role such relationships play in aligning IT with the business.

Research in this field has shown that relationships between IT professionals and their end users are intriguing and complex, and should be seen and managed as a multidimensional environment. The objectives of the research were, among other things, to identify and describe the most important elements involved in *relationships* between the IT department and the end user (referred to in the rest of the chapter as *IT-end user relationships*) which will enhance a supportive culture. Furthermore the research focused on the role and effects *transacting* has in the forming of *IT-end user relationships*. Lastly, the research was aimed at creating a better understanding of the *social nature* and characteristics of the different relationships between IT and its end users while IT is performing its duty as service and support agent.

Theories of how relationships between an IT department and its end users should be managed, or how it can improve alignment between IT and the business, are scarce. Those that do address issues in this regard (Wike et al., 1984; CSC research foundation, 1994; Beard & Peterson, 1988) do not look into soft issues, or give substance to the contents of such relationships. The effects such relationships have on alignment are not addressed at all.

In the next section the cause and nature of poor relationships between IT departments and their end users are briefly described to give the reader proper perspective regarding the problem and the negative effects of poor relationships.

IT-END USER RELATIONSHIPS: HISTORICAL FOUNDATIONS

For many years the *culture gap* between IT departments and their end users has been characterized by unfortunate differences like distrust, scepticism and cynicism. This situation impacts negatively on the relationship of IT departments with their end users, and as such on their ability to produce service and support of high quality.

Historically the gap was caused mainly by the difference in management culture, as well as human behaviour problems on both sides. Umbaugh (1991) states in his argumentation of organizational imbalances that too often IT exists as an adjunct to the organization and not as an integral part of the whole. This situation unfortunately still exists today and contributes to the so-called *culture gap* between IT departments and their end users. Du Plooy (1995) explains this gap as follows:

"...the 'culture gap' should be understood as a gap of misunderstanding in the sense of two different organizational 'cultures' that, according to Grindley, coexist in most organizations. The two cultures under discussion here are the 'culture' of the IT profession and the 'culture' of the rest of the organization."

The culture on both the IT department side and the business side is also an important obstacle in building mutual trust, and eventually in building *sound relationships* between IT and its end user environment, and as such in creating alignment between IT and the business. According to Moad (1994), the IT professional has been fighting for recognition and relevance at the CEO level for the last 25 years. He gives many examples illustrating the kind of culture that exists which could be described as the main reason for misunderstandings and misconceptions about IT among today's end users.

When a user initially gets involved with the IT department, he/she is introduced to one or more IT professionals who will specifically deal with his/her problem(s). Normally a sense of mutual understanding and trust grows out of this *relationship,* which will definitely get disturbed the moment elements of such a relationship change without the knowledge or approval of the role players. In practice end users very seldom get involved in the management of change which will influence a *relationship* in which they are involved, or even get properly informed of changes that take place on the IT side. Practice has indicated that this is a typical reason for distrust and criticism against IT departments from the end user environment.

A review of literature on the history of relations between end users and their IT departments in the data processing industry and how they were treated, tells a very sad tale. The attitude or behaviour of IT departments or the so-called DP professionals was one of "we know the best", or "we know what the end user needs and therefore we don't need to try and get the end user involved". Furthermore, many people on the business side of an organization have never been exposed to computer technology and are totally computer illiterate, which makes them uncertain and in many cases the "prey" of an IT department. As a result of this attitude few attempts were made to keep communication with the end user on a sound basis while developing a system.

Although many efforts were made in the past to address these issues, the emphasis mainly fell on putting structures and procedures together in order to get out of the end user what his basic needs are. Thereafter the IT department normally followed a lonely journey through the last phases of the systems development life cycle.

In the rest of the chapter the nature of and theory behind IT-end user relationships are examined. Furthermore, the way in which the paradigm of IT-end user relationships enhances alignment between IT and the business is discussed.

THE NATURE AND THEORY OF IT-END USER RELATIONSHIPS

The above paragraphs briefly describe the history of how poor relationships emerged over the years between IT departments and their end users, as well as some basic characteristics of such poor relationships. The question one can ask is, what are the characteristics of sound relationships between IT departments and their end users, and how are they established. To answer the question, this section:

- gives a definition of IT-end user relationships,
- discusses the theory behind IT end user relationships, and
- explains what is meant by sound relationships.

Definition of IT-End User Relationships

A relationship between IT and the end user consists of two dimensions, namely a *physical dimension* and an *abstract dimension*. The physical dimension describes those elements which are necessary in order to enable contact between IT and its end users, whereas the abstract dimension describes the soft issues of a relationship. These two dimensions enable one to fully describe the holistic[1] nature of such a relationship and encapsulate the important elements of a support-oriented organization, namely mutuality, belonging, and connection, as mentioned by Pheysey (1993) in her book *Organizational Cultures*. The basic components of such a relationship are illustrated in Figure 1.

Without going into all the detail of the different elements of the *physical* and *abstract* dimensions as described by Leonard (1998), the chapter focuses on describing the most important characteristics of these elements. This will give the reader enough understanding of the social nature of IT-end user relationships.

Physical elements

As far as the *physical dimension* is concerned, the following elements could be seen as the most important:

- People[2]: A relationship consists of all the responsible people who are in-

Figure 1: The Basic Components of an IT-End User Relationship

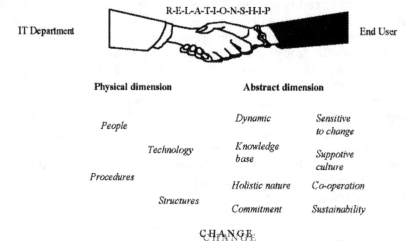

volved in the systems development life cycle at a given time. "Responsibilities are negotiated and shared between systems developers and users" (Dahlbom & Mathiassen (1993)).

- Technology: Technology may be seen as one of the most important elements in such a relationship, enabling the people who participate in the relationship to communicate with one another. The importance of proper communication structures, both vertically and horizontally, are emphasized by Bommer *et al.* (1991) and could be seen as one of the most important organizational characteristics associated with unethical activity. Apart from the normal communication technology, facilities like *help desks* and *Internet* are of the most important factors in this regard.

- Procedures: Two types of procedures are of importance, namely organizational procedures (such as standards and policies) which already *exist* and which can be seen as a given, and *new* procedures that are being created by people because of their interaction with the given procedures and technology (DeSanctis & Poole, 1994).

- Structures: Depending upon the "type" of end user, and therefore the service and support that will be offered, relationships will differ in content as far as *formal and informal* social communication structures are concerned. The most common of these structures are project meetings, JAD sessions and end user group meetings.

Abstract elements

As far as the *abstract dimension* is concerned, the following elements are the most important:

- They are dynamic: The nature of the relationships between the IT department and its end users will, among other things, depend upon the *type* of end user, as well as upon regarding the end user as a human being. According to Stokes (1991), when talking to end users, the IT professional should always bear in mind their concerns, problems, environment, and responsibilities in terms of opportunities for IT services and support. Furthermore, he says, continuous contact with end users gives IT the opportunity to gain more insight into their problems.

- They are sensitive to change: Because of the social nature of relationships, any form of change initiated on either the IT or the end user side may disturb a relationship. It is argued that any kind of change having an effect on any of the elements of both the *physical* and *abstract* dimensions of a relationship will in fact disturb the relationship because of its holistic nature, which will be described later.
- They have a knowledge base: The complex world of perceptions, attitudes and approaches towards developing software products by IT professionals for the end user, forces us to a point where it can be said that in order to overcome the most serious problems during this communication process in a relationship, a knowledge base of some kind is required before entering a relationship.
- They have a supportive culture: In order for a relationship to be sound, continuous support and mutual understanding, among other things, need to be elements of such a relationship. According to Pheysey, a support-oriented organization has the elements of mutuality, belonging, and connection. Furthermore, an appreciative form of control should be applied, which means: "management is seen to be a process focused on maintaining balance in a field of relationships" (Gadalla and Cooper, 1978, quoted by Pheysey).
- A cooperative behaviour pattern is followed by the participants: Cooperation is not a fixed pattern of behaviour, but a changing, adaptive process directed to future results. The representation and understanding of intent by every party is therefore essential to cooperation, and as such emphasizes the importance of communication during cooperation (Clarke & Smyth (1993)). Cooperation can also create new motives, attitudes, values and capabilities in the cooperating parties, which will help create and maintain a supportive culture.
- They have an holistic nature: The important elements making up a relationship between the IT department and its end users at a given time should be organized together as a whole. If any of these elements are disturbed in a negative sense, the whole relationship between the IT department and its end users is undermined. In other words, the relationship as a whole is more than the sum of its elements and therefore one can say that it has an *holistic* nature.
- Sustainability: A most obvious characteristic of the abstract dimension is its sustainability over a period of *time*. In this regard time refers to the life span of an IT-end user relationship. One can therefore argue that out of an information systems viewpoint, a relationship of this kind will only last until the product or service reaches the end of its life cycle.
  In this regard Introna (1994) states: "Structures as relationships are contingent, it appears and disappears. It could be brief (a few seconds) or long lasting (several years)."
- Commitment: Kinlaw (1989) states that one of the primary tasks of a manager

is to create commitment and focus in employees. He furthermore states that managers who help employees increase their knowledge, skill and experience also are building employee commitment.

In this regard it is important that managers should take note of the four sturdy supports of commitment, namely: (a) clarity of goals and values; (b) employee competencies that ensure success; (c) the degree of influence that employees have; and (d) the expressed appreciation given to employees for their contributions. Commitment should be seen as a solid block that rests on these four sturdy supports or legs (Kinlaw, 1989).

Commitment has been defined by Newman & Sabherwal (1996, referring to the work of Staw (1982) as a state of mind that holds people and organizations in the line of behaviour. It encompasses psychological forces that bind an individual to an action. Commitment has been argued to greatly affect the persistence of behaviour (Newman & Sabherwal, 1996, referring to the work of Salancik, 1977).

All the elements described above form important sub-dimensions of the *physical* and *abstract* dimensions. Each of these elements plays a specific social role in an IT-end user relationship environment, which impacts on the soundness of such a relationship as well as the success of alignment between IT and the business. The way in which the application of this paradigm could enhance alignment is addressed in the following paragraphs.

The Theory Behind IT-End User Relationships

At this stage it is necessary to ask, what is behind the construction of IT-end user relationships? In other words, what happens between the IT department and end users that is actually responsible for the establishment and maintenance of such relationships.

Although the record of service and support of IT departments was sketched as a very poor picture, interaction between the IT departments and their end users took place on a continued basis, because of the need to computerize different kinds of business systems. Over the years this ensured that relations between these two environments were established, in the sense that business people became more involved in computer projects, and consequently more computer literate. On the other hand, computer people were forced by the nature of many "computerization" projects to learn the business environment and therefore developed a better understanding of business needs.

According to Introna (1994, referring to the work of Giddens, 1984), the structure of social systems emerges from interaction. Interaction establishes relationships. Structure is a set of relationships: communicative relationships, power relationships, etc. Structure as relationship is contingent, it appears and disappears. It could be brief (a few seconds) or long lasting (several years).

This is not only true of the structure, but also of the actors. As they redefine the structure (through interaction) they themselves get redefined. This implies that social structures (and the actors) not only emerge once, but are in a continual state of "becoming". This becoming flows from a pattern of interaction. It is an unfolding drama with no predefined script. This dramatic "human history" is created by intentional activities, but is not an intended project; it is persistently eluding efforts to bring it under conscious direction.

The process of becoming, of creation and recreation of structure is what Giddens (1984, p.25) calls the *duality of structure.*

Thus, society is truly *historical.* Social systems emerge from a pattern of interaction over time. They are shaped by it, and shape it. Any attempt to dismember an act or pattern of actions (relationship) from its historical context would be to do violence to the very being of self and society (see Figure 2).

In the marketing research area much research has been done in the field of relations between manufacturers and customers. In this regard Pitt & Bromfield (1994) state that managers interact in a number of so-called *dyads* in their everyday work. They define a dyad as: "...the smallest relationship unit, involving a one-on-one relationship between two parties."

This definition also relates to the idea of "user involvement transactions" introduced by Roode & Smith (1989). It follows that in the case of a project team consisting of IT professionals and end users, a number of dyads (*sub*relationships) exist between the different individuals in such a team. Therefore, when *transacting* takes place whereby information between two or more parties is exchanged in order to determine for example the nature of the service requested by the end user(s), *dyads* are formed between the parties, but especially between IT professionals and end users.

The different dyads form the building blocks of an IT-end user relationship that emerges from the initial contact or transaction (exchange) made between an end user and an IT professional. Although transactions are regarded by Ciborra (1993) as the basic organizational relationship in which conflict of interest may take place, it is argued that *transacting* takes place before a dyad is formed. In this regard Ciborra himself states that one of the major purposes of a transaction, or exchange, is to search for a potential partner. This is illustrated in figure 3.

IT-end user relationships could therefore be seen as *social structures* emerging when an IT professional and an end user starts to negotiate or communicate the elements (contents) of a specific service/support activity. In this regard Ciborra (1993) argues that some of the purposes of transacting are to signal willingness to exchange information, to establish the terms of the contract, and to serve as a base for maintaining communication during bargaining. It was also pointed out that the social process of transacting forms the basis from which dyads and eventually IT-end user relationships emerge.

Figure 2. The Structuration Process (Based on Giddens, 1984)

The environment in which this takes place is provided by the IT department (institution) as a basis for IT-professionals and end users to perform planning, design, implementing and training, etc. "Social structures serve as templates for planning and accomplishing tasks" (DeSanctis & Poole, 1994).

The most important advanced structures used by an emerging relationship are composed of the *physical* and *abstract* dimensions thereof. In other words, an infrastructure (physical environment) has to be

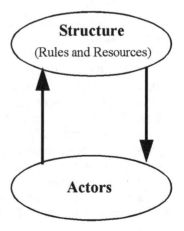

Figure 3. The Building Blocks of an IT-End User Relationship

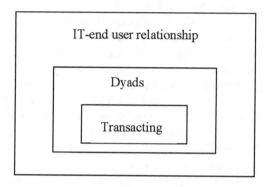

used by the actors (participants) of an emerging relationship to interact, and a knowledge base of the elements of the abstract dimension is required to direct behaviour. The construction of an emerging relationship is illustrated in figure 4.

The Meaning of Sound IT-End User Relationships

So far the term *soundness* has been used in order to indicate "that everything goes well with a relationship". This is actually a rather abstract term which is very difficult to measure. In real life situations, for example, when one asks a project team member how things are with the team (meaning the team spirit), the typical response to such a question is "fine thank you". For any outsider, like a manager or any other person who does not belong to the team (and is therefore not involved in the relationship), it is even more difficult to give an objective answer. This type of question, as well as the response to it, is normally quite subjective. One reason for this is because people play *politics* in the sense that they do not want to portray the situation as it really is - especially when things are not going that well. According to Agyris (1990) *politics* are in many cases the reason for the existence of "undiscussables", preventing people to talk about things that really matter. Pitt & Bromfield (1994) state that political clout, rather than merit, can dictate the final decisions that may have a negative or destructive influence on the soundness of a relationship.

One of the important elements which plays a prominent role in the continuity of a relationship, and which also has a direct influence on the soundness thereof, is *trust* (Anderson & Weitz, 1989; Humphrey, 1990). Many elements, like the "end user type" (in other words, whether the right end user is involved in the relationship) the "culture", communication etc. have an influence on the soundness of relationships, and therefore form determinants of trust in a relationship. In other words, these elements may be described as those that help to establish trust or mistrust in a relationship. Anderson & Weitz state that elements like reputation, support, cultural similarity and power imbalance are important determinants in building mutual trust levels in a dyad, and therefore in a relationship.

In the next section the impact of and role played by the IT-end user relationship paradigm is discussed in terms of the alignment model developed by Henderson and Venkatraman (1992). Furthermore, a conceptual framework is discussed by

Figure 4. The Construction of IT-End User Relationships (Based on DeSanctis & Poole, 1994)

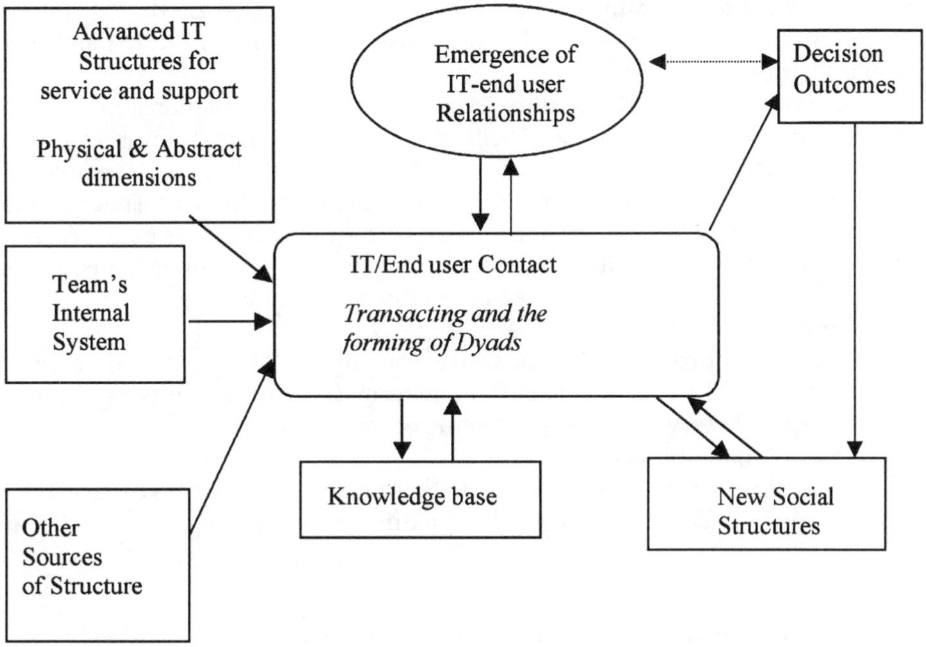

means of which sound relationships are established and maintained.

ALIGNMENT MODEL FOR APPLYING THE IT-END USER RELATIONSHIP PARADIGM

The theoretical construct of strategic alignment (Henderson and Venkatraman, 1992) indicates that in terms of alignment there are two distinct linkages, namely a strategic fit and functional integration. According to the model strategic fit is the vertical linkage concerned with the integration of the external environment in which the firm competes (e.g. partnerships and alliances) and the internal environment which focuses on administrative structure (e.g. human resources and product development). Functional integration, according to the model, is the corresponding horizontal link between business and IT. These two linkages are used to determine the relationships between IT and business (Papp, 2000).

It is clear that the paradigm of IT-end user relationships, which is based on two dimensions, namely the *physical* and *abstract* dimensions (as described above), addresses the two lower domains indicated by the dotted rectangle in Figure 6. In other words, the paradigm enhances alignment in terms of organizational infrastructure and processes, and IT infrastructure and processes. The *physical dimension* addresses structures, skills, and processes while the *abstract dimension* addresses all the soft issues required to ensure that relationships prevail. Therefore, it is argued that if the paradigm of IT-end user relationships is applied when service and support activities[3] are performed by IT professionals, it will enhance the *functional integration* between IT and the business. This is the case because all the elements of the physical and abstract dimensions are of a sound nature[4], which directly impacts on structures, processes and skills in the infrastructure domains of the alignment model in Figure 5.

It is furthermore argued that if the paradigm of IT-end user relationships is applied during service and support activities, it will establish and maintain strong infrastructure domains on both the business and the IT side. This in itself will support the process of assessment for alignment, which is based on identifying strong domains. The conceptual framework of IT-end user relationships consists of the following three main processes, each of which has subcomponents explaining the internal operations of each process. The basic conceptual framework is illustrated in Figure 6.

- **relationship initiation process**
  The initiation process should be seen as the process taking place when the end user and the IT department start negotiating the terms and means of supplying a specific service or support to the organization.
- **relationship activities process**
  During this phase of the relationship three major activities take place, which impact on or which are affected by the different elements in the *physical* and

Figure 5. The Role and Impact of IT-End User Relationships in the Alignment of Business and IT Department (Based on the work of Henderson & Venkatraman, 1992)

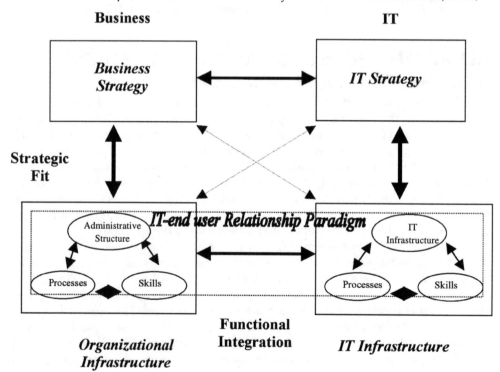

abstract dimensions. These activities are: assimilation of participants, service and support (for example, designing a system or maintaining an existing system) and the decision-making process.

- **Feedback and control process**

  This is a continuous process affording all participants the opportunity to give their own evaluation (feedback) of how they experience the activities of a specific relationship in which they are involved. "Individuals learn as a result of their *experience, and so do organizations.*" (Robey & Sales, 1994). Furthermore, it allows participants to have control over the progress of a specific service and support activity (project).

The detailed conceptual framework in which all the different activities in each process and their relationship to one another is explained, falls beyond the scope of this chapter.

So far IT-end user relationships have been discussed in terms of a *stable* environment, where little or no change is involved. In other words, an environment with little or no turbulence. This is of course an unrealistic situation. As we all know, situations in an IT environment are normally very turbulent and changes take place almost every day. These changes may occur, for example, in the form of organizational restructuring, new technology, and changes in manpower in terms of employees leaving and new employees joining the IT department. Changes of this nature normally disrupt one or more of the elements of either the physical or abstract dimension of a relationship, and therefore the whole relationship (Leonard, 1998).

The question therefore is, how can sound relationships be maintained, and how can one ensure that a *functional integration* will be maintained. According to the theory of IT-end user relationships, change should be managed in such a way that whenever changes in the relationship environment cause disturbances to any of the elements in either the physical or abstract dimensions, these elements should go through a *process of transformation* (Leonard, 1998). This implies that the disturbed elements should be rectified, so that there will again be commitment and focus among all participants of any

Figure 6. A Basic cConceptual Framework for IT-End User Relationships Showing the Main Processes Inside the Dotted Rectangle of Figure 5.

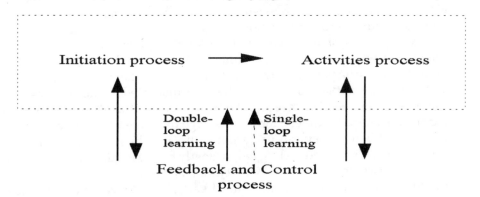

such relationship.

The main purpose of the transformation process will be to *help* participants[5] within the relationship to adapt to the new change(s) influencing their working relationship. It is of course true that one or more participants of a specific relationship could be quite happy (satisfied) with a specific change that affected the IT-end user relationship they belong to. These participants can be regarded as having gone through the transformation process without formal *help*. What is important in such a case, is that these participants should take the responsibility to support those who need *help* as explained below.

The principles behind the transformation process are:
- Strengthen the participants' *commitment* to the project.
- Ensure that the *focus* of every participant in the relationship, but especially that of the team as a whole[6], which has been flawed by the change(s), is fixed or adjusted.
- Serve as *forum* for those individuals in a relationship who understand and who have accepted the change to *support and motivate* other members.
- Support the *champion* in evaluating whether focus has been adjusted, so to continue with the "normal" activities of the team.

The conceptual framework for the transformation of the elements of an IT-end user relationship is illustrated in figure 8 and is explained in the rest of the chapter. Figure 7 is an example of a summarized conceptual framework, illustrating all the processes required to establish and maintain sound IT-end user relationships under changing conditions.

This conceptual framework for the transformation process illustrates three major components, namely:
- **Disrupted relationship**
  This component indicates that one or more of the elements in a given IT-end user relationship have been *disrupted*. These elements form part of either the *physical* or *abstract* dimensions. The term *disrupted* is used to indicate that one or more of the elements in a given relationship have undergone certain changes. Participants (people, the "living" element of any relationship and which form part of the *physical* dimension) in particular, normally experience major uncertainty. Kelly (1991) states that it normally forces participants of a team to address their fundamental expectations, goals, norms, and ground rules. Furthermore, participants' emotions normally have a direct impact on *abstract* elements like the knowledge base and commitment.
  Should the current communication system for example be replaced by a new communication system which is not working properly yet, the participants (people) as well as the communication system (technology) are disrupted, both of which form part of the *physical* dimension. Furthermore, it follows that elements in the *abstract* dimension will also be disrupted by such a change, for example the knowledge base and the level of commitment. In other words, participants need to understand (knowledge base) the new communication system first before they can use it optimally and the new communication system needs to be fixed (debugged) properly before it can be used to its full potential. Furthermore, it would be reasonable to say that a poor communication system will most probably affect participants' level of commitment,

Figure 7. A Summarized Integrated Conceptual Framework for IT-End User Relationship Showing all the Processes Taking Place in the Dotted Rectangle of Figure 5.

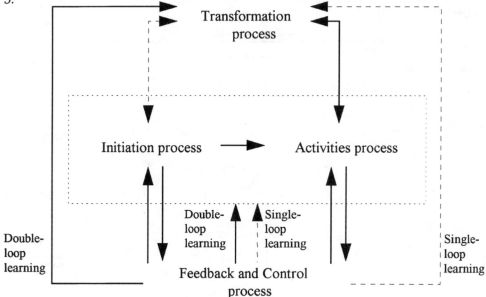

which forms part of the *abstract* dimension.

- **The transformation process**

  The purpose of this component is to take all elements of a disrupted IT-end user relationship through a process of *transformation*. In this regard it is important to realize (as was explained under the previous component) that if a physical element (apart from people) has been disrupted, the problem should be rectified as part of the *transformation* process. In other words, it is not only the people element that has to be *transformed*, but all elements, in order to ensure that the holistic nature of an IT-end user relationship would not have a counter effect on the transformation process. In order to ensure that commitment to the relationship is reinstated, Kinlaw (1989) states that it is important to give serious attention to the four "supports" of commitment.

  The activities involved in the transformation process will of course depend on the nature of the change that occurred, but should consist of the following basic framework:

- **Analysis of current reality**

  It is important to give all role players the necessary opportunity to analyse the new situation in order to become familiar with their *new* circumstances.

- **Desired state**

  After a proper analysis of the current state, it is important to start working

Figure 8. Conceptual framework for the transformation of all elements in an IT-end user relationship environment to maintain alignment (functional integration) between the infrastructures of IT and the business (Based on the work of Caperelli (1996) and Newman & Sabherwal, 1996)

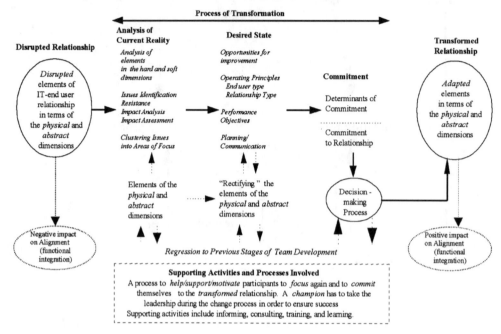

towards the desired state. This could imply that the type of relationship has to change, and by implication also the end user type. Furthermore, it is important to focus on performance objectives, as this is normally an aspect that gets damaged by change. Plans of action should be implemented to do the necessary "transforming".

Last but not least, the transformation process should be regarded as a learning process, not only to ensure that mistakes are not repeated, but also to improve on similar situations in future.

- **Commitment**

  Much has been said about commitment. The purpose of this activity in the transformation process is to ensure that all participants in the relationship *recommit* themselves to the relationship before they can continue with normal relationship activities.

- **Decision making**

  It is the responsibility of all role players to ensure that all participants in the relationship take part in decision making. Furthermore, it is the responsibility of the *champion* to ensure that all participants have recommitted themselves before the important decision is made to go on with the *normal* relationship.

- **Team development**
  In terms of the effects of change, it is important to take note of the effect it has on the level of development of any team. After a certain period of time in a relationship it would be reasonable to say that the participants (team members) would have gone through all stages of team development. In this regard Kelly states that "all teams will generally go through all stages". Unfortunately, research done by Kelly indicates that the moment certain kinds of changes affect a team, it seems that the development level of the team is also affected by this, and therefore the team will have to "rebuild" itself.

- **Adapted IT-end user relationship**
  This component indicates that all the elements as described in the *physical* and *abstract* dimensions of the IT-end user relationship, in particular the people (participants), have adapted to the changes, and now the relationship can continue with its normal activities. It could, of course, be argued that in the real world a relationship which was disturbed by change, could not be put in a "box of transformation" and when it comes out of that box, everything is *all right* again. This argument holds substance and in this regard it is important that the *monitoring system* be used, so as to evaluate the elements of the *physical* and *abstract* dimensions on a continuous basis to ensure that this kind of problem can be managed.

CONCLUDING SUMMARY

In this chapter the paradigm of IT-end user relationships was defined in terms of its *physical* and *abstract* dimensions. It was argued that these two dimensions enable one to fully describe the holistic nature of such relationships. Furthermore, in terms of business IT alignment, it was argued that the paradigm applies in the infrastructure domains (both IT and the business) and will therefore enhance alignment in terms of *functional integration*.

The factors that impact on the *soundness* and *sustainability* of relationships were discussed. It was pointed out that because of the *holistic* nature of IT-end user relationships, any of these factors which may be in a "poor" state may affect the soundness or sustainability of the relationship as a whole, and as such have a negative impact on the functional alignment.

Special emphasis was put on those changes typically taking place in an IT department and which will normally have a negative effect on IT-end user relationships. It was further pointed out that changes can affect elements of both the *physical* and *abstract* dimensions of a relationship. Furthermore, it was pointed out that it is important that the change management process should not only concentrate on the *transformation* of the participants (human beings) but also on *rectifying* physical elements, such as technology and structures, that have a negative impact on a relationship. A conceptual framework was proposed for the management of change with respect to the IT-end user relationship environment so to ensure that functional alignment will be maintained.

END NOTES

1 Under the description of the abstract elements the term 'holistic' is described in broader terms.
2 As human beings, people are viewed in this regard as the *physical enablers* who initiate, create, participate and maintain relationships, because of their inter-action with one another during transacting. This is in line with the adaptive structuration theory of DeSanctis & Poole (1994). See also Orlikowski (1992)..
3 Normal system development activities or any other types of support IT can give its end users.
4 This is true in terms of the *holistic* nature of *sound relationships*.
5 People form an important element of the physical dimension of IT-end user relationships.
6 The holistic nature of IT-end user relationships is of relevance here.

REFERENCES

CIO (1997). "Relationship Matter", (August).

Anderson Erin, Weitz Barton(1989). *Determinants of Continuity in conventional industrial channel Dyads.* Marketing Science,8(4), 310-323.

Argyris C. (1990). *Overcoming Organizational Defences: Facilitating organizational learning*, Prentice Hall, Englewood Cliffs, NJ.

Badaway K Michael (1994). Electronic Business Buyer, *Getting the most from cross-functional team*, 20(8), 65-69.

Beard Jon W. and Peterson Tim O. (1988). A Taxonomy for the Study of Human Factors in Management Information Systems (MIS). In Carey M J.: *Human factors in management information systems*, Ablex Publishing Corporation, USA.

Boar, Bernard, H. (1994). *Practical steps for aligningInformation Technology with Business Strategies: How to achieve a competitive advantage.* John Wiley & Sons, Inc. New York.

Bommer Michael, Gratto Clarence, Gravander Jerry & Tuttle Mark(1991).*A Behaviour Model of Ethical and Unethical Decision Making.* In Dejoie Roy, Fowler George, Paradice David. *Ethical Issues in Information Systems.* Boyd & fraser publishing company.

Caperelli David (1996). Management Corner: Leading the company through the chokepoints of change, *Information Strategy: The Executive's Journal*, Spring, 36-44.

Ciborra, Claudio U (1993). Teams, markets and systems Business Innovation and Information Technology, Cambridge University Press, UK.

Clarke, A A & Smyth, M G G (1993).A co-operative computer based on the principles of human co-operation: *International Journal of Man-machine studies*, Vol. 38, 3-22.

CSC Foundation (1994). *Future roles and responsibilities for the IS Department*, Final Report 96.

Dahlbom B, Mathiassen L. (1993). *Computers In Context; The philosophy and Practice of Systems Design.* Blackwell Publishers, Cambridge UK.

DeSanctis, Poole M S (1994). Capturing the Complexity in Advanced Technology Use: Adaptive Structuration Theory, 5(2).

Du Plooy NF (1995). *Overcoming the culture gap between management and IT staff,* Paper delivered at Conference on "HR Management of IT staff", IEC, Jan Smuts, March .

Giddens, A. (1984). *The Constitution of Society.* Berkeley, University of California Press.

Henderson JC & Venkatraman N. (1992). Strategic Alignment: A Model for Organizational Transformation Through Information Technology. In *Transforming Organizations.* Kochan TA, Useem M. Oxford University Press. New York.

Humphrey, Watts S (1990). *Managing the software process,* Adison-Wesley Publishing Company, Reading, Massachusettes.

Introna Lucas D. (1994). *Giddens, Emergence and Social Intervention.* Paper presented at the International Conference on Systems Thinking and Progressive Social Change, University of Cape Town, South Africa, 2-15.

Kelly, Mark (1991). *The Adventures of a Self-Managing Team,* Pfeiffer & Company, San Diego.

Kinlaw, Dennis C. (1989). *Coaching for Commitment: Managerial Strategies for Obtaining Superior Performance,* University Associates, Inc.,USA

Leonard AC (1998). Information Technology-End User Relationship In A Changing Environment, Thesis (D.Com.(Informatics))-University of Pretoria. Unpublished.

Moad Jeff (1994). Does your CEO get it?, *Datamation,* September.

Newman Michael & Sabherwal Rajiv (1996). Determinants of Commitment to Information Systems Development: A Longitudinal Investigation, *MIS Quarterly,* March, 23-54.

Orlikowski WJ (1992). The duality of technology: Rethinking the concept of technology in organizations, *Organizational Science,* August, 399-427.

Papp, Raymond (2000). Alignment of business and information technology strategy: How and why? *Information Management,* 11(3/4).

Pheysey, Diana C. (1993). *Organizational Cultures,* Routledge, New York.

Pitt, Leyland F & Bromfield, Derek, 2nd ed (1994). *The marketing decision maker: From MkIS to MDSS,* Juta, Kenwyn.

Reich, B,H, Benbasit, Izak (1999) Factors that influence the social dimension of alignment between business and information technology objectives. By the Society of Information Management (SIM) and the Management Information Systems Research Center (MISRC).

Robey, Daniel & Sales, Carol A. (1994). *Designing Organizations,* Richard D. Irwin, Inc., USA

Roode J D, A J Smith, User involvement in systems development: *South African Journal of Economic and Management Sciences,* Vol. 2, November 1989, 7-20

Stokes, Stewart L (Jr) (1991). A Marketing Orientation for End-User Computing Support. In Umbaugh R E, *Handbook of IS Management (Third Edition),* Auerbach Publishers, Boston and New York, 125-134.

Umbaugh R E (1991). *Handbook of IS Management (Third Edition),* Auerbach Publishers, Boston and New York.

Wike W R, Andersen A & Co. (1984). Service management. CMG XV *International conference on the management and performance of computer systems: Conference proceedings*, San Francisco, USA, 534-540.

Chapter XIII

Strategic Human Resource Forecasting for an Internal Labor Market[*]

Wilfred S.J. Geerlings, Alexander Verbraeck and Pieter J. Toussaint
Delft University of Technology, The Netherlands

Ron P. T. de Groot
Royal Netherlands Navy, The Netherlands

ABSTRACT

Every organization needs a staff appropriate for its tasks in order to accomplish its business objectives, both now and in the future. To gain insight in the quality and number of staff needed in the future, human resource forecasting models are being used. This chapter addresses the design of a simulation model for human resources forecasting, which is being developed for the Chief of Naval Personnel at the Royal Netherlands Navy. The aim is to provide their Director of Naval Manpower Planning with tools that give insight into the effects of strategic decisions on personnel build-up, and the effects of changes in personnel on reaching the organization's business objectives. This chapter introduces the major aspects of human resource forecasting. After that, the kinds of models that have been developed so far are presented, together with their merits and shortcomings. It is shown that a new way to investigate the future needs of manpower in an organization might be more effective than the current practice. The new models rely heavily on the use of simulation, and actually try to imitate the internal labor market and the external influences.

[*] The Royal Netherlands Navy has sponsored this research. We especially thank John van Beusekom and Gino J.A.A.M. Damen for their devotion to the project.

INTRODUCTION

Nowadays organizations operate in ever-changing environments. The impact of new technology, changing demands of customers, political factors and many others lead to organizations that have to transform their products, services, and internal processes on a continuous basis. These changing policies imply new ways of working, new job contents and other qualifications needed to carry out the organization's functions (Pettigrew & Whipp, 1991; Tyson, 1997). For an organization to survive in these dynamic circumstances, a long-term policy is needed. It is striking that when most organizations develop their long-term policy, they just focus on the products or services. Almost no attention is given to implications for the workforce or the allocation of employees to future tasks in the organization. When the new policy has already been carried out, many problems arise with staffing the new function structure with qualified employees.

The question is whether an organization that tries to implement a new policy has the right workforce to be able to support and sustain that policy (Batstone, Courlay, Levie & Moore, 1987; Burack, 1988). Restructuring the workforce takes much more time than implementing changes in technology, strategy, or the organization of work (Schein, 1978; Sluijs & Kluytmans, 1996). In other words, having the right number of skilled employees at the right time to carry out the organizational policy is on the critical path. The success of an organization depends heavily on the availability of correctly qualified employees (Evers, Laanen & Sipkens, 1993; Rahman bin idris & Eldridge, 1998). According to this, it is of importance for an organization to have insight into the characteristics of its workforce and into the effects of changes in policy on its workforce.

It can therefore be easily seen that there will often be a mismatch between the business strategy executed by an organization on the one hand and an lack of support on the other hand because of the organizational infrastructure. In their strategic alignment model Henderson and Venkatraman (1990) refer to the linkage between these factors as the strategic fit. Business strategy refers to business scope, business governance and the distinctive competencies of an organization, whereas organizational infrastructure consists of administrative structure, skills of employees and of processes. To improve the strategic fit more attention has to be drawn to strategic human resource planning methods.

Strategic human resource planning concerns all activities to provide the right number of employees having the right skills at the right moment in time, on the basis of the policy and plans of the organization (Zeffane & Mayo, 1994; Khoong, 1996). Within strategic human resource planning two tasks can be distinguished. First is manpower planning or short term planning, which answers questions about which employees will occupy what functions over the next couple of weeks or months. This chapter is focused on the second task, human resource forecasting. This is defined here as a forecast of the number of people per function group within an organization, their skills, and the time path of their movements between these function groups. These forecasts provide insight into the right quantity and quality of the workforce to carry out the proposed changes in the business strategy.

Over the past few decades, forecasting techniques in the field of human resources can be characterized by the addition of more and more sophisticated mathematical tools (Bartholomew, Forbes, & McClean, 1991) without any changes in the basic assumptions of these tools. These techniques are of no use, however, as long as they cannot be converted into practical tools usable within organizations (Parker & Caine,1996). The lack of usable tools is one of the reasons why the strategic fit between business strategy and organizational infrastructure regarding needed skills in a future configuration of the organization is often not realized

The focus of this chapter will be on new concepts to develop usable tools that provide insight into the effects of a changed business strategy on the needed workforce of the organization. As a consequence these tools will enable a better strategic fit between business strategy and organizational infrastructure. A case study at the Royal Netherlands Navy will be used to illustrate the current problems and the impact of the new way of thinking.

CURRENT PRACTICES IN HUMAN RESOURCE FORECASTING

Forecasting models of human resources did not evolve much over the last few decades. The methods and techniques used are well known (Burack, 1988; Bechet, 1994a). Within these models three parts can be distinguished: personnel supply, personnel availability and integration models. Two methods to estimate personnel buildup are used:

- *Extrapolation*
  The assumption is that personnel supply can be derived from trends from *the past. The main variable in these models is time.*
- *Correlation models*
  These models are based on relationships between personnel supply and explanatory variables such as turnover, sales volume or production. If for

Figure 1. Pull Flows and Push Flows in Current Models

example the turnover changes, the personnel supply will also change by a known factor.

The above models view employees simply as numbers that are apart from that completely void: only their quantity changes. Nothing can be said of the qualifications or functions the employees have over time. Furthermore these models give only the number of employees that are needed at a point in time. No information is provided if these prediction can be met with the current workforce.

Personnel availability techniques add dynamics. Dynamic systems models "attempt to predict the life movements of people within a closed system and their interactions with other systems" (Yelsey, 1982).

Two kinds of dynamics can be distinguished: a push-flow and a pull-flow, as is depicted in Figure 1. In a push-flow, movements between cells occur regardless of a job opening existing in that cell. If the transition rate from first mate to skipper is 4 percent per year and the number of first mates is 50, each year two first mates will be promoted to skipper. The pull-model takes into account the availability of a job opening. If one skipper position is free and the transition rate is ten percent per year, then only one first mate will be promoted. In practice, the rates are calculated on the basis of historical data to forecast the flow of staff between the functions in the future.

The most recent Royal Netherlands Navy human resource forecasting model (PBAS) was based on these techniques. Within a model like this, movement of employees is based on past behavior of groups of employees. There is no matching between employees and functions in the system, but only a movement of groups of employees through predestined job ladders. Employees do not change over time in these dynamic models.

The third category of models consists of integration models such as goal models. These models are mainly based on linear programming methods. Based on constraints the model finds the optimal solution. The disadvantage of these models is that for reaching the optimal solution and the desired occupation of functions, these functions often have to be understaffed and overstaffed. This is often not applicable in organizations. Furthermore it shares the disadvantages mentioned before.

For an in-depth overview of the kind of models that have been developed over the last two decades see Niehaus (1985) and Ward, Betchet & Tripp (1994).

The information provided by the these models are for particular moments in time only. At 1 January 2002 there are e.g. 100 employees available to fill the functions in the organization, and at 1 January 2003 we expect that number to have risen to 110. Nothing can be said of the development of the employees or changes in the organization between these points. The granularity of the time steps in the model defines the minimal time period between two observations. The steps are discrete. The development of the employees and the organization, however, is a continuous process. The current models provide insight into the differences between the supply and demand for two points in time. Insight into what happened between these points is not given. In the next section the manpower arrangement within the Royal Netherlands Navy will be examined. This will illustrate the requirements that a new type of human resource forecasting model must meet.

MANPOWER ARRANGEMENT AT THE ROYAL NETHERLANDS NAVY

The main objective of the Chief of Naval Personnel Royal Netherlands Navy is to provide the Royal Netherlands Navy with sufficient, competent and motivated personnel who will operate effectively in circumstances of war, crises and peace-operations both now and in the future. As mentioned before changing the skills of employees is on the critical path when new business strategies are implemented. To realize change in the required competencies of the Royal Netherlands Navy in time, insight is needed into the effects these changes have on the needed skills. These needed skills have to be compared with the current pool of skills and their development over time, in order to estimate which shortages or surpluses occur in the skills. The Royal Netherlands Navy has chosen an internal labor market as part of its organizational infrastructure. In this paragraph the layout and the consequences of next choice are given.

An internal labor market can be characterized as follows; "fixed ports of entry, internal promotions as main way of filling vacancies and normative, established procedures for hiring, firing and promoting" (Rosenbaum, 1984). Another characteristic is that upward movement in the organization is associated with a progressive development of knowledge and skills (Althauser & Veen, 1995). Mostly these skills are only useful for, and used by, employees within that specific organization. Therefore, another property is linked with an internal labor market. The organization focuses on continuing the contract of employment because of the dependency on gathered skills by the employee (Glebbeek, 1993). Thus, an important effect of an internal labor market is the importance of long-term career possibilities for the employees.

There are several reasons why the Netherlands Royal Navy has chosen an internal labor market. First skill-specific or specialized knowledge only needed within the Navy raises the personnel cost of the organization. An internal labor market is formed to avoid the outflow of employees as much as possible and to spread the cost of education over several years. Second, job ladders are constructed to produce a learning effect in such a way that in every function of the career a number of skills are added that are needed in the rest of the career. Third, the employees have to be accustomed to the specific culture of a militarily organization. And finally, the Navy tries to avoid the ambivalence hypothesis mentioned by Thijssen (1988), which states that organizations have to employ persons who not only function well at the time they are hired, but also have to evolve during the rest of their career within the organization. An employer can follow employees over time to get a clear perspective of their performance. Thereby a firm should be able to minimize the trap of promoting those employees who are not capable of carrying out future functions in their career path.

Inflow of new personnel occurs at two places in the Royal Netherlands Navy hierarchy, as a sailor or as an officer. After being contracted they follow initial courses, after which their naval career starts. The career path consists of a job ladder with corresponding ranks. Employees first get the required training before starting in a new function. Most of the functions require specific knowledge and skills only available within the Royal Netherlands Navy. Therefore they are forced to educate their personnel on the job. The internal labor market arrangement provides an accumulation of knowledge and skills necessary for higher functions in the organization. For example, to reach the rank of captain, a career length of at least twenty years is needed. The other factor is that the future prospects of possible careers within the Royal Netherlands Navy from the employees' viewpoint have to be attractive, otherwise they will leave the organization. This is a loss of invested effort in education and training for an employee who resigns. The Navy therefore "guarantees" their employees they can reach a minimum specified rank if they stay long enough.

The internal labor market within the Royal Netherlands Navy has enormous consequences for its personnel policy. It is not possible to enlist people on short notice in other than the entry positions because new employees lack the knowledge and skills needed for other positions. Therefore, a competent future substitution for a resignation should be enlisted early, for a captain for example twenty years in advance. This implies that a change in organizational policy, proposed for the future, which has implications for the job contents or for the organizational structure, must be checked for its consequences on possible occupation of the new set of functions. That is, the required qualifications for the (future) functions have to match the abilities of the employees that will be available at that time. Also, the effects on career possibilities of the current employees must be investigated. When career paths become less interesting, an additional amount of resigning employees can be expected. This additional outflow of employees usually creates serious problems with the occupation of the vacant functions. For example, if a new ship is introduced in the Royal Netherlands Navy, new functions are created, other functions disappear and job contents change. Information is needed to indicate whether or not the ship can be staffed with enough skilled employees. A sailor-job will not change much, but an operator of a new rocket system needs new skills. Retraining is an option, but limited by the capabilities of the employees, the time available for training, and by the effect the additional training has on the current job of the employee. These changes affect the composition of the job ladder and can lead to the absence of promotion possibilities for a sailor to the function of operator due to lack of preparatory training or due to lack of adequate subsequent functions. Of course, such a scenario could have been anticipated if good models were available. This means that there should be a fit between the labor governance structure of an organization, its division of labor and its career system on the one hand and its human resource planning on the other hand. This leads to three categories – organizational configuration, the type of governance structure and the type of career model – which have to find a place to develop manpower planning support models (Geurts, Evers, & Dekker, 1996).

The need to explore the different effects of proposed changes on structure, policy and job contents of the organization requires a modeling approach which provides insight into the dynamics of the system studied. The human resource forecasting model has to operate within a staff division of the Royal Netherlands Navy to answer a large number of questions. Several of these questions are of the "what-if" type, the most simple one being the "what happens if we do not change anything" scenario. Other questions are of the "how to" type. After having made an inventory of questions the organization expects the model to answer, it turns out that the questions can be divided into the following categories

- *Inflow questions*
  Example 1: Do we have the right kind of people in four years to crew a new ship?
  Example 2: What are the results of employing more or less people on starting positions?
- *Outflow questions*
  Example 1: What length of service is needed to reach a certain level of outflow, given that outflow depends on years of service?
  Example 2: What are the last functions before retirement?
- *Transition questions*
  Example 1: What effects occur if job promotions would be accelerated?
  Example 2: What are the main differences between the departments regarding promotion possibilities and time spent in functions?
- *Occupation questions*
  Example 1: Where does the first shortage of employees occur if a vacancy freeze is in effect?
  Example 2: Which effects occur if a new hierarchy level is inserted in the career ladder?
- *Personnel questions*
  Example 1: Are qualified employees available if the requirements for entering a certain function change?
  Example 2: How many employees reach the rank of first sergeant as their last rank?

The human resource planning model must provide outcomes answering these questions. Such a model should make it possible to detect pitfalls in long-term manpower planning. Furthermore, it must provide possibilities to evaluate different scenarios.

As can easily be deduced from the previous discussion, every organization struggles with these kind of questions when it has to make decisions in which way to develop or change the organizational strategy and it has to judge the effects on the organizational infrastructure. The information needed for this process at the Royal Netherlands Navy is largely equal to that of other organizations. The main difference is that the Royal Netherlands Navy has an wide range of specific skills, which are not available outside the organization. Therefore an internal labor market arrangement has been chosen. In the remainder of this chapter, the Royal Netherlands Navy is used as the case to illustrate the concepts and choices.

One should always keep in mind that the aim is primarily to prevent undesired situations from arising, not just to predict them with high accuracy. "In fact a decision maker is often more interested in obtaining insights and understanding how decisions change with varying conditions or assumptions and much less in a particular numerical value that may be a solution under a restrictive set of assumptions" (Marshall & Oliver, 1995).

FORMULATION OF THE NEW REQUIREMENTS

When applying the type of models mentioned in the "current practices" section to the requirements stated by the Royal Netherlands Navy, the following problems arise. A substantial disadvantage of the current models is that these are created for a more stable environment than the environment in which organizations operate today. Most of these classical models have been developed in times and circumstances where organizational goals were clear and instruments had predictable effects (Edwards, 1983; Evers & Korver, 1996; Bechet, 1994). The Royal Netherlands Navy operates in a frequently changing environment. Effective forecasts are based on assumptions about what will happen in the future. When past budgets allocated by politics and promotional patterns will probably not be repeated in the future, why use past data to project future trends (Bechet (1994b)? Therefore several assumptions on which the current models are based are no longer valid.

First, as a result of the changing circumstances, transition rates based on historical data need not at all be valid for the future (Bechet & Maki, 1987; Evers et al., 1993). After a change in the organizational structure, for example, the introduction of a new set of functions—historical data to model the accompanying transition rates between the new functions—is not available. The normal practice is to estimate the needed rates to overcome this lack of data. The outcomes of models that operate in such a way provide the users only with an answer how their own estimates of the forthcoming situation have worked out. We call this the prediction paradox: in order to provide transition rates, users should have insight into the results of changes in the organization, and using the model, try to gain insight in the personnel flows in the changed organization. The solution to solve this prediction paradox is that a human resource forecasting model has to use other mechanisms, independent of historical data, to allocate employees to functions.

Second, an implicit assumption is that when a transition between functions exists, the employees who flow between the functions are indeed qualified for their next job. If a function changes, requiring new qualifications of the employees, there is no possibility of accommodating these in the current models other than by a change of transition rates. The actual transition rates for the new situation will, however, be dependent on the qualifications of the employees in the functions that have a transition to the changed function. For the Royal Netherlands Navy it is important to know if employees are available within the organization who satisfy the new required qualifications. The conclusion is that additional parameters are needed to match function requirements and employee qualifications in order to be able to study the distribution of employees over the changed functions.

Third, through the explicit definition of push or pull transitions between functions, an inflexible model arises. Studying a possible change in the organization structure will therefore take a lot of effort, since changing the model is labor intensive. Related to this, because of the amount of policy changes in the Royal Netherlands Navy, the maintenance of the model will be difficult.

The conclusion is that other methods to allocate employees to functions are needed, as the information and flexibility, which the current models provide, are not sufficient in the context of the Royal Netherlands Navy. The information delivered is not rich enough to get insight in the changes that occur. The current models are not capable bridging the gap in the strategic fit, as they don't accurately describe the processes within the organizational structure of the Royal Netherlands Navy. Therefore, the proposed business strategy changes cannot be evaluated in a correct manner. This leads to discrepancies between the predicted human resource needs and the needs observed in reality. In the next paragraph a new approach is proposed which will provide a better insight into the effects of changes in the organization on the occupation of functions, and on the enlisted employees with their characteristics over time.

COMPETENCE APPROACH

As recognized in the section 'current practices in human resource forecasting", the current models abstract employees to empty entities or just to numbers. The availability of correctly skilled employees in time is taken as an – often wrong – assumption. As a consequence, these models can only give a valid outcome at best if the right amount of employees is indeed available. This is insufficient if one wants to evaluate the effects of organizational changes on personnel requirements. In this section we will describe a forecasting approach based on the differences in employee qualifications and job requirements.

To accomplish the goals of an organization, a certain set of competencies is needed (Lado & Wilson, 1994; Grundy, 1997). Three levels of competencies can be distinguished according to Sluijs & Kluytmans (1996), see Figure 2.

The first level concentrates on the individual perspective. An employee can be seen as a resource with specific competencies. These competencies are defined here as the whole of qualifications gained through education and through job experience. The employees supply the organization with their competencies to be able to reach its goals.

The second level emphasizes the internal organization of the resources. This internal organization consists of the specific competencies of employees together with their mutual relationships with procedures, processes, production technol-

Figure 2: Competence Scheme

Figure 3. Matching Present and Needed Competencies

ogy and knowledge systems (Nordhaug, 1993). The structure of the organization must be specified here in terms of an administrative structure with specified functions. From these functions the organization can derive its demand of competencies.

On the third level, the characteristic properties of the organization are addressed. Through a unique combination of knowledge, skills, formal structure, used technologies and processes, the organization is able to reach and hold a competitive advantage with respect to its competitors. To perform well on the third level, an organization has to identify the right organizational structure and division of labor on the second level. Derived from these decisions, the organization can identify the necessary competencies of individual employees on the first level. The objective of human resource forecasting is to give insight into the match between competencies provided by the employees and the demand for competencies within the organization.

Figure 3 gives an example of matching on the first level. The question that can be answered after carrying out this matching process is whether the organization has employees with the right competencies to carry out its policy. If a match cannot be realized, changes can be made on all three levels of competencies. In the remainder of this chapter, the assumption is that an organization has made its choices concerning the composition of competencies on the third and second level. This serves as input to deduce the necessary competencies on the first level.

A CONCEPT FOR HUMAN RESOURCE FORECASTING

As mentioned in the introduction, a mismatch exists between the demand of competencies based on the business strategy and the current competencies or skills within the accompanying organizational infrastructure through missing insights in the processes of manpower movements in the organization. In this paragraph a new concept will be presented to reach a strategic fit between business strategy and organizational infrastructure. This concept will be implemented in an simulation model.

As mentioned in the previous section, an employee can been seen as a resource with specific competencies. The objective of human resource forecasting is to give insight into the match between the competencies of the employees and the demand for competencies of the organization. To manage an organization effectively, it needs a long-term personnel policy, because changing the competencies of their manpower is on the critical path. To get insight whether bottlenecks occur by unaltered or by new policies, it is necessary to judge the effect of policies on possible staffing of the functions in the organization. A possible view on how to do this is

Figure 4. A Supply and Demand Model for Personnel Planning in Organizations

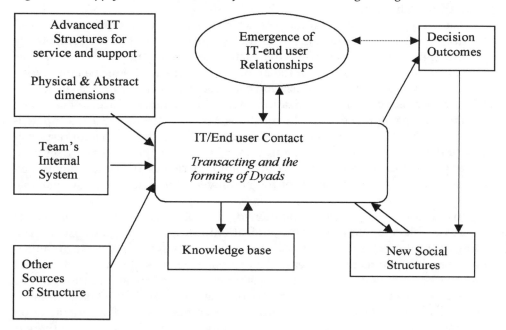

given in Figure 4.

The starting point of the simulation has to be the demand of the organization, in terms of needed competencies, and based on the organizational goals. Therefore, the following information is needed of the organization on the second level of competencies: first, a characterization of the organizational infrastructure, a list of functions that are available within the organization to be able to carry out the activities of the organization.

Second, the organization must provide a characterization of required competencies for carrying out a function. When combined with the needed number of employees in the functions, it defines the demand for competencies in the organization. To model the flow of employees through the organization, conditions for promotion such as a minimum time served in a function have to be determined. As mentioned earlier, education is important to develop the skills of the employees within an internal labor market. The possibilities for an employee to take courses are limited by the number of persons allowed and by the frequency the course is given. The organization must decide which range and quantity of education they offer to their personnel.

The supply side for personnel forecasting consists of the set of competencies for employees. Their competencies can change (and usually increase) continuously. The increase can have different causes. One cause for changes in the competencies of employees is gaining experience by working in a function. This competence growth through experience is an autonomous process. The organization can only influence it by changing the job-contents of the functions of the employees. Additionally, employees can be trained by taking internal or external courses. As the knowledge of the employee increases, the employee is better prepared for other functions.

The competencies of the employees, which are useful for the organization, can also decrease due to several causes. In the first place, a shift in the competency demand of the organization arises after each form of reorganization. The number of employees stays the same, but the amount of competencies of the employees, which are still valid for the organization can decrease. As these competencies are no longer necessary for the organization, they are not taken into account anymore when matching employees with the functions. Second, the employee's competencies become out of date after some time. Fighting obsolescence is a joint responsibility of the employee and the organization. Solutions can be to take courses or to change position in the organization to gain new experience. The factors mentioned here do not change the quantity of the employees, but just the set of available competencies.

In addition to the processes mentioned, three other factors have an influence on the available competencies in an organization: inflow, outflow, and absence. The inflow of employees creates a growth in competencies available for the organization. The other two factors decrease the competencies. Insight into the trends of absence (through illness, vacation, and other causes), inflow and outflow can be gained by analyzing historical data and by looking at the developments on the labor market. These three factors change the available competencies in the organization by changing the quantity of employees within the organization. Of course there is a difference between inflow in the 'lowest' functions in the organization and horizontal inflow in higher functions. In the latter case, one can expect the new employees to have a larger set of suitable competencies for the organization. In organizations with an internal labor market, employees usually only enter the organization at the bottom in a fixed set of functions. The inflow can be controlled by the organization, but of course it depends on the status of the labor market. Outflow and absence can only be influenced indirectly.

This model covers the development of competencies within the organization over time and measures to influence them. By defining functions as a set of demands for competencies, every function structure of an organization can be modeled. As a function and an employee are defined in terms of the same variable (i.e. competencies), they can be compared directly. Demand and supply are also integrated in one model, which provides an easy overview of shortages and surpluses of competencies in the organization. In the next section a simulation based implementation is introduced to provide the needed level of detail and accuracy for modeling the aspects proposed above.

NEW FORECASTING TOOL

In this section we will show a conceptual design of a forecasting model, based on object oriented simulation, to support human resource decisions. The object oriented modeling approach has been chosen because it allows detailed modeling of the interactions between different parts of the model: functions and employees for example are objects with their own behavior. This makes it possible for employees to have individual development characteristics over time, and it makes it easier for functions to have different competency demands after reorganization. The new design is composed of four parts:

- *Employee model*
  Autonomous developments of the employees over time. Furthermore, an inflow and outflow sub model are part of the employee model.
- *Function model*
  Job structure and changes therein.
- *Matching model*
  Algorithms to match job vacancies and their requirements with the employees and their qualifications.
- *Formal rule structure*
  Rules governing allocation decisions.

The employee model is concerned with the status of an employee, which changes over time. The competencies of the employees change during the simulation run as a result of acquiring new functions, aging, and obtaining more experience. A second aspect of the employee model refers to the education of an employee, which might be influenced by the possible functions that are "open" for the employee after additional training. The frequency, capacity and admission requirements of the courses are known. Therefore it is possible to detect which employees are eligible for certain training at a certain point in time. This enables the investigation of the effects of changing, for example, education possibilities and course contents for employees as well the functions they might obtain under a new policy. The outflow of employees can be based on extrapolating historical data on contract duration and on the relation between outflow and items such as age or labor market characteristics. Experimenting with these trends can give insight in whether or not it makes sense to invest in trying to keep employees longer. The inflow can be modeled in several ways: an immediate inflow whenever there is a vacancy that cannot be filled by internal employees, an inflow after a certain amount of time that depends on the status of the labor market, or an external inflow in certain functions only. The employee model can work independently of the matching model or the function model, but in that case no insight can be obtained in function related experience and in training driven by job vacancies.

The core feature of the function model is that it contains no relationships based on historical data that determine the transition possibilities of employees between functions. Functions can be any clustering of competency demands, from very rough – a few clusters for an entire organization – to a detailed level where each function describes the needed competencies for one person. A 'function' contains the following attributes:

- The minimum number of employees needed in the function for the organization to operate at all.
- The optimal number of employees needed in the function for the organization to operate properly.
- The maximum number of employees that can be allowed because of resource constraints.
- The function requirements, i.e., the competencies that employees must have to enter the function. Examples are age, rank, education, training and experience.

It is possible to define valid and non-valid functions in time, so organizational changes can be accommodated in the function model.

The matching model takes care of the assignment of employees to functions. The matching occurs between the available competencies of the employees and the required competencies of a function. On the one hand, if functions are valid for the current point in time and when they do not have the minimum number of required employees, they notify the matching model of their vacancies. On the other hand, there might be employees who are free to take another job. A matching strategy could be to consider those employees who have gathered enough experience in their current function for new functions. The matching model will match the required competencies of the valid functions with the competencies of the employees who are available. Another matching strategy could be that if a function is understaffed, employees whose competencies match regardless of the experience gathered have to be found immediately. In case one would like to incorporate horizontal inflow, the matching model can notify the inflow model of remaining vacancies. A final and interesting matching strategy is searching for a completely new match every year, as if all persons in the organization are free to look for a completely new job they can do best every year. This gives a lot of insight into qualifications that are really missing in the organization. Other algorithms to match the function requirement of a specific function against the qualifications of employees can easily be incorporated due to the object-orientation nature of the simulation model.

The formal rule structure represents the organization's policy. The rules that are modeled here influence and overrule properties of the three mentioned models. An example is the set of rules for retirement of employees, which influence the outflow submodel of the employee model. The availability of these rules makes it possible to construct scenarios for studying the effects of changing the retirement policy on the occupation of functions by employees in a straightforward way. For example: what are the effects of increasing the retirement age in the Royal Netherlands Navy from 55 years to 58 years as announced in the Defense White Paper in November 1999?

The operating procedure of the simulation is an event driven one with variable steps (not fixed steps of such as one year). During the simulation, employees will age over time, obtain education and hold functions. When an employee acquires a new function, the new function description will be added to the career history of the employee. One attribute of the function changes, being the total number of employees in the function (for an in depth description of the operation procedure, see Geerlings, Verbraeck, Vries, Beusekom & Groot, 1998).

Several outcomes can be immediately observed from the simulation, for any wanted timeframe or point in time:
- functions that are fulfilled;
- functions with a shortage of employees;
- employees who hold a function;
- employees who do not hold a function;
- competencies of employees that are not needed by the organization.

The decision makers can immediately use this information. If function requirements are fulfilled, the organization has enough employees with the right competencies. The inflow question, "Do we have the right kind of people in four years to crew a new ship", can be answered directly by using the model. Functions with a shortage of employees will cause serious problems with respect to the organization's objectives. In other words, the current manpower and the inflow and education policies cannot provide the right amount of competent employees in time. The organization now has to study how to solve this shortage. The different solutions devised lead to new scenarios that can be tested with the help of the simulation model. Example questions are: "What is the result if the inflow of employees is increased?" "Will a change in the competencies required for a function or changing the amount of courses for employees decrease the shortage?" Employees who occupy a function have competencies that are needed by the organization. If employees do not occupy a function this can have two reasons: their possible functions are occupied or they have a set of competencies that do not match the demands of the available functions well. Questions to consider include: "Are there any functions that aren't fulfilled ?" and "Is it possible to train the employees without a function for the vacant functions to make them useful for the organization?"

IMPLEMENTATION

This section will give an outline of a possible implementation of the employee model, matching model, and function model by adopting the object oriented modeling method. The employee object forms the core of the simulation model. Instances of this object can be in several states. These states are depicted in Figure 5 that summarizes the behavior of employees" object instances.

As depicted, the employee object possesses five possible states. The first one, not employed, means the employee is not yet part of the organization. Within the Royal Netherlands Navy, twice a year new sailors enlist and follow initial courses. The amount of sailors who enlist is based on historical data and labor market surveys. In the simulation, these employees are created and have a date of enlistment equal to the starting date of their initial training. If the simulation clock reaches the enlistment date the state of each of these employees changes to "employed active". Moreover, an "employed active" employee is available for a function and will get one in the matching process. Over time, the characteristics of the employee will change, for example the function history and the time spent in a function. A third state is an employee who is "being educated" and therefore not available for a function. After the duration of the education, the state of the employee changes back to "employed active". Furthermore, the educational record of the employee is updated. Through this education, the employee might be more suited for other functions. The illness chance and duration for state 4 "ill" are derived from historical data and depend on the kind of occupied function, the age of the employee, and maybe other attributes. After the illness duration, an employee becomes "employed active" again. If the period of illness is too long, the employee might leave the organization entirely with disability pension. It is also possible that an employee dies after a term of illness. The final state an employee reaches is discharge. Several grounds for dismissal can be recognized, such as end

Figure 5. State-Transition Diagram for the Life-Span of an Employee-Object

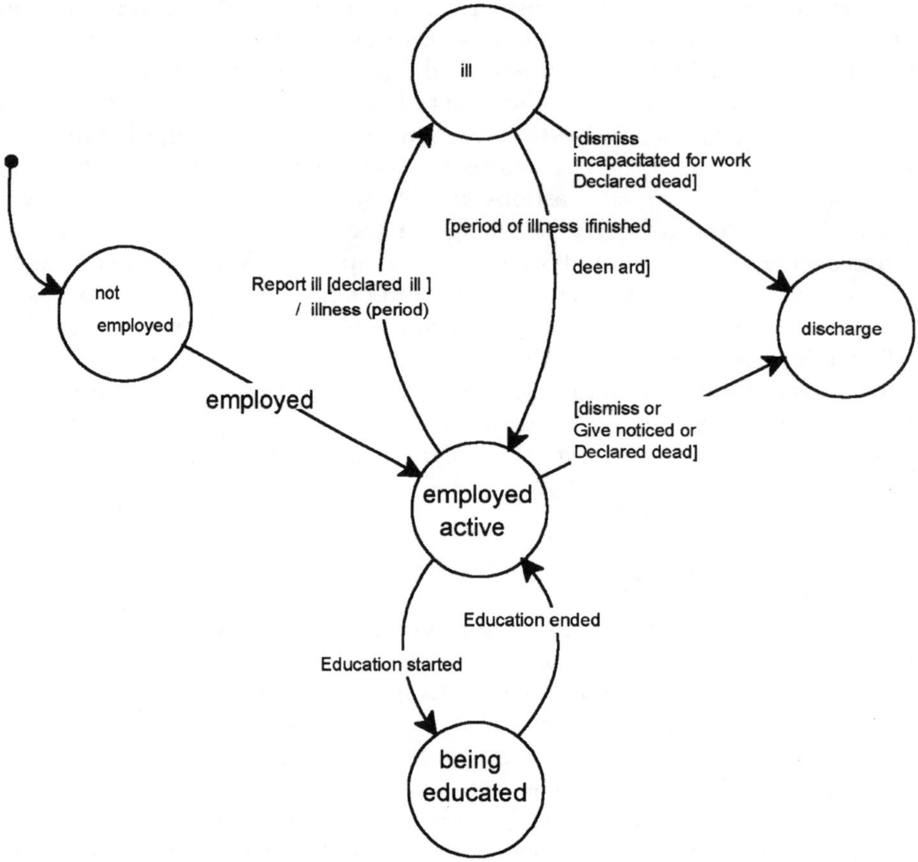

of contract, discharge by the organization, resignation by the employee, long illness, or death. The five states cover the complete life of an employee relevant for the organization. At every moment in the simulation, an overview can be given of the states of the employees. For the Royal Netherlands Navy, this means that there are always about 15,000 active employee objects in the model.

The current (old) models match supply and demand in an implicit way by the transition rates between functions. The assumption is that the promoted employees match the requirements of the next function. In our proposed model, the matching will take place explicitly. A match will occur between the present competencies represented by the employee objects and the necessary competencies required by the organization to fulfil their business goals (see forgoing section for details). Figure 6 depicts the matching process.

The objective of the matching is to avoid the rigid connections and placement of employees that we see in old flow models, and to allow for a flexible structure of matching supply and demand of competencies.

Functions can be described as static objects that need a number of employees with correct competencies to carry out the function. Functions give the information

Figure 6. Matching Process

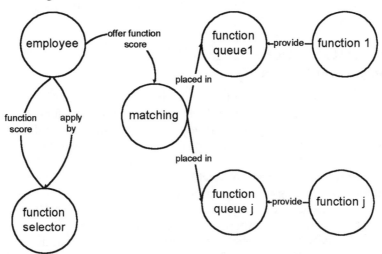

of competencies to a selector object. Their purpose in the simulation is to ask if there are suitable employees to carry out the vacant function. In order to judge the suitability of the employees, they obtain a weighed score of their competencies. These scores are being calculating by an object function selector and give back a score to the employee. Through this construction, the employee actually does not know for which function he is qualified. The employee enters the matching by his given score. The matching algorithm can represent several scenarios for example:

- Best employee occupies organizationally important function (BEOF). The employee gets the function that has the highest priority.
- Best employee gets the most suitable function (BESF). The employee gets the function that suits him best
  A brief example is worked out in Figure 7.

The employee is ignorant of the strategy used, he just enters the matching process and will be placed on a function queue. The higher the score the higher the ranking will be for the employee in the queue. The function notifies the function queue that it needs an employee to fill an occupation. If a function content changes, new weights for the competencies and new competencies will be stored in the object function selector. Functions and employees have no fixed connections. If a function

Figure 7. An Arithmetic Example with Two Strategies

Function : commander of a vessel.
Employees : A,B,C

Way of allocating employee regarding both strategies. Each function requests one employee

Employee	Frigate	Minelayer	Submarine
A	80	90	40
B	70	60	100
C	60	40	70

Commander	Priority	Strategy BEOF	Strategy BESF
Frigate	1	A	C
Minelayer	2	B	A
Submarine	3	C	B

is disabled, the employee gets no score for that function. This makes it possible to simulate several organizational scenarios regarding valid functions with the same set of employees.

IMPLICATIONS FOR THE ROYAL NETHERLANDS NAVY

We began this chapter with the observation that the Royal Netherlands Navy has difficulties gaining insight in which way the proposed long-term strategy affects the availability of required employees and the needed qualifications over time. An investigation has been made of the usability of current human resource forecasting models. It turns out, roughly said, that these models produce only numbers of employees placed on functions, based on historical data. This is also true for their current long term personnel planning systems.

As a solution, a new way of describing the organization's needs and resources has been introduced, the competencies approach. As a consequence the Royal Netherlands Navy should translate their current organizational descriptions into a competency-based description. Three dimensions can be distinguished:

- A description of all functions with the requirements that must be matched to enter a function.
- The employees within the organization with their current competencies.
- The ways employees can develop their competencies over time.

A new, flexible simulation tool based on the competencies approach has been designed for the Royal Netherlands Navy and has been implemented in the object oriented simulation language Modsim III. The tool incorporates employee developments, changes in functions requirements and changes in the formal rule structure over time. Therefore the interaction with the support tool takes place on a much lower abstraction level when comparing it with the old tools. This pays off in an increased information richness of the output provided by the model. All questions of the Royal Netherlands Navy that were mentioned in the section, "Manpower arrangement at the Royal Netherlands Navy", can be addressed. In addition to the questions the organization had in the past, many other issues can be studied and many other variables can be investigated for their effects on the match between competency demand and supply. This new angle on manpower forecasting provides more insight in the processes that influence personnel movements through the organization. Therefore more knowledge is gained by the personnel planners an policy makers on the effects of their proposed policy changes. When they take this into account for their future decisions, the entire organization can benefit from the increased insight.

CONCLUSIONS

In this chapter, a description has been given of the problems that arise within the Royal Netherlands Navy for getting insight in how to reallocate their manpower in the best way possible under changing circumstances. An overview has been given of current human resource forecasting models. The information the current models provide does not match the needs of the Royal Netherlands Navy. Current flow-oriented human resource forecasting models have several drawbacks:

- They depend heavily on historical data to predict transition rates between functions, while this data may no longer be applicable in a changing world.
- They lack data on transition rates when new functions appear in the organizational structure.
- The models report only on numbers of employees in functions.
- Insight into the effects of new requirements to enter functions cannot be made visible.

Therefore it is impossible for the current models to give an accurate insight into the future allocation of functions to employees.

The introduced competencies approach distinguishes between three levels, and it creates the opportunity to describe the effects of a new business strategy on the future demands for competencies. The demand can be described in detail on the third level where the needed competencies for individual functions are given. On the second level the internal organization of the function structure must defined. Relations and amounts of personnel needed are specified here. These two levels of competencies cover the demand side of the organization. The supply side of the organization are the employees and their skills. Their competencies are described on the first, individual, level. As a result the demand and supply are measured on the same scale. Proposed shifts on the demand side can directly be matched with the supply side to forecast their effects.

In order to implement this new approach, a conceptual simulation based model that is matching-oriented, was introduced. In this model, transitions between functions occur on the basis of matching the current competencies of employees with the current required competencies of functions. New functions do not pose a problem, because the requirements of new functions can be specified in advance. Transitions of employees take place automatically, and do not follow the outdated job ladders. The observed inflexibility to changes in the job-structure of the flow-model through explicit specification of transitions between functions has also disappeared in the matching model. Functions have no mutual relationships anymore. The matching between functions and employees is based on their respective properties. The signaled impossibility to incorporate job contents, and thus changes in job contents, in the flow-model can also be solved by specifying changing requirements of a function. The only parts of the model for which historical data is needed are absence generators, the voluntary outflow of employees, and, in case of organizations with an internal labor market like the Navy, the inflow. As a result the matching-oriented model is less dependent on historical data.

To analyze the effects of different scenarios on the organization, only the set of new functions with their requirements needs to be known. The matching process between employees and functions will now result in an occupation of functions by employees automatically. Thus, the simulation itself generates the patterns of personnel flows through the changed organization. The result depends on the chosen matching model which can still originate from the employee (push), the function (pull), or both (job center or job application analogy). Future research will therefore focus on the effect of different matching algorithms on forecast results, and on valid modeling of the current personnel policies of an organization in terms of matching rules.

The main conclusion is that the matching-oriented approach to human resource forecasting promises to provide better insight in the dynamics of the occupation of functions and the allocation of employees to functions over time. Therefore organizations can get a better insight into the impact of proposed changes to the organization, which leads to a more underpinned long-term human resource policy. As a consequence the Royal Netherlands Navy now has the possibility to investigate and evaluate the consequences of their proposed strategy changes. Therefore, the strategic fit between the business strategy and the organizational infrastructure is expected to be much tighter from now on.

REFERENCES

Althauser, R., Veen, K. van (1995). "An algorithm for identifying career lines from job history data", *Journal of Mathematical Sociology*, 20(2-3), 89-107.

Bartholomew, D.J., Forbes, A.F. & McClean, S.I. (1991). *Statistical techniques for manpower planning*, 2nd ed., Chichester: Wiley.

Batstone, E., Courlay, S., Levie, H. & Moore, R. (1987). *New technology and the process of labor regulation*, Oxford: Clarendon Press.

Bechet, T.P. (1994a). *Concepts of modelling*. In D. Ward, T.P. Becht & R. Tripp (Eds.), *Human Rsource forecasting and Modeling*. New York: HRPS, New York.

Bechet, T.P (1994b);"Breathing new life into old techniques: trends in human resource forecasting", In D.Ward, T.P. Becht & R.Tripp (Eds.), *Human resource forecasting and modeling, the Human Resource Planning Society*, 53-60, New York.

Bechet, T.P. & Maki, W.R. (1987). "Modeling and Forcasting focusing on people as a strategic resource", *Human Resource Planning*, 10(4), 209-218.

Burack, E.H. (1988). *Creative Human resource planning and applications : a strategic appraoch*. Englewood Cliffs, NJ: Prentice-Hall.

Edwards, J. (Ed.) (1983). *Manpower Planning*, Chichester: Wiley.

Evers, G.H.M., Laanen, Ch.C.M. van & Sipkens G.J.J. (1993). *Effectieve personeelsplanning*. Deventer: Kluwer Bedrijfswetenschappen. (in Dutch).

Evers, G.H.M. and Korver A.; (1996) "Mobiliteit en personeelsplanning", WESWA congress (in Dutch).

Geerlings, W.S.J., Verbraeck, A. Vries, D.K. de, Beusekom, J. van & Groot, R.P.T. de (1998). "Simulation support for strategic human resource forecasting; a conceptual model". In: A. Bargiela & E. Kerckhoffs (Eds.) ESS98 - Simulation technology: science and art. Ghent / San Diego: SCS, 556-563.

Geurts, T.W.; Evers, G. H. M., & Dekker R. J. P.(1996)." Human Resource Planning: A Contingency Approach", Work and Organization Research Center Paper, Tilburg, 2.

Glebbeek, A.C. (1993). Perspectieven op loopbanen, Doctoral Thesis, Groningen University, The Netherlands. (in Dutch)

Grundy, T. (1997). "Human resource management – a strategic approach", *Long Range Planning*, 30(4), 507-517.

Henderson, J., & Venkatraman, N. (1990)."Strategic alignment: A model for organization transformation via information technology." Working Paper 3223-90, Sloan School of Management, Masschusetts Institute of Technology.

Khoong, C.M. (1996). "An integrated system framework and analysis methodology for manpower planning", *International Journal of Manpower*, 17(1), 26-46.

Lado, A.A & Wilson, M.C. (1994). "Human resource systems and sustained competitive advantage: A competency-based perspective", *Academy of Management Review*, 19(4), 699-727.

Marshall, K.T., & Oliver, R.O. (1995). *Decision Making and Forecasting.* London, McGraw-Hill.

Nordhaug, O. (1993). *Human capital in organizations: competence, training and learning.* Oslo: Scandinavian University Press.

Niehaus, R.J. (Ed.). (1985). "Strategic human resource planning applications". *Symposium on strategic human resource planning applications,* New York: Plenum Press.

Parker, B. & Caine, C., (1996)." Holonic modelling: human resource planning and the two faces of Janus", *International Journal of Manpower*, 17(8), 30 – 45.

Pettigrew, A. & Whipp, R. (1991). *Managing change for competitive success,* Oxford: Blackwell.

Rahman bin idris, A. & Eldridge, D. (1998). "Reconceptualising human resource planning in response to institutional change", *International Journal of Manpower*, 19(5), 343-357.

Rosenbaum, J.E. (1984). *Career mobility in a corporate hierarchy*, Orlando: Academic Press Inc.

Schein, E.H. (1978). *Career dynamics: matching individual and organizational needs,* London: Addison-Wesley.

Sluijs, E. van & Kluytmans, F. (1996). "Management of competencies", *M&O*, No. 3, 201-221.

Thijssen, J.G.L.C. (1988). *Bedrijfsopleidingen als werkterrein,* Den Haag: Vuga/ROI (in Dutch)

Tyson, S. (1997). "Human resource strategy: a process for managing the contribution of HRM to organizational performance". *The International Journal of Human Resource Management*, 8(3), 277-290.

Ward, D., Bechet, T.P. & Tripp, R. (Eds.) (1994). *Human resource forecasting and modeling,* New York: HRPS.

Yelsey, A. (1982). "Validity of human resource forecast designs", *Human Resource Planning*, 5(4), 217-224.

Zeffane, R. & Mayo, G. (1994). "Planning for human resources in the 1990s: development of an operational model", *International Journal of Manpower*, 15(6), 36-56.

Chapter XIV

Strategic Alignment for Electronic Commerce

Christian Bauer
Electronic Commerce Network, Western Australia

ABSTRACT

The dynamic nature and flexibility of electronic commerce increases the importance of the alignment of business strategy and information technology further. This chapter presents an extension of the strategic alignment model with an integration of the external domains of business and information technology strategy, thus keeping the focus on the competitive environment and shifting the responsibility for information technology to top management level. The application of the proposed hypothesis through a framework of the competitive environment is demonstrated within the context of the retail banking industry.

INTRODUCTION

This chapter investigates the relationship between business and information technology strategy of organizations in the new economy transformed by electronic commerce and on-line distribution. The following discussion of suitable reactions to these trends for strategy formulation is based on Henderson and Venkatraman's strategic alignment model. The model is adjusted to reflect the requirements imposed by the new economy. Subsequently, the impact of emerging electronic distribution on the strategic environment in general, and the competitive environment in particular, is formalized in a staged industry framework. The application of this framework in conjunction with the revised strategic alignment model is then demonstrated for the on-line retail banking industry.

On-line distribution will lead to dramatic changes in the competitive environment over the next few years. Information technology and telecommunication networks provide new opportunities to reach consumers more efficiently. However, if firms neglect the challenges associated with these opportunities, they risk losing customers and giving up competitive advantages to faster competitors. While consumers will enjoy the freedom of open networks and standards, companies struggle to incorporate the Internet challenge into their corporate strategy. Organizations have to respond to the success and the potential of on-line distribution. The implementation of open standards and resulting areas for differentiation and competition will change industry structures and entry barriers. Thus, the optimal alignment of the business strategy with the information technology strategy becomes a critical success factor for organizations of all sizes.

STRATEGY ALIGNMENT FOR ELECTRONIC COMMERCE

The analysis of suitable alignment models leverages the existing strategic alignment model by Henderson and Venkatraman. However, the substantial advancement of information technology in the electronic commerce era necessitates a revision of the strategic alignment model to reflect the increasing requirements on strategy formulation in the new economy. These necessary changes are directed at the analysis of the external domain for both the business and the information technology area and are presented in detail a bit later on.

The Strategic Alignment Model for Information Technology

The impact and importance of information technology on a firm's competitive advantage (Porter & Millar, 1987) and the corporate strategy formulation (Keen, 1991; Scott Morton, 1991) has been acknowledged by academia and practitioners for some time now. Despite doubts about the strength of productivity gains through information technology innovation (Strassman, 1990), information technology management theory and practice focused on "shaping" and "reengineering" business functions (Hammer & Champy, 1993; Venkatraman, 1994).

Henderson and Venkatraman (1999) proposed the "Strategic Alignment Model" as a theoretical framework for the alignment process between information technology and corporate strategy. Subsequently, the Strategic Alignment Model has been empirically applied and revised by several other authors (Luftman, Lewis & Oldach, 1993; Papp, 1995).

As emphasized in Henderson and Venktraman's work, and even more important in electronic commerce, is the inherently dynamic nature of strategic alignment. The evolutionary nature of electronic commerce requires organizations to constantly adjust their strategies, business processes, and deployed information infrastructure and applications (Bauer, Glasson & Scharl, 1999). Clearly, the "compressed" Internet time leads to added pressure for the adoption of a strong position on strategic alignment. In terms of a subject description of strategic alignment, Henderson and Venkatraman (1999) propose: "... a strategic fit between the position of an organization in the competitive product-market arena and the design of an appropriate administrative structure to support its execution".

The Strategic Alignment Model identifies four separate strategic domains along two dimensions:
  • Distinction between business strategy and information technology strategy; and

Figure 1: The Four Domains of the Strategic Alignment Model
(adapted from Henderson and Venkatraman, 1999)

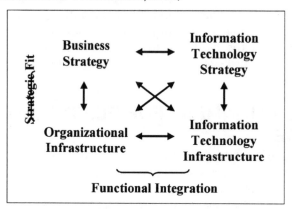

- Distinction between external (on products, markets and sourcing environments, and competitive advantage in general) and internal focus (on design of administrative structure and critical business processes).

These two distinctions result in four domains, as depicted in Figure 1. Functional integration is the linkage between business and information technology domains, while strategic fit is the linkage between internal and external domains.

The number of linkages between all four domains totals six (see black arrows between strategic domains in Figure 1), which require strategic alignment to yield optimal economic results. In theory, each of the domains could be aligned to the other three domains separately. However, the complexity of the alignment task (and the dynamic nature of strategy formulation and environment) generally does not allow such an approach. Consequently, several different alignment perspectives (as described in chapter 1) exist.

The Strategic Alignment Model and Electronic Commerce

The commercialization of the Internet and the rise of electronic commerce further strengthened the link between business strategy and information technology strategy. A major impact of electronic commerce has been to further elevate the information technology-related issues of strategy from inward focused support functions to critical success factors. Through electronic commerce, information technology is not only achieving cost savings through the elimination of process inefficiencies, but is also a driver for future revenue opportunities. The absolute necessity for alignment of business and information technology strategies is consequently becoming more and more the focus of attention (Papp, 1998).

The external focus of any strategic analysis in the information technology area becomes particularly important because it is no longer the support function of information technology that is in the center of attention, but the opportunities arising from a changing marketplace, the new "marketspace" (Rayport & Sviokla, 1995). The importance of electronic commerce initiatives and the strength of the market forces that are driven by information technology require business strategy to be linked closer to information technology than other corporate areas. Electronic commerce evolves continuously and requires fast response from organizations according to market and technical innovation. The business strategy can therefore only be formulated based on the external information technology strategy. Likewise, the information technology strategy needs to be based on the business strategy. Thus changes in the competitive environment in electronic commerce necessitate that organizations first assess the technology—business functional integration (competitive potential perspective) followed by the business strategy—infrastructure strategy fit (strategy execution perspective). By cycling through these perspectives (see chapter 2) electronic commerce can successfully integrate business and technology strategy. Figure 2 provides an overview of this new information technology alignment perspective.

Of particular importance is the role of top management in formulating a strategy for the new economy, since it requires a business visionary that understands the fundamental laws of the new economy and the technical foundations driving success in this arena. Simply shifting strategy responsibility (or parts thereof) from top management to information technology management (i.e., from the CEO to the CIO) is doomed to fail, since such an approach lacks alignment with other functional areas within the organization and organizational "power" for strategy execution. The next section will present a framework that empowers decision makers to assess the market situation and formulate their business strategy in line with the market landscape shaped by the forces of electronic commerce.

A FRAMEWORK FOR THE ASSESSMENT OF MARKET COMPETITION IN THE NEW ECONOMY

The decision makers in global organizations are faced with rapid development in the information technology area. Alternative distribution channels for

Figure 2: New Alignment Perspective (integrated)

services and products, namely direct and/or electronic delivery channels, have a significant impact on the industry structure and therefore the overall corporate strategy. In a recent *Harvard Business Review* article, Evans and Wurster predict (1997, p. 71):

> "Executives —and not just those in high-tech or information companies —will be forced to rethink the strategic fundamentals of their business. Over the next decade, the new economics of information will precipitate changes in the structure of entire industries and in the ways companies compete."

The economies and principles of new business models are opening up more opportunities for such changes to occur (Evans & Wurster 1997). The areas, where such opportunities will appear, are inherently tied to the characteristics of new distribution channels. Figure 3 represents a framework to structure these areas into stages, or layers. It distinguishes between the physical network, transmission standards, distributed data and object models, basic functions (routine and mass transactions) and special functions (value-adding services). Focus on competitive strategies in "lower" layers will become less important when these layers have been standardized. Standardization occurs at all layers due to customer pressures, transaction efficiencies, and/or economies of scale. However, it is generally easier to achieve standardization at the lower layers, and it can therefore be observed at the lower layers first. These interdependencies introduce a sequential element into the framework, resulting in the layers effectively becoming stages. At any point of time, the stage of the industry determines the scene where the strategic plays will take place. The formulation of the corporate strategy cannot be carried out success-fully without the determination of the current stage of the industry according to the framework in Figure 3.

The proposed framework consists of the following stages (bottom up in Figure 3):

Figure 3: Framework of Competition Stages for On-line Distribution (modified from Bauer, 1998; compare also Dratva, 1994)

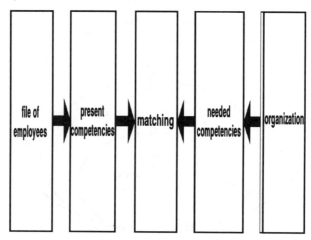

1. *Physical Network*: The accessibility of electronic channels for customers is an obvious precondition for alternative distribution. Before the emergence of the commercial Internet, access to (proprietary) telecommunications networks was determined to a large extent by the physical access to terminals or other end-user equipment providing connection to the networks. With the global connectivity of the Internet the focus of physical network access has been clearly shifted to consumer and end-user adoption rates and available Internet bandwidth.

2. *Transmission Standards*: Physical connectivity is only one requirement of (tele) communication. As it becomes clear from layered communications models such as the ISO/OSI (International Standardization Organization/Open Systems Implementation) Reference Model (Tanenbaum, 1989), the interconnection of information systems requires higher level protocols. The convergence of media and the success of TCP/IP as a de-facto standard already reduce the barriers in this area significantly. The origins of the phone network for primarily voice communication information and the Internet for primarily data transmission are early examples of current convergence processes. The security of electronic distribution channels is another concern to business operations and again leaves the choice between proprietary and open solutions (Bhimani, 1996).

3. *Distributed Object and Data Models*: Specifications on the format of the transaction data are a first step to create complete interoperability (i.e., multi-vendor capability). Customers can then access various vendors with the same software and customized interface. The standardization can also be formulated as object models with attributes and methods, which extend the specification beyond the simple definition of content to process.

4. *Basic Functions*: At this stage, standardization is not restricted to pure technology any more. Standardization of products and services is needed to meet the requirements of virtual business models (for example, trust in an on-line business relationship) and to enable automated tools, like agent technology. For the purposes of this chapter, basic functions comprise essentially all routine mass transactions.

5. *Special Functions*: Besides the basic (mass) functions, companies fulfill a wide variety of specialized functions for their customers. These functions are usually of a more complex nature and involve some form of advising and consulting. The delivery of special functions involves a different set of competencies and client communication, setting it apart from the provision of basic functions.

Both information technology and business strategy need to consider these competition stages (layers). The framework allows identifying areas of the competitive environment where business strategy can leverage (internal) business and information technology infrastructure capabilities. The following section will demonstrate strategy considerations and formulation within this framework.

THE RETAIL BANKING INDUSTRY AS AN ILLUSTRATION

The retail banking industry is presented as an example and illustration of the effects and application of the competitive framework introduced in the previous section. The retail banking industry has been chosen as a proven pioneer of alternative distribution channels. After an investigation of the impact of Internet banking utilizing the framework for competition stages, the strategic choices for decision makers in financial services organizations in the current market situation and with current technological infrastructure are evaluated. A critical evaluation of available strategic theories led to the selection of Porter's model of competitive strategy as the most suitable for this illustration. The application of the competitive framework to a more traditional business strategy model serves as an illustration for the actual decision making in the current market situation.

An Overview over the Retail Banking Industry

The Financial Services industry, and in particular retail banking, is a leading pioneer in exploring the opportunities of the Internet and in implementing on-line solutions for consumers. For an industry with high information intensity in both product content and value chains (Porter & Millar, 1987), the early adoption is not surprising and awareness of on-line trends is a necessity to all companies competing in such an area. In this section current trends of on-line retail banking will be used to illustrate the importance of the Internet for the Financial Services industry.

Physical branch networks are the traditional distribution channels for retail banking. Retail banks are increasingly confronted with high fixed costs incurred by this mode of distribution. The cost of mass transactions (e.g., cheque processing, money transfers, account statements or cash withdrawal) increases and can hardly be recovered from customer fees. The shift from interest-based to commission-based revenues implies a greater emphasis on efficiency of business processes. Additionally, financial deregulation leads to more fierce competition with new competitors from within the industry (foreign and direct banks) and from outside (e.g., technology leaders or insurance companies). Banks challenged by this dynamic environment are actively looking for alternative distribution channels. Besides more "traditional" concepts still involving human-to-human interaction, for example mobile or telephone banking, retail banks have started to offer a variety of electronic delivery channels. A study from the Bank Administration Institute (Yan & Paradi, 1998) reports that in the U.S., 32 % of customer interaction is done physically (branches and ATMs), 58 % through phone and mail, while 10 % is already making use of electronic systems. A classification of currently available electronic distribution systems includes: Phone-banking (automated); Self-service with kiosk-systems; electronic banking directly via PC/modem-connection; electronic banking via on-line services; and Internet banking (Bauer, 1998).

Moving toward a virtual delivery channel offers advantages for banks and customers: sharp reduction in costs (Bauer, 1998; Booz Allen & Hamilton, 1996), new types of services (e.g., real-time trading), and the convenience of anytime, anywhere banking services. The growth figures of the Internet banking market indicate a success story. In a 1998 survey, 69 % of American households with personal computers were willing to adopt on-line financial services for a small monthly fee (Cyberdialogue, 1999) and similar figures can be assumed in other developed countries (KPMG, 1998). At the same time, more and more banks are starting to establish an on-line presence and the number of worldwide banks with on-line account access jumped from 55 in 1996 to 625 in 1998 (KPMG, 1998). Banks are starting to direct their investments in electronic distribution channels primarily at Internet banking.

Anecdotal Evidence from the Retail Banking Industry in Support of the Competition Framework

The physical connection or accessibility of consumers has traditionally been associated with branch networks in retail banking. Retail banks are trying to keep their accessibility high, but have changed their distribution strategy from building large branch networks to providing several alternative distribution channels, for example ATM networks, phone banking, or electronic banking. The introduction of Automated Teller Machines (ATM) and the linking of bank's ATM networks is a prime example of the radical impact of electronic distribution channels on competitive strategies. The ATM became the primary interface between the bank and the customer leading to declining consumer brand loyalty (Rayport and Sviokla, 1994) and giving customers access to the bank wherever an ATM was located. Naturally, the location of the nearest bank branch became less important to customers, changing the rules of competition, entry barriers and the industry structure radically. Banks began to focus on the content of their products rather than the simple provision of access services.

Another example can be drawn from phone banking. In 1989, FirstDirect, a stand-alone direct bank serving their customers only through (operator assisted) phone banking started operation in the United Kingdom. FirstDirect quickly gained 500,000 customers by combining excellent service with an inexpensive fee structure (Devlin, 1995; Bosco, 1995) and building a defensible business model. Accessibility, transmission standards and protocols, and the data interface (manual in this case) could all have been duplicated fairly easily. However, by concentrating on basic and special functions, FirstDirect differentiated itself from followers.

In proprietary electronic banking, for example the PC-banking solutions relying on proprietary client software introduced in the 1980s, each solution typically relied on singular transmission standards and protocols, preventing a uniform set-up of telecommunications equipment for access to multiple banks. The emergence of Internet-based solutions forced banks into providing more open solutions with multi-banking capabilities. This resulted in a radical shift, since uniform (open) transmission protocols and later data interfaces provided customers with a wider choice of banking services. The key to signing up customers was no longer to connect them to the bank's system more easily, but rather the basic and special functions that were offered.

The Strategy Formulation Process Illustrated
Generic business strategy

Strategic concepts and models of strategic thinking have played a most important role in the scholarly research into business theory (e.g., the PIMS project,

Buzzell & Gale, 1987) and in the work of major consulting groups (e.g., The Boston Consulting Group) in the 1970s and 1980s (Hamel, 1998; Prahalad & Hamel, 1994). Porter's work on competitive strategy (Porter 1980) and competitive advantage (Porter, 1985) became very influential in business schools and industry. The focus shifted in the early 1990s to an emphasis of the process of strategic thinking (Hamel, 1996), management role (Mintzberg, 1994) and operational improvement (Hammer & Champy, 1993). Recently a swing back to acknowledge the importance of strategy (Hamel, 1998) and Porter's structured strategic concepts (Surowiecki, 1999) can be observed. This chapter looks at the impact of the general corporate strategy on the on-line distribution strategy and therefore needs to analyze the strategic position of the examined organization. Therefore, Porter's model of generic competitive strategies has been identified as the most suitable for the purpose of this study.

In Porter's view of modern markets, five forces that drive industry competition can be identified (Porter, 1980; Porter, 1979): Threat of new entrants into the industry, bargaining power of buyers, threat of substitute products and services, bargaining power of suppliers and rivalry among existing firms. These structural determinants of the industry influence an organization's position and determine its strategy in response to this position. Porter (1980) identifies three possible generic competitive strategies —cost leadership, differentiation and focus. An organization failing to fully commit to any one of these generic strategies ends up "stuck in the middle" —an extremely poor strategic position (Porter, 1980). The three generic strategies can be characterized as follows:

- *Overall cost leadership*: The basic objective of this strategy is to outperform competitors industry-wide in terms of product cost. Managerial attention to cost control is a necessity for this strategy. High revenues can still be achieved through low-cost positions and high relative market shares.
- *Differentiation*: This strategy requires a unique position in an industry through providing value to customers that cannot be offered by any competitor. The potential areas of differentiation range from technology to brand image and distribution networks. Porter (1987), concerned about the failures of organizations to succeed, offers a detailed framework to assess the benefits of this strategy in advance.
- *Focus*: A particular buyer group can be targeted specifically by market segmentation. Superior competitive position can be achieved through both lower cost and/or differentiation.

Next, an attempt will be made to classify corporate business strategies according to these generic strategy types.

Standardization processes in Internet banking

The goal of widespread integration into client software (financial management software, Web interfaces, etc.) requires financial transaction specifications to be open and publicly available. Customers can then access accounts at multiple banks with the same software. Economies of scale in providing software solutions, market power and software integration led soon to a concentration on a small number of standards, with Open Financial Exchange (OFX) from Intuit, Microsoft and Checkfree and Integrion Gold from IBM, Visa and a number of high profile retail banks as the most prominent survivors. Plans have already been announced to merge these last two remaining financial services standards (BITS, 1998). In the current version 1.6 (Open Financial Exchange, 1998) OFX supports a variety of banking functions and object specifications.

At this stage the standardization is not restricted to the information (or the specification thereof), but also covers the essential banking functions. Where possible, these functions need to be standardized and a certain service level needs to be guaranteed to allow client software to rely on (back-end) banking applications and to establish "trust" in a virtual world. The implementation and processing of basic banking functions, such as:

- account information,
- credit card management,
- inter- and intrabank funds transfer,
- electronic (bill) payments, and
- investment and money market information

will be required to satisfy certain minimum standards. Only retail banks that oblige to these criteria will be allowed to participate in on-line distribution systems and electronic markets.

Strategic options according to the competitive environment in Internet banking

For the illustration of the strategy formulation process we will focus on the competition stage that shows the most recent development: distributed data and object models. As outlined before, the competing standards in this area are OFX and Integrion GOLD, which allow the customer to access banking services through the Internet with the client software of her choice. The occurrence and widespread implementation (both in client software and bank gateways) of these open financial transactions standards requires retail banking institutions to choose between adoption and non-adoption. Opting out of on-line delivery completely, without offering an Internet-based alternative, will only be feasible for organizations in narrow niche markets where customers are not Internet-literate or where services cannot be enhanced through on-line communication channels.

The top of Figure 4 shows this relationship between the business strategy and the Internet (distribution) strategy. The three business strategies according to Porter (cost leadership, differentiation and focus) on the left hand side have been discussed previously. As depicted on the right hand side of Figure 4, the on-line distribution strategies (or information technology strategies in the more generic strategic alignment model) can take the form of one of three options: adoption of open standards, implementation of a proprietary solution or non-adoption of on-line distribution. How can a sensible alignment of a business strategy with an on-line distribution strategy be achieved? The answer to this question can only be found by analyzing the market development—what information technology stage is the industry in, what are the technical drivers— and applying the desired business strategy to the problem. The simultaneous alignment of both externally focused strategies will then determine the options for the infrastructure implementation.

For the infrastructure categorization of the strategy of a particular organization, the pricing of transaction fees serves as a proxy to reflect the generic strategy.

Figure 4: Strategic Choices for On-line Distribution and their Operationalization in the Retail Banking Industry

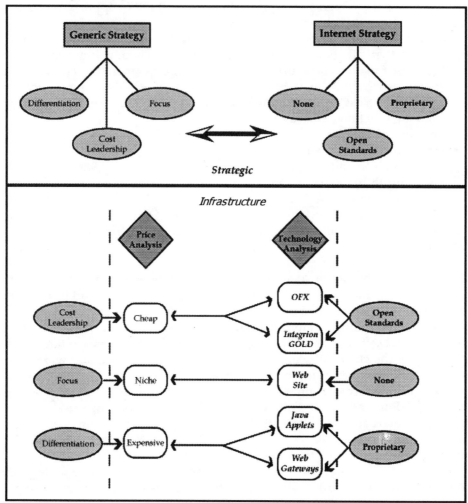

Clearly, cost leaders will have to offer the most inexpensive rates to their customers. On the other hand, retail banks concentrating on differentiation will introduce a more expensive fee structure as compensation for their superior services. Focused banks will take either one of two forms: smaller, regional banks or private banks concentrating on only the wealthiest clientele. Protected by entry barriers, these banks are expected to charge the highest fees. However, they will be separated from the other banks (and classified as "focus" banks) prior to the categorization.

As explained above, organizations can respond to the emergence of an industry-wide standard for electronic transactions with three mutually exclusive strategies. On an operational level, these strategic Internet options translate into certain actions on the marketplace and in the adoption of specific information technologies:

- *Proprietary software* is custom-made for the requirements of the institution and its customers and becomes the single point of access via the Internet. Retail banks opting for a proprietary strategy will implement their own Internet applications and data interfaces. Available technologies include HTTP gateways, JAVA-Applets or stand-alone applications utilizing an Internet socket.
- Adoption of an *open* standard provides customers with a choice of client software and reduces implementation and maintenance cost for the financial institution. Currently OFX appears to emerge the dominant open standard for Internet banking transactions. In this option banks would therefore adopt OFX (or the competing standard Integrion Gold).
- *Denial* or non-delivery and concentration on traditional distribution channels avoids competing on the Internet. Retail banks that choose not to offer electronic transactions delivery over the Internet will most likely still operate a small Web site with some information and for advertising and public relations purposes.

Broad industry adoption is crucial to the establishment of any standard. Retail banks with better service and higher fees will choose proprietary solutions, price leaders will opt for OFX and focused retail banks will not offer electronic transactions on the Internet. Crowston (1996) predicts similar behaviour and strategic options for the development of Internet buying agents.

CONCLUSION

This chapter analyzed the impact of electronic commerce on strategic alignment. The hypothesis that the new economy requires organizations to integrate the external domains of both the business and information technology in their strategy formulation process has been discussed in the context of the strategic alignment model. The application of these theories was illustrated with practical examples from the retail banking sector. The key points for the application and extension of the presented framework are:

1. Electronic commerce elevates the importance of information technology to top management level. Strategic decisions cannot be made without considering current developments in the market environment and information technology. In fact, it can be argued that with electronic commerce the market environment becomes information technology. Therefore information technology has to be elevated over other functional corporate areas for successful business planning (see chapters 1 & 2).
2. The alignment of strategy with the external domains, namely the business and information technology environment, is equally important. The competitive framework implies that a strategy can only be successful if it is aligned with the stage the industry is in. Therefore the strategy can only be determined after the industry has been assessed.
3. The competitive framework provides a tool for decision makers to analyze the competitive situation in an on-line environment and identify the areas (layers) that require particular attention. As it has been shown for the retail banking industry, current strategic options and analysis tools do still apply in

the new economy, but have to be supplemented by additional tools and frameworks to remain valuable for electronic commerce.

The importance of the on-line distribution strategy for the success of an organization becomes obvious when the Internet remains the only direct link to the customers. This importance requires decision makers to integrate information technology into their business strategy and align it with the business strategy. Strategic problems that arise from these newly established relationships have been presented. Based on theoretical models for competitive strategy and strategic alignment, the framework for competition stages provides a conceptual model to analyze the competitive and technological environment. The illustration of these strategy formulation processes in the retail banking industry can serve as a recommendation for industry on how to address this problem.

REFERENCES

Bauer, C., & Scharl, A. (1999). Acquisition and Symbolic Visualization of Aggregated Customer Information for Analyzing Web Information Systems. *Proceedings of the Thirty-Second Annual Hawaii International Conference on System Sciences (HICSS-32)*, Maui, Hawaii, USA.

Bauer, C. (1999). Financial Institutions and the Internet: Issues and Trends. In C. Romm and F. Sudweeks (Eds.), *Doing Business On The Internet: Opportunities and Pitfalls*. London, Springer, . 65 - 76

Bauer, C., B. Glasson, & Scharl, A. (1999). Evolution of Web Information Systems: Exploring the Methodological Shift in the Context of Dynamic Business Ecosystems. In C. Romm and F. Sudweeks (Eds.), *Doing Business On The Internet: Opportunities and Pitfalls*. London, Springer, 53 - 64.

Bauer, C. (1998). *Internet und WWW für Banken: Inhalte, Infrastrukturen und Erfolgsstrategien*. Deutscher Universitats-Verlag, Gabler, Wiesbaden.

Bhimani, A. (1996). Securing the Commercial Internet. *Communications of the ACM*, 39(6), 29 - 35.

BITS, O. F. E. a. I. (1998). *BITS, Publishers of Open Financial Exchange and GOLD Team Announce Timetable for the Publication of Converged Specification*. Available: http://www.ofx.net/ofx/pressget.asp?id=17 [01/99].

Booz Allen & Hamilton (1996). *Consumer Demand for Internet Banking*. New York.

Bosco, P. (1995). Branchless Banking: First Direct Holds the Phones. *Bank Systems and Technology*, November, 1995, 26 - 27.

Buzzell, R. D. & Gale, B., T. (1987). *The PIMS principles: linking strategy to performance*. The Free Press, New York.

Crowston, K. (1996). Market-Enabling Internte Agents. In *Proceedings of the 17th international Conference on Information Systems (ICIS)*, Cleveland, USA, pp. 381 - 390.

Cyberdialogue (1999). *Cybercitizen Finance*. Available: http://www.cyberdialogue.com/pdfs/promotional/finance/ccf_brochure.pdf [01/1999].

Devlin, J. F. (1995). Technology and innovation in retail banking distribution. *International Journal of Bank Marketing*, 13(4), 19 - 25.

Dratva, R. (1994) WWW-based Homebanking Services in Switzerland: A Case Study. In *Proceedings of the 2nd international World Wide Web Conference*, pp. 289 - 299.

Evans, P. B., & Wurster, T. S. (1997). Strategy and the New Economics of Information. *Harvard Business Review*, September - October 1997, 71 - 82.

Hamel, G. (1996). Strategy as Revolution. *Harvard Business Review*, July-August, 69-82.

Hamel, G. (1998) Strategy Innovation and the Quest for Value'. *Sloan Management Review*, Winter 1998, pp. 7 - 14.

Hammer, M., & Champy, J. (1993) *Reengineering the corporation: a manifesto for business revolution*, Nicholas Brearley, London.

Henderson, J. C., & Venkatraman, N. (1999). Strategic alignment: Leveraging information technology for transforming organizations. *IBM Systems Journal*, 38 (2 & 3), 472 - 484.

Keen, P. (1991). *Shaping the Future*. Boston, USA: Harvard Business School Press.

KPMG 1998, *Internet Home Banking Report Australia*.

Luftman, J., Lewis, P., and Oldach, S. (1993). Transforming the Enterprise: The Alignment of Business and Information Technology Strategies. *IBM Systems Journal*, 32 (1), 198 – 221.

Mintzberg, H. (1994). Rounding out the Manager's Job. *Sloan Management Review*. Fall, 11 - 26.

Open Financial Exchange (1998). *Open Financial Exchange (OFX) Specification 1.5*, Available: http://www.ofx.net/ofx/noreg.asp [01/99].

Papp, R. (1998). Alignment of Business and Information Technology Strategy: How and Why, *Information Management*, 11(3/4)..

Papp, R., & Luftman, J. (1995). Business and IT Strategic Alignment: New Perspectives and Assessments, *Proceedings of the Inaugural Americas Conference on Information Systems*, August 25 - 27, Pittsburgh, USA. Available: http://hsb.baylor.edu/ramsower/acis/papers/papp.htm [02/00].

Porter, M., & Millar, V. E. (1987). How information gives you competitive advantage. *Harvard Business Review*, July-August, pp. 149-160.

Porter, M. (1979). How Competitive Forces Shape Strategy. *Harvard Business Review*, March-April,137 - 145.

Porter, M. (1980). *Competitive Strategy. Techniques for Analyzing Industries and Competitors*. The Free Press, New York.

Porter, M. (1985). *Competitive Advantage. Creating and Sustaining Superior Performance*. The Free Press, New York.

Porter, M. (1987). From Competitive Advantage to Corporate Strategy. *Harvard Business Review*, May-June, 43 - 59.

Porter, M. (1996). What Is Strategy? *Harvard Business Review*, November-December, 61 - 78.

Prahalad, C. K., & Hamel, G. (1994). Strategy as a Field of Study: Why Search for a New Paradigm?, *Strategic Management Journal*, vol. 15, 5 - 16.

Rayport, J. F., & Sviokla, J. J. (1994). Managing in the marketspace. *Harvard Business Review*, November-December 1994, 141-150.

Scott Morton, M. S. (1991). *The Corporation of the 1990s*. Oxford, UK: Oxford University Press.

Strassman, P. (1990). *Business Value of Computers*. New Canaan, Connecticut, USA: Information Economic Press.

Surowiecki, J. (1999). The Return of Michael Porter. *Fortune*, 135 - 138.

Tanenbaum, A. S. (1989). *Computer Networks*. (2nd ed.). Englewood Cliffs, New Jersey: Prentice-Hall.

UNISYS (1999). *The Unisys Finance Barometer*, Available: http://www.internet-banking.com/barom.html [01/1999].

Venkatraman, N. (1994). IT-enabled Business Transformation: From Automation to Business Scope Redefinition. *Sloan Managment Review, 1994* (Winter), 73 - 87.

Yan, G., & Paradi, J. (1998). Internet - The future Delivery Channel for Banking Services? In *Proceedings of the 31st Hawai'ian International Conference on Systems Sciences (HICSS-31)*, IEEE, Los Alamitos, USA.

Chapter XV

Strategic Significance of Information Technology to Developing Countries

Muhammadou Kah
Rutgers University-Camden, USA

INTRODUCTION

The growth of information technology use in developing countries will depend on a number of factors, such as effective economic policies, the IT human capital stock, and an adequate telecommunications infrastructure. However, it is difficult to say which aspects will play the most significant roles. The definition of a new economic sector has emerged (the information or the knowledge sector/economy) as economies of the world witness the growth of the information industry. The fading of the industrial revolution into the dawn of the information revolution has transformed the world economy into a truly global one. However, the emergence of this new sector has started to create a wider gap between the information-rich and the information-poor, thus creating a wider gap between developing and more developed economies.

The strategic integration of information technology planning and strategy within sectors of governments and businesses in developing countries and the strategic use of information systems is key to economic efficiency and development in these countries. Most business processes and economic activities are performed mainly by government agencies or the public enterprise organized in the form of Ministries. For example, Ministry of Education, Ministry of Trade and Economic Planning, Ministry of Finance etc. Ministries consist of departments, divisions and agencies which conduct the economic activities in these developing countries.

In most cases, these ministries are not interconnected, causing duplication of efforts and redundancies contributing to inefficiencies. However, this situation is changing slowly with the diffusion of information technology and the Internet in ministries or government agencies in developing countries. The issue faced here is not an issue of availability of information technology infrastructure, rather, its appropriate and strategic use within organizations in developing countries coupled with inadequate skilled IT professionals in most of these countries. Further, the strategic fit of information technology in these organizations/government agencies "needs' is often misaligned, resulting in under usage of the existing information technology infrastructure. These "needs" are neither static nor uniform across government agencies or businesses in developing countries. The convergence of computers and communications technologies, and the more widespread use of databases, networks and enterprise resource systems could help alleviate these issues if effective planning and information technology strategy is implemented. These must include strategies to increase the pool of skilled IT human resources in organizations in developing countries. Given the improving telecommunication infrastructure in developing countries and the increasing use of the Internet in these countries, innovative "Web education" could be implemented through strategic partnerships with firms offering these services in developed countries. This will be very cost effective and would help increase the IT human stock in developing countries needed for strategic use, planning and implementation of appropriate information technology.

Developing countries, including those in Africa, have become more detached from the global economy, largely due to lack of a sustainable and appropriate information technology strategy and poor telecommunications infrastructures, resulting in inadequate information technology resources. While the information technology sector could be viewed as a source of productivity growth in all sectors of the economy, this is a significant infrastructure and an industry in its own right. Governments in developing countries can play a catalytic role in developing this infrastructure and in piloting and demonstrating various services to utilize it and to stimulate the effective use of these services in support of economy-wide competitiveness. The value of information resource and its intimate connection with strategy and structure were recognized in the 1970s (Mason 1984). Most business strategic planning in the developed world then, did not take information technology into consideration, it was merely an exercise in resource allocation generated from the lower levels of the organization. It was not fitted to the overall business strategy or business "needs" (Ward et al. 1990; Remenyi 1991). This, however, changed in the 1980s following Porter's (1980, 1985) analysis of industry competition. Porter and others used the forces of industry competition, generic strategies (Parsons 1983; McFarlan, 1984; Cash and Konsynski 1985), the value chain, and industry variations in information intensity (Porter and Millar 1985) to shed light on the connections between IT and business strategy. McFarlan suggested the strategic grid, in which the implications for investment, management control and structure, attitude to risk, and corporate strategy were shown to vary according to the role that information systems played in firms (Gerstein, 1987; Synnott, 1987; Atkins 1994). In the late 1980s, organizations used information systems strategically. In light of these studies, the following strategic applications are suggested for adoption in developing countries:

- linking government agencies/ministries via technology-based systems to its customers/consumers and/or suppliers;
- improved integration of internal value-adding processes in these government agencies;

- enabling the government agencies/ministries to develop, produce, market and deliver new or enhanced products or services based on information;
- top management support (i.e. Office of the Presidents, the Ministers, Permanent Secretaries , Managing Directors etc.)

Whether information technology can be a catalyst to economic development in developing countries is a moot point in many of these economies, where the telecommunication infrastructure is extremely poor or not widely available, and where computers are a rarity. Plagued by barriers of poverty, poor health, low life expectancy, military governments, civil unrest, illiteracy, and little access to tertiary education, African economies must compete with advanced countries in a highly competitive global economy.

So just what does the information revolution mean to developing economies? Economic growth in these economies has stagnated or has been increasing very slowly. The gap between these economies and that of the developed counties continues to widen yearly. Can they ever take advantage of the economic benefits that the information revolution *could* bring to them? Well, policy makers in most developing countries are renewing their attitudes, strategies, and perception towards the role of telecommunications and information technology in economic growth and development.

The role of IT in developing countries is already significant, but among the many issues that restrict the further diffusion of IT is low educational attainment. One must focus on the low literacy rates in these economies, in some countries they are at about 40 percent of the population. Among those who are literate, most cannot gather information for problem solving or decision making. Consequently, for IT to be of significance to the economic well being of developing countries, aggressive educational activities are required. This chapter argues that IT education is the main solution for building indigenous capacity in developing countries, and that governments have major roles to play in the diffusion of information technology into the entire educational sector. Appropriate use of existing Internet gateways is crucial. The existence and growth of Internet connectivity in developing countries gives them a tantalizing glimpse of the global knowledge resource just waiting to be tapped.

Thus, telecommunications infrastructures and services play an essential role in both the modernization and social development of a nation. They have become indispensable as they enable countries to compete on equitable terms in an international community governed by interdependence and a global economy.

Developing countries such as those in Africa and Latin America have enormous potential for development. African policy makers are setting objectives, with the aid of the World Bank, to address the needs of this area – an area characterized by sharp contrasts in its telecommunications development. Factors such as the state of the national economy, education, technology, culture, demography, and geography are all interrelated with telecommunications development. Studies such as those by Kaplinksky (1987), Bhatnagar (1992), and the World Bank (1992) have argued that telecommunications infrastructure is an essential element in the future economic and social development of African economies. Information technology is clearly diffusing rapidly into all industrial and service sectors and must now be seen as one of the most crucial technologies affecting economic growth in developing countries.

Despite this, no evidence, whether empirical or otherwise, has been put forward regarding the telecommunications sectors in most of these developing economies. In particular, not much has been done to investigate the restructuring, reforms, and policy shifts that have taken place in developing countries in Africa with relatively modern telecommunications infrastructures. If this were to take place, however, the following questions would surely be raised:

- Is there a relationship between investments in telecommunications and economic growth in developing countries?
- What is the political economy of developing countries' telecommunication reforms and policies?
- Is there a relationship between international telecommunications and international movements of factors such as exports, imports, and tourists in developing countries?
- What is the information technology strategy in some of these developing countries?

Information Technology and Economic Growth: The Connections

The global gap between the rich and poor widens every day says the Human Development Report 1996, published for the United Nations Development Program (UNDP). According to an administrator of the UNDP "the world has become more economically polarized, both between countries and within countries and if present trends continue, economic disparities between industrial and developing nations will move from inequitable to inhuman." The report shows that, despite a dramatic surge in economic growth in 15 countries over the past three decades, 1.6 billion people have been left behind and are *worse* off than they were 15 years ago. In those countries where people are better off than they were 10 years ago, governments have stressed not just the degree of growth (the quantity), but also its quality. They have provided some measure of equity—improved health, education, and employment opportunities for their citizens. Early investment in building people's capabilities creates a climate, as in East and Southeast Asia, for the forging of strong links between growth and human development. The above-mentioned findings show that more economic growth will be needed to advance human development, particularly for those countries that have not achieved much growth thus far. The report looks at uneven growth and poverty, however, clearly shows that there are no simple links between economic growth and human development and employment.

According to an adviser to the administrator of the UNDP, Mr. Richard Jolly, "short-term advances in human development are possible—but they will not be sustainable without further growth. Conversely, economic growth is not sustainable without human development. A strategy for economic growth that emphasizes people and their productive potential is the only way to open opportunities. It is increasingly clear that new international measures are needed to encourage and support national strategies for employment creation and human development, especially in the poorer countries." Finally, the report suggests that there is no *one* formula through which all countries will succeed. Former Socialist countries now in transition need to combine the most rapid economic growth possible with human development, if they are not to slide back on both fronts. Countries exhibiting fast growth, such as the tiger economies of Asia, need to take care to combine their concern for growth with an attack on poverty and a "boosting" of human development policies if they wish to ensure future gains. Industrial countries, too, will have to find new approaches to employment, equity, and energy-consuming lifestyles, as well as improving social services for mothers and children, the working poor, and the growing post-retirement population.

In sub-Saharan Africa and the less developed countries (LDCs), the emphasis must be on building a solid platform of human development while accelerating growth in order to sustain that development. The report estimates that at the current slow rates of improvement, countries like Cote d'Ivoire, which is losing ground in education, may require 65 years to reach the Human Development Index level of industrial countries, and that those further behind, such as Mozambique and Niger, will take more than two centuries to achieve this, without changes in policy and/or much more help from the outside. Such priorities call for debt relief, access to foreign markets, and well-targeted development assistance.

The changes discussed above dictate a major adjustment—information adjustment—to achieve macroeconomic and political balance in an environment of uncontrolled information flows and global competition, trade, and investment. Societies all over the world correctly see major challenges and opportunities from advances in information technology. National strategies that recognize the importance of information for development have appeared in Turkey, Mauritius, Singapore, Vietnam, South Korea, the United States, the Netherlands, Canada, and elsewhere. In the best-known example, Singapore's Tradenet system was implemented as a key component of the country's export-oriented economic strategy. The Asian Tigers, without exception, treat information as a strategic priority. Europe has an urgent strategy to make the European Union into an information society, and the United States, despite its aversion to industrial planning, formulated a national strategy for deploying an information infrastructure. Also, the United Nations Economic Commission for Africa (UNECA) formulated an African information society.

It is vital for developing countries, especially those in Africa to adjust or suffer exclusion from the global economy and severe disadvantages in the competitiveness of their goods and services. They are threatened with a new and dangerous form of information poverty that could further widen the gap in economic status and competitiveness.

Allaire (1994) argues further that "those nations that establish (their information) infrastructure can develop a broader range of applications first and will have a tremendous competitive advantage over those that lag behind. This advantage will accrue not only to the telecommunications industry, but also to such industries as manufacturing, banking, and entertainment and to such activities as education and healthcare."

Bangemann (1994) argues that the first countries to enter the information society will reap the greatest rewards. They will set the agenda for all that must follow. By contrast, countries that temporize, or favor half-hearted solutions, could, in less than a decade, face disastrous declines in investment and a squeeze on jobs.

Hudson (1995) makes this same argument a little differently. She says that information is critical to the social and economic activities that comprise the development process. Basically, telecommunications, as a means of sharing information, is not simply a connection between people, but a link in the chain of the development process itself.

Information Technology and Economic Development: The International Experience

Knowledge and information are critical in determining a nation's international competitiveness. According to Lopez and Vilaseca (1996), nations with infrastructures that facilitate the gathering and analysis of information on international markets, trends, consumer needs, production costs, and competitors, are transformed into "knowledge hubs," from which they can determine how to best adapt to changes in international economic and technological conditions.

They also contend that most developing countries face huge external debts, information poverty, obsolete infrastructures, trade barriers, and poor commercial development. This hinders efforts to develop their information technology base and tests their abilities to cope with global changes and trends, thus the importance of a strategic information technology framework for these countries. In addition, they contend that the level of economic development in these developing countries mirrors the level of information technology application in these economies.

However, it is to be noted that they too feel that IT and a modern telecommunications infrastructure could help developing countries to "leapfrog" to par with the developed countries at a far lower cost. This is because, as mentioned earlier, the initial research and development costs have already been borne by the developed nations.

Kah (1999), then, argues that for developing economies such as those in Africa, to rectify the failure of current national, social, and economic development plans and programs and be a part of the global economy, they must utilize appropriate information technology—a process that cannot be undertaken without improvements in their telecommunication infrastructures. This is because the telecommunications component of information technology (IT) serves as a foundation for infrastructure development and is a key factor in generating exports and attracting foreign investments. Kah (1999) found that several studies show that exports of products characterized by seasonal demands requiring close contact with customers such as auto parts are particularly dependent on reliable and abundant telecommunications infrastructures.

This new attitude has stimulated an increase in investment in the telecommunications infrastructure and has precipitated and rejuvenated sectoral reform in developing countries. Telecommunications reform is a prerequisite for developing countries to be effective players and partners in the information economy and the global economy at large. The entire worldwide telecommunications sector is experiencing a dynamic transformation—a transformation manifested in the convergence of telecommunications and computers, the participation of local companies in the long-distance market, the development of multimedia, and the advent of wireless, mobile, and cellular communications.

However, policies in support of economic development cannot be reduced to pure technological issues with which the primary objective is to increase the efficiency and productivity of certain sectors. Rather, it requires a broad base of infrastructure and support in education transfer, technical services of all kinds, research and development, technology transfer, linkage with the manufacturing sector, marketing, and management. This should be done within the overall context of maintaining macroeconomic stability and within an economic development plan that promotes the productive use of labor, and provides basic social services, education, and protection of the environment and natural resources, especially water and land. Once these policies are developed, governments should be committed to following them through.

The emergence of this new society, with its pervasive information capabilities, makes it substantially different from an industrial society. This information society is much more competitive, more democratic, less centralized, less stable, better able to address individual needs, and friendlier to the environment. For African countries, these changes dictate the need for a major adjustment in order to harness information for economic and social development. Such an adjustment requires urgent new policies, regulatory and institutional reforms, and investments.

Information Technology and the Global Labor Market

The effect of information technology on employment patterns is complex and shifting. Because of lower wages, developing countries are gaining skilled jobs from industrial countries largely due to telecommunications. However, according to Tolero and Gaudette (1996), this advantage is only temporary for any particular country, because wages for skilled service jobs in developing countries will rise with demand, the knowledge content of these jobs will increase, and the advantage might shift to other countries that are more effective in building knowledge and skills. This argument is well enunciated by Peter Drucker (1994b) when he says that developing countries can no longer expect to base their development on their comparative labor advantage—that is, on cheap industrial labor. The comparative advantage that now counts is in the application of knowledge (Drucker 1994a). Drucker explains why the application of knowledge has become more important than cheap labor by saying that the segments that comprise the world economy—the flows of money and information on the one hand, and trade and investment on the other - are rapidly merging into one "transaction." They increasingly represent different dimensions of cross-border alliances, the strongest integrating force of the world economy, and both of these segments are growing fast. These two significant economic phenomena—money flows and information flows— are not even transactional; they are non-national.

Most countries of the world are moving toward progressive forms of market economies. Developing countries such as those in Africa, however, are lagging behind - in part because most of their telecommunication sectors are state-owned and controlled while in the developed world and Latin America the shift toward markets (privatized PTTs) is likely to continue and even accelerate. Thus, the private sector has become the primary engine of growth worldwide, substantially changing the role of government. According to de Soto (1993), those countries that have market economies have prospered so much more than those that have not that, today, nobody dares propose a solution to underdevelopment that disregards the market.

International trade in goods has increased to the point where global production and outsourcing prevail. International trade in services is increasing as a share of total trade, and developing countries are catching up by exporting high-skill and low-skill services. Investments and money flow globally through an increasingly integrated, and volatile, financial market. Information systems built on telecommunications are essential for this expanded global market (Tolero & Gaudette, World Bank, 1996). Tolero and Gaudette expound on this by using Drucker's arguments (1994b) that money flows in the London Interbank Market, and trades on the main currency markets exceed by several orders of magnitude what would be needed to finance the international transactions of the real economy. An unambiguous lesson of the last 40 years is that increased participation in the world economy has become the key to domestic economic growth and prosperity (for industrial economies). Integration is the only basis for an international trade policy that can work, and the only way to rapidly revive a domestic economy in turbulence and chronic recession.

According to Richardson (1994), software production from "tele-ports" in Bangalore, India, yields annual exports worth $300 million (as of mid-1994). About 150 of 600 firms operate on global contracts only, mainly from the USA and Europe. Conversely, before 1989, few firms worked internationally. Citicorp, Microsoft, Oracle, and others have software operations inside India, and most firms have leapfrogged traditional development approaches straight to the latest programming technologies, such as object-oriented development and client server systems.

Competition increases through the globalization of trade and investments and the entry of developing countries into markets formerly dominated by industrial nations. Markets for industrial countries expand as incomes rise in developing countries. Competition between low-value-added goods and services intensifies with new entrants, technological progress, and skill-based efficiencies. As profits erode, developing countries with low labor costs can exploit this advantage only temporarily. Without flexible labor markets, developing countries cannot base development strategies on these products. Investment in training to develop a skilled labor force, pursued with the elimination of barriers to entry and exit, can propel the whole economy into a dynamic growth pattern, and fast growth is extremely common in developing countries. According to a World Bank (1994a) study, nine out of ten countries achieving export growth rates of over ten percent, from 1980-92, were developing countries, among them China, Colombia, the Republic of Korea, and Botswana. During this period, China and Korea were the fastest growing economies with average per capita GNP growth rates of 7.6 and 8.5 percent, respectively.

Drucker (1994a) argues that knowledge, the new resource for economic performance, is not in itself economic. It cannot be bought or sold. The acquisition of knowledge has a cost, as has the acquisition of anything. However, the acquisition of knowledge has no price. Economic interests can therefore no longer integrate all other concerns and interests.

Reorganizing Society: The Role of Information Technology

The changes brought on by the information revolution go far beyond economics and technology and affect society in broader ways. As a great social leveler, information technology ranks second only to death. It can raze cultural barriers, overwhelm economic inequalities and even compensate for intellectual disparities. According to Pitroda (1993), high technology can put unequal human beings on an equal footing, and that makes it the most potent democratizing tool ever devised. Society is being reorganized as, when information is ubiquitous and inexpensive, social and organizational control based on closely held information is no longer possible. Democracy and decentralization rise, and hierarchical organizations flatten. Travel, work, and consumption patterns change as electronic networks replace stores, factories, and workplaces that exist largely to facilitate information exchanges. Products and services of all kinds become information-intensive, and uncontrolled flows of information increase, creating opportunities for social reorganization.

Tolero and Gaudette (1996) explain how IT reduces information and income inequalities. The relationship between access to information and level of income is strong and becoming stronger at both the national and international levels. The information revolution threatens to increase inequity, but it also provides tools to reduce poverty. An agenda of technology-improved access to education, health care, and information is increasingly possible for developing countries. Rural and poor urban communities can be integrated into economic life, and thereby have their income levels raised, through information services. Appropriate regulatory incentives can be designed to encourage the provision of rural telecommunications on a commercial basis. Satellite networks, wireless communications, public telephones, and community information centers are effective arrangements. Intellectual and artistic products of national cultures can be preserved and disseminated with information technology.

Drucker (1994a) further argues that neither governments nor employing organizations should take care of the social challenges of the knowledge society. A separate and new social sector—the non-governmental organization (NGO)—rises to prominence as it slowly replaces government in the social agenda. In the early 1990s, about a million organizations were registered in the United States as non-profit or charitable organizations involved in social sector work. Government demands compliance; it makes rules and enforces them. Business expects to be paid; it supplies. Conversely, social sector institutions aim at changing the human being. The 'product' of a school is the student who has learned something. The 'product' of a church is a churchgoer whose life is being changed. The task of social sector organizations is to create human health and well being. Increasingly, these organizations of the social sector serve a second and equally important task, though—they create citizenship.

Information Technology and Public Administration

Human development and poverty alleviation—long established goals of economic and social development—are increasingly a prerequisite for international competitiveness. Communities everywhere, informed through television about how others live, aspire to higher standards of living and place increasing demands on their leaders. Victims of disease and malnutrition recognize their plight mainly as economic and political problems, creating pressures for change that reverberates internationally. Consequently, the demand for institutional accountability increases. Spurred on by the increasing availability of international information, the public is ever more unwilling to allow public and private organizations to operate in secrecy. At the same time, the spread of democracy creates new opportunities for people to participate in public decisions. Institutions of all kinds, but chiefly government, must promptly change their roles and must operate under conditions of permanent scrutiny by their stakeholders

Successive changes in the governments of Ghana, Congo, Brazil, Venezuela, India, and elsewhere in the last few years have been spurred by investigations into the conduct of government and the propriety of the personal transactions of ousted leaders. The increased accountability of private enterprises through financial market disclosure requirements is worth taking note of in this regard: capital flows worldwide on portfolio investments generate a demand for credible financial reports, corporate audits, and credit ratings.

Information technology makes governments more efficient, accountable, and transparent. Large productivity increases in government services are possible with information systems, which simultaneously increase speed, volume, quality, transparency, and the accountability of transactions. According to Tolero and Gaudette (1996), well-designed information systems can become major instruments of public policy—powerful tools with which to implement, enforce, and evaluate policy reforms. Moussa (1995) enunciates this point well. He argues that public administration is, by its very nature, highly information-intensive. Government business can be considered as a series of systems, such as education, health, defense, public revenue and expenditures, natural resources management, social security, etc., and public administration relies heavily on the use of information and communication technologies to gather, process, and diffuse information within both public and private domains. For example, each night a developing country can determine its cash and foreign exchange positions. Every fiscal transaction is validated every day against budget and public liquidity. This system eliminated the need to maintain a substantial no-interest float and created many secondary capabilities. According to Hanna (1993), successful reaping of the benefits of information technology by governments depends on many factors, including strictly centralized transaction controls, compatible public policies, a highly skilled workforce and substantial long-term investments.

According to Moussa (1995), in Morocco, the Ministry of Finance computerized tax administration, auditing, and control, and information systems are used for public investment planning and public debt management. Computer-based modeling is also used in macroeconomic monitoring, external trade management and industrial promotion.

Information technology increases the effectiveness of economic reforms. Economic reforms often fail in implementation due to weak compliance. Good monitoring mechanisms can help here, and information systems designed in conjunction with reforms are most likely to be effective. Through information systems, it is possible to embed policy reforms into institutional processes and transactions, which can then be readily monitored and audited.

This point is well illustrated by Singapore's Tradenet system, which is a key component of an open, export-oriented, market economy. Though strategic decisions and policy reforms related to trade were fundamental to Singapore's success, information systems were the vehicle for the implementation and enforcement of these strategic decisions and policy reforms. The combination of trade policy changes and computer support was rapidly and widely accepted by the trade industry.

Information technology can be used to better monitor and protect the environment in developing countries. Environmental monitoring, inherently data-intensive, is more effective using information technology, and primarily geographic information systems. These systems are already practical and are becoming increasingly inexpensive and, with developing countries already facing an environmental hazard (as the sea moves inland – ever closer to for example, Banjul, The Gambia, West Africa), IT could help in the monitoring, forecasting, and solving of this potential environmental threat.

Information Technology and Education

In the 1996 Human Development Report prepared by the World Bank, education is recognized as a basic human right and the path to higher incomes. According to a study by the UN, economic growth has failed a quarter of the world's population and 89 countries are worse off, economically, than they were 10 years ago.

The influence of telecommunications on education has already been observed through grassroots connections in the region. In Western Africa, the Economic Organization of West African States (ECOWAS) is involved in developing regional networks. Similar organizations also exist in North Africa. All of these organizations should be interconnected, appropriately, in order to maximize their value and utilization throughout the continent. Internet connectivity could improve the efficiency and value of these regional base organizations in Africa and, more importantly, their effectiveness and value to member states. The Organization of African Unity (OAU) could benefit tremendously from an appropriately "wired" Africa. Currently, most of these regional organizations are *not* enjoying the benefits of networks.

Too narrow a definition of "appropriate technology", of course, ignores the profound social implications of technology and risks consigning the world's poor to a life of third-rate capacity and opportunity. Information technology, when designed for the right job, can be deployed even in regions that lack adequate water, food, and power. This technology can be effective for many tasks, including human and economic development. In fact, this technology is often indispensable in meeting basic needs. For example, information technology makes it possible to educate more people, and support lifelong learning, because it plays primary and supporting roles in the delivery of education. Information systems can provide efficient administration, low-cost delivery, and the production of appropriate educational materials; while computer-based training is an effective tool for the sort of lifelong learning outlined above.

In a study conducted by Wooldridge (1992), education correlates with employment, income, and opportunity. His study suggests that, in industrial countries, the well educated are more likely to be employed. He also showed that in the U.S., in 1989, the unemployment rate was 9.1 percent for those with less than or equal to a high school education, and 2.2 percent for those with college degrees. In Japan these figures were 7 percent and 2.3 percent, respectively. The well educated earn more, and the gap is widening. In the US, in 1980, the earnings gap was 31 percent; in 1988 it was 86 percent. The well educated land jobs that provide them with more training; the uneducated are locked out from opportunities to improve their skills.

Distance education in Africa (defined to include print, broadcasting, and limited face-to-face education) has been used to pursue entirely unconventional educational ends. This could be a very valuable, cost-effective option that developing countries' policy makers could include as they conceptualize the first University of developing country, anticipated opening its doors in 1999. Developing countries are not well endowed with qualified personnel to teach University level courses. Therefore, for her University to achieve some degree of stature, it must have qualified faculty and administrators. In addition, it would not want to repeat the mistakes of most African universities, i.e., find itself short of adequate resources, and thereby provoke the students and faculty into striking. It is my view, given the adequate telecommunications infrastructure in place, that the opportunity exists for developing countries to model their higher education using information technology as a catalyst with which to build capacity. Alliances with major universities could be forged via long distance learning for appropriate and sustainable course offerings. With the Internet gateway in place in Gambia, this country has a competitive edge in higher education compared to most African economies, by appropriately using the Internet not only in universities, but also throughout the educational system. However, this is an enormous challenge for developing countries policy makers from a cost and knowledge point of view. Most developing countries' policy makers, of course, have inadequate knowledge of, and exposure to, information technology. Consequently, they may find it difficult to appreciate what IT can achieve, and thus effectively align it with economic agents such as education. Nevertheless, it is crucial that policy makers attempt this for, though the initial investment may be costly, the payoffs are likely, in the long run, to be great, particularly for a developing economy such as The Gambia, West Africa. As Perraton (1992) puts it, the main advantages of using information technology in education is that it is cheaper, more flexible, and suitable for widely scattered student bodies.

Information Technology and Agriculture

Much of Africa still depends heavily on agriculture, and other developing countries are no exception. Though agriculture is the largest employer, this sector has faced very difficult challenges in the past, ranging from old-fashioned and inefficient farming methods to drought, which can in turn cause social, political, and economic instability. Such instability has sometimes resulted in competition springing up between local groups for resources, which often results in civil wars. International assistance to Africa continues to dress the wounds of hunger and civil war, culminating in a stage of "donor fatigue." Given this scenario, it is evident that innovative ways to achieve better food security, and new ways to interact among African countries and local citizens, can become bases from which we can break this vicious cycle.

Internet connectivity has a vital role to play in improving interaction by delivering critical information to farmers, extension workers, and researchers fighting poverty. According to Benzine and Gerland, electronic networking in colleges—where people of diverse backgrounds and expertise share resources, knowledge, and experience—is of particular relevance here. Their implication for research in Africa is bidirectional. Networking breaks the isolation of researchers and African research from the global community, it empowers local researchers by making them both recipients and generators of global information; and stimulates researchers to upgrade the standard of African higher education. In addition, long-distance learning provides access to resources from the developed countries at a cheaper cost and thus enhances access at all levels.

Satellites are increasingly being used to provide early warnings regarding infestations of insects, such as desert locusts and tsetse flies, by combining satellite data about vegetation patterns, moisture levels, and weather, with ground-based data. The images are expensive, and interpretation requires deep technical exper-tise. However, dependable, timely predictions of pest infestations can help to prevent serious damage to health and agriculture[1].

Hudson (1995) also argues that, in many parts of the developing world, women do much of the agricultural work. They may take crops to market or negotiate prices for their crops or livestock. In such cases, the benefits of telecommunications in getting information about prices and markets and in getting expert advice from extension agents would be very helpful to women. A steadily increasing body of evidence suggests that girls' education is probably the single most effective invest-ment that a developing country can make. According to Sandstrom (1994), educat-ing women: (1) reduces child mortality, (2) reduces maternal mortality, (3) reduces fertility, (4) improves family health, (5) increases the educational attainment of their children, (6) has important environmental benefits, and (7) increases productivity (Sandstrom 1994).

Information Technology and Manufacturing

Information technology increases diversity in information-intensive indus-tries. Markets for information goods and services are young, growing, and excep-tionally mobile. In this dynamic situation there are many opportunities and success-ful models for creating new industries in developing countries. These industries can provide information products, such as components and equipment, custom soft-ware, or export provision of services. They can also help to improve the information components of traditional products, a fast-growing aspect of many industries. According to Hanna (1993b), the software industry in India has been able to take advantage of its low-cost, highly skilled work force and with the benefit of interna-tional communications links has become a major producer of software. India ranks second among competing countries in software/services exports. India's software exports have grown from $24 million in 1986-87 to $225 million in 1993-94.

The ability to disseminate, widely and cheaply, very detailed design information is changing the traditional manufacturing process. Making an original design for a product can account for half of its life-cycle cost. Computer-aided design can dramatically cut cost and time requirements and improve accuracy. Developing countries may be able to skip entire stages of industrialization if they are able to incorporate computer-aided design, information systems, and flexible manufacturing into their nascent industries.

Managing Information Technology for Economic Growth: Challenges in Developing Countries

Though the impact of technology could be substantial, implementation issues would be a challenge for developing countries. Obstacles would include delays, conversion problems, cost overruns, lack of local skilled labor and technical support, and a lack of acceptance by end users. In fact, obstacles such as changing from the "old way " of doing things/processes, end-user training, and poor power supply warrant consideration in the early adoption phases of new technologies. Active participation at different levels of government and society is very important if any tangible impacts and positive returns on investment are to be seen. It is particularly important to note that the acceptance of information technology has a "generation gap" component in developing countries. The younger the generation, the more exposure they have had to technology.

According to Hanna (1994), though information technology can have positive effects on the economic development of a country, it can fail to fulfill the high expectations placed on it if the process is not adequately managed from its inception. He further suggested that information technology's impact on the labor force is an aspect of IT integration that warrants maximum attention. Automation has decreased the direct labor share of production costs but requires a highly skilled labor force—often a scarce resource in less-developed countries. Nevertheless, information technology provides developing countries with automated alternatives, which lessen the need for highly skilled personnel in professional applications, such as computer-aided design in engineering and architecture etc., thus relieving these countries of handicapping constraints.

Hanna (1994) cautions that African economies will be challenged by the political implications of the existence of these infrastructures (telecommunications and IT). They would have to wrestle with issues such as "foreign ownership" of these important infrastructures, which are high revenue earners and will be the nerve of their economies. The need for better skills and education, and less labor-intensive human involvement, will also represent an enormous challenge for developing countries, with its excess labor and low skills base. In order to combat this, developing countries' governments must ensure that unrealistically high expectations are not developed and that, over the long term, the education and training needs for full participation in their country's information technology platform are available to all. There will be a need to retool the educational system, too, especially if they are to facilitate the education and training of information technology.

Trends in recent years show a reduction in the costs of information technology. This is the driving force behind the increased popularity and use of information technology; however, African countries should avoid the temptation to buy older technology in order to compensate for rising peripheral costs without first ensuring that the selected technology can evolve within its planned technology platform. It is very important to identify the information technology platform at an early stage, as this will protect the users of these technologies against premature obsolescence. In determining which platform to select, it is important to evaluate the benefits of new technology versus costs over its projected life cycle. These costs include maintaining and upgrading technology as it approaches maturity. Upgrading technology in developing countries does not imply leapfrogging from obsolescence to a state-of-the-art technology platform. Two approaches that could be adopted are: (1) to utilize the existing technology and to continue technological development by integrating new technologies; and (2) to totally replace the technology they currently possess.

Through IT-led economic development, developing countries could achieve macroeconomic balance, political stability, and growth amidst global information flows, competition, trade, and investment. Developed countries and the NICs are rapidly adjusting their economies to remain competitive in the global economy. Therefore, developing countries governments must also adjust or risk exclusion from the global economy and suffer severe competitive disadvantages in the sale of goods and services.[2]

Telecommunications has been described in the literature as both the core and infrastructure of the information economy. It's described as the core since major economic activities, such as financial services, are themselves mostly information processing and transmission and other services such as transportation, traveling, and publishing also depend on these facilities. Telecommunications itself has become a large and rapidly growing business—telecommunications operating revenues worldwide exceeds $500 billion, which is roughly equal to the GNP of Canada or two to three times that of Africa. Telecommunications systems have been effectively deployed in the extension of social services and regional development:

- to support human resource development through distance education and training and to facilitate health services in rural areas through linkages to interactive medical information networks;
- to extend and consolidate government administration to regions;
- to enhance agricultural development and resource management by enabling farmers to access such information as market trends, weather reports, and modern crop growing techniques; and
- to support the mobilization of aid for disaster relief operations, among other things.

Since new technologies such as wireless local loops and satellites are promising cost-effective capabilities with which to access remote areas, the use of telecommunications systems for promoting regional and economic development is likely to intensify in the future and help in the alleviation of poverty in developing countries. This is because telecommunication facilitates market entry, improves customer service, reduces costs, and increases productivity in *all* sectors of the economy. It has become a strategic investment to maintain and develop a competitive advantage at all levels - the firm, the region, the country, and the continent.

Despite Africa's poor telecommunication infrastructure, Africa's policy makers and donor agencies are realizing the impact of Internet connectivity on economic development. A recent study by Rorissa (1996), funded by the International Development Research Council (IDRC), surveyed the African countries of Senegal, Zambia, Uganda, and Ethiopia regarding the impact of electronic communication. It suggested that users are realizing the potential of a full Internet connection. In another study, by the National Research Council (1996), it was found that academic and research institutions have been able to conduct effective collaborative projects. This suggests that wider connectivity would improve the overall knowledge bases of many countries and promote positive changes in their economic development processes.

In order for this to be effective, developing countries' governments must cooperate and interact with users, private entities, non-governmental organizations (NGOs) and donor agencies. The government needs to create the environment for Internet connectivity by improving its telecommunications infrastructure. NGOs, donor agencies, and interested multinational corporations (MNCs), should recognize the diversity of technological levels, policies, and national settings, and come up with different solutions and support strategies. International organizations such as the International Telecommunication Union (ITU) and the United Nations (UN) already play a significant role exerting pressure on African governments to liberalize their telecommunications infrastructure to allow competition. As noted earlier, training will be crucial, as will be sensitizing developing countries' policy makers to the fact that improvement of telecommunications infrastructure, and investment in Internet connectivity, is vital for the economic viability of developing countries.

There is a proliferation of low-cost communication networks instituted by donor agencies such as the UN, World Bank, IDRC and NGOs, paving the way for the development of Africa's national information infrastructures. There is no doubt that for Africa to compete and be viable in this global economy, and to attract investment and spur economic activity, it needs to be "wired."

This section tackles a number of issues revolving around one major question: namely, why is it necessary to "wire" developing economies given there rising and pressing economic and social problems?

- Is improved telecommunication infrastructures and Internet connectivity a solution to the recurrent socio-economic problems?
- What are the implications of the information superhighway and the approaching global information economy to developing country?
- What are the challenges in attempting to "wire" a developing country?

The current advancement in telecommunications and information technology has transformed and elevated developed and East Asian economies. According to Bangemann et al, (1994) technological progress now enables us to process, store, retrieve, and communicate information in whatever form it may take, unconstrained by distance, time, and volume. In this global economy, information is an asset to—a very vital ingredient in—the information economy; and its proper management, and efficient use, enhances economic development and activity. Information technology has transformed the traditional ways in which we work, organize, and govern, and has reduced cycle times and transaction costs, all aspects that developing countries have not yet fully enjoyed.

Internet connectivity will be of great value in assisting in the management of the economic and social crisis confronting developing countries and the alleviation of poverty that is stifling developing countries' economic growth. Numerous projects funded by international agencies such as USAID, UN, the World Bank, and IDRC provide for the exchange of crisis-related information. Internet connectivity could improve regional collaboration and competitiveness and research efforts. The Common Market for Eastern and Southern Africa (COMESA) and the United Nations Conference on Trade and Development (UNCTAD) have realized the impact of trade information networks on inter-regional and intra-regional trade. UNCTAD is setting up trade information focal points called "trade points," in many African countries. COMESA is developing regional trade networks between its member states.

In order to make developing countries viable economic and competitive powers in this information economy, they must conceive and implement national information technology strategies to further their economies to move-up the value-added chain by driving and aligning information technology into all sectors of their economies. This will facilitate the process of appropriate and sustainable computerization and then informatization in developing countries. A strategic IT for developing countries also facilitates the role of government to develop appropriate IT infrastructure and to maintain a positive investment climate to attract investors as well as sophisticated users.

REFERENCES

Atkins, M.H. (1994) 'Information Technology and Information Systems Perspectives on Business Strategies', *Journal of Strategic Information Systems*, 3(2):123-35

Bangemann, Martin (1994). Bangemann et al. Europe and the global information society. Unpublished recommendations to the European Council. 26 May 1994.

Cash, J.J., and Konsynkski, B.R. (1985). ' IS Redraws Competitive Boundaries' , *Harvard Business Review*, 85: 132-42

De Soto, Hernando(1993). " The future surveyed: The missing ingredient- what poor countries will need to make their markets work" *The Economist*, Special 150th anniversary issue, 11 September.

Drucker, Peter(1994a). "The Age of Social Transformation" *The Atlantic Monthly*, November.

Drucker, Peter (1994b). "Trade Lessons from the World Economy." *Foreign Affairs* vol 73, no 1, Jan/Feb 1994.

Gerstein, M. (1987) *The Technology Connection: Strategy and Change in the Information Age* (Reading, Mass.: Addison-Wesley).

Hanna, Nagy (1991). "The Information Technology Revolution and Economic Development". World Bank, Washington, DC. 1991.

Hanna, Nagy and Sandor Boyson (1993a). *Information Technology in World Bank Lending: Increasing the Developmental Impact*. World Bank Discussion Papers #206. World Bank, Washington, DC. 1993.

Hanna, Nagy (1993b). *Exploiting Information Technology for Development - A Case*

Study of India. World Bank Discussion Papers #246. World Bank, Washington, DC. 1993.

Hanna, Nagy Ken Guy, and Erik Arnold (1994).. *Information Technology Diffusion Policies in OECD Countries - Lessons for Developing Countries*. World Bank Discussion Papers to be published by Asia Tech Dept. World Bank, Washington, DC. Not yet published as of 1994.

Hudson, Heather (1995). *Economic and Social Benefits of Rural Telecommunications: A Report to the World Bank*. Unpublished report, World Bank, Washington, DC. March 1995.

Hudson, Heather (1995).. Economic and Social Benefits of Rural Telecommunications. A Report to the World Bank, March 1995.

Kah, Muhammadou M.O. (1999). An Econometric Analysis of Telecommunications, Information Technology, And Economic Growth in Africa: A Case Study of Developing Country

McFarlan, F.W. (1984) ' Information Technology Changes the Way You Compete', Harvard Business Review, 84: 98-103

Mason, R. (1984) 'IS Technology and Corporate Strategy - Current Research Issues', in F.W. McFarlan (ed), *The Information Systems Research Challenge* (Boston: Harvard Business School Press).

Moussa, Antoun and Robert Schware (1992). "Informatics in Africa: Lessons from World Bank Experience." *World Development*, Vol 20, No 12, 1992.

Moussa, Moussa (1995).. "Information and Telecommunications Technologies in the Public Sector." Unpublished topic paper prepared for this project, World Bank, January 1995.

Parsons, G. L. (1983) 'Information Technology: A New Competitive Weapon', *Sloan Management Review*, 3- 14

Perraton, Hillary, ed.(1986). "Distance Education: An Economic and Educational Assessment of its Potential for Africa." World Bank, Discussion Paper, Education and Training Series Report no. EDT 43. World Bank, Washington, DC., December.

Pitroda, Satyan (Sam) (1993). "Development, Democracy, and the Village Telephone." *Harvard Business Review* Nov/Dec .

Pitroda, Satyan D.(1976). " Telecommunication Development – The Third Way." IEEE Transactions on Communication. 24(7). .

Porter, M.E. (1980). Competitive Strategy: Techniques for Analyzing Industries and Competitors (New York: The Free Press).

_____ (1985) Competitive Advantage (New York: Free Press).

_____ and Millar, V.E. (1985) ' How Information Gives You Competitive Advantage', Harvard Business Review, 85: 149-60

Remenyi, D. (1990). Strategic Information Systems: Development, Implementation, Case Studies (Manchester and Oxford: National Computing Center/Blackwell).

Sandström, Sven (1994). "The Most Effective Investment in the Developing World: Educating Girls." Address to the Economic Development Institute Workshop on Girls' Education, 13 October 1994, World Bank, Washington DC.

Synnott, W.R. (1987). *The Information Weapon: Winning Customers and Markets with Technology* (New York:Wiley)

Talero, Eduardo (1994).. "A Demand-Driven Approach to National Informatics Policy". In Duncan and Krueger (ed). *IFIP 13th World Computer Congress Vol 3.* Elsevier Science.

Ward, J., Griffiths, P., and Whitmore, P. (1990) *Strategic Planning for Information Systems* (Chichester: Wiley)

World Bank (1992a). Internal World Bank report. Policy Research Working Paper. 2/1/92.

World Bank (1993a). World Bank. *The East Asian Miracle: Economic Growth and Public Policy.* Published for The World Bank by Oxford University Press, New York. 1993.

World Bank (1993b). World Bank. *Turkey: Informatics and Economic Modernization.* A World Bank Country Study. World Bank, Washington, DC. 1993.

World Bank (1994a). *World Development Report 1994.*

World Bank (1994b). "Telecommunications Sector Background and Bank Group Issues: Joint World Bank/IFC Seminar." Presented to the World Bank Executive Directors on February 16, 1994.

World Bank (1994c). Internal World Bank report. Policy Research Working Paper. 12/1/94.

World Bank (1994d). Internal World Bank report. Jordan, National Information Systems Assessment, IDF Request. 1994.

World Bank (1994e). Internal World Bank report. Staff Appraisal Report. Tanzania, Third Telecommunications Project. 1994. (SAR #11539-TA).

World Bank (1994f). Internal World Bank report. Staff Appraisal Report. Colombia, Public Financial Management Project. 1994.

World Bank (1994g). Internal World Bank report. Executive Project Summary. Mauritius, Service Sector Modernization Project. 1994.

World Bank (1995a). *Global Economic Prospects and the Developing Countries.* 1995.

World Bank (1995b). *Mauritius: Information Technology and the Competitive Edge.* To be published 1995.

World Bank (1995c). Internal World Bank report. Draft Staff Appraisal Report. Indonesia, Telecommunications Sector Modernization Project. 1995.

World Bank (1995d). Internal World Bank report. Annual Report on Portfolio Performance - Informatics. January 1995.

World Bank (1995e). Internal World Bank report. Performance Indicators for the Telecommunications Sector. May 1995.

ENDNOTES

1 This was illustrated in an article in *The Economist* (August 12, 1993)

2 see, Talero and Gaudette- World Bank, 1996).

About the Authors

Raymond Papp is an associate professor in the Lender School of Business at Quinnipiac University. Before pursuing his PhD, Dr. Papp worked as a computer programmer, senior analyst and management consultant. His research interests include strategic impacts of information technology, Internet-based learning, strategic alignment and emerging information technologies. His publications have appeared in several academic and practitioner journals, and he has presented research at professional and executive conferences.

Dr. Papp completed his doctorate in information management at Stevens Institute of Technology. His dissertation, "Determinants of Strategically Aligned Organizations: A Multi-Industry, Multi-Perspective Analysis" is an empirical investigation into the determinants of strategic alignment, specifically addressing the impact of title/function, industry and firm performance.

* * *

David Bahn is an assistant professor of management information systems at Metropolitan State University in Minneapolis/St. Paul. He received his PhD in information and decision sciences from the Carlson School of Management of the University of Minnesota and his MBA from the Stern School of Business of New York University. Dr. Bahn teaches systems analysis, electronic commerce and business strategy. A former systems analyst, Dr. Bahn is also a consultant on information technology and electronic commerce for business and government organizations. He is currently researching "clicks and mortar" business strategy: how firms balance the imperatives of operating "brick and mortar" business operations with electronic commerce channels.

Christian Bauer started his academic career at the MIS department of the Vienna University of Economics and Business Administration in 1995 as an assistant professor/lecturer. He completed his doctoral research on reference modeling of mass information systems for the banking industry in 1997. Thereafter he accepted a postdoctoral fellowship from Curtin University and joined the Electronic Commerce Network in Western Australia. Research areas include Web information systems development and on-line financial services.

Katherine Boswell is currently a PhD candidate in the MIS program at the University of Mississippi. Her research interests include strategic information systems, electronic commerce and appropriate use policy. She has work published in the *Southwest Decision Science Institute 2000 Conference Proceedings*.

Mary Brabston is assistant professor of MIS in the Faculty of Management at the University of Manitoba. She received her PhD from Florida State University, her MBA from the University of Alabama at Birmingham, and her BA from Vanderbilt University. Previous work has been published in *Human Relations*, the *Journal of Computer Information Systems*, the *Journal of Information Systems Education*, and the *Journal of Computer and Information Technology* among others. Her current research interests include electronic commerce applications for executives, strategic information systems planning, and organizational impacts of technology.

John R. Carlson received his PhD from Florida State University in 1995 and serves as an assistant professor of information systems in the Hankamer School of Business at Baylor University. Recent work has appeared in the *Academy of Management Journal*, the *Journal of the American Society for Information Science* and the *Information Systems Journal*. His current research interests include computer-mediated communication, computer-supported decision making and ethical issues related to information systems.

Yolande E. Chan is an associate professor of management information systems at Queen's University. She holds a PhD from the University of Western Ontario, an MPhil in Management Studies from Oxford University, and SM and SB degrees in Electrical Engineering and Computer Science from the Massachusetts Institute of Technology. She is a Rhodes Scholar. Prior to joining Queen's, Yolande worked with Andersen Consulting as an information systems consultant. Yolande currently conducts research on knowledge management, the alignment of information systems strategy and business strategy, and the business performance impacts of information technology investments. She has published her research in a number of refereed books and journals such as *Information Systems Research*, *Journal of Management Information Systems*, *Journal of Strategic Information Systems*, and the *Academy of Management Executive*.

Ron de Groot works at the Department of Personnel Planning at the Royal Netherlands Navy. He manages a small group of IT-specialists who are involved in developing a variety of tools to provide the Royal Netherlands Navy with information how to get sufficient, competent and motivated personnel, who operate effectively in circumstances of war, crises and peace-operations now and in the future.

Wilfred Geerlings has an MSc in sociology from the University of Groningen (1996). In his study his focus was on research methodology and simulation in the field of labor and organizations. Currently he is working as a PhD student at the systems engineering group of the faculty of technology, policy and management of Delft University of Technology. The subject of his PhD research is to develop simulation models to support strategic human resource forecasting processes in organizations. Research results so far have been presented at several international conferences.

Petter Gottschalk is an associate professor at the Norwegian School of Management. Dr. Gottschalk has been the CIO of ABB Norway and the CEO of two major Norwegian corporations. He has published in *Information & Management*, *Journal of Global Information Technology Management*, *Journal of Knowledge Management* and *Journal of Information, Law and Technology*.

Gareth Griffiths is a senior lecturer in the business information technology department within the Manchester Metropolitan University, UK. He has extensive industrial experience gained from being a consultancy manager with Hewlett Packard both within the US and England. His research areas include strategic information systems, e-commerce and the adoption of new technologies within Eastern Europe. He has published numerous articles in leading national and international conferences and journals. He is currently the course director for a business information technology honours degree and has taught on a variety of undergraduate and post graduate degree programmes throughout Poland, Croatia, Bulgaria as well as the UK. He has also been a reviewer for a number of conferences and journals including the Academy of IS (UK), ICIS and the *Journal of Strategic Marketing*.

Ray Hackney is director of business information technology research within the Manchester Metropolitan University, UK. He holds a Cert Ed, BSc (Hons), MA and PhD degrees from leading universities and has contributed extensively to research in the field of information systems with publications in numerous national and international conferences and journals. He has taught on a number of MBA programmes including MMU, Manchester Business School and the Open University. He leads the organising committee for the annual BIT and BITWorld Conference series and is a member of the Strategic Management Society and Association of Information Systems. Dr. Hackney has served on the board of the UK Academy for Information Systems since 1997 and is also the vice president of research for IRMA (USA), associate editor of the *JGIM*, *JEUC*, *JLIM* and *ACITM*. He is also a reviewer for a number of publishers, journals and conferences and was an associate editor for ICIS'99. His research interests are the strategic management of information systems within a variety of organisational context.

Chi Hwang is currently a member of the information systems faculty at California State Polytechnic University—Pomona. Prior to earning his doctorate at the University of Mississippi, Dr. Hwang spent ten years in industry as a systems analyst and consultant. His current research interests include group decision support systems, strategic information systems, and intelligent text-based information systems. He has published research articles in *Journal of Information Science, Journal of International Information Management, International Journal of Information and Management Science,* and *Information & Management.*

Muhammadou M.O. Kah is currently an assistant professor of management —MIS/e-commerce at Rutgers University, School of Business-Camden. Between 1996-2000, he was a faculty member at Howard University, School of Business, Department of Information Systems & Analysis. He taught as an adjunct at the George Washington University information systems' graduate program and also at Saint Mary's University Halifax, Canada's extension program in The Gambia, West Africa. Dr. Kah received his bachelor's, master's, advanced graduate certificate in human factors and a PhD in information management (systems) from Stevens Institute of Technology, Hoboken, NJ. He also recently received a master of science in finance (MSF) from George Washington University, Washington, DC. Dr. Kah is currently a consultant at The World Bank, consulted for GAMTEL (The Gambia Telecommunication Company LTD.) and Fannie-Mae. Dr. Kah previously worked at Strand Management Solutions, Inc., AT&T Bell Laboratories and Education Testing Services (ETS). He was also director of institutional research and strategic planning at Bloomfield College, NJ. His research interest includes economics of information technology and telecommunication, strategic use of IT in organizations and governments of developing countries; electronic business and electronic commerce infrastructure use and valuation; knowledge management and data mining; real options and financial engineering.

Awie Leonard was born in Nigel, South Africa, and matriculated at the Technical High School in Brakpan. He obtained the degrees BSc, majoring in computer science and mathematics, in 1974 and BSc (Hons) in 1975, both at the Potchefstroom University for Christian Higher Education. He obtained the degree MSc information systems at the University of South Africa in 1981. Having spent a few years in the private sector as systems analyst and designer and project leader, he joined the Department of Informatics at the University of Pretoria as senior lecturer in 1992, where he also obtained the degree Dcom (informatics) in 1998.

Jerry Luftman is the executive director and distinguished service professor for the graduate information management programs at Stevens Institute of Technology. His twenty-two year career with IBM included strategic positions in management (IT and consulting), management consulting, information systems, marketing and executive education. Dr. Luftman played a leading role in defining and introducing IBM's consulting group. As a practitioner he held several positions in IT, including a CIO. Dr. Luftman's research papers have appeared in several professional journals and he has presented at many executive and professional conferences. His doctoral degree in information management was received at Stevens Institute of Technology.

Makoto Nakayama is an assistant professor at DePaul University's School of Computer Science, Telecommunications and Information Systems. His work experience includes software engineering, software product development management and strategic planning. His research focuses on strategic use of interorganizational systems and e-commerce impact on business-to-business relationships in retail marketing channels. Dr. Nakayama earned a BS in physics from Science University of Tokyo, an MBA from University of Texas at Austin, and a PhD in management from University of California, Los Angeles.

Mark R. Nelson received his BS from Saint Michael's College and both an MBA in marketing and a PhD in information science from the University at Albany (SUNY) where his dissertation on cross-functional integration between IT and marketing units won a distinguished dissertation award upon completion. He has taught several information systems management courses and has several professional publications. Dr. Nelson served in a high-level administrative position for a small liberal arts college and worked as a management consultant to higher education institutions in the areas of performance measurement and quality assessment. Currently he is an assistant professor at Rensselaer Polytechnic Institute.

Anne Powell is an assistant professor of computer management and information systems at Southern Illinois University—Edwardsville. She has an MBA and will be completing her PhD in MIS from Indiana University Kelley School of Business. Her current research interests include organizational and individual impacts of virtual work and user acceptance of information technologies.

Brian J. Reithel is currently an associate professor of management information systems at the University of Mississippi. His research interests are in the areas of quality of user-developed applications, strategic use of information systems and modern information systems development techniques. His articles have been published by *Decision Support Systems, Data Base, The Journal of Systems and Software, Public Administration Quarterly, The Journal of Computer Information Systems* and other business research journals. In addition, he has been the author of numerous papers for regional, national and international conferences. He received his PhD in management information systems from Texas Tech University. Dr. Reithel currently serves as the area coordinator for the MIS/POM area at the University of Mississippi.

Pieter Toussaint has been working at the research department of a software company in the field of hospital information systems. He was involved in a number of research projects on electronic patient records funded by the European Commision. In 1998 he received his PhD on the subject of integration of information systems. Currently he is involved in an electronic patient record research project funded by the Dutch government. He has published in several international journals on medical informatics issues, and has given several international presentations. Currently he is employed as an assistant professor at the faculty of technology, policy and management of the Delft University of Technology.

Alexander Verbraeck has an MSc in mathematics (cum laude, 1987) and a PhD in computer science (1991) from Delft University of Technology in the Netherlands. He worked as assistant professor in information systems until 1995, when he was appointed associate professor in the systems engineering group of the faculty of technology, policy and management (TPM) of TU Delft. He teaches courses on information systems, project management, discrete mathematics, logistics and simulation to undergraduate and graduate students. In addition, more than 60 MSc thesis projects in industry have been coached. Alexander Verbraeck carried out a large number of industry funded research projects, in which simulation and logistics played a central role. Examples of successful research projects are real-time control of AGVs using simulation, decision support for long-term personnel planning and the development of generic, object oriented simulation libraries. Research results have been published in books and journals and they have been presented at many international conferences.

Robert Zmud is professor and Michael F. Price Chair in MIS in the division of MIS, Michael F. Price College of Business, University of Oklahoma. His research interests focus on the organizational impacts of information technology and on the management, implementation, and diffusion of information technology. He is currently a senior editor of *MIS Quarterly* and serves on the editorial board of *Management Science* among others. He is a fellow of the Decision Science Institute, the research director for the Advanced Practices Council of SIM, International, and previously served as general conference chair for the 1993 ICIS and as program chair for the 1986 ICIS. He holds a PhD (management) from the University of Arizona, a MS (management) from MIT, and a BAE (aerospace engineering) from the University of Virginia.

Index

A

acceptance 97
Advanced Practices Council of the
    Society for Info 56
agriculture 284
alignment 94, 219
assessing alignment 12
assessment of systems 178
awareness frameworks 171

B

balanced scorecard 48
business performance 56
business process reengineering
    192
business strategic orientation 59
business strategy 1, 274
business structure 61
Business Workbook 64
buyers 140

C

change 223
change leader 155
chief architect 155
chief information officer 152
chief operating strategist 155
coach 155
commitment 223
communication 45, 95
communication channels 95
competencies 245
competitive advantage 178, 201
competitive force/marketing mix
    201

competitive potential perspective 7
competitive strategies 262
consultant 155
corporate strategy 135
critical success factor 187
cross-domain alignment 4
cross-functional integration 40
culture 89
culture gap 220

D

decisional roles 152
double loop model 186
dyads 225
dynamic models 240
dynamic processes of IT alignment
    185

E

e-commerce 185, 186
e-commerce strategies 180, 191
economic growth 285
economic policies 273
economic sector 273
economic/financial status 88
education 283
efficient consumer response 194
employee model 248
enabler 25, 155
entrepreneur 155
environment 88
environmentalist 155
envisioning process 87

F

financial services 264
forecasting 239
formal rule structure 248
formalization of IT planning 89
function model 248
functional integration 57
fusion framework 175

G

generation gap 286
global gap 276
goal models 240

H

human resource planning 238

I

implementation 176
information adjustment 277
information technology
        infrastructure 3
information technology strategy 3
informational roles 151
innovator 155
integration 40
integration hierarchy 41
intellectual dimension 219
internal labor market 241
Internet banking 266
Internet connectivity 288
interpersonal roles 152
IS leadership roles 155
IS literature 136
IS performance 56
IS strategic orientation 60
IS strategy 135
IT alignment 40
IT alignment model 185
IT human capital stock 273
IT management success 89, 93
IT resource alignment 188
IT vision 93
IT-end user relationships 219, 221

K

knowledge base 223

L

linkages 3

M

management 261
management commitment 177
management implications 12, 50,
    164
manufacturing 285
marketing and IT 41
marketing information systems 212
matching model 248
middle management 178
Mintzberg 151

N

new entrants 140, 203

O

on-line distribution 258
opportunity frameworks 172
organization size 89
organizational capability 186
organizational context 89
organizational infrastructure 2
organizational learning 186
organizational planning 83
organizational policy 238
organizational strategic vision 94
organizational structure 185
outsourcing 136

P

people 221
performance 58
perspective of organizational
    learning loops 185
planning 169
Porter's framework 136
positioning frameworks 171

potential strategic value 88
power of buyers 203
procedures 222
product developer 155
project structure 178
public administration 281
pull-model 240

R

research implications 51
rivalry 203
rivals 140
Royal Netherlands Navy 241

S

service level perspective 8
social dimension 219
standardization 266
strategic alignment 1, 56, 163
strategic alignment model 1,
    136, 258
strategic and structural alignment
    56
strategic information system 169,
    201
strategic integration 273
strategic IT vision 83
strategic planning 136, 172
strategic use of IT 202
strategic value of IT 93
strategic vision 83
strategic weapon 136
strategist 155
strategy 185
strategy execution perspective 5
structural alignment 56
structure 89
structures 222
substitute products 140, 203
suppliers 140, 203
supply chain management
    186, 191

supportive culture 223
sustainability 173, 223
SVIT 83
synergy 59
system maintenance 155

T

technologist 155
technology 222
technology potential perspective 5
technology provocateur 155
telecommunications infrastructure
    273
transacting 225
transactional information
    processing 191

W

Web-based consumer transaction
    applications 186
Web-based consumer transaction
    systems 191
World Bank 275